Theophilus F. Rodenbough

Autumn Leaves from Family Trees

Historical, biographical and genealogical materials relating to the Cauffman, Chidsey, Churchman, Foster, Montgomery, Rodenbough, Shewell and affiliated families

Theophilus F. Rodenbough

Autumn Leaves from Family Trees
Historical, biographical and genealogical materials relating to the Cauffman, Chidsey, Churchman, Foster, Montgomery, Rodenbough, Shewell and affiliated families

ISBN/EAN: 9783337370145

Printed in Europe, USA, Canada, Australia, Japan

Cover: Foto ©Andreas Hilbeck / pixelio.de

More available books at **www.hansebooks.com**

Autumn Leaves

from Family Trees: historical, Biographical and Genealogical Materials relating to the Cauffman, Chidsey, Churchman, Foster, Montgomery, Rodenbough, Shewell and affiliated families. ✻ Gathered and pressed, for whom it may concern, by a Kinsman, Theo. Francis Rodenbough. ✻ Illustrated ✻ A. D. 1892 ✻

ELIZABETH SHEWELL WEST
(AND SON RAPHAEL)
After the portrait by Benjamin West, P R A

Very truly yours

J. F. Rodenbough

To

John W. Jordan Esq

The edition, with the exception of a few presentation copies, is in stiff paper covers.

No 1 EAST FIFTY-FIFTH STREET

May 5 1892

Dear Sir

I owe you an apology for my delay in replying to your note of the 13th ult. It reached me at a time when I was engrossed with an important research, was mislaid, and so escaped my mind.

Now as to your query. It seems that there is a conflict

ask as to his grandmother's maiden name and the name of Stephen Shewell's wife, as it appears in "Autumn Leaves". The materials for Robert Shewell's line (father of Stephen) were either of the Siraff and Lorraine families. I note that Elizabeth Fordham's dates of birth and death are given; an evidence of more than mere traditional information. You will also note that Stephen's sister married a Bickley. There's also the possibility that E.F. was a widow née Bickley (E) At a more convenient

original MSS. with the view of discovering the source of my information on that point. If anything more definite appears it will give me pleasure to send you word. I hope you will do me the favor to advise me of any other item needing explanation; doubtless errors have crept into the book, and I would like

I am, dear Sir, Very truly yours L.J. Rosenberg

Contents.

Prologue—"Autumn."	7
"To My Kindred."	9

Cauffman.
Births, Marriages and Deaths.	13
A Medical Student's Letters.	25
An Impartial Judge.	30
The Memory of the Just.	31
Loss of the U. S. S. *Randolph*.	32

Chidsey.
Births, Marriages and Deaths.	37
An Upright Man.	44

Churchman.
Births, Marriages and Deaths.	47
A Quaker Missionary.	51

Foster.
Births, Marriages and Deaths.	56
A Colonial Indian Fight.	71
Craigie House.	79
"The Yellow Elms."	85
Church Row—Cambridge.	86

CONTENTS.

"The Old Clock on the Stair." 90
A Relic of Seventy-six. 93
Fosteriana. 94
A Franco-American Leaf. 96

Montgomery.

Births, Marriages and Deaths. 100
"Patriot, Officer and Gentleman." 123
One of the Old Navy. 140
"The Ship that Sailed." 144

Rodenbough.

Births, Marriages and Deaths. 148
Easton to New Orleans, 1825. 158
"A Mother in Israel." 172

Shewell.

Births, Marriages and Deaths. 174
An Ancestor's Letter-Book. 203
Reminiscences of Painswick Hall. 209
The Founder of a Creed. 215
"Abou Ben Adhem." 219
Anglo-American Notes. 220
An Early English Shewell. 223
A Waterloo Survivor. 224
A Balaclava Hero. 225
"Captain Sword and Captain Pen." 238
"Who Sent out his Argosies." 244
The Mother of Leigh Hunt. 247

ILLUSTRATIONS.

Introduced to his Ancestors.	251
"Cupid Swallowed."	254
An Elopement by Proxy.	255
Leaflets—Social and Scientific.	265
A Pennsylvania Loyalist and George III.	270
Napoleon and Benjamin West.	274
Benjamin West's Funeral.	275
"Lost Names."	277
Index.	279
"To a Missal of the XIII. Century."	281

Illustrations.

1 Elizabeth Shewell West and Son. (after West.)—*Frontispiece.*	
2 Laurence Cauffman, 1769–1850.	13
3 Gateway of St. Joseph, R. C. Ch. (Philadelphia.)	25
4 Russell Smith Chidsey, 1802–1865.	37
5 Penn's Treaty with the Indians. (after West.)	47
6 Bossenger Foster, 1742–1805.	56
7 Craigie House—Cambridge.	79
8 Boston in 1768.	93
9–10 John Berrien Montgomery, 1794–1873.	100, 123
11 U. S. S. *Portsmouth*.	135
12 Charles Rodenbough, 1797–1872.	146
13 Easton in 1825.	158
14 Robert Shewell, 1740–1825.	174

ILLUSTRATIONS.

15	Leigh Hunt, 1784–1859.	247
16	The Elopement.	255
17	A Family Group. (after West.)	265
18	Benjamin West, 1738–1820.	275
19	Emblematic Title.	279
20	Page from a Missal, *fac-simile*.	280
21	William Penn's Seal, *tailpiece*,	55
22	Foster Pedigree, *folded plate*.	71
23	Entrance to Craigie House. *tailpiece*	89
24	"Old Clock on the Stair," *headpiece*.	90
25	Spanish Merino Ram, *tailpiece*.	99
26	Montgomery Arms, *full page*.	122
27	Washington-Berrien Card Table, *tailpiece*.	121
28	"Old Ironsides." "	145
29	Easton from Canal Locks. "	171
30	Memorial Font. "	173
31	British Stamps, 1765. "	203
32	Seal. S. P. G. F. P. "	218

Autumn.

What a glory doth this world put on
For him who, with a fervent heart, goes forth
Under the bright and glorious sky, and looks
On duties well performed, and days well spent!
For him the wind, aye, and the yellow leaves,
Shall have a voice, and give him eloquent teachings.
He shall so hear the solemn hymn that Death
Has lifted up for all, that he shall go
To his long resting-place without a tear.

LONGFELLOW.

To My Kindred.

> "Of all the affections of man, those which connect him with Ancestry are among the most natural and generous. They enlarge the sphere of his interests, multiply his motives to virtue, and give intensity to his sense of duty to generations to come, by the perception of obligation to those which are past."—JOSIAH QUINCY.

SOME light should, perhaps, be thrown upon the character of the Work which is, hereby, respectfully dedicated to Posterity. It has been compiled under the inspiration of the beautiful words of America's greatest bard and in the sincere belief that the contemplation of this record, of "duties well performed and days well spent," must give to *these* "yellow leaves" a "voice," and "eloquent teachings," to which we and our descendants cannot be insensible.

A marked feature of this family group is its social and religious breadth. In amicable propinquity may be found the descendants of Papist and Puritan, Anglican and Quaker, Noble and Commoner, Cavalier and Roundhead. In occupation the Merchant predominates; next, perhaps, the Farmer; then the Soldier and Sailor; followed by the Bench, the Bar, Medicine, the Church, Literature and Politics in the order named. Martyrs and exiles for conscience sake; pioneers and "sons of liberty"; defenders of the flag by land and sea; magistrates and advocates; cabinet ministers; commercial princes; law-makers;

scientists and men of letters ; bishops, priests and deacons, are here joined in the bonds of clanship. In each sphere of action there have been distinguished representatives ; and many, who, if falling short of the goal, have left indelible traces of their honorable existence. The laurel and the bay have been, often, won and worn by the individual, to the honor of the family, the welfare of the community and the glory of the country ; while the vine, oak and ivy symbolize the pure women and strong men whose memories may herein be kept forever green.

In a historic-biographical sense the scope of this book is not less broad. Commencing with the Norman conquest, it touches upon subsequent events in England, France and Scotland, including Waterloo and Balaclava ; it crosses the ocean with Penn and Conant ; tarries awhile in New England and Pennsylvania, during the colonial period ; affords glimpses of "the times that tried men's souls," of the second war with Great Britain, and of our short campaign in Mexico and California ; and, finally, records the services of some who fought in the War for the Union. There are also peaceful triumphs to chronicle : of International strife averted, of a National industry inaugurated, of the fostering of old, and the founding of new creeds ; of the engrafting of American genius upon British stock. It is a feast of good things, to which each family contributes something, and of which "all whom it may concern" are invited to partake.

The genealogical data is often incomplete, owing to the loss of church registers, the destruction of family papers, or the indifference of those who possess valuable information. Nevertheless, it is believed that sufficient material has been collected to stimulate "Posterity" to take up the thread and spin it into a complete fabric.

TO MY KINDRED.

For valuable assistance, grateful acknowledgment is due, and is here made, to THEOPHILUS FRANCIS CAUFFMAN, Esq., THOMAS FASSITT SHEWELL, Esq., JOHN A. MCALLISTER, Esq., THOMAS HARRISON MONTGOMERY, Esq., and JAMES HENDRIE LLOYD, M.D., all of Philadelphia; Hon. CHARLES FRANCIS CHIDSEY and EDWARD CLEMENT SWIFT, M.D., of Easton, Pa.; THOMAS ROBERTS SHEWELL, Esq., of Boston, Mass.; Paymaster JOSEPH FOSTER, U. S. Navy; Rev. THEODORE BOGERT FOSTER, of Great Barrington, Mass.; Miss KATE MCCREA FOSTER, of New York; Mrs. SAMUEL P. HAZARD, of St. Louis, Mo.; Gen. JAMES GRANT WILSON, Prest., and EDWARD TRENCHARD, Esq., Asst. Librarian of the N. Y. Genealogical and Biographical Society, and to MARTIN I. J. GRIFFIN, Esq., of the American Catholic Historical Society. I have the honor to remain,

Explanatory Note.

THE work is arranged as follows: (1st.) There are seven *divisions*, one for each family, in alphabetical order of family names. (2d.) Each division consists of two *subdivisions:* one comprises "Births, Marriages and Deaths": the other biographical and historical sketches relating to the family. (3d.) A "Table of Contents" and an "Index.". For those unfamiliar with genealogical methods, it may be stated that, under the head of "Births, Marriages and Deaths," the earliest ancestor known is first mentioned; for instance, "Cauffman"—" I. Joseph Theophilus " (in *bold faced* letters) followed by a brief personal sketch and the names of children (in smaller type) with dates of their births, marriages and deaths. Immediately preceding each child's name is printed a Roman numeral indicating the order of birth; if there is to be more extended mention, elsewhere, a small Arabic numeral appears outside of and on same line as the Roman numeral, thus: "2. I. Joseph, b. Phila., 1755 : d. at sea Mar. 7, 1778." By referring to a corresponding *Arabic numeral, in bold faced type,* in margin of a following page, further mention will be found—*e. g.* 2. Joseph[2] (Joseph Theo.[1]); the Christian name in brackets is that of the paternal ancestor and the small figures, *over* the names, signify the generation.

ARTOTYPE, E. BIERSTADT, N. Y.

Cauffman.

AUFFMAN is the name borne by the descendants of JOSEPH KAUFFMAN of Alsace, Germany, who arrived at the port of Philadelphia, in the Province of Pennsylvania, in September, 1749. Some time after he had taken up a residence in that city, it was found that certain deeds of land, belonging to him, had been, through a clerical error, recorded under the surname of *Cauffman*, and, thereafter, he adopted that form of spelling the name.

Births, Marriages and Deaths.

1 **Joseph Theophilus Cauffman**[1] was born at Strasburg, Germany, in 1720. He received a good education and, soon after reaching his majority, came (1749) to America and settled in Philadelphia. Having excellent credentials and some means, he became prosperous and influential. He was a Roman Catholic and, notwithstanding the legal obstacles at one time in the way of persons of that faith becoming landholders,* invested largely in lands in the counties of Philadelphia, Chester, Bucks, Westmore-

---

* *Province Penna.*, *May 26, 1769.* " The Governor laid before the Board a bill entitled, ' An Act to enable JOHN COTRINGER and JOSEPH CAUFFMAN to hold lands in this province,' which was sent to him by the Assembly, for his concurrence during its sittings in Feb. last, and retained under his consideration. The Board having considered that the persons mentioned in the bill are Roman Catholics and being of opinion that any act for naturalizing said persons, as to enable them to hold lands, would be repugnant to an act of Parliament passed, advised the Governor to refuse his assent to said bill, and the Secretary was directed to carry it back to the Assembly with a message that he cannot agree to it." (Records Am. Cath. Hist. Society.)

land, Indiana, Blair and Montgomery, in Pennsylvania. The ground now bounded by Arch, Race, 11th and 12th streets, Philadelphia, was offered to Mr. Cauffman shortly before the Revolution; he declined to purchase, but lent the requisite amount to another investor. He took an active interest in charitable and religious works, being one of the founders (1764) and a director (1765-67) of the German Society for the relief of German emigrants; a prominent member of St. Joseph's, the first Roman Catholic Church in Philadelphia*; and one of the contributors (£55) towards building St. Mary's R. C. Church (1762) in the same city.† When the struggle for American Independ-

---

* Hildreth, the historian, says: "St. Joseph's, founded 1732, was the only place in the original thirteen states where the mass was permitted to be publicly celebrated prior to the Revolution." A writer in 1837 said: "The faithful and even many *non-Catholics*, of Philadelphia, have as profound a feeling of veneration for this church as if it were an ancient shrine. They are heard calling it '*the sweet old church*.'"

† Mr. Cauffman also gave the land upon which it was first designed to establish a province of the Franciscan Order in this country. The following extract, from the Records of the American Catholic Historical Society of Philadelphia, gives the terms of the conveyance: "1806, August 9th, Joseph Cauffman, gentleman, of Philadelphia [Recorded in Indiana County, Book I.,p. 132, etc.], conveyed to Mark Willcox and Rev. Matthew Carr the piece of ground called Rodesheim (also spelled Rodesham in another place in same deed), situated on south branch of Yellow Creek, above and adjoining Anthony Grove, in late Westmoreland, now Indiana, County, containing 332¾ acres, ' to Mark Willcox and Matthew Carr, and the survivor of them and the heirs and assigns of such survivor, in trust and confidence nevertheless, as a site for a House of Religious Worship and Parsonage and for a Burial place for the use of the Religious Society of Roman Catholics, in the township in which the said land and premises lie and the vicinity thereof, and for the support of the clergyman or clergymen for the time being who should officiate at the said Religious Society, and in confidence that they, the said Mark Willcox and Matthew Carr and the survivors of them and his heirs, would permit and suffer the land and premises and buildings thereon, to be erected, to be at the disposal and under the care, regulation and management of the said Religious Society, in or near the said township ; provided always, that the clergyman or clergymen officiating for the time being at the congregation should be of Reverend Brethren of the Order of St. Francis, and would be appointed by the Bishop of the diocese in which the land should be for the time being. But in case none of the reverend members of the

dence began, it found Mr. Cauffman with pronounced loyalist opinions. He took no part in the War, but suffered the loss of a son (Joseph), a surgeon in the Infant Navy of the United States, who was blown up while serving on board the U. S. S. *Randolph*, during an engagement with a British frigate, March 7, 1778.* After the War, Mr. Cauffman removed to one of his farms in Providence township, Montgomery County, near Norristown, Pa. He died in Philadelphia, February 12, 1807, and was buried in St. Mary's R. C. Churchyard. He married (1st),† about 1754,

ANNA CATHARINE ———.

They had:

2   I. JOSEPH, b. Phila. ——— 1755; d. at sea, Mar. 7, 1778.

---

said Order could be obtained, in which case, but not otherwise, it should be in the power of the Bishop, but not otherwise, to appoint other Roman Catholic priests to officiate at the congregation.'"

The mendicant order of friars, called *Franciscans*, was founded in Spain, in the year 1208, by St. Francis d'Assisi, and subsequently were introduced into France by St. Louis of Gonzaga. They were also called " Récollets," from the Latin word *Recollectus* signifying " meditation " and, also, " gathering." Their chief works were teaching, nursing the sick and ministering to the poor, whose wants they supplied out of the alms which they received. The " Récollets " were most liberal toward other religious denominations, for it is recorded in the *Quebec Gazette* of May 21, 1767, that "On Sunday next, divine services, according to the use of the Church of England, will be at the Récollets' Church and continue for the summer season, beginning soon after eleven. The drum will beat, each Sunday, soon after half an hour past ten, and the Récollets' bell will ring, to give notice of the English service, the instant their own is ended."

*The U. S. S. *Randolph*, 32, Capt. N. Biddle, sailed from Phila. Feb. 1777; soon after caught in a gale and dismasted ; put into Charleston, S. C., refitted, and sailed. In one week returned with several prizes ; was believed to be the first vessel in our Navy that carried a lightning-rod conductor. She sailed again, in company with four small vessels, belonging to State of South Carolina, placed under her command. On the night of March 7, 1778, while closely engaged with H. B. M. Frigate *Yarmouth*, 64, Captain Vincent, the *Randolph* blew up ; four of the crew only, out of 315 men, were saved ; the other vessels escaped. (For particulars, see App. " Loss of the *Randolph*.")

† As the Registers of St. Joseph Church, prior to 1758, have disappeared, it is impossible to supply dates of certain births, marriages and deaths. Both of Joseph¹ Cauffman's wives were Protestants.

II. JAMES (or JACOB?) b. Phila. Aug. 14, 1758; bapt. Sept. 17, 1758; d. ———.

3. III. ANNA MARY, b. Phila. Apr. 25, 1761; bapt. May 10, 1761; m. ——— 1786, Mark Willcox; d. Ivy Mills, Feb. 6, 1821.

4. IV. JOHN, b. Phila., Apr. 30, 1764; bapt. May 1, 1764; d. 1820.

V. CATHARINE, b. ——— m. ——— John Schriner and had: MARY (b. ——— m. ——— Paul).

JOSEPH THEOPHILUS,[1] married (2d) Nov. 27, 1768, MARY BARBARA ARNOLD (widow of Capt. Edmund Buttler, who was lost at sea). She was born at Phila. in 1741, and died at Philadelphia, August 8, 1787, and was buried in the burying ground in Franklin Square.

They had:

5. VI. LAURENCE, b. Phila. Aug. 8, 1769; d. Phila. July 4, 1850.

VII. GEORGE, b. ———; d. Phila. ——— 1793.

VIII. MARGARET, b. Phila. Nov. 24, 1773; bapt. Nov. 25, 1773; d. Jan. 8, 1827. (Was a pewholder, St. Augustine's R. C. Ch., Phila., 1801-1808 and 1814-20.)

IX. JAMES, b. Phila. Nov. 13, 1778; bapt. same day; "sponsor, the priest"; d. in infancy.

X. ANN THERESA, b. Phila. ———, 1782; d. Phila. March 4, 1822.

The following obituary is taken from Poulson's *American Daily Advertiser* (Philadelphia), March 23, 1822. "Died, March 16, in the 41st year of her age, Miss Ann Theresa Cauffman, of a lingering pulmonary affliction. Her patience in suffering and unexampled submission to the Divine Will, has been rarely surpassed. The widow's and orphan's tears, are the best testimonials of her worth. She, faithfully, followed the example of her beloved Saviour in searching out the habitations of wretchedness and sorrow, relieving the one, and commiserating with the other."

"Her mind was tranquil and serene,
"No terrors in her looks were seen,
"A Saviour's smiles, dispelled the gloom,
"And smoothed her passage to the tomb."

2 **Joseph**[2] (Joseph Theo.[1]) was born at Philadelphia, Pa., 1755. At the age of eleven he was sent to school at Bruges, remaining there four years under the care of Father Rector, a Jesuit priest. In 1771 he entered the University at Vienna, where, in 1776, he took the degree of M.D., and after a brief experience in the hospitals of London and Edinburg, he returned to Philadelphia in 1777, and accepted the appointment of Surgeon in the new Navy of the United States. In the latter part of the same year he was assigned to duty on board the U. S. S. *Randolph*, 32, Captain Nicholas Biddle, and was blown up, with all hands, during an engagement with H. B. M. frigate *Yarmouth*, 74, off the island of Barbadoes, March 7, 1778.*

3 **Anna Mary**[2] (Joseph Theo.[1]) was born at Philadelphia, Pa., April 25, 1761, and was baptized at St. Joseph's R. C. Ch., May 10, 1761, "sponsors, John Cotringer and Catharine Spengler." She married, in the year 1786, MARK WILLCOX, and resided thereafter at Ivy Mills, Delaware County, Pa., where she died Feb. 6, 1821. Mr. Willcox died Feb. 17, 1827, aged 82 years, 5 months, 29 days.

MARK and ANNA MARY (Cauffman) WILLCOX had:

    I. JOSEPH CAUFFMAN, b. Aug. 8, 1787; d. Jan. 14, 1815.

6.   II. JAMES, b. Apr. 12, 1791; m. (1) Elizabeth Orne; (2) Mary Brackett; d. ———, 1854.

    III. ELIZABETH, b. May 1, 1793; d. March 22, 1811.

7.   IV. JOHN, b. April 15, 1799; m. ———, Elizabeth Brackett; d. July 16, 1827.

4 **John**[2] (Joseph Theo.[1]) was born in Philadelphia, Pa., April 30, 1764, and was baptized May 1, 1764, at St. Joseph's R. C. Church, and died about 1820. He married (at St. James P. E. Church, Perkiomen), April 2, 1793, Margaret Wade, and had:

8.   I. SARAH, b. ———, 1798; m. John Carrell of Phila.; d. St. Louis, Mo., 1848.

    II. CATHARINE, b. ———, 1801; d. Ivy Mills, Pa., 1852.

    III. JOSEPH, b. ———, 1803; d. ———, 1823.

    IV. THEOPHILUS FRANCIS, b. ———, 1805; d. Mt. St. Mary's College, Emmittsburg, Md., 1818. (Accidentally killed.)

---

* See App. "A Medical Student's Letters" and "Loss of the *Randolph*."

5 **Laurence**[2] (Joseph Theo.[1]) was born in Philadelphia, Pa., Aug. 8, 1769. He was educated in that city and upon attaining his majority entered the counting-room of Robert Morris (the famous financier of the American Revolution). In 1796, Governor Mifflin appointed him Justice of the Peace for Bucks County, Pa., where he resided for some years. Returning to the city, in 1802, he engaged largely in the importation of china and glassware, retiring from business in 1846 with a comfortable fortune. He died at Philadelphia, July 4, 1850.

LAURENCE[2] CAUFFMAN was married at Painswick Hall, Bucks Co., Pa., April 23, 1796 (by Rev. William White), to SARAH FALCONER, daughter of ROBERT SHEWELL.[2] (See " SHEWELL.")
They had:

9. I. CAROLINE, b. " Painswick Hall," April 20, 1801 ; m. May 5. 1825, Hopewell Hepburn of Easton, Pa. ; d. Aug. 20, 1879.

II. ROBERT SHEWELL, b. " Painswick Hall," Oct. 11, 1803. He was educated at St. Augustine's Academy, Phila., (1811-15) and at private schools and entered his father's counting-room at an early age. He married (1st) Sept. 26, 1832 (by Rev. John Rodney), SUSAN H. dau. of DANIEL RODNEY of Lewes, Del.; she died suddenly at Germantown, Pa., May 22, 1846. He married (2d) July 3, 1855, LOUISA M. SHADWELL, of Manchester, England. He was fatally injured by being thrown from his carriage, died at his residence, Roxborough, Pa., May 10, 1856, and was buried in St. Luke's P. E. Churchyard, Germantown, Pa.

III. EMILY, b. Philadelphia, May 6, 1806; m. May 16, 1836, Charles Rodenbough of Easton; d. Dec. 11, 1876, at Easton, Pa. (See " RODENBOUGH.")

IV. JULIA, b. Philadelphia, Jan. 21, 1809; m. April 26, 1843, Robert Churchman of Chester, Pa.; d. April 9, 1887, at Philadelphia, and was buried at Woodlands Cemetery. (See " CHURCHMAN.")

10. V. THEOPHILUS FRANCIS, b. Phila. Jan. 12, 1815; m. June 13, 1839, Henrietta M. Guernsey.

11. VI. MARY WILLCOX, b. Philadelphia, Aug. 15, 1818; m. Sept. 4, 1841, Robert Poalk McCullagh of Philadelphia ; d. Germantown, Pa., Nov. 16, 1869.

6 James M. Willcox[3] (Anna Mary,[2] Joseph Theo.[1]) was born at Ivy Mills, Pa., on April 12, 1791, and died at Phila., March 4, 1854.

He married (1st), 1813, ELIZA ORNE, (b. 1792; d. Jan 28, 1817) and had: MARK (b. Aug 24, 1814; d. ———, 1883) and WILLIAM J. (b. Oct. 27, 1815; d. Jan. 14, 1845.)

He married (2d), 1819, MARY BRACKETT (b. Sept. 9, 1796; d. Jan. 28, 1865) and had: MARY (b. ———, 1820; d. ———,), THOMAS B. (b. Oct. 5, 1822; d. March 25, 1840), JAMES (b. ———, 1824), JOHN (b. Sept. 9, 1827; d. March 1, 1846), JOSEPH (b. ———, 1829), MARY ELIZABETH (b. Aug. 15, 1831; d. Jan. 6, 1846), EDWARD (b. ———, 1834; d. ———, 1890), HENRY (b. ——— 1838), and ELIZA (b. ———, 1840).

7 John Willcox[3] (Anna Mary,[2] Joseph Theo.[1]) was born at ———, April 15, 1799, and died at Ivy Mills, July 16, 1827. He married ———, 1823, ELIZABETH BRACKETT.

They had:—ELLEN (b. May 14, 1824; m. May, 1852, Howard Golder of Baltimore, Md.), and CAROLINE (b. May 17, 1826; m. Oct. 17, 1855, William Seal of Philadelphia).

ELIZABETH B. WILLCOX, married, (2d) November, 1830, JOHN MARSTON, U. S. Navy, who was born at Boston, Mass., February 26, 1796. He was the son of Col. John and Anna Randall Marston. Entered the Navy as Midshipman, April 15, 1813, and was promoted to the grades of Lieutenant, 1825; Commander, 1841; Captain, 1855; Commodore, 1862; and Rear Admiral 1866. He served during three wars (1812, Mexican War and War for the Union) and is entitled to great credit for his action in connection with the affair of the *Merrimac* and *Monitor*.* He

---

* "The facts of the case are these. Commodore Paulding had been ordered by the Department to send the *Monitor* to Hampton Roads, and she left New York under these orders. She had, however, been gone but a few hours when another order was received by Commodore Paulding, from the Secretary of the Navy, directing him to send the *Monitor* to Washington. Commodore Paulding immediately dispatched a fast vessel to overhaul the *Monitor*, with orders to proceed to Washington, but it was too late, the *Monitor* had gained too great a distance to be overtaken and the dispatch vessel returned to New York without accomplishing her object. At this time I was in command at Hampton Roads, some two or three days before the *Merrimac* came down from Norfolk.

was placed on the Retired List, December 21, 1861, and died at Philadelphia, April 9, 1885.

JOHN and ELIZABETH B. (Willcox) MARSTON had :
I. JOHN, b. Sept. 21, 1831 ; d. Feb. 28, 1833.
II. JOHN,* b. Phila., Dec. 15, 1833 : m. ———, ANNA RANDALL MARSTON of Bristol, R. I., and had : John (b. Sept. 13, 1856), Henry Ward (b. March 6, 1859), Mary Van Weber (b. June 7, 1863), Katie Lincoln (b. July 10, 1866), and Anna Randall (b. April 28, 1875).
III. MATTHEW RANDALL, b. Phila., Oct. 13, 1835 ; m. ———, MARY EMMA LOUISA SHAW of New Orleans. He entered the U. S. Army as 2d Lieut. 1st Infantry, April 26, 1861 ; 1st Lieut. May 14, 1861 ; Captain, Jan. 10, 1862 ; was breveted Major, July 4, 1863 for gallant and meritorious services at Vicksburg, Miss., and died of injuries received in a steamboat explosion on the Mississippi, Jan. 13, 1869.
IV. JAMES HENRY, b. Phila., March 14, 1838 ; d. ———, 1842.
V. FRANK DU PONT, b. Phila., Aug. 9, 1847 ; m. June 29, 1886, KATE LEE GALLAGHER, of Bloomfield, N. J.

8 Sarah[3] (John[2], Joseph Theo.[1]) was born at Philadelphia in 1798. She married JOHN CARRELL of Philadelphia and moved

---

I received from the Navy Department four telegrams ordering me, most peremptorily, to send the *Monitor* to Washington immediately on her arrival. On the night of the 8th of March (the day on which the *Merrimac* came down and sank the *Cumberland*, and the *Congress* was burned) at about nine o'clock the little *Monitor* arrived. Captain Worden immediately came on board the *Roanoke* and reported himself to me. I inquired into his condition, which was not a very favorable one ; his men were all green, they knew nothing of that peculiar armament then on board the *Monitor*. A few moments' reflection, however, determined me as to the course I should pursue. I informed Captain Worden that my orders were very positive to send the *Monitor* to Washington, but that I was going at the risk of my commission to disobey those orders and send him up to Newport News to look out for the *Merrimac*. In this Captain Worden most cheerfully acquiesced, and, on the following day, the result was known to an astonished and admiring world." (Letter of Admiral Marston to *Harper's Weekly*, dated January 25, 1879.)

* General Agent N. E. Mutual Life Ins. Co. (Phila.)

to Louisville, Ky., and died (while on a journey) at St. Louis, Mo., in 1843.

JOHN and SARAH C. CARRELL had: EDWARD JOHN, (b. 1826; d. New Orleans, 1853. He was a graduate of St. Louis University, was associated with Geo. D. Prentice on the *Louisville Journal*, and became, successively, Editor of the *Memphis Eagle* and N. O. *Crescent*; he was also a barrister-at-law); ANNA MARGARET, (b. 1826, and became a Sister of Mercy); FIELDING LUCAS (b. 1828; d. 1833); CATHARINE JOSEPHINE (b. 1830; became a *religieuse* in the Society of the Sacred Heart of Jesus); MARY ELENA (b. 1833; m. William H. Gray of Frankfort, Ky.); and HENRY CAREY (b. 1835; d. New Orleans, 1853).

9 **Caroline**[3] (Laurence,[2] Joseph Theo.[1]) was born at Painswick Hall, Bucks Co., Pa., April 20, 1801; married (by the Rev. John Rodney) May 5, 1825, Hopewell Hepburn,* of Easton, Pa. He was President Judge of the District Court of Allegheny County, Pa., 1846–51, and President of the Allegheny Bank 185–. Judge Hepburn resided in Philadelphia for a few years until his death, which occurred there, February 14, 1863. Mrs. Hepburn died at Spring Lake, N. J., August 20, 1879, and was buried at Woodlands Cemetery, Phila.

HOPEWELL and CAROLINE (Cauffman) HEPBURN had:

I. MARY, b. ——— 1827; m. ——— 1855, L. Clark Wilmarth of Pittsburgh, Pa.,

II. SARAH CAUFFMAN, b. Easton, Pa., May 25, 1828; bapt. June 22, 1828.

III. LAURENCE CAUFFMAN, b. Easton, Pa., March 3, 1830; bapt. Aug. 19, 1830; Lafayette Coll. (———); m. Sarah E., dau. of David Wagener, Esq., of Easton, Pa.; d. Sept. 2, 1880.

IV. JAMES FRANCIS, b. Easton, Pa., Dec. ———, 1832; bapt. Feb. 9, 1834; d. Roxborough, Pa. May 6, 1856.†

V. JULIA, b. Easton, Pa., June 11, 1837; d. in infancy.

VI. ELENA MARIA, b. Easton, Pa., Aug. 4, 1839.

---
* See App. "An Upright Judge."
† Was thrown from a carriage with his uncle, Robt. S. Cauffman, and both were killed; he was engaged in business at Pittsburgh, Pa., was extremely popular with all classes, and his interment was one of the largest private funerals of the day.

10 **Theophilus Francis**[3] (Laurence,[2] Joseph Theo.[1]) was born at Philadelphia, Pa., Jan. 12, 1815. He was educated at private schools, four years being spent in the classical school of Professor Espy, noted for his theory of producing rain. In 1832 he entered the counting-room of A. G. Ralston & Co., remaining until 1837, when he formed a partnership with James H. Brackett of Rock Island, Ill. He returned to Philadelphia in March 1844, and, together with his brother Robert, was for many years successfully engaged in the importation of china and glassware. He retired from business in 1877. Mr. Cauffman married at Rock Island, Ill., June 13, 1839 (by Rev. Albert Hale), HENRIETTA M. (born June 30, 1821), daughter of Hon. Daniel G. Guernsey* of Western New York. They had:

12. I. EUGENE LAURENCE, b. Rock Island, Ill., July 5, 1841; m. Dec. 3, 1867, Lydia Cloud Aldrich.

13. II. EMILY HUDSON, b. Phila., Oct. 28, 1844; m. Oct. 19, 1871, Jonathan Knight Uhler, M.D.

14. III. FRANK GUERNSEY, b. Phila., March 8, 1850; m. Oct. 28, 1878, Sarah Byerly Hart.

IV. HARRY FALCONER, b. Phila., Oct. 22, 1855. Educated there and at Chambersburg, Pa. Entered, as Cadet, the service of the Pacific Mail S. S. Co., October 1874; he resigned in 1876 and accepted the position of First Officer, in the service of the American S.S. Line. running between Philadelphia and Liverpool.

---

* DANIEL G. GUERNSEY, was born at New Canaan, N. Y., June 17, 1779, and died at Gonanda, N. Y., in 1851. He was educated and began the practice of the law at Waterford, N. Y. While still young, he removed to the western part of the State, then almost a wilderness, where he founded the village (now the city) of Dunkirk. During the administration of John Quincy Adams he represented the Whigs in Congress, as a representative from the district composed of the counties of Erie, Niagara and Chautauqua, procuring the first appropriation from the United States for the improvement of the harbor and erection of the lighthouse at Buffalo, as well as appropriations for other points on Lake Erie. In 1831 he removed to Michigan and, as a pioneer, was instrumental in the establishment of a new town, Battle Creek. He was, subsequently, appointed Postmaster and Government Superintendent of Public Works near Detroit and Ypsilanti. With characteristic energy he continued his course westward to Rock River, Illinois, extending the old town of Stevenson, that part

11 **Mary Willcox**[3] (Laurence,[2] Joseph Theo.[1]) was born at Philadelphia, Pa., Aug. 15, 1818. She was married Sept. 4, 1844, (by Rev. Benjamin Dorr, D.D., Rector of Christ Church), to ROBERT POALK MCCULLAGH of Philadelphia, (one of the founders and, for many years, Secretary and Treasurer of the Philadelphia Trust and Safe Deposit Company), died at Germantown, Pa., Nov. 16, 1869, and was buried there in St. Luke's P. E. Churchyard.*

ROBERT POALK and MARY WILLCOX (Cauffman) MCCULLAGH had:

I. WILLIAM, b. Phila., Jan. 21, 1846; d. Germantown, Pa., June 27, 1866.

II. LAURENCE, b. Phila., Aug. 9, 1847; d. Phila., Aug. 2, 1848.

III. SUSAN RODNEY, b. Phila., Aug. 11, 1849; d. Germantown, Pa., Sept. 8, 1851.

IV. FRANCIS HEPBURN, b. Germantown, Pa., Nov. 25, 1853; was for some years connected with the shipping house of Peter Wright and Sons, of Philadelphia, but in 188– removed to California and became a banker; m. June 10, 1880, MARY ELIZABETH EVANS of Germantown.

V. MARY, b. Germantown, Pa., Sept. 9, 1855.

12 **Eugene Laurence**[4] (Theo. Francis,[3] Laurence,[2] Joseph Theo.[1]) was born at Rock Island, Ills., July, 1841. Educated in Philadelphia, Pa. Entered the military service of the United States as Sergeant of the 3d Regt. Pa. Cavalry in July, 1861; was promoted 2d Lieut. after the battle of Antietam, 1862, and 1st Lieut. at Kelly's Ford, Va., 1862, and was honorably discharged Aug. 24, 1864, having participated, with distinction, in the principal battles (excepting "Gettysburg") of the Army of the Potomac. He married, at Phila., Dec. 3, 1867 (by Rev. J. W. Claxton), LYDIA CLOUD, daughter of Henry Aldrich of Wilmington, Del., and had: LAURENCE, (b. Roxborough. Pa., Oct. 27, 1869) and THEOPHILUS FRANCIS (b. Roxborough, Pa., Dec. 22, 1872).

---

now comprised within the limits of the city of Rock Island. In 1841 he was appointed by President Harrison, Receiver in the Land Office at Dixon, Ill. He was a man of great physical and mental activity and personal popularity—numbering among his intimate friends the great statesman, Henry Clay.

* See App. "The Memory of the Just."

13 Emily Hudson[4] (Theo. Francis,[3] Laurence,[2] Joseph Theo.[1]) was born at Philadelphia, Pa., Oct. 28, 1844; baptized by the Rev. Dr. Dorr of Christ Church; married at Roxborough, Pa., Oct. 19, 1871, (by Rev. J. W. Claxton), JONATHAN KNIGHT UHLER, M.D. (son of Geo. and Rebecca K. Uhler), who died suddenly at Bryn Mawr, Sept. 29, 1878.

JONATHAN K. and EMILY H. (Cauffman) UHLER had: EMILY HUDSON (b. at Falls Schuylkill, Aug. 6, 1873; d. May 12, 1881); JONATHAN KNIGHT (b. Falls Schuylkill, Aug. 24, 1874); FLORENCE (b. Falls Schuylkill, Pa.. Nov. 30, 1878—last hour of day, of week, of month).

14 Frank Guernsey (Theo. Francis,[3] Laurence,[2] Joseph Theo.[1]) was born at Philadelphia, Pa., March 8, 1850; baptized by Rev. Kingston Goddard, D.D., Church of the Atonement; educated at private schools, became a musician (possessing a fine baritone voice, he was connected for several seasons with the Strakosch Opera Co.) ; is now (1891) an architect. He was married at Philadelphia, Oct. 28, 1878, (by Rev. R. N. Thomas, Holy Trinity Chapel) to SARA BYERLY, daughter of James H. Hart of Philadelphia, and had : STANLEY HART (b. Roxborough, Pa., Nov. 1, 1880) ; FRIEDA (b. Roxborough, Pa., Sept. 9, 1886; d. Sept. 12, 1886).

GATEWAY, ST. JOSEPH'S R. C. CHURCH, PHILA.

A Medical Student's Letters.*

VIENNA, *27 December, 1773.* I've made my entrée at the Ambassador's, having had the honour of being invited to dine with him, whom I found a very amiable gentleman. As to the state of studies here, I've given you too exact an account, in my preceding, to need any addition. I have met several English doctors, on their travels, who commonly make little or no stay here. . . . Chymistry is most excellent here, far surpassing many other Universities in this branch. It is my particular study, being very much adapted to my disposition and humour. . . .

12 September, 1774. I should have answered your letter immediately, if you had not injoined my writing at the same time to Dr. Morgan,† which made me defer it till now, being necessitated to advertise our correspondents, at London, to remit me the said gentleman's letters, before I could write to him. . . . Thus you behold the inevitable of my remaining some time longer at Vienna, and I'm thoroughly persuaded that so great a connoisseur of affairs as Dr. Morgan will most readily assent. . . . I cannot help taking notice of your continually intreating "Surgery! Surgery!" Remember, Dr. Father, that surgery is both the least and most easily attained part of Medicine, it being but a result of the latter. One, well learnt, is the most easy introduction to the other. . . . During the scholas-

---

* Extracts from the letters of JOSEPH CAUFFMAN[2] to his father, 1773–76.

† *John Morgan* (b. Phila. 1725 ; d. there Oct. 15, 1789) was grad. at the Coll. of Phila. (now Univ. of Penna.) 1757. In 1760 he attended lectures in London and Edinburgh, where he received the degree of M. D., 1763. After visiting the Continent he returned (1765) to Philadelphia and was appointed the first Professor of the theory and practice of Medicine, Coll. of Phila. He was Director General of Hospitals and Physician-in-Chief of the American Army (1775–77). He was a member of certain foreign learned societies, was one of the founders of the Am. Philosophical Soc. (1769), and the author of many medical essays. Doctor Morgan was the first man in Philadelphia to carry an umbrella. Dr. Chancellor and the energetic Tory, Parson Duché, afterward kept him company, and, though at first every one sneered at them as effeminate and full of airs, they won the day in the end. Dr. Morgan also refused to compound or carry his own medicines, and sent to the apothecary for them, an innovation even more startling than the umbrella.

tic year which is just elapsed, I was chiefly occupied in the study of Pathology, but the following year I intend to frequent the hospitals in the environs of Vienna. . . . Dr. de Haën continues, with the greatest affection, his civilities towards me. I have just bought his works. I beg you'd write to him immediately in most amiable style, in French, (as he is deficient in the German language) thanking him for his kindness towards me and recommending me to his future attention. It will prove very acceptable to him, for, as the expression runs, "Old Men tho' they creep, still they are always a Tiptoe." I have gained the acquaintance of several eminent practitioners here, and, perhaps, if occasion should serve, I may be so happy as to attend, soon, one of them in his visits. . . . I'm very sorry I can't make use of Dr. Morgan's letters of recommendation, as in reality they would have been very serviceable, being directed to very able Doctors at London.

28 March, 1775. Personal merits are not sufficient, now-a-days, to pave the way to honour and preferment, but a knowledge of making proper use of the occasions that occur thereto is requisite, which is always commendable as far as it does not exceed the bounds of honesty. I have attained the 20th year of my age, which I've mostly spent far from friends and home, subject and an eye-witness of the different intrigues which ambition employs in her way to the Temple of Fame, and, accordingly, I hope that my sentiments, on my own welfare, will be as little despised as strictly followed. Scarce had I attained my 11th year, when you thought proper to send me abroad amidst the dangerous rocks of intrigue, wickedness and an insnaring world. However, conducted by the fear due to the counsels of a parent, I passed untouched, and finished my studies at Bruges with that success which, you so often confessed, proved agreeable to you. This was but the first stadium of infancy and childhood. At length, whilst still young and weak, you resolved, a second time, to commit me to foreign climes, to reconnoitre, with eyes more clear, the dangers past and render myself more firm in the knowledge of the world by applying to that study of Nature, viz., Medicine. Even here, as letters from Father Rector concerning my conduct have sufficiently demonstrated, I've executed your commands with that applause which, heretofore, I have always envied. I am at present just three years passed at Vienna, in which time I've not only completed my two years of Philosophy, but likewise almost a general course of Medicine.

Continual application and assiduity to my studies have, hitherto, prohibited me from considering where and how I may put, to the best advantage, my sweat and labour, but now, since I am once launched out into the deep, I begin to look about to reach the most convenient shore. You informed me, in one of your former letters, that a fortune is scarce to be made in Pennsylvania, at present, by a young physician, it being already overstocked with them. However, it can be answered, a physician who really understands his business is as scarce in Europe as in America, and in reality a doctor's fortune in many parts of Europe, unless he be very eminent in his sphere, is as small and precarious as in America. In truth, unless I was persuaded of surpassing our common quacks of Pennsylvania, I would never expect better success than they. Notwithstanding all this, it is not to be denied but that a physician, though he be an able man in his profession, often meets with poor success either through want of money, friends or backwardness of the occasions thereto. This is no doubt the case of many. What course is here to be taken? I answer for myself. My fortune is either to be made in Europe or America; both, perhaps, easily if well considered. I can never hope, at least in the beginning, to make the appearance or hold the equipage becoming a practitioner in Europe, as Providence has denied me the means. The only refuge, therefore, is my own merits and a way of exposing them, that is of procuring myself, thereby, a name and reputation so absolutely necessary to a physician. The only method in America to show the world that I have not received an education in vain, but that I am able in every respect to answer the duty of an intelligent man in my profession, would be by giving public lectures, on some branch or other, in Medicine, at a low rate in the beginning in order to engage more auditors; secondly, the better to endear myself to my countrymen, and the easier to signalize myself in my sphere. The best way of coming to great practice, either in Europe or America, is by understanding my business as well as possible, which I think would be best done as follows: I've frequented Dr. Haën's colleges with that assiduity that I flatter myself that I have derived all possible good therefrom; the only thing remaining is to confirm what I've already learnt, by frequenting continually the sick, with some able physician of this city, which I think I can do the next scholastic year. I'm acquainted with several eminent practitioners here who, I am certain, will with pleasure conduct me to all their patients. By this means I shall see that Theory, which I've been continually exhausting, combined and confirmed by Practice, which certainly is the most essential point for one who desires to make any proficiency in this science. After being thus once strengthened in all the difficulties of practice, I think a further removal, then, would be absolutely necessary; and indeed the most adapted plan thereto would be London, where, according to my opinion, I could repeat what I intend to do here, viz.: of practising under some renowned doctor of that city, not only to render myself quite firm and solid in my profession, but likewise, if misfortune is designed in Europe, I may acquire a name and reputation which at one stroke will answer all my wishes. . . The doctor under whom I should practice in London is Dr. Fothergill, to whom Dr. Morgan has been pleased to recommend me, who, I flatter myself after my leaving Vienna, if recommended by Dr. Morgan, will not refuse to accept of me as an assistant. . . Whether I am destined for Europe or America, I think this last seems the best, for then I shall be capable of acting the part of an able physician in every part of the world. . . Dr. de Haën, my particular friend, has been pleased, in a private conversation, to bestow upon me such encomiums as would create a thought of pride even in the most senseless soul. I delivered your French letter to him which caused him much satisfaction. . . .

15 July, 1776. I received your letter dated February 28, 1776, which afforded me singular satisfaction, as I had reason to apprehend that all communication between England and America was cut off. I wrote you, some time ago, a pretty long letter which, I am informed by Messrs. Pigot and Booth, has not been sent to you for want of a proper occasion in the present tumult. In this letter I explained myself, diffusely enough, concerning future measures to be taken and my present situation. In the first place I mentioned the impossibility of taking my degree at Vienna, as no one could be admitted to his examen unless he had adequately studied, first, the two years of Philosophy, and then, during five entire years, applied himself to Medicine. For which reason I entreated you to lay aside all thoughts of this kind. I likewise remarked that it would be most prudent to send me to Wurtzburg in order to study surgery, where I was told it was in a very flourishing condition, after which you might have sent me to Edinbourg to take my degree in Physics. You will be surprised to find me talk in another strain in the present. . . . Dr. Stoll has already commenced his lectures. In duty to our intimacy I could not help communicating your intentions about taking my degree at Vienna. He expressed much satisfaction at my desire of being promoted here, and assured me he would speak to the President, Baron Störck, for an allowance to undergo my examen here, though I have studied medicine scarce three years, a term for being examined, hitherto unknown in this University. As for my part, I am willing to enter my examen although, perhaps, it is by far the most rigorous here of any University in all Europe. I believe whatever can be pretended from diligence, ardour and the short time I study Physics, I have sufficiently effected. Dr. Stoll has entreated me to remain one half year after having taken my examen in his hospital, which is the best, by far, at Vienna. . . . Dr. Stoll is a most able man in his profession, full of ardor and fire to promote the Science of Medicine, my true friend, and who, upon every occasion, will give me all possible assistance, declare his open sentiments on a disease, or the imbecility of its theory, or the insufficiency of the method of curing it. This I never can expect to enjoy either in France, England or Scotland. For most practitioners, especially professors of Medicine, are very backward in giving their own sentiments on a disease either to avoid the trouble or hide their ignorance. . . . Weigh things well and inform me briefly of your intentions. . . . Time is pressing ; the disputes between England and America require quickness and dispatch, and indeed to give my opinion on the matter, the most prudent step would be to order your correspondents to furnish me with requisite money when called upon. . . . I am much indebted to Dr. Benjamin Rush* for his kind offer to recommend me to the professors of Edinbourg, and could wish myself in the opportunity of testifying my gratitude for the honour done me. I often read his

---

* BENJAMIN RUSH, M. D., LL. D. (b. Bybury, near Phila., Jan. 4, 1746, d. Phila. April 19, 1813), graduated Princeton Coll. 1760 and studied medicine in Phil., Edinburgh, London and Paris. Professor of Chemistry, Phila. Coll. (1769) ; Member of Prov. Conference of Penna. 1776, and Chairman of Committee that reported expediency of a declaration of independence ; Member Continental Congress and one of the signers of the "Declaration" 1776. Succeeded Dr. Morgan (1789) as Prof. Theory & Practice of Medicine, University of Penna. His eminent services during yellow fever epidemic (1793) were recognized by the King of Prussia (1805) and Emperor of Russia (1811) ; one of the founders of Dickinson Cottage and author of medical text books and essays.

name in the newspapers, and cannot help, pardon the expression, envying the great merits he accumulates himself by serving his country so essentially. I should be very proud of his correspondence; perhaps I could, now and then, communicate things in the chemical way worth notice, as the Austrian Dominions furnish numberless matters to engage the attention of a natural philosopher. I beg particularly to be remembered to Dr. Bond.* I should have interrupted some of his precious moments, with a line or two, was I not convinced his time was much better employed in the intricacies of practice than in reading the scrawl of a young, confused Tiro: however, tell him I am grown very audacious of late, and may on a sudden undermine him with a letter. . . . I hope you will answer me immediately, if not by the way of England, in the present disturbances, at least by some other way; for example, by some merchant in France, Spain or Holland.

I wish you, dearest Father, all happiness and prosperity, and believe me to be your truly affectionate and most dutiful son,

Jos. Cauffman.

An Impartial Judge.

HOPEWELL HEPBURN† succeeded Charles Shaler as Associate Judge and R. C. Grier as President Judge of the District Court. He was born in Northumberland County, Pa., Oct. 28, 1799. In his youth he attended the Academy taught by Mr. Grier, where their acquaintance began, which probably led to his appointment as Judge Grier's Associate. He graduated at Princeton College; read law with his brother, Samuel Hepburn, at Milton, Pa., and was admitted to the bar at Easton in 1822 or 1823. He practised law at Easton until appointed Associate Judge of the District Court, Sept. 17, 1844. When Judge Grier was advanced to the Supreme Court of the United States, he was commissioned as President Judge, August 13, 1846. He held that position until November 3, 1851, when he resigned.

The first election of Judge in this State was in October 1851, under the amended Constitution of 1850. Judge Hepburn had been on the

---

* Thomas Bond, b. Maryland in 1712: d. in Phila. 1784. He was a distinguished practitioner and delivered the first chemical lectures in the Pennsylvania Hospital.

† See "Cauffman."

bench of the District Court for seven years. He had given entire satisfaction to the people and bar by his promptness in the dispatch of business, his fidelity to duty, his integrity, learning and legal ability. His qualifications and fitness for the position were acknowledged by all. But he was a Democrat. The office had been elective. Party leaders immediately drew party lines. The Democrats nominated Hepburn, the Whigs, Walter Forward ; and the Whigs having a majority, elected Forward. The inevitable tendency to carry politics into an elective judiciary was seen also in the case of Chief Justice Gibson. He had been thirty-seven years on the bench of the Supreme Court, eleven years as Associate Justice, and twenty-six years as Chief Justice, and was universally acknowledged to be a jurist of transcendent ability. Yet he could not get the nomination of the Whig party of the State.

After Judge Hepburn retired from the bench, he practised law at Pittsburgh for a few years, then withdrew from the practice, accepting the presidency of the Allegheny Bank, which he held for three years, but his health failing, he removed to Philadelphia and died there February 14, 1863. ("The Judiciary of Allegheny Co." J.W. F. White, *Penn. Mag. Hist. and Biog.*, V. 7, No. 2.)

The Memory of the Just.

DIED in Germantown, Pa., Nov. 16th, MARY WILLCOX, wife of ROBERT POALK MCCULLAGH, Esq.

For the refined and extended circle of which this departed Christian lady was a cherished member, it would not be necessary to say anything, in a public manner, with reference to the many graces of her character and the excellent fruits of her life. To others, however, who did not enjoy the privilege of her acquaintance, we may be allowed to speak of her as a happy illustration of the beauty of Christian truth and purity and benevolence.

In full communion with St. Luke's Episcopal Church in Germantown, her whole life, whether social or domestic, was radiant with the pleasant activities of an intelligent, cheerful faith. Eminently cultivated and refined, she ministered largely to the gratification of her friends by her exquisite taste in whatever is beautiful in nature or in art ; and with an active charity that bespoke its own source to be the love of God alone, in the Name and in the Spirit of the Saviour Himself, she went about, everywhere, doing good.

Faithful and complete in all her domestic relations, she yet lived largely for the relief and comfort of the poor. No nation, no race, no persuasion, stood beyond the reach of her tenderest sympathies. Specially the neglected poor, whom others had overlooked or forgotten, were sure to come within the light of her inquiring eye, and to rejoice in the prompt, the judicious, the systematic benefactions of her ready hand.

Rich in devising and in executing liberal things, her path, like the light, was ever shining more and more unto the perfect day.

The Orphans' Home in Germantown and the department of that Institution devoted to the care of the aged poor, were objects of her free and untiring charity. There, doubtless, and in the private homes of many of the needy, to whom she was long known as an angel of mercy, the tear of unaffected sorrow has often fallen for her decease, and hearts and hands have been lifted up, invoking the blessing of God upon her memory and her name.

She died as she had lived, in the Lord. The memory of the just is blessed. [Obituary, *Germantown Telegraph*.]

Loss of the U. S. S. Randolph.

THE year 1777 opened with new prospects for the American cause. The recent movements of Washington, in New Jersey, had restored the drooping confidence of the nation and great efforts were made to follow up the advantage. Most of the vessels authorized by the laws of 1775 had been built and equipped during the year 1776, and America may now be said for the first time to have had something like a regular navy, although the service was still, and, indeed, continued to be throughout the war, deficient in organization, system and unity.

One of the first, if not the very first of the new vessels that got to sea was the *Randolph* 32. Captain Nicholas Biddle* was appointed

---

* Nicholas Biddle was the sixth son of Wm. Biddle of Philadelphia, where he was born in 1750. He was at one time a Midshipman in the British Navy and served in the Phipp's Arctic expedition. He and Nelson were both made coxswains at the same time and in the same ship. Subsequently he returned to

to this ship on his return from his successful cruise in the *Andrea Doria* 14. The *Randolph* was launched at Philadelphia in 1776 and sailed on her first cruise early in 1777. Discovering a defect in her masts as well as a disposition to mutiny in his people, too many of whom were volunteers from among the prisoners, Captain Biddle put into Charleston for repairs. As soon as the ship was refitted, he sailed again, and three days out he fell in with and captured four Jamaica men, one of which, the *New Briton*, had an armament of twenty guns. The *Randolph* returned to Charleston with her prizes in safety. Here she appears to have been blockaded by a superior English force during the remainder of the season. The authorities of South Carolina now added four small vessels of war of their own; the *Gen. Moultrie* 18, the *Polly* 16, the *Notre Dame* 16, and the *Fair American* 14, to Captain Biddle's command.

With three vessels in company Captain Biddle sailed early in 1778 in quest of the British ships, *Carysfort* 32, *Perseus* 20, *Hinchenbrook* 16, and a privateer which had been cruising off Charleston for some time. When the American squadron got into the offing, no traces of the enemy were to be discovered.

BRITISH ACCOUNT.*

BARBADOES, March 17, 1778. "I take the opportunity of the January packet sailing from here, to-morrow morning, directly for St. Johns, Antigua, of acquainting you of my having on the 7th inst. at half past five P. M. discovered six sail in the S. W. quarter on a wind standing to the northward; two of them, ships, three brigs, and a schooner. We were then fifty leagues to the east of this island. We immediately bore down upon them, and about nine got close to the weather quarter of the largest and headmost ship. They had no colours hoisted, and, as ours were then up, I hailed her to hoist hers or I would fire into her, on which she hoisted American and immediately gave us her broadside, which we returned, and in about a quarter of an hour she blew up. It was fortunate for us that we were to windward of her; as it was our ship was in a manner covered with parts

---

America, joined her cause. In the action with the *Yarmouth*, Captain Biddle was severely wounded in the thigh, and is said to have been seated in a chair with the surgeon, Joseph Cauffman, examining his hurts, when his ship blew up.

* From the *Remembrancer* (London), 1778, V. I, p. 143.

of her; a great piece of a top timber, six feet long, fell on our poop; another large piece of timber stuck in our fore-top-gallant sail (then upon the cap); an American ensign, rolled up, blown in upon the forecastle not so much as singed. Immediately on her blowing up, the other four dispersed different ways. We chased a little while, two, that stood to the southward, and, afterwards, another that bore away right before the wind, but they were soon out of sight; our sails being torn all to pieces in a most surprising manner. We had five men killed and twelve wounded. But what I am now going to mention is something very remarkable; the 12th following, being then in chase of a ship steering west, we discovered a piece of a wreck with four men on it, waving; we hauled up to it, got a boat out and brought them on board. They proved to be men who had been in the ship which blew up; and who had nothing to subsist on, from that time, but by sucking the rain water that fell on a piece of a blanket which they luckily had picked up. They informed us the ship blown up was called the *Randolph*, of thirty-six gun, and 305 men; the other ship was the *Gen. Moultrie* of twenty guns; and the other three, armed brigs; and sailed from Charleston, South Carolina, about a month before. I resumed the chase, but she was too far away to get up with her; however, I continued it, in order to draw her at least off the station, until eleven that night, when we made this island, having lost sight of her." (Letter from Captain Vincent, H. B. M. S. *Yarmouth* to Admiral Young, R. N.)

AMERICAN ACCOUNT.*

Captain Blake who commanded the marines on board the *Moultrie* (one of same squadron with the *Randolph*) thus describes the engagement in which the *Randolph* was blown up.

Dear Sir: Agreeable to your request, I would endeavor to recollect and state what happened during the unfortunate cruise in which the *Randolph* was blown up. I was ordered with a detachment of the 2d South Carolina Regiment to embark on board the *Gen. Moultrie*, and sailed in company with the *Randolph* and the brigs *Notre Dame*, *Fair American* and *Polly*, in the month of February, 1778. The object of this armament was understood to be an attack on the *Carysfort* frigate, *Perseus*, twenty-gun ship, and *Hinchenbrook*, brig of six-

* From " Autobiography of Charles Biddle, Vice-President Sup. Ex. Council Penna., 1745–1821." Phila., 1883.

teen guns, who had for some time annoyed the trade of this place, and so completely blockaded it that very few vessels escaped them either bound in or out. Our little squadron was some time detained in Rebellion Roads by contrary winds, and the want of a full tide to carry the *Randolph* out; her draft of water being eighteen feet. The first chance that offered we proceeded to sea, and were over the bar by eight o'clock in the morning, and after discharging the pilots, stood to the eastward. . . . From this time nothing extraordinary happened till our arrival in the West Indies, when we cruised to the eastward and nearly in the latitude of the Barbadoes, and for several days had stopped and examined a number of French and Dutch vessels. The only English vessel that we saw was a schooner, from New York to Grenada, who mistook us for an English squadron, and never discovered the mistake till she spoke the *Polly*, who took possession of her. The day this capture was made I dined on board the *Randolph*, when, I recollect, Captain Biddle expressed himself to this effect:

"We have been cruising here for some time and have spoken a number of vessels, who will no doubt give information, and I should not be surprised if my old ship should be sent after us; but as to anything that mounts her guns on one deck, I think myself a match for her." I don't recollect her name, but understood her to be a fifty or sixty-gun ship, which he had formerly served on board of and which was then supposed to be the only two-decker the British had in the West Indies. Two or, perhaps, three days after this, about 3 o'clock in the afternoon, a signal was made from the *Randolph* for a sail to windward; in consequence of which the squadron hauled on the wind and stood for her. It was near 4 o'clock before she could be seen from our quarter deck, when I could plainly discover through a glass that she was a ship. About 6 o'clock I again looked at her through the glass, and if I had not before satisfied myself of her being a ship, I should without hesitation have declared her to be a large sloop. At this time she had neared us so much that her topsails were out of water, and her top-gallant sails being handed and she coming down before the wind, she had the appearance of a large sloop with only a square-sail set.

About 7 o'clock the *Randolph* being to windward, hove to; the *Moultrie* being then about 150 yards astern and rather to leeward also hove to, the *Notre Dame* rather astern and to leeward of us. I don't recollect the situation of the other brigs. About 8 o'clock the British ship fired a shot just ahead of us, and hailed asking what ship it was. The answer was "the *Polly*." " Where are you from ? " " From New York." She took no further notice of us, but immediately hauled her wind and hailed the *Randolph*. At this time, and not before, we discovered her to be a two-decker. One or two questions being asked and answers returned, as she was ranging up alongside of the *Randolph* and had got on her weather quarter, I heard Lieutenant Barnes very distinctly call out, " This is the *Randolph*," who immediately began the action. The British ship's stern being then clear of the *Randolph*, the captain of the *Moultrie* gave orders to fire, and in consequence of it three broadsides were fired, the last of which I am satisfied must have gone into the *Randolph*, as the enemy had shot so much ahead as to bring her between us. I then mentioned, with some warmth, to our captain that instead of assisting we were firing into the *Randolph*, in consequence of which we immediately made sail to go ahead and engage her on the bow, but before this could be effected the *Randolph* blew up. . . .

I am, with regard, dear sir, yours truly,

J. BLAKE.

Charleston, 7 Oct., 1804.

TO THOS. HALL, ESQ.

Yours
R. S. Chilsey

Chidsey.

HIDSEY,* from the Saxon "Ceort's Eye" (Chertsey), the name given an island in the river Thames, England, from whence came families with the names of Chertsey, Chadsey, Chedsey, Chidsey, which were, originally, one name. The town of Chertsey is twenty miles S. W. of London. It is said that it arose from a monastery founded in 666 A. D. and rebuilt in the year 964 by Edgar and the Benedictine monks. During the heptarchy the South Saxon Kings resided at Chertsey. Here, too, the famous Charles James Fox and the Poet Cowley resided. During the reign of Charles I., and five years before his execution, JOHN CHIDSEY and ELIZABETH, his wife, left Chertsey and came to America, becoming members of the New Haven Colony. He was born at Chertsey, England, in 1621—one year after the landing of the Pilgrims on Plymouth Rock, and twenty-three years afterward he was chosen Deacon of the First Church in New Haven, Connecticut. He is the ancestor of all the Chidseys in America.

---

*This account of the Chidsey family, beginning with John Chidsey's arrival in America in 1644, is taken from authentic memorials of them. That part relative to the Chidseys *in England*, their origin, etc., is obtained, mainly, from tradition. While some of this part may be apocryphal, it is known that the name has undergone various orthographic changes, and that the original name was that of a town in England. The preponderance of evidence is, that *Chertsey* was that town. Credit is due to the "East Haven Register," a book published in 1824, by Rev. Stephen Dodd, for much valuable information in the preparation of this chapter. C. F. CHIDSEY.

Births, Marriages and Deaths.

1 **John Chidsey** was born in England, 1621. He came to America in 1644 and died at East Haven, Conn., Dec. 31, 1688. He married Elizabeth and had: MARY,* JOHN, ANNE,* JOSEPH,* DANIEL, MARY, CALEB, HANNAH, EBENEZER,* ELIZABETH and SARAH.

2 **Caleb**[2] (John[1]) was born at East Haven, Ct., Nov. 20, 1661, and died there Feb. 20, 1713. He married (1) ANNA THOMPSON, May, 10, 1688, and (2) HANNAH DICKERMAN, July 6, 1693, and had: DANIEL, CALEB, ABRAHAM and MARY.

3 **Caleb**[3] (Caleb,[2] John[1]) was born at East Haven, Ct., May 9, 1697, and died there Sept. 6, 1785. He married ABIGAIL SMITH and they had: ISAAC and CALEB.

4 **Isaac**[4] (Caleb,[3] Caleb,[2] John[1]) was born at East Haven, Conn., Nov. 8, 1731, and died there July 30, 1814. He was spoken of subsequent to 1775, as "Captain" Chidsey and, as there is no reference to East Haven people in the Revolutionary annals examined by the writer, it is supposed he commanded a company of colonists in that war. In a list of deaths appears "Andrew, servant of Captain Isaac Chidsey, died March 17, 1789."†

He married SARAH BRADLEY (1752) and they had: SARAH, SAMUEL,* ABIGAIL, LYDIA, CALEB, LOUIS, ANNE, SAMUEL and ISAAC.*

5 **Samuel**[5] (Isaac,[4] Caleb,[3] Caleb,[2] John[1]) was born at East Haven, Ct., April 24, 1773, and died there Aug. 2, 1861. He was always called "Captain" and is said to have held that commission in the War of 1812. He married, Jan. 26, 1800, BETSEY HOLT.‡ They

---

* Died in infancy.
† East Haven Register, 1824.
‡ BETSEY HOLT was born at East Haven, Conn., Oct. 2, 1781, and died there March 8, 1866. She was a lineal descendant of William Holt, born in England 1624, who came to America in 1644 and settled in Connecticut: Sir John Holt, Lord Chief Justice of the Court of King's Bench, during the reign of William III. and Anne, was, as far as can be learned, a relative—probably a nephew of William the Emigrant.

had: SARAH, RUSSELL SMITH, HARRIET, LORINDA, ANNA, SAMUEL, ALMIRA, BETSEY, LYDIA, ABIGAIL and HANNAH.

6 **Russell Smith**[6] (Samuel,[5] Isaac,[4] Caleb,[3] Caleb,[2] John,[1]) was born at " Foxon,"* East Haven, Conn., June 4, 1802, and died at Easton, Pa., December 1, 1865.† He married (1st) August 14, 1831, ELIZA WOODIN‡ of Green River, Columbia County, N. Y., who died at Easton, Pa., March 17, 1846.

They had:

7.   I. GEORGE WOODIN, b. Green River, Columbia Co., New York, May 15, 1832; m. March 21, 1858, Sarah Walters; d. at Elizabeth, N. J., March 15, 1874.

8.   II. HENRY RUSSELL, b. Easton, Pa., June 16, 1834; m. Aug. 11, 1869, Matilda Butz; d. Easton, Pa., July 21, 1870.

9.   III. MYRA LOUISA, b. Easton, Pa., Oct. 27, 1836; m. June 11, 1857, William H. Armstrong of Easton, Pa.

10. IV. ANNA ELIZA, b. Easton, Pa., Nov, 9, 1838; m. Oct., 20, 1858, Charles Stewart of Easton, Pa.

11. V. EMILY HARRIET, b. Easton, Pa., Jan. 25, 1842; m. Oct. 5, 1865, Joseph S. Rodenbough of Easton, Pa.

12. VI. CHARLES FRANCIS, b. Easton, Pa., Dec. 25, 1843; m. July 7, 1869, Katharine A. Williams of Little Falls, N. Y.

RUSSELL SMITH CHIDSEY[6] married (2d) Sept. 16, 1847, LUCY MORRIS STREET § of East Haven, Conn., and had:

---

* " Foxon " was the name of an Indian Sagamore, who once lived there.

† For biographical sketch of Russell Smith Chidsey, see App., " An Upright Man."

‡ The Woodins, in America, are of English descent, coming from the Isle of Wight. Eliza Woodin was born at Green River, Columbia County, N. Y., Sept. 26, 1804. Her grandfather, Peter Woodin, came from Massachusetts, where he was born 1738. His son Daniel married Thankful, daughter of Stephen Graves of Fairfield, Conn., and had eight children, of whom Eliza was the youngest. Combining the graces of the Christian mother and kindly neighbor, her sudden death was a loss to the community. She was called a *beautiful* woman, both as to person and character; and many an old employé of her husband has had " tears unbidden start " while speaking, years after her death, of the many virtues and excellent qualities of Eliza Woodin Chidsey.

§ Rev. Nicholas Street of England was ordained Teacher in the First Church

13. VII. ANDREW DWIGHT, b. East Haven, Conn., Sept. 30, 1848; m. Oct. 7, 1875, Emily Stewart McKeen of Easton, Pa.
14. VIII. EDWARD HART, b. East Haven, Conn., Aug. 3, 1850; m. (1st) April 15, 1873, Elizabeth Riegler (died June 29, 1879) ; m. (2d) Nov. 10, 1881, Jennie E. Snyder of Easton, Pa.

7 George Woodin[7] (Russell S.,[6] Samuel,[5] Isaac,[4] Caleb,[3] Caleb,[2] John [1]) was born at Green River, Columbia Co., N. Y., May 15, 1832. Educated at Nazareth Hall and Vanderveer's Academy, and for a short time at Lafayette College, Easton. In California in early life, (wrecked on the *Georgia* in the Pacific Ocean just outside the Golden Gate) as a miner and miller, and subsequently shipping agent at Elizabethport, N. J., for the Thomas Iron Co. He married, March 21,1858, SARAH WALTERS of Easton and died March 15, 1874.

8 Henry Russell[7] (Russell S.,[6] Samuel,[5] Isaac,[4] Caleb,[3] Caleb,[2] John) was born at Easton, Pa., June 16, 1834. Educated at Vanderveer's Academy and for a short time at Lafayette College, Easton. Succeeded his father in business, became Director First National Bank, and was President of the Town Council of Easton at time of his death, July 21, 1870.* He married Aug. 11, 1869, MATILDA BUTZ of Easton.

9 Myra Louisa[7] (Russell S.,[6] Samuel,[5] Isaac,[4] Caleb,[3] Caleb [2] John [1]) was born at Easton, Pa., Oct. 27, 1836. Educated at Dow's Seminary and the Misses Graves' School, Bergen Heights, N. J. She married, June 11, 1857, WILLIAM H. ARMSTRONG,†

---

at New Haven, Ct., 1659; died 1674. He had Samuel, who graduated at Cambridge University, Eng., 1664, and was ordained Pastor of the Church at Wallingford, Conn., in 1674. His tenth child was Elnathan, born 1695. He had Rev. Nicholas, born 1730, graduated at Yale College, 1751, and ordained Pastor of the Church at East Haven, Conn., 1755. He had Elnathan, his eighth child, born Feb. 16, 1774, at East Haven, Conn. Elnathan was the father of Lucy Morris Street, the second wife of Russell Smith Chidsey. She was born at East Haven, Conn., ———, 1811, and now (1891) resides at New Haven, Conn.

* As a mark of respect to his memory the merchants of Easton closed their stores on the day of his funeral.

† Col. Armstrong is the author of " Red Tape and Pigeon-hole Generals" and a number of sketches.

Attorney at Law, of Easton, Pa., (afterward Captain 1st Pa. Vols.
and Lieut.-Col. 129 Regt. Pa. Vols.) also Deputy Secretary of
the Commonwealth (under Gov. Curtin) of Pennsylvania. He
was born at Lewisburg, Pa., Feb. 10, 1833.

WILLIAM H. and MYRA (Chidsey) ARMSTRONG had:

I. ELLIOTT CHIDSEY, b. Easton, Pa., March 24, 1858; m. May
11, 1887, Mary McNeal of Easton and had: Margaret
(b. ———). He took Douglas prizes 1876–77, and 3d J. O.
prize 1878, and graduated at Lafayette College (1879),
Union Theological Seminary, N. Y. (1886), became a Presbyterian clergyman (June 1, 1886,) and is now (1891) pastor of the Grove Pres. Church, Danville, Pa.

II. WILLIAM RUSSELL, b. Easton, Pa., June 3, 1860; m. Dec. 3,
1890, Theresa Jeannette Frohock of Philadelphia. He
graduated, Phila. High School (1878), was Captain of the
Athletic Club of the Schuylkill Navy, Phila. (1889), a
merchant in the West for a short time and is now (1891)
in chemical manufacturing business in Philadelphia.

III. HARRY KNOX, b. Easton, Pa., May 15, 1864; m. July 31,
1890, Nellie Williams of Beatrice, Neb., and had one
daughter. He is in business at Beatrice, Neb. (1891).

VI. FRANK WOODIN, b. Easton, Pa., April 16, 1870. He graduated at Lafayette College (1890) and is a law student at
Easton (1891).

10 **Anna Eliza**[7] (Russell S.,[6] Samuel,[5] Isaac,[4] Caleb,[3] Caleb,[2] John[1]) was born at Easton, Pa., November 9, 1838. Educated at Dow's Seminary. She married, October 20, 1858, CHARLES STEWART, M. D., of Easton, a graduate of Miami University, Ohio (1847). Received degree of M. D. at University of Penna. (1853) but did not practice, devoting himself, instead, to commercial pursuits.

CHARLES and ANNA (Chidsey) STEWART had:

I. RUSSELL CHIDSEY, b. Sept. 2, 1859, at South Easton, Pa.; m.
Jan. 21, 1885, Mathilda Seitz of Easton, and had Anna
(b. ———). He took Second Junior Orator prize in 1877
and graduated at Lafayette College (1878); studied law at
Columbia College Law School, N. Y., was admitted to the

Bar, Jan. 1881, and became District Attorney, Northampton Co., Pa. (1887–90), and Secretary, National Bar Association (1888).

II. JOHN, b. South Easton, Pa., Oct, 2, 1865; m. Dec. 4, 1884, Fannie Dale of Phillipsburg, N. J. Left Lafayette College in junior year of class of 1884, and entered the office of Stewart & Co. (wire manufacturers) South Easton, Pa.

11 **Emily Harriet**[7] (Russell S.,[6] Samuel,[5] Isaac,[4] Caleb,[3] Caleb,[2] John[1]) was born at Easton, Pa., Jan. 25, 1842. Educated at Lawrenceville Female Seminary, N. J. She married, Oct. 5, 1865, JOSEPH SWIFT RODENBOUGH of Easton and had CHARLES RUSSELL (b. June 26, 1867), ALBERT CHURCHMAN (b. July 4, 1870) and FRANCES JOSEPHINE (b. Feb. 28, 1875). (See " RODENBOUGH.")

12 **Charles Francis**[7] (Russell S.,[6] Samuel,[5] Isaac,[4] Caleb,[3] Caleb[2] John[1]) was born at Easton, Pa., Dec. 25, 1843. Graduated, Easton High School (1859) and Lafayette College (1864). Served in War for the Union, as Private 129th Pa. Vol. Inf. and 1st Lieut. 38th Pa. Vol. Inf. President Board of Education (1876–77). Member of Town Council (———). Prison Inspector (———); first Mayor, City of Easton, Pa., (1887–88); Republican Candidate for Congress 10th Pa. Dist. (1884); in business in New York City, Phillipsburg, N. J., and Easton, Pa.; Director, Warren Foundry & Machine Co. (1871–75); Commander, Lafayette Post, G. A. R. (Easton) 1890; Deacon American Reformed Church and Trustee First Presbyterian Church. He married, July 7, 1869, KATHARINE A. WILLIAMS of Little Falls, N. Y., (who d. Easton, Pa., June 28, 1891, aged 47), and had:

   I. RUSSELL WILLIAMS, b. May 7, 1870, at Easton. Pa.; graduated as M. D. University of Penna., May 1, 1890, also took medical course College of Physicians and Surgeons, N. Y., and became a physician.

   II. EMILY HEIDELBERG, b. Heidelberg, Germany, ("Pension Schildecker" No. 101 Plückstrasse) Oct. 10, 1871. Graduated Easton High School (1890); took an honor grade and was Valedictorian.

III. KATE, b. Little Falls, N. Y., Nov. 13, 1873; Graduated Easton High School (1890) having an honorary essay. At Seminary, Hollidaysburg, Pa., (1891).
IV. CHARLES FRANCIS, b. Easton, Pa., Sept. 21, 1875.
V. DUDLEY KIRK, b. Easton, Pa., April 18, 1885.

13 **Andrew Dwight**[7] (Russell S.,[6] Samuel,[5] Isaac,[4] Caleb,[3] Caleb,[2] John[1]) was born at East Haven, Conn., Sept. 30, 1848. He was educated at Lawrenceville, N. J., and at Yale College (Sheffield Scientific Dept.). Engaged in the stove business and became a Director of Easton National Bank, Easton Trust Co., a deacon in the American Reformed Church and Trustee of the Second Presbyterian Church at Easton, Pa. He married, Oct. 7, 1875, EMILY STEWART McKEEN of Easton, and there had: HELEN STREET (b. July 5, 1876), ANDREW DWIGHT (b. Oct. 7, 1879), THOMAS McKEEN (b. Jan. 26, 1884) and HAROLD (b. June 1, 1889).

14 **Edward Hart**[7] (Russell S.,[6] Samuel,[5] Isaac,[4] Caleb,[3] Caleb,[2] John[1]) was born at East Haven, Conn., Aug. 3, 1850. Educated at Easton and Lawrenceville, N. J., and at Russell's Military School, New Haven, Conn. Engaged in stove business at Easton, of which place he served, for one term, as a member of the Town Council. He married (1st) April 15, 1873, ELIZABETH RIEGLER (who died June 29, 1879), and had: MORRIS DWIGHT (b. June 6, 1876; d. June 21, 1879). He married (2d) Nov. 10, 1881, JENNIE SNYDER and had: JOHN RUSSELL (b. May 5, 1883), EDWARD HART (b. May 7, 1886) and HENRY R. (b. Oct. 25, 1890). All born at Easton, Pa.

An Upright Man.

RUSSELL SMITH CHIDSEY.* Born at Foxon, town of East Haven, Connecticut, June 4, 1802. Taught school 1821-22. Served as deputy-sheriff and constable 1823. Left home, to make his own way through the world, 1824. First in permanent business at Geneva, N. Y., 1827-28-29. Removed to Easton, Penna., 1830. Married (1st) to Eliza Woodin of Green River, Columbia Co., N. Y., Aug. 14, 1831. Joined the First Presbyterian Church, Easton, and made a public profession of faith in 1833. One of the founders of the Protestant Reformed Dutch Church of Easton, now the Second Presbyterian, which was organized July 26, 1851. Elected Deacon 1853. Ordained an Elder in 1861, which office he held until the day of his death. Married (2d) to Lucy Morris Street of East Haven, Conn., Sept. 16, 1847. One of the founders of the Thomas Iron Co., Hokendauqua, Pa., which began business about the year 1852. A Director of it during the rest of his life. One of the originators of the Warren Foundry and Machine Company of Phillipsburg, N. J. (established in 1856), a member of the first Board of Directors and the third President of the Company. One of the organizers of the Farmers and Mechanics Bank (now the First National) of Easton, Pa., and a Director until his death. He held large moneyed interests in these three establishments, besides investments in the mines and railroads of the West. He was particularly interested in the Chicago and North-Western Railroad, always predicting for it a great and prosperous future. He placed one of his sons (Charles) in the financial office of the Company in New York, when it was just budding into importance as a great railway. He was an uncompromising enemy to slavery. During the great Rebellion (1861-65) he was an active Unionist. He gave one son (Charles) to the Union Army; and by example and precept did his full share in upholding the cause of his country. He was one of the chief supporters of a local organization to aid and comfort the soldiers, in the field, who had gone from Easton and vicinity. At the organization of the Thomas Iron Co., R. S. Chidsey was chosen to introduce the new-comer to the markets of the country. He soon relinquished his stove and tin-ware business at Easton, to his second son, Henry Russell, and then, until his death, he gave all his time and energy as Agent of the Thomas Iron Company, and as

---
* See "CHIDSEY."

Director, to place the concern on a substantial financial basis, and to make its success assured. In this effort he succeeded ; and just as he saw the two establishments, which he had helped to start, viz., " The Thomas Iron Co." and " The Warren Foundry," beginning business careers that betokened a prosperous and important condition in the near future, the end came ; and Mr. Chidsey, by a terrible collision on the Central Railroad of New Jersey, December 1, 1865, was called away, suddenly, from the duties of time to the everlasting joys of eternity. His death caused a thrill of pain to pass through the community ; and such was the esteem in which he was held, by the people of Easton, that all places of business were closed on the day of his funeral. A large concourse of friends—many from a distance, who had been with him in his varied business enterprises—attended his remains to the Easton Cemetery. Mr. Chidsey left a widow and eight children—three daughters and five sons.

From " Easton's Prominent Citizens " (Copp) we quote as follows in reference to Mr. Chidsey : " He had an excellent physique, tall, full-breasted, broad-shouldered, well developed in form, straight as an arrow, and active as an athlete, he commanded not only respect but admiration." " In his business affairs whatever he undertook he pushed forward with a determined will and tenacity of purpose that recognized no such thing as failure." " He was regular in his attendance in the sanctuary. In twelve years he was absent but twice, once on account of illness, and once, absence from home." " He realized the value of dollars and cents ; and while he was liberal in supporting all good causes of a religious or charitable nature, he never squandered his means on anything not essential to his own, or the real welfare of others." " He was gentle and companionable, a kind husband, affectionate father, and a good citizen ; and with all his extensive business transactions and his success in temporal affairs, he was the embodiment of honesty and integrity."

From a " Memorial Sermon by Rev. Dr. C. H. Edgar " we quote : " On his monument it may be truthfully inscribed ' He died wept by many good men.' " " A man of good sense and an independent mind." " It is as a Christian, that his surviving friends and his bereaved family are most comforted in thinking of him now." " It is his domestic life that most beautifies his character and best embalms his memory." " That which is the brightest gem in this memorial is, that he never gave his mother an unkind word."

From the action of the Great Consistory of his Church we quote: " By his faithful discharge of all duties, civic, social, and religious, he has, through divine grace, embalmed his name in our inmost hearts." " We will revere his memory and endeavor to imitate his example." " His influence has been marked and should be perpetuated." " In the departed, grace reigned through Jesus Christ."

All the local newspapers contained eulogistic articles at the time of his death. R. S. Chidsey was a silent man, saying little, but doing much. His industry was incessant. Work was the remedy prescribed by him for every fancied ailment of his children. He used to say "There is no such word as 'tired.' The word to use is 'lazy.'" He had served his apprenticeship on a New England farm, and there was no better school for hard work, anywhere, at the time. The wonderful 19th century was but an infant, when Mr. Chidsey was born, too young to give the slightest promise of its marvellous history. Toil was the inheritance of every young man in those days. Mr. Chidsey received his share without a murmur; and his whole life was passed in sturdy, honest toil. As a result, he received the blessing of God; and bequeathed to his children good health, strong wills, stout hearts, an ample fortune and a good name. All of them rise up to-day and " call him blessed."

After Benjamin West. PENN'S TREATY WITH THE INDIANS. *Copyright, Century Company.*

Churchman.

CHURCHMAN, in America, is the name of a family of Friends, descendants of JOHN CHURCHMAN[1] of Saffron-Walden, Essex, England, who, in the seventeenth year of his age, migrated to Pennsylvania (1682) and eventually settled in East Nottingham about 1704. The townships of East and West Nottingham were cut through by Mason and Dixon's line in 1766–67 : the southern parts were attached to Cecil County in Maryland, the northern were left in Chester County, Pennsylvania.

Births, Marriages and Deaths.

1 **John Churchman** was born in 1665, at Saffron-Walden, Essex, England. He came to Pennsylvania in 1682, settled at East Nottingham (1704) having married in 1696, HANNAH, daughter of Thomas Curry of Astor, and died October 1724.

They had: GEORGE (b. July 13, 1697 ; d. June 29, 1769) ; DINAH, (b. June 7, 1699); SUSANNAH (b. July 15, 1701) ; JOHN (b. June 4, 1705 ; m. Nov. 27, 1729, Margaret Brown ; d. July 24, 1775).

2 **John**[2] (John[1]) was born in Nottingham, Chester County, Pa., June 4, 1702. He was a studious youth, utilizing to the utmost the few opportunities for obtaining an education, and at an early age manifested a deeply religious turn of mind. He became a famous preacher and missionary of the Society of Friends, travelling throughout the American colonies and in Europe, 1731–57.* He

---

* See App. "A Quaker Missionary."

married on November 27, 1729, at East Nottingham, Pa., MARGARET BROWN, daughter of William and Esther Brown, and died July 24, 1775.

They had: GEORGE (b. Aug. 28, 1730; m. May 28, 1752; d. Nov. 18, 1814).

3 George[3] (John,[2] John[1]) was born at East Nottingham, Pa., Aug. 28, 1730. He married, May 28, 1752, HANNAH ———, and died Nov. 18, 1814.

They had: JOHN (b. May 29, 1755; d. at sea July 17, 1805); EDWARD, (b. Feb. 6, 1757; m. Rebecca Pierce, Sept. 18, 1782, d. Sept. 5, 1834); MORDECAI, (b.———, m. June 2, 1790, Sarah West, at Phila.; d. March 1830); MICAIJAH, (b. Dec. 20, 1758; d. Jan. 1, 1788); MARGARET, (b. Dec. 12, 1760, went with Jane Haskins to Virginia; d. Oct. 26, 1837); GAINER, (b. Nov. 20, 1762; d. Oct, 7, 1822); GEORGE (b. Dec. 29, 1764; d. March 14, 1837); JOSEPH, (b. Oct. 15, 1767; m. Hannah Pierce; d. Nov. 21, 1837); HANNAH (b. Aug. 3, 1772; d. Feb. 4, 1855).

4 John[4] (George,[3] John,[2] John[1]) was born at East Nottingham, Pa., May 29, 1755. He was a Land-Surveyor and Geometrician. About the year 1778, he executed a Map of the Peninsula, between the bays of Delaware and Chesapeake, including the State of Delaware and Eastern Shore of Maryland and Virginia. About the year 1790, he constructed a Variation Chart, or Magnetic Atlas, and stereographic Projection of the Spheres, on a plane of the first magnetic medium, on a new plan, with a book of explication; on which account he met with strong opposition from some characters of eminence in the learned world (as appears by publications yet extant), who could not relish that an obscure and self-taught genius should acquire ideas which had so long escaped the penetration of men who had been familiar with the illuminations of Science. But while he was thus discountenanced, and annoyed, in the land of his nativity, he maintained an encouraging correspondence with Sir Joseph Banks, President of the Royal Society, at London; H. Parker, Secretary of the Commissioners of Longitude; also, with the Commissioners and Secretaries of several learned Societies, and Academies, at Hamburg, Copenhagen, St. Petersburg, Lisbon, Cambridge, Paris, etc.; and also with George Washington,

Thomas Jefferson, and other liberal-minded men in America,—who were pleased to say, they highly approved of his very laudable design of improving magnetic observations; that they acknowledged the originality and usefulness of his ideas and scheme; that the subject would derive no small increase from his ingenious works; that it was an enterprise of great merit and might be of material service in navigation, that they advised him to pursue with diligence a subject, wherein the progress authorized a reasonable hope that science would derive real benefit from it, etc. In 1792, he embarked on a voyage to England and France, in order to pursue his researches,—as also with a view to apply his scheme to find out the Longitude at sea. Having received an invitation from a learned Society in Russia, he visited Copenhagen, and thence to St. Petersburg—where he met with great attention; was elected a member of the Imperial Academy of Arts and Sciences, and received a gold medal with diplomatic honors thereof. Some time after this, he proceeded to London,—still pursuing his studies with unfaltering diligence. He received, also, a silver medal from a learned Society, as an acknowledgment of some ingenious topographical labors. Sitting up late, one night, at his accustomed pursuits, he was found fallen in a paralytic, or apoplectic state,—from which, after a few months he so far recovered as to embark for home. He never arrived; but died on board the ship, at sea, July 17, 1805, aged about 50 years.*

5 **Edward**[4] (George,[3] John,[2] John[1]) was born at East Nottingham, Cecil County, Maryland, February 6, 1757; died Sept. 5, 1834. He married, September 18, 1782, REBECCA, daughter of Caleb and Anna Pierce, of Thornbury, Delaware County, Pa.

They had: CALEB (b. Nov. 4, 1783; m. Martha Shelley); OWEN (b. Oct. 14, 1785; m. Mary Pennell); PHOEBE (b. Sept. 20, 1787; m. Nov. 18, 1807, Wm. Painter; d. Nov. 30, 1866: they had MILTON† (b. Jan. 7, 1815; d. Oct. 6, 1888); ANN (b. July

---

* "Chester County Men."—by Darlington. Chester, Pa., May 25, 1861.

† MILTON PAINTER, m. Oct. 24, 1849, Sarah A. Hickson, and had: Frances Churchman (b. Sept. 27, 1850; d. July 11, 1853), Lillian Churchman, (b. Feb. 23, 1853; d. July 9, 1884), Francis Bennet (b. July 12, 1855; d. April 1, 1879), Armstrong (b. March 1, 1858; d. Feb. 2, 1860), Charles Armstrong (b. Oct.

17, 1789; m. Seth Smith); MICAJAH (b. Aug. 7, 1791; m. ——, Sinclair); HANNAH (b. Jan. 18, 1794; d. ——); ROBERT (b. Mch. 5, 1797 *; m. Oct. 22, 1834, Martha J. Reed; (2d) April 26, 1843, Julia Cauffman† ; d. Phila., October 23, 1873); MARY (b. April 6, 1800; m. Peter Wilson); REBECCA (b. Dec. 13, 1804; m. Bartholomew Fussell, M.D.); MARGARET (b. June 8, 1807; m. Wm. White Mendenhall).

6 Robert[5] (Edward,[4] George,[3] John,[2] John[1]) was born March 5, 1797. He resided for many years at Naaman's Creek, Pa.; removed to Philadelphia in 1849; entered largely into the manufacture and sale of lumber and retired in 1865 with an ample fortune.

He married (1st) Oct. 22, 1834, MARTHA J. REED (dau. A. W. and Mary Reed) who was born May 1, 1815 and died Oct. 13, 1838. They had: MARY REED (b. Nov. 17, 1835; d. Sept. 26, 1856); EDWARD (b. April 15, 1838; d. Feb. 21, 1853). ROBERT CHURCHMAN[5] married (2d) April 26, 1843, JULIA (daughter of Laurence Cauffman, Esq., of Philadelphia,†) who died April 9, 1887. They had: ALBERT (b. April 4, 1844; d. Phila., Nov. 28, 1869). ROBERT CHURCHMAN[5] died at Philadelphia, Oct. 23, 1873.‡ All of the above named were buried at Woodlands Cemetery in that city.

30, 1860; d. Nov. 22, 1877), Edward Lynne (b. Feb. 27, 1863), Evelyn (b. Aug. 4, 1866; d. June 6, 1883), Margaret Churchman (b. Sept. 20, 1870).

* The ancient family bible (in possession of Miss Painter) gives R. C.'s birth, March 20: the R. Churchman bible, March 5.

† See "CAUFFMAN."

‡ St. Mark's P. E. Church, Phila., contains a Memorial Window placed there by Mrs. Julia C. Churchman, as a tribute in remembrance of her husband and son.

A Quaker Missionary.*

WHILE I was in the city, the Governor summoned the members of Assembly together, and in pressing terms laid before them the defenseless state of Pennsylvania, in order to prevail with the House to grant a sum of money to station a ship of war at Delaware Capes, also to encourage the building a battery below the city, which was begun some time before by subscription, but likely to be too heavy for the undertakers. One night as I lay in my bed, it came very weightily upon me to go to the House of Assembly, and lay before the members thereof the danger of departing from trusting in that divine power which had hitherto protected the inhabitants of our land in peace and safety. The concern rested on me several days, which occasioned me with earnest breathings to seek the Lord, that if this was a motion from him, he would be pleased to direct my steps therein, so that I might be preserved from giving just cause of offense to any. It seemed to be a very difficult time, many, even of our Society, declaring their willingness that a sum of money should be given to the king, to show our loyalty to him, and that they were willing to part with their substance for his use, though as a people we had a testimony to bear against wars and fightings. I made no man privy to my concern until nearly a week had passed; when one morning it became so heavy upon me, that I went to the house of an intimate friend, and as we sat together he had a sense that something of weight was upon me, and asked if I was concerned about the Assembly. I asked him if he ever knew of any Friend going to the Assembly with a concern to speak to them? He answered "Nay," adding: "But I have often wondered that they have not, for I have understood it was formerly a common practice for them to sit in silence a while, like solemn worship, before they proceeded to do business." . . .

PREACHING TO THE LEGISLATURE.

Being pressed in mind, I went directly to the State-house before I took breakfast, and got there just as the Speaker was going in; I beckoned to him, and he came to me. I requested the

---

* Extracts from "An Account of the Gospel Labors, etc., of John Churchman." Phila., 1873 (see "CHURCHMAN").

Speaker to go in and inform the members that a countryman was in waiting who had a desire to be admitted, having something to communicate to them, and if they refused, he would be clear. He readily and affectionately answered he would, and soon brought me word that they were willing. There was a great awe over my mind when I went in, which I thought in some measure spread, and prevailed over the members beyond my expectation. After a silence of perhaps ten or twelve minutes, I felt as though all fear of man was taken away, and my mind influenced to address them in substance after the following manner :* . . .

THE INDIANS IN PENNSYLVANIA.

In the year 1756, I attended our general spring meeting in Philadelphia, at which we had the company of our dear friends, Samuel Fothergill and Catharine Payton, from Great Britain, and her companion, Mary Peasley, from Ireland, and it was a solemn, edifying meeting. The Indians having burnt several houses on the frontiers of this province, also at Gnadenhutten, in Northampton county, and murdered and scalped some of the inhabitants, at the time of this meeting, two or three of the dead bodies were brought to Philadelphia, with an intent, as was supposed, to animate the people to unite in preparations of war, to take vengeance on the Indians, and destroy them. They were carried along several of the streets, many people following, cursing the Indians, and also the Quakers, because they would not join in war for the destruction of the Indians. The sight of the dead bodies and the outcry of the people were very afflicting and shocking to me. Standing at the door of a Friend's house, as they passed along, my mind was humbled and turned inward, and I was made secretly to cry, " What will become of Pennsylvania?" for it felt to me that many did not consider that the sins of the inhabitants, pride, profane swearing, drunkenness, with other wickedness, were the cause why the Lord had suffered this calamity and scourge to come upon them. The weight of my exercise increasing as I walked along the street, a length it was said in my soul, "This land is polluted with blood, and in the day of inquisition for blood, it will not only be required at the frontiers and borders, but even in this place where these bodies are now seen." I said within myself, " How can this be ? since this has been a land of peace, and as yet not

---

*The limited space, available, causes the omission of the speech.

much concerned in war"; but, as it were in a moment, my eyes were turned to the case of the poor enslaved Negroes. And however light a matter they who have been concerned in it, may look upon the purchasing, selling, or keeping those oppressed people in slavery, it then appeared to me, that such were partakers in iniquity, encouragers of war and the shedding of innocent blood; which is often the case, where those unhappy people are captivated and brought away for slaves. . . . .

TEEDYUSCUNG AND THE EASTON TREATY.

ON the 12th of the Seventh month, this year, I left home in order to attend a treaty to be held between the Indians and our government, at Easton, in Northampton county; and proceeded to Philadelphia, where I was present at several conferences with Friends; the Governor having declared his dislike to their attendance at that treaty, or their distinguishing themselves by giving the Indians any presents. The result, was, that as mutual tokens of the revival of ancient friendship had passed between Friends and the Indians, with a view to promote a general peace, it would be of bad consequence now to neglect or decline attending on this important occasion; though it was judged necessary for Friends to act with great caution. We, therefore, set forward, and taking a meeting at Gwynnedd in the way, reached Easton on Fourth-day, the 21st of the month, the Governor having arrived about two hours before us; but did not enter on business that day.

Many friends from Philadelphia and other parts being here collected, we held a meeting on Fifth-day, which was low and dull, things appearing very dark. In the afternoon the Indians with Teedyuscung,* their king, or chief man, went to the Governor and signified the sincerity of their intentions to promote the good work of peace; when he delivered several strings and belts of wampum, in order to certify the full power and authority given to Teedyuscung for that purpose, who also desired that as things had heretofore been misunderstood or forgotten, he might have the liberty to choose a clerk to take the

---

* TIDIUSCUNG—Meaning "one-who-makes-the-earth-tremble" was a large, portly man, brave and eloquent; he was, however, a great drunkard and used to say that after he had drunk a half gallon of rum he was a match (intellectually, he meant) for the (then) Governor of Pennsylvania.—Denny. (*Penna. Mag. Hist. and Biog*, IX., 335.)

minutes of the transactions at this treaty, on behalf of the Indians; which was put off by the Governor at that time.

Next morning Teedyuscung renewed the same request, but was again put by; then the Indians began to be very uneasy, from an apprehension that some people from the Jersey side of the river were likely to rise, with a design to destroy them; but on going to converse with them, and giving them some pipes and tobacco, which they were told were a present from Friends, they became more quiet, and seemingly pacified; this day and the next there was little business done.

On First-day, the 24th of the month, Friends held a public meeting in the treaty-booth, to pretty good satisfaction, to which a great number of people came, two Friends having acceptable service therein. In the afternoon, Friends met again; but there seemed so great a cloud over the meeting, by reason of a raw careless spirit prevailing over the minds of the people, as though there was no God, notwithstanding his judgments are so conspicuous, especially in these parts of the country, that life did not arise in this meeting. About sunset this morning, we heard that the Mohawk Indians had requested to have a fire made to dance round, which the Governor allowed, as he had the evening before to the Delawares, with both which we were very uneasy, as the tendency thereof was to make the Indians drunk; but no endeavors of ours could prevent it.

On Second-day morning, the Governor agreed to allow the Indian king to choose himself a clerk, which he did, and about one o'clock that day, the treaty was first opened in public, when Teedyuscung was desired fully to inform, with an open heart, wherein he apprehended the Indians had been defrauded by the proprietaries, to which he answered that he would to-morrow; but they must first clean up the blood, as he expressed it, and bury the dead bodies. Next day being again met, the king said, that according to his word, he had met some of the several nations to do what they could for settling peace; but in the first place he had seen and considered the black cloud that hung over the land, the blood and bodies of the people who had suffered. " I have gathered up the stained leaves; the blood and dead bodies, and looked round about; when all seemed terrible, so that I could find no place to hide them; but looking up, I saw the great and good Spirit above. Let us heartily join in prayer to Him, that he may give up power to bury all these things out of sight, that neither the evil spirit, nor any wicked person may ever be able to raise them; that we may love like brethren, and the sun may shine clear upon us, that we, our wives, our young men and children, may rejoice in a lasting peace, that we may eat the fruits of the earth, and they may do us good, so that we may enjoy peace in the day-time, and at night lie down and sleep in it." Gave a belt of seventeen rows of wampum.

By another belt he told the Governor, that he took him by one hand, and the Five Nations of Indians and their allies took him by the other; therefore, said he, "let us all stand as one man, with one heart and one mind, and join in this good work of peace. When we intend to lift or remove a great weight we must be strong; if all do not exert themselves we never can do it; but if all heartily join, it is easy to remove it. Our forefathers did not proceed right when they met together; they looked at the earth and things present, which will soon pass out of sight; but did not look forward to the good of posterity. Let us set out right, and do better than they did, that a peace may be settled which may last to our children."

He next acquainted the Governor, that one of the messengers who had gone on a late message to the Indians afar off, meaning Moses Tatamy's son, was shot on his return by one of our young men and lay in a dangerous condition; and by a string of wampum insisted, that if he died, the other should be tried by our law, and suffer death also; and that some of their people should be present, to be able to inform the other nations of Indians of the justice done. He also revived the ancient agreement, that if any of them should commit the like offense, the criminal should be delivered up to be tried according to our laws, and suffer death in the same manner.

From Harper's Magazine.—Copyright, 1870, by Harper & Brothers.

Foster.

OSTER comes from the word *forester*, indicating occupation; is also spelled *Forster* and *Forrester*. It is found in England, Ireland and Scotland: from Great Britain it was brought to America by the Pilgrims and, to this day, the name is more common in New England than in any other part of the United States. The family whose American pedigree is here set forth, and which was at one time prominent in Boston and Cambridge, Massachusetts, it known to have descended * from

Births, Marriages and Deaths.

1 **Thomas Foster**, who was born in Cornwall, England, about 1660 and came to New England in 1690. He married Mary Bossenger who died at ———, in England.
  They had:

2. 1. THOMAS, b. Cornwall, England; m. (1st) Susan Howell of Boston (daughter of ——— Howell, who came from Wales; m. (2d)———, dau. of ——— Sumner; d. Boston, 1752.

2 **Thomas**[2] (Thomas[1]) was born in Cornwall, England. He came with his father to New England. He married (1st) Susan, daughter of ——— Howell of Boston (who came from Wales) and had:

3. 1. THOMAS, b. Boston, in 1711; m. Mary Banks of Boston; d. Boston, ———.

---

* As further research, necessary to complete the account of the first three generations of this family, would delay the publication of the book, the Editor has concluded to print the data already at hand. (See, also, folded " Pedigree.")

From a miniature.

II. BOSSENGER, b. Boston, ———; d. unmarried.
  III. EDWARD, b. ———; m. ———; d. ———.
  IV. ELIZABETH, b. ——— ; m. John Hurd * of Boston ; d. ———,
  178–.
  THOMAS² FOSTER married (2d) ——— Sumner. He died at
  Boston, ——— 1752 (buried in Dorchester).

3 **Thomas³** (Thomas,² Thomas¹) was born in Boston, July 13, 1713.†
He married Dec. 14, 1740, MARY,‡ only daughter of John Banks
of Boston, "Merchant," (who went from England) and had :

  I. THOMAS, b. Boston, July 4, 1738 ; m. Lucy, daughter of Captain Dwight and had Thomas and William ; d. at Halifax,§ 1770, and was buried there.
  II. JOHN, b. Nov. 28, 1741 ; d. in infancy.
4. III. BOSSENGER, b. Boston, June 3, 1742 ; m. (1st) Nov. 6, 1766, Elizabeth Craigie ; (2d) Feb. 26, 1779, Mary Craigie ; d. Cambridge, April 23, 1805.
  IV. SARAH,‖ b. ——— ; m. John Gare of Boston ; d. ———.
  V. MARY, b. ——— ; m. Rev. Timothy Hilliard of N. H.
  VI. HANNAH,¶ b. ——— ; m. Captain Nathaniel B. Lyde.
5. VII. WILLIAM, b. Boston, Sept. 28, 1745 ; m. Sept. 1, 1768 Grace, dau. of Nathan Spear of Boston ; d. ———.

---

  * JOHN HURD was a member of the Massachusetts Assembly, and m. (2) Mary, dau. Richard Russell of Charlestown, widow of Dr. Isaac Foster, Director-General of Hospitals, Cont. Army, 1776–80. (N. E. H. G. R., XXV. 67.)
  † According to the "*Curio*" Pedigree of the Foster family, (see list of illustrations) Thomas³ was born about 1711–12. In Paige's Hist. of Cambridge, under head of "Foster" (genealogical notes) the marriage of "Thomas Foster and Ann Bossenger, 1711" is mentioned as found in the official records of "the town of Boston": the coincidence of the names of FOSTER and BOSSENGER and the date (1711) in this item, taken together with the date of birth of Thomas³ (in "*Curio*" Pedigree) possesses a curious interest and invites further research. (See also the "Haskin," Foster Pedigree, on folded sheet.)
  ‡ She was living in 1783, aged 62.
  § Clerk in H. M. Naval Office, there.
  ‖ A widow, living in London, in 1783.
  ¶ Living, 1783 at Boston.

VIII. TIMOTHY,* b. ———; d. ———.

6. IX. JOSEPH, b. ———; m. (1st) April 10, 1783, Miriam, dau. of John Cutler of Boston; (2d) mother of W. D. Sohier, Esq., of Boston; d. Jan. 25, 1835.

"The Sons of Liberty," an ante-Revolutionary association, celebrated the discomfiture of the "Stamp" project by anniversary dinners. At one of these dinners, held at the "Liberty Tree," Dorchester, Mass., Aug. 14, 1769, among 355 subscribers, appear the names of Timothy Foster, Bossenger Foster and William Foster (sons of Thomas³ Foster).

From the Minutes of the Selectmen of Boston, Dec. 7, 1774, it appears that " The Committee to prepare a list for a Committee of Inspection, and to carry the Resolutions of the Continental Congress into Execution, reported the following names: The Honble. Thos. Cushing, Esq., Honble. JOHN HANCOCK,† Esq., Mr. SAMUEL ADAMS, William Phillips, Esq., Col. Thos. Marshall, Mr. Thomas Wendell, Dr. BENJ. CHURCH,‡ Dr. JOSEPH WARREN,§ Mr. PAUL REVERE,‖ Mr. John Winthrop, Capt. John Marston, Mr. BOSSENGER FOSTER, Capt. Samuel Partridge, Jonathan Williams, Esq., and others."

4 **Bossenger**⁴ (Thomas,₃ Thomas,² Thomas¹) was born at Boston June 3, 1742. He married (1) Nov. 6, 1766, ELIZABETH CRAIGIE (sister of Andrew Craigie, Apothecary General of the Continental Army, 1777). Bossenger Foster was active in the patriotic measures of Revolutionary times,¶ resided at Cambridge

---

* Unmarried in 1783.

† The famous Revolutionary Governor.

‡ Subsequently charged with treasonable correspondence with the British, and removed from the position of Director-General of Hospitals, Continental Army.

§ Who fell at Bunker Hill.

‖ The hero of the famous ride.

¶ " On a Motion, Voted—That the town will now Come to the choice of ten members of the Committee of Correspondence, Inspection and Safety in the room of those who have resigned or are looked upon by the Town as ceasing to be members of said Committee, since their being chosen Representatives, viz., Nathaniel Appleton, Oliver Wendell, William Dennie, Caleb Davis, William

(in what was afterward known as "the Batchelder house") where he died of gout, April 23, 1805. ELIZABETH CRAIGIE FOSTER d. ———.

BOSSENGER and ELIZABETH (CRAIGIE) FOSTER had:

I. BOSSENGER, b. Boston ———, 1768, graduated, Harvard College, 1787 ; d. Jan. 17, 1816.

7   II. ELIZABETH CRAIGIE, b. Jan. 23, 1770 ; m. March 6, 1799, Samuel Haven, d. Feb. 10, 1826.

BOSSENGER FOSTER married (2) Feb. 26, 1779, MARY CRAIGIE, and had:

8   III. ANDREW, b. Sept. 7, 1780; m. Nov. 19, 1813, Mary Conant ; d. Cambridge, May 17, 1831.

IV. JOHN, b. July 4, 1782 ; graduated, Harvard College, 1802 ; d. Cambridge, Nov. 3, 1836.

V. THOMAS, b. Nov. 9, 1784; graduated, Harvard College, 1805, became a physician and Town Clerk, 1827 ; d. Cambridge, Feb. 4, 1831.

VI. JAMES, b. April 23, 1786 ; graduated, Harvard College, 1806, was admitted to the Bar and became Register of Probate; d. Cambridge, Aug. 27, 1817.*

VII. GEORGE, b. May 6, 1790; graduated at Brown University, 1811, became a lawyer ; d. Cambridge, Sept. 4, 1817.*

VIII. MARY CRAIGIE, b. Cambridge, Dec. 3, 1795; d. Feb. 18, 1811.

5 William⁴ (Thomas,³ Thomas,² Thomas¹) was born, Boston,

Cooper, John Brown, John Pitts, Esqrs., and Mr. John Sweetser. It was further Voted that the choice of the ten Members for the Committee of Correspondence be by separate Votes. The Votes being brought in accordingly, upon sorting them it appeared that Mr. James Bowdoin, Mr. Ezekiel Price, Mr. Joshua Blanchard, Mr. William Davis, Capt. Gustavus Fellows, Jonathan Williams, Esq., Capt. Eleazer Johnson, Mr. Hermain Brimmer, Mr. BOSSENGER FOSTER, Mr. Ebenezer Dorr, were chosen Members of the Committee of Correspondence, Inspection and Safety for the remainder of the year." (Records of Boston Committee of Corr., Insp. & Safety, Aug. 20, 1776.)

* GEORGE and JAMES FOSTER were engaged to be married to Elizabeth and Sarah, daughters of Richard Dana Esq. of Boston ; but both brothers died within a week of the day fixed for the wedding.

Sept. 28, 1745.* He was in London, England, April 8, 1783, the date at which letters patent were issued to him authorizing certain changes in his coat-of-arms. He was a prominent merchant and public-spirited citizen of Boston about the time of the Revolution.† The following extract from the Minutes of the Selectmen of Boston (Oct 31, 1768,) illustrates the dawn of an anti-slavery feeling in Massachusetts:

"The Several Constables of the Watch directed, by the Selectmen, to be watchful of the Negros and to take up those of them that may be in gangs at unseasonable hours: Zachary Johonnot, Esq., Messrs. Nathan Spear, William Foster and others, enter their Complaint with the Selectmen against John Willson, Esq., of the 59th Regiment of Foot for practising on their Negro servants to induce them immediately to enter into a dangerous conspiracy against their Masters, promising them their freedom as a reward, whereupon Mr. Justice Ruddock was desired by the Selectmen to take the several Affidavits relative to the above mentioned complaints. In consequence of the above, the Selectmen lodged a Complaint in Writing with the Worshipful Richard Dana, Esq., and John Ruddock, Esq., two of his Majesty's Justices of the Peace for the County of Suffolk, and the quorum."

WILLIAM FOSTER[4] married (pub.) Sept. 1768, GRACE, daughter of Nathan Spear‡ of Boston (who was b. 1751; d. June 12, 1816).

---

* Other dates and details relating to William[4] and his children were not forthcoming in time for insertion in this edition.

† From the Minutes of the Selectmen of Boston, Feb. 14, 1776, it appears that "William Foster has imported 700 barrels of flour for the use of the inhabitants" (being one of six persons agreeing to supply 3000 barrels during the siege of Boston).

‡ NATHAN[3] SPEAR (b. Boston, 1728; m. Grace Willis; d. Aug. 30, 1800), was grandson of George[1] "the emigrant" who settled at Braintree, Mass., about 1650. Nathan[3] had seven children. In 1768 he, William[4] Foster and others complained to the selectmen of Boston "against John Willson, Esq., of the 59th Regt. of Foot, for inducing our negro servants (slaves) to enter into a dangerous conspiracy against their masters, promising them their freedom as a reward." Nathan[3] was foreman of a jury, 1779. His brother Gershom, a sea captain, commanded (1760) the British brig, *Anson*, and, in a contest with a French ship in the Mediterranean, handled his ship so skillfully and gallantly that he was received at Gibraltar with public honors. In 1784 Nathan[4] Spear visited France in company with William[4] Foster (who had married his sister

They had: SALLY (b. Boston, Jan. 10, 1770; m. March 3, 1790, Harrison Gray Otis,*, d. Philadelphia Sept. 6, 1838†), WILLIAM‡ (b. Boston, Jan. 10, 1772; m. 1792, Marie Hortense Grace). Mrs. Adams (the wife of John Adams) in a letter to her friend, Mrs. Cranch, dated July 6, 1784, describing passengers on board the ship *Active*, in which she sailed for London, writes of " Mr. Foster, a merchant, a gentleman soft in his manners, very polite and kind, loves domestic life and thinks justly of it: I respect him on this account. . . Mr. Spear brings up the rear, a single gentleman, with a great deal of good humor, some wit and much drollery, easy and happy, blow high and blow low; can sleep and laugh at all seasons. . . Mr. Spear reading ' Thomson's Seasons,' with his hat on." (N. E. H. G. R. XVIII, 160.)

*HARRISON GRAY OTIS⁶ b. Oct. 8, 1765; m. May 31, 1790, SALLY, daughter of William Foster, merchant of Boston. She was b. Jan 10, 1770 and d. Sept. 6, 1838, aged 66 yrs., 8 mos. He d. Oct. 28, 1848, at 2 A. M., at his residence, Beacon St., Boston, aged 84. They had: Elizabeth Gray (b. 1791; m. Geo. Lyman, had 3 sons, 2 dau.; d. 1821) Harrison Gray (b. 1792; m. Eliza Boardman and had 4 children—1. Arthur, in U. S. N.) Sally (b. 1793; m. Israel Thorndike and had 1 son, 3 dau.), Mary Foster (b. 1795; d. 1796), Alleyne (b. 1796; drowned 1806), Sophia Harrison (b. 1799; m. Andrew Ritchie, and had 2 sons, 1 dau.), James William (b. 1800; m. Martha Church, and had 5 children, resided in 1850 in N. Y.), William Foster (b. 1801; m. Emily Marshall and had 3 children), Alleyne (b. 1807, resided, 1850, in Boston), George Harrison (b. 1810). In a letter to Hon. Charles S. Daveis of Portland, Me. (Boston, 3 Nov., 1845), giving his recollections of Gen. Knox, of the Revolution, Mr. Otis writes: " I notice the postscript respecting ' Harry Otis and Sally Foster.' The prediction contained in it was fulfilled, and followed by five and forty years of conjugal happiness. *Hinc illæ lachrymæ*." " The family of Mr. Otis was remarkable for great intelligence and personal beauty. I well remember numerous parties at the fine old mansion-house in Beacon Street, with its spacious hall and the beautiful rooms en suite, decorated with pictures by Copley, Blackburn, and Smybert, which threw over the place the air of good old colony times. There Mr. Otis, surrounded by his children and grandchildren and their friends, moved, the ruler of the revels. After an experience of more than forty years in such matters, I have never seen Mr. Otis surpassed in the perfection of his dress, his equipage, his entertainments, or his manners. He always reminded me of a fine old French nobleman, one of those we read of as uniting wit with learning, and great elegance with profound acquirements" (Aug. T. Perkins, A. M., in Mem. Biog. N. E. H. G. Society).

† Haskin " Pedigree " says, " m. March 30, 1790; d. Sept. 4, 1834."

‡ WILLIAM and MARIE H. (Perron) FOSTER, had: MILLITE, FRANCES A.

Perron, b. 1780; d. Feb. 14, 1838, of Morlaix, France; d. Boston, Feb. 23, 1863). GRACE (b. Sep. 22, 1774; m. Col. John T. Apthorp,* of Boston; d. Dec. 30 1795). MARY SPEAR* (b. Sep. 22, 1774; m. Jan. 15, 1797, Col. Apthorp; d. March 9, 1854). CHARLES CHAUNCY (b. Feb. 18, 1785; m. (1st), Sarah Borland; (2d) 1816, Catharine Cabot†). LEONARD (b. July 24, 1787; m. Lydia Geaubert‡). JOHN FRANCIS (b. 1789; d. Feb. 17, 1812). CHARLOTTE WILLIS (b. 1792; m. April 25, 1822, Jeremiah Van Rensselaer; d. March 7, 1852).

6 Joseph[4] (Thomas,[3] Thomas,[2] Thomas,[1]) was born at Boston; married (1) April 10, 1783, MIRIAM, dau. of John[3] Cutler§ of

(m. Aug. 6, 1845, Henry Tudor and had 3 children), VIRGINIA (m. April, 1845; Coppinger). See App. "A Franco-American Leaf."

*JOHN T. APTHORP (b. Dec. 24, 1770; d. April 7, 1849); was (1796) one of the Wardens of Christ Church, Cambridge, Mass. By his second m. he had 9 children.

† CHARLES CHAUNCY and CATHARINE (Cabot) FOSTER had: KATHARINE BORLAND, (b. April 29, 1817; d. Sept. 1887). CHARLES FRANCIS (b. May 16, 1818; m. 1st, Emma, dau. Bradford Sumner of Cambridge, and 2d, Mary Wells of Greenfield, Mass., and had Charles Chauncy.) SARAH LLOYD (b. Feb. 10, 1820), and SUSAN CABOT (b. Aug. 19, 1823; m. Frank Batchelder and had 2 children.

‡ LEONARD and LYDIA (Geaubert) FOSTER had: FRANCIS CHARLES (b. March 17, 1829; m. Nov. 24, 1857, Marion, dau. Edward Padelford, of Savannah, Ga., b. 1832, and had Leonard, b. Nov. 17, 1858; d. Oct. 27, 1884; Caroline Padelford, b. April 7, 1861, and Francis Apthorp, b. Sept. 21, 1872). MARY GRACE (b. March 24, 1834; m. Edward Graham Davis of New Berne, N. C., and had 7 children) and WILLIAM LEONARD (b. Jan. 3, 1837).

§ JOHN CUTLER[3] (1725-1805) was the grandson of "Johannes de Mesmaker chirurgeon," who came from Holland in 1674, settled at Hingham, subsequently took the name of CUTLER (English translation of Mesmaker) and removed to Boston, where he established a profitable practice. John[3] (father of Miriam) fell heir to part of his grandfather's estate including the "splendid mansion on Marlboro Street, built in 1693, three stories high, the rooms being fitted with leather hangings." He was a prominent and public spirited citizen, hospitable and charitable. He was a good musician and frequently played the organ in Christ Church, of which his son-in-law was Rector. He was Grand Master of the Masonic order. His children intermarried with the families of Appleton, Foster, Hoppin, Sullivan Fanueil, Parker, Prince, Lawrence, Sumner, Ward and McAllister.

Boston, and had: JOSEPH * (b. Dec. 10, 1786; d. July 18, 1855), and MARIA (b. ———; d. ———).

JOSEPH FOSTER married (2) Mrs. SOHIER of Boston.*

7 **Elizabeth Craigie**[5] (Bossenger,[4] Thomas,[3] Thomas,[2] Thomas,[1]) was born at Boston, Mass., January 23, 1770. She married, May 6, 1799, Hon. SAMUEL HAVEN of Dedham, (b. April 5, 1771; bapt. April 7, 1771; d. Sept. 4, 1847) and died at ——— Feb. 10, 1826.

SAMUEL and ELIZABETH (FOSTER) HAVEN had:

I. ELIZABETH CRAIGIE, b. Dedham, Jan. 26, 1800; d. 1806.

II. CATHARINE DEXTER, b. Dedham, Jan. 4, 1802; bapt. Jan. 10, 1802; m. July 26, 1831, FRANCIS HILLIARD of Cambridge (b. Cambridge, Nov. 1, 1806; d. Worcester, 1878); d. Morristown, N. J., March 10, 1888. FRANCIS and CATHARINE DEXTER (Haven) HILLIARD had:

(1) FRANCIS WILLIAM, b. Lowell, Mass., July 18, 1832; m. May 12, 1857, Maria Nash Johnstone and had: Francis (b. Edenton, N. C., March 3, 1858; d. Cheyenne, Wyo., Feb. 3, 1876), Margaret Bergwin, (b. Edenton, N. C., June 25, 1859), Catharine Haven (b. Plymouth, N. C., Jan. 15, 1861), Samuel Iredell Johnstone (b. Chapel Hill, N. C., May 1, 1862; d. Erie, Pa., Feb. 20, 1878), George Johnstone (b. Chapel Hill, N. C., April 4, 1864; d. Pocomoke, Md., Aug. 29, 1881), Haven (b. Edenton, N. C., Aug. 1866; d. same day), Elizabeth Haven (b. Edenton, N. C., Oct. 3, 1867), Foster Haven (b. Edenton, N. C., Oct. 1, 1869), Maria Nash (b. Theresa, N. Y., Aug. 16, 1871), Iredell (b. Theresa, N. Y., Dec. 1, 1872). (2) ELIZABETH CRAIGIE HAVEN, b. Dedham, Oct. 2, 1833. (3) CATHARINE LYDIA, b. Dedham, May 17, 1835; m. April, 1859, Frederick G. Burnham of Morristown, N. J. (no chil-

---

* JOSEPH FOSTER, Esq., d. Somerville, 18 July, 1855; b. Boston, 10 Dec., 1786. He was clerk in the State Treasury office 35½ years, "being appointed, Aug. 1815, under Treasurer Apthorp, and continued through his term and the terms of Sargent, Mitchell, Sewall, Barnard Wilder, Russell, Mills, Barrett and Bradbury, resigning on his 64th birthday." (N. E. H. G. R. IX., 373.) [Am inclined to think this is the "Joseph Foster" mentioned by Hoppin as one of the wardens of Christ Church, Cambridge, 1829-1835.—ED.]

dren). (4) SAMUEL HAVEN, b. Cambridge, Mass., Dec. 13, 1838; m. May 19, 1870, Alice Anne Johnstone of London, England, and had: Haven Johnstone (b. North Conway, N. H., Aug. 6, 1871), Frederick Burnham (b. North Conway, N. H., Sept. 22, 1872), Herbert Beeton (b. Erie, Pa., Dec. 6, 1875), Edmund Bayfield (b. Washington, Pa., Feb. 5. 1878). (5) SARAH MCKEAN, b. Roxbury, Mass., Dec. 21, 1840; m. May 1871, Frederick S. Pratt of Worcester, Mass; they had: Francis Hilliard (b. 1872; d. 1872), Frederick Haven (b. Worcester, 1873), Catharine Chase (b. Worcester, 1875), Robert Gage (b. Worcester, 1878), Elizabeth (b. Worcester, 1882).

III. SAMUEL FOSTER, b. Dedham, Mass., May 28, 1806. He graduated at Harvard College in 1826, was admitted to the bar in Middlesex County, and for some time practised law in Lowell. He was appointed Librarian of the American Antiquarian Society of Worcester, Mass., Sept. 23, 1837, a position held by him until his death, Sep. 5, 1881. Mr. Haven received from Amherst (1826) the degree of Doctor of Laws, and from Harvard (1852) that of Master of Arts. He was a very scholarly man, a learned archæologist and the author of several able works, including "The Archæology of the United States,"* and a "History of Dedham." He was a member of many scientific and historical societies.†

---

*Smithsonian Institute, 1855.

†"On the day following the last monthly meeting of this Society, the remains of our late honored associate, Dr. SAMUEL FOSTER HAVEN, of Worcester, were committed to Mount Auburn Cemetery. Our esteem for him, our estimation of his high and attractive character, and of his many virtues, and our appreciation of his devoted labors and his great accomplishments in his chosen fields of history, archæology and bibliography, require of us a further sympathetic reference. . . . If the word Librarian means merely a custodian of books, it is a wholly inadequate title for Dr. Haven ; for he was himself the catalogue, the interpreter, the commentator, the appraiser of the contents and value of that rich collection of treasures which had so largely gathered under his administration. Among the portraits of all the worthies which adorn the walls of the Library in Worcester, beginning with that of the discoverer of the Continent, there is not one which more becomes its place than does that of Dr. Haven." (Memoirs, *Mass. Hist. Society*, 1881.)

He married (1) May 10, 1830, LYDIA GIBBS, daughter of Rev. Freeman Sears, of Natick. She died March 10, 1836.
They had: SAMUEL FOSTER * (b. Dedham, May 20, 1831; d. Fredericksburg, Va., Dec. 3, 1862). Doctor Haven married (2) Dec. 3, 1872, FRANCES W. ALLEN of Worcester.

8 Andrew[5] (Bossenger,[4] Thomas,[3] Thomas,[2] Thomas[1]) was born in Boston on Sept. 7, 1780. He was graduated at Harvard College (1800) and became a physician in Dedham. He was at one time Professor of Botany at Harvard, and is said to have first demonstrated the value of the tomato as an article of food.†
He married (at Dedham, Mass.), Nov. 19, 1813, MARY (daughter of Samuel‡ and Mary§ Parker (Conant) of Charlestown, Mass.,

---

* SAMUEL F. HAVEN, JR., M. D., was graduated Harvard College (1852) and Boston Medical College (1855); continued his studies in London, Paris, Vienna and Berlin and settled in Worcester. When the war for the Union broke out he joined the 15th Mass. Vol. Infantry as Assistant Surgeon. "He was regardless of personal exposure and in the engagement at Fredericksburg, Dec. 13, 1862, was killed, by a shell, while engaged in performing an operation." " In him the Army will mourn the loss of a surgeon of unwonted skill and fidelity; his profession a member certain to attain distinction, and his intimate acquaintance a pure minded, simple hearted, devoted friend."

† In Felt's "Annals of Salem" there is a note which says (under date of 1802, Oct. 12) "Mr. Corne is endeavoring to introduce the Tomatoes. He finds it difficult to persuade us even to taste of them, after all his praise; being a native of South America, it was carried to Europe and raised in England before 1600; still for a long period it was no favorite in our Northern States." It was known to the Indians of Mexico by the name, *tomatl*. N. E. H. G. R. XX, 1373,

‡ SAMUEL CONANT[8] (b. Charlestown, Mass., 1755; m. March 7, 1782, MARY PARKER of Portland, Me.) was a lineal descendant through Samuel[7] (b. Charlestown, 1730), Roger[6] (b. Charlestown, 1701), Roger[5] (b. Beverly, Mass., 1668), Lot[4] (b. Nantasket, Mass., 1624), Roger[3] (b. East Budleigh, Devonshire, England, 1592) and Richard[2] (b. same place, 1548) from John[1] (b. Gittisham, Devonshire, England, 1520), a prominent citizen and churchwarden of East Budleigh, 1577 (in which place, in 1643, the father of Sir Walter Raleigh held the same office). John[1] " was descended from ingenious parents of Gittisham, near Honiton, whose ancestors for many generations had been fixed here but were originally of French extraction." Roger[3] was born at East Budleigh

and died at Cambridge, May 17, 1831. Mary (Conant) Foster was born Charlestown, July 17, 1785, and died at New York, Nov. 4, 1854.

They had:

9. I. ANDREW, b. Dedham, Mass., Jan. 5, 1815; bp. March 10, 1815; m. Sept. 16, 1849, Delia Henry, dau. of Capt. J. B. Montgomery, U. S. N.; d. Brooklyn, N. Y., Sept. —, 1879.

10. II. SAMUEL CONANT, b. Jamaica Plain, Mass., Oct. 24, 1816; m. Sept. 23, 1857, Mary B. Bogert (b. Sept. 14, 1832, d. Feb. 4, 1880); d. New York, April 18, 1873.

11. III. JAMES, b. Jamaica Plain, Mass., Nov. 20, 1818; m. July 18, 1843, Delia Henry, dau. of Comdr. J. B. Montgomery, U. S. N.; d. New York, Nov. 11, 1847.

England, April 9, 1592, and was the youngest of eight children of Richard[2] and Agnes (Clark) Conant, " who were esteemed for their eminent piety." He landed at Plymouth in 1623 and in 1624 was chosen to govern the Dorchester Company of colonists at Cape Ann, located on west side of Gloucester Harbor, near Stage Head, where are the ruins of a small fort, then called Fort Conant. The house occupied by Roger Conant at Cape Ann was removed to Salem, where the framework still stands (corner Church and Washington streets). Although he is not nominally acknowledged as first Governor of Massachusetts, the colony of which he was the head made the first permanent settlement in Massachusetts territory, and was the germ from which the Massachusetts Bay Colony sprang. Roger's brother, John, was the rector of Lymington, Somersetshire, England, who in 1643 preached a sermon to the House of Commons. Roger[3] m. (at St. Anne, Blackfriars, London) Nov. 11, 1618, Sarah Horton. He died at Marblehead, Nov. 19, 1679. The name of Conant can be traced in England for more than six hundred years, and is derived from the Celtic *Conan*, formerly of Wales and Cornwall. Although spelled Conant it is pronounced in Devonshire, *Connett*. In that county the earliest mention is of "Alexander Connaunt," who was living at Exminster in 1327 and was doubtless of the family here recorded. (*Resumé* from " *The History of the Family of Conant in England and America*, 1520-1887, by F. O. Conant, Portland, 1887.")

§ MARY[6] PARKER (b. Jan. 25, 1759; m. March 7, 1782, Samuel Conant; d. Jamaica Plain, Mass., Oct. 3, 1828) was descended from DANIEL[5] (b. Nov. 20, 1726; m. Oct. 3, 1751, Margaret Jarvis; d. Dec. 31, 1785), ISAAC[4] (b. 1692; m. 1727, Grace Hall; d. 1742), DANIEL[3] (b. 1667; m. Anna Errington of Charlestown Mass.; d. Oct. 16, 1694), JOHN[2] (b. Saco, Me. ——— ; m. August 20, 1660, Mary Fairfield of Boston : is said to have "purchased of the Indians,

12   IV. GEORGE, b. Roxbury, Mass., Oct 5, 1820; m. Nov. 30, 1848, Louisa A. Gibbons; d. Brooklyn, N. Y., Nov. 28, 1866.
   V. MARY CONANT, b. Roxbury, Aug. 25, 1822; d. Roxbury, Nov. 11, 1822.
   VI. MARY CONANT, b. Roxbury, July 13, 1824; d. Roxbury, Aug. 13, 1825.

9 Andrew[6] (Andrew,[5] Bossenger,[4] Thomas,[3] Thomas,[2] Thomas[1]) was born at Dedham, Mass., Jan. 5, 1815 (bapt. March 10, 1815); He was graduated at Harvard College (1833) and became a manufacturer. He married, Sept. 16, 1849, DELIA HENRY, daughter of Capt. John B. Montgomery. U. S. N. and died at Brooklyn, N. Y., Sept. 1879.
   They had:
      I. JULIA, b. Feb. 27, 1831; d. New York, May 3, 1852.

(1657) the territory which comprises the present town of Phippsburgh and part of West Bath, Me., and was the first of the English nation that began to subdue the said tract, from which he was more than once driven off by the Indians"; he and his son James returned to Georgetown and again fled on account of the Indians to Falmouth, Me., where they were both killed at the capture of Fort Loyall, June 1, 1690, and JOHN[1] who with his wife Mary came from Biddeford, Devonshire, England, before 1536, when they were at Saco, Me.). John[1] purchased Parker's Island (now Georgetown, Me.) from the Indians in 1650 and died about 1660. DANIEL[5] PARKER had twelve children: Daniel[6] (b. Jan. 20, 1757; grad. Harvard College, and an officer in the Revolution), Mary[6] (as above); Elias[6] (b. June 3, 1760; d. young); Margaret[6] (b. ——— m. July 29, 1784), Abraham Eustis, who was b. 1757; d. 1788; o. w. a.); Isaac,[6] John[6] and Stephen[6] (all d. young), Sarah[6] (b. April 23, 1766; d. unmarried———) Edward,[6] (lived and d. in N. Y.), Isaac[6] (b. June 17, 1768; Harvard Coll. 1786; Member Me. Legislature, 1791-93-94-95; Member of Congress, 1796, U. S. Marshal, 1799-1803; Judge Supreme Court, 1806; Chief Justice of Mass. 1814-30; m. Margaret Hall and had eight children; d. ——— 1830), John[6] (d. in N. Y.) and Jacob[6] (d. 1789, aged 17). MARY[6] (Parker) CONANT m. (2d) Col. David Wood of Andover.

   Abraham Eustis (brother to William, Surgeon 1776, Secretary of War 1809-12, Minister to Holland 1815, Governor of Mass. 1824-25), m. Margaret[6] Conant and had ABRAHAM (b. 1786; d. 1843) H. C. 1804; Capt. Light Artillery U. S. A. 1808; Colonel 1st Artillery and Bvt. Brig.-Gen. U. S. A. 1834. (*Bangor His. Mag.* I. 126, N. E. H. G. R. VI.)

II. ANDREW, b. Sept. 5, 1856; m. ———.

III. KATE MCCREA, b. Dec. 31, 1860; graduated at Normal College, City of N. Y. (1878).

10 **Samuel Conant**[6] (Andrew,[5] Bossenger,[4] Thomas,[3] Thomas,[2] Thomas[1]) was born at Jamaica Plain, Mass., Oct. 24, 1816. He graduated at Harvard College, 1834, and in Sept. of the same year entered the Medical School at Boston under the care of Directors Channing, Lewis, Ware and Otis. In Sept. 1836, he became a student at Jefferson Medical College, Philadelphia, from which he was graduated, March, 1837. He spent the period 1837–39 in Europe in professional improvement and settled in the city of New York, where he remained in active and successful practice until his death, which occurred April 18, 1873. Dr. Foster married, Sept. 23, 1857, MARY BENEZET BOGERT of New York City (b. Sept. 14, 1832; d. Feb. 4, 1880).

They had:

I. THEODORE BOGERT, b. New York, Aug 10, 1858; m. (1) June 15, 1886, Sarah E. Wells (d. Oct. 27, 1887) and had: Helen (b. Oct. 3, 1887; died March 12, 1888); m. (2) April 6, 1890, Ellen Lincoln, daughter of Hon. T. A. D. Fessenden, M. C., and niece of Hon. William Pitt Fessenden, U. S. Senator for Maine. He graduated at Columbia College (1879), Gen. Theolog. Sem. N. Y. (1882), was ordained Deacon P. E. Church (Oct., 1882), and Priest May 20, 1883. He is (1891) Rector of St. James Ch., Great Barrington, Mass.

II. CONANT, b. July 6, 1860; d. July 13, 1870.

III. MARY CONANT, b. Nov. 22, 1863; m. June 14, 1888, Herbert Woods Harris of New York City, and had: Reginald Foster (b. April 15, 1889) and Florence (b. June 5, 1890).

IV. FRANCES NELSON, b. June 19, 1865; m. July 12, 1890, Elmer Ellsworth Wentworth of Boston, Mass. (Harvard University, 1882).

V. JAMES REGINALD, b. Nov. 23, 1867.

11 **James**[6] (Andrew,[5] Bossenger,[4] Thomas,[3] Thomas,[2] Thomas[1]) was born at Jamaica Plain, Mass., Nov. 20, 1818. He was edu-

cated at the noted schools of Green, of that place, and Wells of Fresh Pond. At an early age he manifested a taste for the sea, and, while yet a mere lad, made a voyage "before the mast" on board a merchant vessel, belonging to an uncle, sailing between Boston and Calcutta. Upon his return he received from President Jackson (through the influence of his cousins, Hon. William Foster* of Boston and Miss Delia Tudor Stewart,† daughter of the late Admiral Charles Stewart, U. S. N.) an appointment to the U. S. Naval School, (then at Philadelphia) from which he was graduated (1838) second in his class. He was commissioned Midshipman (March 2, 1838) and Passed Midshipman (May 20, 1844) and served on board the *Erie* (1838) *Grampus* (1839) and *St. Louis* (1840–42) on the West India station. During part of this time he was employed on Coast Survey duty, for which he had a special aptitude, and for his services received the highest commendation of his superiors, Lieutenant (afterwards Rear Admiral) C. R. P. Rodgers and Lieut. Commander (afterwards Rear Admiral) Charles H. Davis, U. S. N.

While serving on the coast of Mexico in the U. S. S. *Grampus* and in command of the ship's launch, he was seriously injured (September 29, 1838) by the capsizing of the boat, in crossing the bar, off the mouth of the Rio del Norte, near Matamoras. He remained in active service for several years, but eventually succumbed to the effects of this accident and died at New York City, Nov. 11, 1847. The letters of officers of high rank, who knew Mr. Foster, contain evidence of the universal esteem in which he was held, for his unselfish devotion to duty, and express sincere sorrow at the untimely death of one who "gave promise of the highest standing in his profession." He married at Charlestown, Mass. (by Rev. Mr. Buddington) July 14, 1843, DELIA HENRY,‡ daughter of Commander (afterward Rear Admiral) John Berrien Montgomery, U. S. N., and had :

1. MARY, b. New York, N. Y., March 14, 1846; d. New York, Feb. 14, 1849.

---

* See " A Franco-American Leaf."

† Miss Stewart soon after married Henry Parnell, the father of Charles Stewart Parnell, the " Home Rule " M. P.

‡ See " MONTGOMERY."

70   *AUTUMN LEAVES FROM FAMILY TREES.*

  II. ELINOR FRANCES, b. Boston, Mass., April 3, 1847; educated at schools of Madame Ogden Hoffman, (N. Y.), and at Genéva, Switzerland; m. Sept, 1, 1868, Theo. F. Rodenbough,* U. S. A.

12 George[6] (Andrew,[5] Bossenger,[4] Thomas,[3] Thomas,[2] Thomas[1]) was born at Roxbury, Mass., October 5, 1820. He was educated at Harvard College and became a manufacturer. He served during the war for the Union as Captain and Colonel 67th Regt. N. Y. Vols. (1861–64), was twice wounded, and died in New York City, Nov. 28, 1866. He married, Nov. 30, 1848, LYDIA ADELIA CLARK, daughter of George and Mary D. Gibbons Miller, and had:

  I. EDITH, b. Aug, 29, 1849; m. Feb. 25, 1875, d. New York, April 27, 1867.
  II. GEORGE CRAIGIE, b. Oct. 30, 1850.
  III. SAMUEL CONANT, b. April 15, 1852; d. New York, March 8, 1885.
  IV. FITZ GIBBONS, b. April 3, 1860; m. Aug. 4, 1884.

---

* See "RODENBOUGH."

NOTE BY THE EDITOR.—After the first page, relating to the FOSTER family, had been printed, the "Pedigree," compiled by Mr. Haskin of Cambridge, (see folded sheet, following) was received from Francis Apthorp Foster, Esq. It differs in certain respects from the "Curio" pedigree, particularly with reference to the earliest American ancestor who is said to be "EDWARD FOSTER, a lawyer of Scituate in Plymouth colony, as early as 1633; perhaps from Kent, Eng. Representative—1639-40. He m. 8 Apr., 1685, Lettice Hanford and had three children. The evidences in this document of careful research, entitle it to equal credit with the "Curio" pedigree.

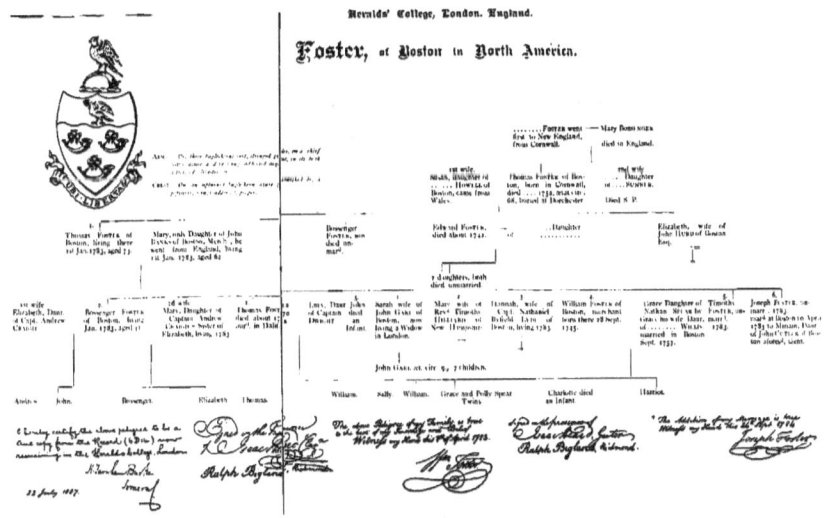

From the "Foster Pedigree," prepared by Mr. Haskin, of Cambridge, Mass.

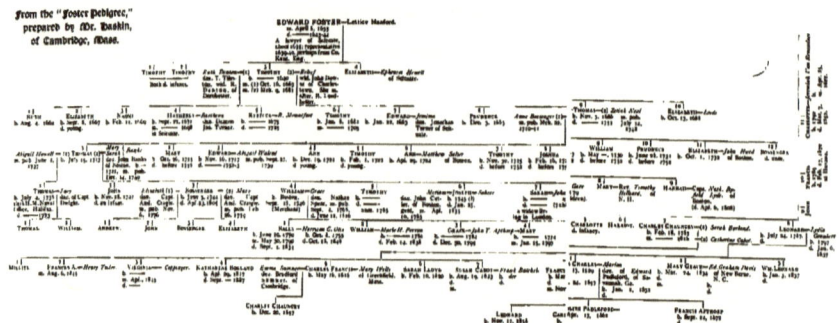

A Colonial Indian Fight.*

AFTER Massachusetts had purchased Maine from the Gorges' heirs, they deemed it necessary, in order to protect the people of Maine from the inroads of the French and Indians, that a strong fortress should be constructed at some prominent easterly location. Falmouth or Casco (called Falmouth by the English and Casco by the French) being the principal town on the frontier accessible by water, was selected as the location. On an eminence overlooking Casco Bay a stout defensive structure was erected in 1680. It comprised a number of buildings, of logs, surrounded by palisades strengthened at intervals by wooden towers for purposes of observation, and pierced by loopholes for musketry and for eight small cannon. In most respects this outpost was like the average frontier army "fort," which until very recently dotted the western borders of the United States. It covered about half an acre and was called Fort Loyall. Among the little cluster of houses occupied by the settlers near the fort were four block-houses called "garrison-houses," each manned by a half dozen men. On these rude defenses depended the safety, not only of Falmouth, but of the whole eastern frontier. In 1681 the General Court of Massachusetts fixed the size of the garrison to be maintained at "a captain, a sergeant, a gunner and tenn private souldiers." The commencement of hostilities against the whites in Maine began in August, 1688, by the Indians killing cattle in the eastern plantations, which caused terror to prevail among the inhabitants; the knowledge that the savages were to be assisted by the French caused them to be insolent to the white settlers. The accession of William and Mary to the English Throne and the removal from office of Governor Andros, caused defections among the frontier garrisons, a fact which was taken advantage of by the Indians. All the inhabitants of the settlement east of Casco Bay were driven from their homes, and sought the protection of Fort Loyall. In June, 1689. Lieutenants Brackett and Ingersol of the foot company at Falmouth wrote to the Massachusetts government urging immediate assistance; they reported that there were but few men in the fort and that "they were worn out with watching; that they had, on hand, but 3½ pounds of

---

* " The Siege and Capture of Fort Loyall, May 20, 1690. By S. T. Hall, Portland, Me., 1885.

powder, 24 hand grenades, 2½ pounds of musket shot, 20 balls for the great guns, a small quantity of match; about 30 cartridge boxes for small arms; not one musket belonging to the fort, and no provisions." In October, 1689, Captain Church, who had distinguished himself as an Indian fighter in " King Philip's War," attacked and whipped the French and Indians at Deering, near Fort Loyall, giving them the first check during that year.

Upon the arrival of the new French Governor in Canada, Count Frontenac, three expeditions were sent against the English provinces ; one was to rendezvous at Montreal, and proceed toward Albany ; another at Three Rivers and make a descent on New York or some point between Boston and Albany ; a third was to leave Quebec and gain the seaboard between Boston and Penobscot. The first party waded through the snow and in the depth of winter fell upon the village of Schenectady and was responsible for the terrible and historic massacre there, February 8, 1689. The second party entered New Hampshire and attacked the settlement at Salmon Falls, March 27, 1690, with a similar result. The third proceeded by a toilsome march through the wilderness and mountain ranges that separate the St. Lawrence and the Kennebec rivers, to attack the Maine settlements. By the time it had reached Merry-meeting Bay, it had been reinforced by the Salmon Falls detachment and troops under Baron de Castine, until its strength aggregated five hundred men, (200 French and 300 Indians*), all under command of Sieur Portneuf. This formidable force arrived in Casco Bay and rendezvoused upon some of the islands near the fort, reconnoitring and making other preparations to attack. Fort Loyall was commanded by Captain Sylvanus Davis and was garrisoned by about sixty men.

Some of the Indian scouts, who were reconnoitring on Penobscot Bay, near the falls, killed and scalped a Scotchman by the name of Robert Greason. His family fled in terror to the protection of Casco, some four miles distant, and that was the first notice the whites had of the expected attack. The alarm cry was sounded. The few soldiers and men of the town gathered at the fort and garrison houses with promptness, and full of courage, ready to defend their homes against the savage foes. They did not wait long, for the Indians finding that they were discovered, made preparations for a

---

* The Indians were of the Abenaquis and Penobscot tribe led by several famous chiefs.

speedy attack. Amid the darkness of the night of the fifteenth of May, they moved their forces from the islands to that part of Munjoy Hill which at this day bears the name of " Indian Cove," near the G. T. R. bridge. Munjoy Hill was then covered with a forest growth, except a portion of it near the present observatory, which was open pasture land, where grazed the cattle belonging to the town. At Indian Cove, the Indians were hid from observation, and in the morning a detachment of them proceeded to the top of Munjoy Hill, and concealed themselves in the low woods and underbrush, to the north of (now) Congress Street, waiting for the opportunity to begin the attack. They did not wait long; they were discovered by some of the soldiers at the Lawrence garrison house, which fact was communicated to Captain Davis at Fort Loyall. The brave officer resolved upon a sortie, and an attempt to dislodge and drive away this (as it was supposed) small party of Indians. Toward noon a party of young men, full of zeal and courage, under command of Lieut. Thaddeus Clark, left the fort, marched up Broad (now India), and through Queen (now Congress), to the foot of Munjoy Hill.

The French account taken from the Paris Documents is as follows:

"At noon thirty men issued from the principal fort, and came to the spot where our people lay, who having discharged their guns at ten paces distant, rushed on them sword and hatchet in hand, and pursued them so hotly that only five of them, all of whom were wounded, entered the fort again. As our men followed, hot foot, they were exposed to the fire of one of the forts, in the proximity of which they happened to find themselves. One Frenchman received a wound in the thigh and an Indian was killed. At night the principal fort was summoned to surrender, but an answer was returned '*that they should defend themselves to the death.*'"

Thus was the commencement of that struggle which lasted four days and nights, and which so redounded to the honor and glory of our ancestors. After the destruction of Clark and his party, the few who were left retreated to the protection of the Lawrence garrison house. This was a wooden block-house in its upper story, with a stone foundation. The inmates defended themselves during the day, and at night the Indians withdrew. The defenders knew that the attack would be renewed in the morning, with an increased force of the enemy, and they being short of ammunition, withdrew, as did the occupants of the other garrison house in the town, during the siege to the protection of Fort Loyall. Before leaving the Lawrence garrison they fired a slow match leading to a quantity of powder in a cask, hoping that after they had left, and the enemy entered, an explosion might take place, which would destroy their assailants. But the first Indian who entered in the gray of the morning, spied the burning match and extinguished it.

During the night of the 16th of May, all the forces from the garrison houses were withdrawn into Fort Loyall; and also all the inhabitants, young and old, the weak and the strong, the mother and her infant children, to the number of two hundred or more, found a hoped for refuge and place of safety, within the wooden walls of this protected fort. The fighting force was not above seventy men. The brave Lieutenant Clark was no more. Captain Davis, Lieutenants Lawrence, Brackett, and others, encouraged and cheered the small band of heroes. It was a time of dread suspense. No hope or expectation of assistance from any quarter could be had. On the next morning, the 16th, the enemy commenced the attack; the flaming torches, setting on fire the deserted houses in the immediate vicinity of Fort Loyall, and the skies were illumined by the conflagration. The houses on Broad (India Street), Thames and Fore streets, were soon in flames. The horrors of the situation can be imagined at this time; the distress and anguish of those in the fort, as they witnessed the destruction of their homes can be conceived. But in this dark hour of despair did our fathers show any lack of courage or want of bravery? No! When the fort was surrounded by the bands of French and savage Indians, who, amid their terrific yells and savage war-whoops, demanded its immediate surrender, according to French accounts, the reply of the commander of the fort was, " *That they should defend themselves to the death!*" Nobly they did it; and nobly they died. The first day of the siege passed with no definite results, the enemy having gained no advantages. The besieged watched every exposed situation, and whenever a gathering of the besiegers was made, the cannon of the fort sent death and destruction among them. The next day, May 17th, the French leaders became satisfied that, notwithstanding their larger force that they had, they could not capture the fort. Having no cannon to make a breach in its walls, they could only with their guns pick off those of its defenders who exposed themselves. The cannon of the fort prevented any attempt being made to take it by storm. It was at length determined to make a breach under the bank to its foundation. In the deserted garrisons they found tools suitable for the purpose, and they began a mine, within fifty feet of the fort, under a steep bank which entirely protected them from its guns. At what part of the fort this trench or mine was dug is at this day a matter of conjecture only. My impression, from a knowledge of its location, before the changes that have since been made there, is that the trench was dug from the India Street side, in an easterly direction; as the rock formation on the other side of the fort would prevent any such work.

During these days of siege the red-crossed banner of England floated over the fort. On both sides the firing was sharp and heavy. The roar of the cannon echoing in the surrounding forests, the reports of musketry, the flaming houses of the inhabitants, the war-whoops and yells of the savages outside the palisades, the cries and fears of women and children inside the fort who saw their husbands and fathers fall before the bullets of the French, or brought in wounded to die in the arms of their loved ones, were scenes of terror that can hardly be described or imagined. The defenders of the fort were but a small and feeble band; but they firmly stood repelling the assaults of the foe. Whenever a Frenchman or Indian exposed himself a musket bullet found its way to him. The English wasted much ammunition in their vain efforts to dislodge their besiegers, who, in undermining the fort, were in such a situation that they were protected from its cannon. Captain Davis encouraged his men to renewed exertions, knowing well that if the fort surrendered to the Indians no quarter could be expected, and they preferred to meet their deaths, defending themselves and families on the walls of the fort, than trust themselves to the mercies of their savage foes. It was found that the mine commenced by the enemy under the walls of the fort was proving a success, that in a day or two the results expected would be accomplished, and a further defense of the fort would be useless. The last day of the siege was May 20th, of which the anniversary was yesterday. Another terror was added to the horrors that surrounded this brave band. At different times during the siege attempts had been made to set fire to the fort and the buildings therein enclosed; flaming arrows and combustibles had been fired by the Indians, but they had been unsuccessful. The flames they kindled had been extinguished. But on the last day of the siege a machine (as the French termed it) had been obtained, which was probably an oxcart, which was filled with combustible materials, including a barrel of tar (birch bark). This cart was pushed up the trench that had been made, close up to the walls of the fort. Those who were pushing it up were protected by the cart from the fire of those in the fort. The flames soon began to crackle and take hold of the logs of which the palisades were constructed. The inmates of the fort then knew that they were doomed, that no choice was left to them but to surrender or be destroyed in the flames. Up to that time the English did not appear to know that there were any French among their assailants, supposing from the equipment and dress that they were all Indians. Some order, given by the French leader in French accent, reached the ear of Captain Davis, which gave him a ray of hope. If there were any whites among their foes would they not respect the rights of war and humanity, and protect them if they surrendered from their savage associates? Up went the white flag of surrender! I here give Captain Davis' account of what was done:

"We then demanded," he says, "if there were any French among them, and if they would give us quarter? The response came back from the leader in command that there were Frenchmen and would give us good quarter. Upon that we sent out to them again to know from whence they came, and if they would give us good quarter, both for our men, women and children, both wounded and sound, and that we should have liberty to march to the next English town and have a guard for our defense and safety unto the next English town, then we would surrender,—and also that the Governor of the French should hold up his hand and swear by the great and everlasting God, that the several articles should be performed. All of which he did solemnly swear to perform, but as soon as they had us in their custody, they broke their articles, suffered our women and children, and our men to be made captives in the hands of the heathen; to be cruelly murdered and destroyed, many of them, especially the wounded men; only the French kept myself and three or four more, and carried us overland to Canada."

The French account of the capture, taken from the French Archives, is as follows:

"The Count was not to attack any fort for fear of losing too many people, but to attend exclusively to laying waste the country. This order could not be executed, all the surrounding places having been abandoned in consequence of notice of the approach of this party having been given by a soldier, who had been with M. Hertel, and had been taken prisoner by the English. Under these circumstances it was unanimously resolved to attack the large fort in force, as it was impossible to capture it otherwise. The entire of the enemy had withdrawn into it; and had abandoned the four smaller ones. Our people lay during the nights of the 26th and 27th (May) on the ocean, within fifty paces of the fort, under cover of a very bold bluff, whence they had no fear of the enemy's continued cannonadings and heavy fire of musketry. On the night of the 28th, the trench (traversée) was opened. Our Canadians and Indians had not much experience in that mode of besieging places. They did not fail to work vigorously, and by good fortune found in the forts that had been abandoned, some implements wherewith to remove the earth. This work advanced with such rapidity that the enemy demanded a parley. In the course of the night of the 28th, they were required to surrender their fort, stores and garrison. They asked on their side for six days to consider their proposals. They were allowed only the night to make up their minds, and the work continued. Their fire redoubled the next morning. They then threw a quantity of grenades without much effect. On arriving by trenches at the palisades, preparations were made to set those on fire by means of a barrel of tar, that had also been discovered, and some combustibles. Seeing this machine approaching very near them, and not being able to prevent it, those who pushed it along being sheltered in the trench, they hoisted a white flag in order to capitulate. Their commander surrendered himself shortly after to Sieur de Portneuf, and the entire garrison, and those of the fort marched out to the number of seventy men, exclusive of women and children. They were all conducted to the camp. A moment after four vessels crowded with people made their appearance, but seeing no English flag flying, they retired. (This statement I do not find authenticated from any other source.) The fort was fired, the guns spiked, the stores burnt, and all the inmates made prisoners. *The Indians retained a majority of them.* Captain Davis, the commander, and two daughters of his lieutenant who had been killed (Thaddeus Clark), were brought hither (Quebec) with some others. Our people decamped on the first of June, after having set fire to all the houses they found within a circle of two leagues, all of which were unoccupied. They arrived here (Quebec) on the 23d of the same month, St. John's eve. One Frenchman had his arm broken by a cannon ball, and an Indian received a wound in the thigh."*

Both of these accounts agree as to the terms of surrender granted by the leader of the French, Sieur de Portneuf, to the brave garrison, and they also agree that the treaty was barbarously and grossly violated. The French account slurs over the massacre, by saying that "*the Indians retained a majority of them,*" the prisoners, which is,

*This French account from which I have quoted, is an extract of a letter from M. de Monseignat, to the celebrated Madame de Maintenon, giving an account of the most remarkable occurrences in Canada, from November, 1689, to November, 1690. Maintenon, Francoise d'Aubigné, Marchioness de, second wife of Louis XIV. of France, was born November 17, 1635 and died April 15, 1719.

that they being given by the French into the hands of the Indians, were cruelly murdered. The notorious Indian chief, Hopegood, is said to have been one of the principal actors in the bloody scene. At least two hundred persons, men, women and children, surrendered. Not more than ten or twelve of them had their lives spared. The savage massacre must always stand as a foul blot upon the reputation of the French officers who commanded at the siege. To the honor of Frontenac, the Governor of Canada, it may be said that when the expedition returned to Canada, and the report was made to him of the murder of the prisoners, he was very angry with Portneuf, and denounced his cruelty, and took all the means in his power to obtain from the Indians the captives they had brought to Canada.

The names of but few of those who died on those days are known. A few names have come down to us from the past. The Lieut. Thaddeus Clark, whose descendants are with us. John Parker * and his

---

She, at the age of sixteen years, married the deformed poet, Scarron. She was at that time extremely graceful and witty. Her husband died in October, 1660. She received from Louis a pension of 2000 francs a year, and in 1669 he made her governess of his children. She was made a Marchioness under the name of Maintenon. The Queen was much attached to her, and died in her arms, July 30, 1683. Some time after, Louis XIV., who had vainly solicited her to become his mistress, was secretly married to her. From that time to his death, the King was greatly under her influence, though she exercised her power with prudence and judgment. After the death of the King, she retired to the Convent of St. Cyr, where she spent the rest of her life in acts of charity and devotional exercises. (Amer. Cyclopedia, XI. 39, 40.)

* Hon. J. H. Drummond has furnished me with the following, viz.: "John Parker was the second son of John Parker, 'the fisherman,' who came from Biddeford in England, and was in Saco in 1636, but went afterwards to Georgetown, and in 1650 bought Parker's Island of the Indians. The date of the father's death is unknown, but it was before July, 1661. The son, John, was born in Saco, according to tradition; he married, Aug. 20, 1660, Mary Fairfield, daughter of Daniel Fairfield, of Boston; he purchased of the Indians nearly all the territory that makes the present town of Phippsburgh; other parties claimed, under other titles, and on July 15, 1684, Richard Wharton made an indenture with him, in which it was recited that John Parker 'for twenty years past has been seized of lands between Kennebec River and Casco Bay, bounded on the north by Winnegance Creek,' and by which Parker's land was conferred to him, in whole and in part. His son James was killed

CRAIGIE HOUSE.

From "Life of Longfellow." Copyright, Houghton, Mifflin & Co.

son James.* They were the ancestors of the late distinguished jurist, Isaac Parker, of Massachusetts. Thomas Cloice, Seth Brackett, son of Anthony. From Danvers were Alsop and Edward Crocker, and George Bogwell; a soldier from Lynn was named Joseph Ramsdell. Lieutenant Lawrence, one of Casco's active men, was mortally wounded. But, of the great majority of them, their names will never be known except on the roll of the Archangel, when " his trump shall awake the dead to life."

Craigie House.†

ALL visitors to Cambridge are familiar with the spacious old-fashioned house, painted in yellow and white, which stands far back from Brattle Street on the right, as one goes from Harvard Square to Mount Auburn. A gateway in the oddly patterned fence opens through a lilac hedge into the long walk, at the end of which, up low flights of steps, the house stands on its grassy terraces. Its ample front of two stories extends, including the broad verandas, to a width of more than eighty feet. There are large clumps of lilac bushes upon the greensward, and, on the left, an aged and lofty elm-tree throws its shadows upon the house, and sighs for its companion, killed many years ago by canker-worms and too vigorous pruning. An Italian balustrade along the first terrace is a late addition; but the roof is crowned with a similar railing, of the old days. Between the tall white pilasters which mark the width of the hall-way, the front door still retains the brass knocker which announced many a visitor to the ancient hospitalities, and which, even now, occasionally answers to the hand of a stranger, or the small boy who does not see the modern bell-knob, and whose wonder is duly aroused by the cum-

---

with him; his daughter, Elizabeth, then unmarried, administered on his estate in 1700; he left another son, Daniel, the great-grandfather of Isaac Parker, the celebrated Chief Justice of the Supreme Court of Massachusetts. According to the deposition of John Phillips, John Parker had three other daughters, but it is quite certain that he fell into the error of confounding another John Parker, who had three daughters, with this John Parker."

* John Parker was the gr. gr. gr. grandfather of Mary Conant. (See " FOSTER.")

† The description of Craigie House is taken from " Life of H. W. Longfellow." Ticknor & Co., Boston, 1886.

brous old lock, with its key that might almost have belonged to a Bastile. In the white-wainscoted hall is a handsome staircase, with broad, low steps, and variously twisted balusters. On the left opens the drawing-room, which, with its deep window-seats, its arched recesses, its marble mantel surmounted by a broad panel set in an architectural frame, remains a fine specimen of a "colonial" interior. Opposite to this is a similar room, of much simpler, but still substantial, style,—in all the later years the poet's study. Beyond is a spacious apartment, now used as a library, whose windows command the garden and grounds. Above are the chambers, whose broad fire-places are framed in old-fashioned Dutch tiles.

The history of this house is also familiar. Built by the wealthy Colonel John Vassall, in the last century,—the accepted date is 1759, —in the midst of his large inherited estate of between one and two hundred acres, it was left by him on the eve of the Revolution, when taking, or keeping, the side of the king, he went to England, and erased from his family coat of arms the motto, "Always for my country, often for my king" (*Semper pro republica, saepe pro rege*). Then it was confiscated to the State. When, after the battle of Bunker Hill, the American army gathered about Boston, the Marblehead regiment was quartered under its roof. Then Washington came to Cambridge to take command, and after a short stay in the "President's house" (now known as the Wadsworth House) established his headquarters in this Vassall House, which had been meanwhile put in order for him.*

Here he remained nine months, till the evacuation of Boston by the British troops. And here Mrs. Washington joined him and spent the winter. If tradition is trustworthy, the drawing-room remembers the gayety of a Twelfth Night party given by her. The south-eastern room, now the study, was used, according to the testimony of one of the General's aides, as the dining-room.† The chamber over it was Washington's private room.

---

* In Washington's Account Book is the following entry in his own handwriting: "July 15, 1775. Paid for cleaning the House which was provided for my Quarters, and which had been occupied by the Marblehead Regiment, £2 10s. 9d."

† MS. Letters of Colonel John Trumbull, who, in 1775, when just graduated from Yale College, at the age of nineteen, was made aide-de-camp to

> Once, ah, once, within these walls,
> One whom memory oft recalls,
> The Father of his Country, dwelt.
> And yonder meadows, broad and damp,
> The fires of the besieging camp
> Encircled with a burning belt.
> Up and down these echoing stairs,
> Heavy with the weight of cares,
> Sounded his majestic tread ;
> Yes, within this very room
> Sat he in those hours of gloom,
> Weary both in heart and head.

wrote the poet when he had made that chamber his (first) study. Yet, serious as were those days, and often weary with the weight of cares, we are glad to know that they were not without their enlivenment. Among the traditions of the house are two stories of "Washington's laughter." In the first, an old woman had one day been arrested in the American lines as a spy, and brought before General Putnam. He thought the matter important enough to be referred to the Commander-in-Chief, and took the woman to headquarters. Arrived at the gate, she refused to go in. Whereupon Putnam seized her, and lifting her on his back, bore her up the pathway to the door. This, Washington, looking from his window, beheld, and laughed heartily at the spectacle of "Old Put." and his burden. At another time, the second story runs, several of the generals were at the Vassall House when word was brought that the British were making a demonstration from Boston. The officers rushed for their accoutrements, and General Greene's voice was heard calling to the barber, "My wig! where is my wig?" "Behind the looking-glass, General," said Lee; and the mirror revealed that Greene's wig was already on his head. Again Washington joined in the general laugh.

After Washington's departure to follow southward the fortunes of the war, the house came into the brief possession of Mr. Tracy, of Newburyport, of whose wealth and luxury there are fabulous tales; and then of Mr. Russell, a Boston merchant. On the first of January, 1793, it was purchased, with one hundred and fifty acres of land (in-

---

General Washington. He was afterwards well known as a painter of persons and scenes of the Revolution.

cluding what is now the Observatory Hill), by Andrew Craigie.* His wealth and style won the hand, if not the heart, of the beautiful Miss Shaw, of Nantucket, whose young lover had gone to seek his fortune on the seas, and came back only to find her married. Mr. Craigie, it is believed, built the western wing of the house, with its kitchen and dependencies, and being a giver of dinners, enlarged the square northeastern room to its present spacious dimensions, and adorned it with columns to serve as a grand dining-room. Here he entertained the merchant-princes of Boston; and once, according to tradition, a prince of diplomats, Talleyrand, with whom Mrs. Craigie, much better educated than her husband, could converse in his native French. Nor was a royal prince wanting. Tradition again avers that the Duke of Kent, father of Queen Victoria, was once a guest at this table, and adds that, when the Royal Duke had left Boston, Mr. Craigie purchased his carriage and horses.†

Mr. Craigie—having, as he said, "lost himself" in his house, its grounds, greenhouses, equipages, and hospitalities (not to mention

* ANDREW CRAIGIE, the son of Andrew and Elizabeth Craigie, was born in Boston, June 7, 1743. He was appointed Apothecary General of the Northern Department of the Continental Army, serving in that capacity until December 31, 1780. Was one of the earliest members of the Society of the Cincinnati. He married Elizabeth, daughter of Rev. Bezaleel Shaw (H. C. 1762), a relation of Chief Justice Shaw. At the close of the Revolution he made large investments in real estate in the neighborhood of Boston, and did much to develop the present city of Cambridge, Mass. At one time he owned nearly all of East Cambridge, and was the principal projector and one of the corporators of the bridge bearing his name, connecting West Boston and Lechmere's Point. Out of Mr. Craigie's efforts to build the bridge and to open up new streets in the village of Cambridge, grew a protracted controversy and much litigation. It terminated in an important decision (said to be the first of the kind in the Commonwealth of Massachusetts) establishing the principle of law that "the damages which a landowner sustained by the taking of his land for a highway and the benefit which he derived from its construction shall be equitably adjusted and offset against each other: and if the benefit be equal to the damage, he shall receive nothing more." Andrew Craigie was one of the Wardens of Christ Church, Cambridge, in 1796. He died at Cambridge, September 19, 1819. (Paige's "History of Cambridge.")

† *Boston, September 5, 1792.* A large carriage and four horses took our travelling party out into the country. We set out immediately and passed over the new Charles River Bridge, through the town of Medford, over the weirs

outside speculations, such as the bridge which still bears his name)—departed this world, leaving to his widow a life interest in the estate. Left alone in the large house with a very small income, Mrs. Craigie reserved certain rooms for herself and let the others to various occupants, among whom Jared Sparks and Edward Everett, it is remembered, brought their brides to these chambers. The writer of this remembers very well visiting Mrs. Craigie, in his early college days, to beg some autograph letters of Revolutionary personages, of which she had a store. She sat in her south-eastern parlor, in white muslin turban and gray silk gown, with the sun shining among her window plants and singing birds ; and as often as he took his leave she said, "Be good; I want you to be good." There was an awful whisper in Cambridge circles that she read Voltaire in the original. At any rate, her copy of his works remained in the library of Craigie House.

The story of Mr. Longfellow's coming to live in the house has been often told, especially in the charming sketch by Mr. George William Curtis in "Homes of American Authors." The reader may like to read the Professor's own account, as written from his dictation many years ago :

"The first time that I was in the Craigie House was, on a beautiful summer afternoon, in the year 1837. I came to see Mr. McLane, a law-student, who occupied the south-eastern chamber. The window blinds were closed, but through them came a pleasant breeze, and I could see the waters of the Charles gleaming in the meadows. McLane left Cambridge in August, and I took possession of his room,

---

and down through Menotomys to the house of Mr. Craigie in Cambridge, where we were cordially received and hospitably entertained by the modest and opulent proprietor. We walked up to his summer-house, a pretty piece of ornamental architecture situated on an eminence, once a reservoir of ice. Our Maryland gentlemen were perfectly enchanted with this delightful seat. I think one may safely assert that, after Beacon Hill in Boston, this point presents the most beautiful, extensive and variegated landscape in the world. . . . . *September 10*, dined with Dr. Craigie, met there Mr. Gerry, one of the members of Congress this State, and several other gentlemen. The entertainment was elegant and variegated, and genuine, unceremonious hospitality gave it an additional zest. . . . *September 19*. We took a walk out to Cambridge, and breakfasted with Mr. Craigie, who received and entertained us, as he does all the world, with good humor and hospitality. (Journal of Nathaniel Cutting, who visited Boston in 1792.)

making use of it as a library or study, and having the adjoining chamber for my bedroom. At first Mrs. Craigie declined to let me have rooms. I remember how she looked as she stood, in her white turban, with her hands crossed behind her, snapping her gray eyes. She had resolved, she said, to take no more students into the house. But her manner changed when I told her who I was. She said that she had read "Outre-Mer," of which one number was lying on her side-board. She then took me all over the house and showed me every room in it, saying, as she went into each, that I could not have that one. She finally consented to my taking the rooms mentioned above, on condition that the door leading into the back entry should be locked on the outside. Young Habersham, of Savannah, a friend of Mrs. Craigie's, occupied at that time the other front chamber. He was a skillful performer on the flute. Like other piping birds, he took wing for the rice-fields of the South when the cold weather came, and I remained alone with the widow in her castle. The back part of the house was occupied, however, by her farmer. His wife supplied my meals and took care of my rooms. She was a giantess, and very pious in words; and when she brought in my breakfast frequently stopped to exhort me. The exorbitant rate at which she charged my board was rather at variance with her preaching. Her name was Miriam; and Felton called her 'Miriam the profit-ess.' Her husband was a meek little man.

"The winter was a rather solitary one, and the house very still. I used to hear Mrs. Craigie go down to breakfast at nine or ten in the morning and go up to bed at eleven at night. During the day she seldom left her parlor, where she sat reading the newspapers and the magazines, occasionally a volume of Voltaire. She read also the English Annuals, of which she had a large collection. Occasionally, the sound of voices announced a visitor; and she sometimes enlivened the long evenings with a half-forgotten tune upon an old pianoforte.

"During the following summer the fine old elms in front of the house were attacked by canker-worms, which, after having devoured the leaves, came spinning down in myriads. Mrs. Craigie used to sit by the open windows and let them crawl over her white turban unmolested. She would have nothing done to protect the trees from these worms; she used to say: 'Why, sir, they are our fellow-worms; they have as good a right to live as we have.'

"Mrs. Craigie was eccentric to the last. In matters of religion she was a 'free-thinker.' She used to say that she saw God in nature, and wanted no mediator to come between Him and her. She had a passion for flowers, and for cats, and in general for all living creatures. A day or two before her death she said to me, ' You'll never be married again; because you see how ugly an old woman looks in bed.' She had a great hatred for the Jews; and when Miss Lowell said to her, 'Why, Mrs. Craigie, our Saviour was a Jew!' she answered, ' I can't help it, ma'am.' Shortly before her death she burned a large quantity of papers, which she had stowed away in an upper chamber, and among them the letters of her young lover."

Whether or not she knew of the letters hidden away in the back staircase, which many years afterwards came mysteriously dropping one by one upon the cellar stairs below, history does not record. These proved to be letters—not of love, but of duty—from a young girl, a ward of Mr. Craigie, absent at school. Why one of the stairs should have been made into a box for holding them, it is not easy to see; probably it was originally constructed for some other purpose.

THE YELLOW ELMS.*
BY BESSIE CHANDLER.

She lay within her chamber, pale and ill,
    Bound to her bed by cruel bonds of pain ;
Outside the leaves were falling—all was still
    Save for the dripping of the dull, sad rain.

The elms that year were yellow all the way
    From tops to those low boughs that fringe and grace
Their tall, straight trunks, like little curls that stray
    And cling, caressing, o'er a woman's face.

And through the leaves, as through a yellow pane,
    The light shone in, all golden, on her bed,
And every morn, unwitting of the rain,
    " Another sunny day," she, smiling, said.

She never knew how gloomy, dark, and gray
    Those long days were. In time we came to bless
The elms, that gave her sunshine every day,
    And robbed the rain of all its dreariness.

---
* *Scribner's Magazine*, March, 1888.

"Church Row," Cambridge.

FROM a charming paper entitled "Old Cambridge and New"* by the late Thomas C. Amory of Boston, the following description of famous houses, formerly the homes of Bossenger Foster, and Joseph Foster, is here reprinted.

Farther along on the road to Mount Auburn, beyond where Judge Story so long resided and opposite the above mentioned church † stands, in admirable preservation, one of the most interesting, as it is one of the most ancient mansions in Cambridge. It is now owned and occupied by our excellent and venerable fellow-citizen, Samuel Batchelder, whose generous hospitalities often throng its many apartments with youth and beauty, the worth and wisdom of Cambridge and its neighborhood. It is still an elegant as it is a commodious dwelling, and presents towards the lawn and river, as towards the road, elevations of unusual stateliness. Its large dimensions, sombre tints and venerable appearance, suggested to college companions something uncanny, which impression was heightened by the rumors afloat in its neighborhood of tragedies that had taken place beneath its roof. An acquaintance from the south in the law department had taken up his abode in what is now the dining-room, and sitting by the summer moonlight at its windows it was not difficult to conjure up, out of what was known or conjectured, many a weird vision of its ancient inhabitants.

Early in the last century it belonged to the Belchers. The estate passed from the Belchers in 1720, through Mercy Tibbetts, in 1736, to John Vassall ‡ son of Leonard, who, two years after his first wife died in

---

* N. E. Hist. Gen. Reg. XXV. 3.

† St. John's.

‡ JOHN VASSALL, b. West Indies, Sept. 7, 1713, H. C. 1732; m. (1st) Elizabeth, daughter of Lieut.-Gov. Spencer Phips (1734), and (2d) Lucy dau. of J. Barron; was descended from John[1] an Alderman of London; who (1588) fitted out and commanded two ships of war to oppose the Spanish Armada. He erected the "Batchelder House" and sold it to his brother Henry, Dec. 30, 1741. He died at Cambridge, Mass., Nov. 27, 1747 and is "supposed to have been buried in the tomb which he erected in the graveyard at Cambridge. The monument over it is a massive freestone slab resting upon five columns:

1739, conveyed it to his brother Henry. Henry died in 1769. The house passed through James Pitts in 1779, Nathaniel Tracy and Thomas Russell, in 1792, to Andrew Craigie, who owned and occupied the Longfellow mansion opposite, while his brother-in-law, Mr. Bossenger Foster, for several years was the occupant of this, which was purchased by Mr. Batchelder in 1842.*

It bears no inscription, only the heraldic emblems of the family—the vase and sun—and forms one of the most conspicuous features in the cemetery. It passed with the estate into the hands of ANDREW CRAIGIE, Esq., and is now owned by his heirs. An examination was made June 24, 1862. Twenty-five interments have been made in the vault, and in almost every case the coffin was found to be entire. Those which from their position at the farthest end of the vault were supposed to contain the remains of Colonel Vassall and his first wife were in fine preservation. Besides these the tomb is known to contain the remains of JOHN FOSTER, died Nov. 1, 1836 (aged 52); ANDREW FOSTER, M.D., died May 17, 1831 (aged 50); THOMAS FOSTER, M.D., died Feb. 4, 1831 (aged 46); JAMES and GEORGE FOSTER, died, Aug.-Sept., 1817; ELIZABETH C. HAVEN, died Feb. 10, 1826; Mrs. LYDIA G. HAVEN, died Mar. 10, 1836, and ANDREW CRAIGIE, Esq." (N. E. Gen. His. Reg. V. 17.114.)

* "Thomas Russell conveyed to Andrew Craigie, Jan. 1, 1792, 'a piece of land in Cambridge containing 9 acres, . . . being the late homestead of Henry Vassall, Esq., with the dwelling house, barn and out-houses thereon standing.' Craigie continued to own the estate until his death. During this time by some agreement between Bossenger Foster and Craigie, whose sister Mary was the wife of Foster, and Craigie having no children, the children of Foster would be his legal heirs. Mr. Foster and family moved from Boston and resided in this house some years, until the death of Foster, which probably took place before that of Craigie, who died intestate about 1820. After the assignment of dower to his widow, an agreement was executed Oct. 4, 1821, between Samuel Haven of Dedham, and Elizabeth his wife in her right, and Andrew Foster of Roxbury, physician, and John Foster of Cambridge, gentleman, and Thomas Foster of the same Cambridge, physician, being the heirs at law of Andrew Craigie, late of Cambridge, deceased, intestate, for the partition of the real estate of said intestate in the county of Middlesex, except such parts thereof as have been assigned to his widow as dower. In the execution of this agreement the property was divided into four parts and 'share No. 1' fell by lot to Elizabeth Haven, consisting of the Henry Vassall estate so-called. . . . The present proprietor (Samuel Batchelder) purchased the estate of Messrs. Greenleaf and Hilliard, representing the several parties in the interest, in Dec. 1841, just one hundred years after it was conveyed to Henry Vassall in Dec. 1741."—(" *Title & Hist. of the H. Vassall Est.*" *N. E. H. G. R. July, 1891*).

The house was later occupied by one of the best of men, Mr. JOSEPH FOSTER, as the writer, who on Sundays often dined with him when in college, would be ungrateful not to remember. The first Mrs. Foster was daughter of John Cutler, the popular grand master of the masons, who, as such, officiated at the funeral solemnities in Boston, when Washington died, in 1799. She was one of the numerous family noted for personal attractions largely represented in their descendants. The second, when he married her, was the widowed mother of the late William D. Sohier, long a prominent leader of the Suffolk bar, and well remembered for his professional attainments, practical sagacity, ready wit and kind heart. Mr. Foster had several brothers, one of whom, BOSSENGER, occupied the Batchelder mansion. A daughter of WILLIAM married Harrison Gray Otis, nephew of James, both as pre-eminent for eloquence as the former for the elegance of his manners and social graces; her two sisters were successively wives of Col. Apthorp, and their brothers were William, Leonard and Charles, the latter of whom, at the age of eighty-seven, is the only survivor. Thus widely connected and universally beloved, a large circle of later generations more or less entitled grew up to call Mr. Foster by the endearing appellation suggested by their degree of affinity, one which is more than usually significant where the sentiment as in his case was of such affectionate respect. The house in his time was especially attractive from his cordial welcome and pleasant ways, and one to many of agreeable associations and frequent resort. It was a large and roomy structure, possessing no peculiar feature for remark; but when flung wide open in the summer noonday, the air laden with fragrance from field and garden, hum of insect and song of bird, its fair proportions, simple grace and exquisite order and freshness combined to render it a fitting abode for the genial host and hostess who dispensed its hospitalities. Its ancient memories were carefully cherished, and on a window pane was to be seen an inscription with a diamond by Baroness Riedesel, when she was its occupant.

These several dwellings, occupied by members of the English establishment and attendants of Christ Church, were known as "Church Row."* Tradition informs us that at each of them, annually,

* "*Church Row*" *Costume—1783.* Full dress for elderly persons: a coat of some light colored cloth, small clothes, diamond or paste buckles at the knee and in the shoes, silk stockings, powdered hair; and a cocked hat: in cold

were given social entertainments to the president, professors and tutors of the college, and this from a sense of propriety rather than congeniality or inclination, for the rest of the year they lived among themselves or with their acquaintances and kinsfolk from other places. They were men of education and large fortune. Productive plantations in the West Indies contributed to the princely revenues of some of them, others were rich in lands or other property nearer home. Their houses abounded in rich plate, valuable paintings and furniture of the best; their shelves were laden with books; capacious and well-arranged wine cellars denote their abounding hospitality; the long distances and scanty public conveyances would compel the inference, if tradition were wanting, that their stables were well stocked with the best of steeds. Close by Charles River and Fresh Pond, Mt. Auburn with its forests near at hand and the country beyond of great picturesque beauty, their lot was indeed cast in pleasant places.

---

weather a scarlet cloak. A scarlet cloak and a white head were, in the last century, to be seen at the end of every pew in some of the Boston churches.'' (N. E. H. G. R., Vol. 9—p. 14.)

ENTRANCE TO CRAIGIE HOUSE.

THE OLD CLOCK ON THE STAIR.*

    Somewhat back from the village street
Stands the old-fashioned country-seat.
Across its antique portico
Tall poplar trees their shadows throw ;
And from its station in the hall
An ancient timepiece says to all,—
        " Forever—never !
        Never—forever ! "

---

* In these verses Longfellow describes his home, formerly " The Craigie House."

Half-way up the stairs it stands,
And points and beckons with its hands
From its case of massive oak,
Like a monk, who, under his cloak,
Crosses himself, and sighs, alas!
With sorrowful voice to all who pass,—
    " Forever—never!
      Never—forever!"

By day its voice is low and light;
But in the silent dead of night,
Distinct as a passing footstep's fall,
It echoes along the vacant hall,
Along the ceiling, along the floor,
And seems to say at each chamber-door,—
    " Forever—never!
      Never—forever!"

Through days of sorrow and of mirth,
Through days of death and days of birth,
Through every swift vicissitude
Of changeful time, unchanged it has stood,
And as if, like God, it all things saw,
It calmly repeats those words of awe,—
    " Forever—never!
      Never—forever!"

In that mansion used to be
Free-hearted Hospitality;
His great fires up the chimney roared;
The stranger feasted at his board;
But, like the skeleton at the feast,
That warning timepiece never ceased,—
    " Forever—never!
      Never—forever!"

There groups of merry children played,
There youths and maidens dreaming strayed ;
O precious hours ! O golden prime,
And affluence of love and time !
Even as a miser counts his gold,
Those hours the ancient timepiece told,—
      " Forever—never !
      Never—forever ! "

From that chamber, clothed in white,
The bride came forth on her wedding night ;
There, in that silent room below,
The dead lay in his shroud of snow ;
And in the hush that followed the prayer,
Was heard the old clock on the stair,—
      " Forever—never !
      Never—forever ! "

All are scattered now and fled,
Some are married, some are dead ;
And when I ask, with throbs of pain,
" Ah ! when shall they all meet again ? "
As in the days long since gone by,
The ancient timepiece makes reply,—
      " Forever—never !
      Never—forever ! "

Never here, forever there,
Where all parting, pain, and care,
And death, and time shall disappear,—
Forever there, but never here !
The horologe of Eternity
Sayeth this incessantly,—
      " Forever—never !
      Never—forever ! "

BOSTON IN 1768.

A Relic of "Seventy=six."

WILLIAM EUSTIS to ANDREW CRAIGIE.

ROBINSON'S HOUSE (nr. West Point),
22d Oct., 1779.

DEAR CRAIGIE:—There is so favorable an opportunity by Doctor Foster to remind you of your promise last winter, that I cannot suffer it to pass unimproved. For God's sake (if not for the sake of your friends) let us have the pleasure to hear from you. Acquaint us what methods you pursue in Philadelphia, rather what steps Congress imagine we shall very shortly be obliged to take. Is it not astonishing that, regardless of the decent applications from the medical department, they use us with a neglect which would weary the patience of Job? Do they imagine us stocks and stones? and are we not human nature?

I assure you, my good friend, our ill treatment is not seldom mentioned by officers of the line, and its only palliation is that we have the honor to taste that inattention which the Saviours of this country have long experienced. . . .

One good effect will at least be produced by this, which from its nature must be our last representation to Congress. January will either give us some compensation for five, the most valuable, years in life, expended in the service of the country, or it will send us home with a most useful lesson; and which alternative will conduce most to our advantages as individuals, I am utterly at a loss to determine.

Adieu, my dear friend, and believe me with affection y^r friend and servant,

WILLIAM EUSTIS.*

TO AND^R CRAIGIE, ESQ.

---

* Regimental Surgeon (1776); Member of Congress (1800–1805); Secretary of War (1809–12); Minister to Holland (1815); Governor of Mass. (1824–25); dying in office.

Fosteriana.

I.

BOSSENGER FOSTER, JR., to ANDREW CRAIGIE.

LONDON, June 4, 1797.

MY DEAR FRIEND:—I have written to Bissey to send out the pictures I purchased for you, and also the grape-vines you wished purchased, and to make inquiries respecting the delay about the wine. I thought it had been sent, in the fall, from what I heard from France.

I come now to your observations respecting the proposed loan in Holland. I think, from aught that appears at present, we may calculate on success in the attempt; if anything has had a tendency to impair the probability, it is the late appreciation of property in France, of every kind, and the flattering prospect of its more permanent establishment by the late *great event of Peace*, add to which the growing connection between Holland and France and an increasing connection of interests arising from a similitude of Policy and Law. I do not know whether such effect will be immediately perceptible, but that it must take place, I think is clear. . . .

I was much pleased with the letter I received from Andrew.* He gave me the first intimation of his having entered college. The manner in which he writes, discovers a correctness and strength of mind that I am highly pleased with. I am related to him as a brother, but I am far prouder in considering him as my friend. In considering his situation and advantages, I calculate on the most rapid advancement. I believe I know his mind and talents. If I am not mistaken in conjecture, he will shortly prove himself an invaluable friend, as well as an enlightened, an intelligent, and an interesting companion. He certainly will not need good advice and great advantages; he certainly will appreciate their value and take a due advantage. Speaking, as I would wish to do, without prejudice, I think him, in point of intellectual accomplishment, the finest young man I have seen either in America or Europe, and if we add, in considering his character, the most *amiable of minds*, and connect it with the talents he is unfolding, we cannot but mingle our congratulations on his apparent destiny,

---

* See " ANDREW FOSTER," p. 65.

and look forward with equal satisfaction to the period when his understanding, more ripened by years of study, shall endear him to us as an enlightened friend and intelligent companion. His younger brethren I think equally well of, they have talents and they have advantages. . . .

Intending as I do, if time permit me, to write some other letters to my friends in Cambridge, and particularly to my good and really beloved parents, I shall take my leave of you for the present, by repeating a wish for the continuance of your happiness, as well as of that of those with whom you are the most dearly connected in the world. Yours truly,

BOSS^R FOSTER, JR.

To ANDREW CRAIGIE, Esq.,
Cambridge, Mass.

II.

BOSSENGER FOSTER, SR., TO REV. JASON HAVEN.

CAMBRIDGE, April 22, 1799.

REV'D AND DEAR SIR :—With pleasure I acknowledge the receipt of your very agreeable letter of the 27th ulto, as also the addition of the 11th instant, and I do now, with the greatest sincerity, wish you and Mrs. Haven much joy and happiness in the connection that has lately taken place between our families. Having but one son, you must feel a degree of anxiety for his welfare, more especially in a transaction of such importance as a connection for life. I am pleased with the connection, and think we have every prospect that it will prove happy to the young couple and of consequence to all their connections.

I hope you will realize the satisfaction you anticipate with respect to my daughter, and that she may prove an addition to the happiness of you and Mrs. Haven. I shall esteem it a duty, incumbent on me, to treat your (and now my) son with all that esteem, affection and regard, that I do my other children, and to do everything in my power to promote his interest and happiness.

I am pleased and gratified with his character, and his conduct, since we had the pleasure of an acquaintance with him, bespeaks it justly merited. My earnest wish and prayer is that they may both prove wise, virtuous and happy, and be a source of great comfort and consolation to you in the evening of life. We were sorry your indisposition was such as to prevent our having the pleasure of yours and Mrs. Haven's company at the wedding; it would have been a gratification and great addition to our pleasure. As the weather grows more favorable, we shall hope you will be so much recruited as to be able and disposed to pay us a visit, of a few days, at Cambridge. I am still confined and very weak, but hope soon to be able to ride as far as Dedham, when Mrs. Foster will accompany me to pay Mrs. Haven a visit. In the meantime, we salute you by the title of brother and sister.

I am, Rev'd and dear sir, with great esteem and best wishes for such a renewal of your health, strength and spirits, as will render the remainder of your life comfortable, serene and happy,

Yours affectionately,

BOSSENGER FOSTER.

Mr. Craigie requests his Compliments.

A Franco=American Leaf.

WILLIAM FOSTER[5] (b. Boston, Jan. 10, 1772; d. Boston, Feb. 25, 1863) was the eldest son of William[4] and Grace (Spear) Foster and grandson of Thomas[3] Foster of Boston. His mother was the daughter of Nathan Spear, Esq., of that city. The subject of this sketch attended the Boston schools until he was about fourteen years of age, when he was sent by his father to be employed in the counting house of his correspondent, Barry & Co., of Cadiz, Spain. William remained in Cadiz some years. While there he became acquainted with a Jesuit priest, who took a great fancy to the boy. From this priest he obtained the chief part of his education and became well versed in the Spanish language. After his return to America, when about twenty years old, his father sent him with an assorted cargo to Morlaix, France. He arrived safely at the port and put his business into the hands of M. Perron, a merchant of that place. William became acquainted with the family of M. Perron and concluded to send his vessel home and remain a while in France, for he had become much interested in Mlle. Hortense Perron, a young lady about fourteen years of age. In about a year from that time he married her and continued to reside in France some twenty years. He was there during a part of the French Revolution, and was drawn as a conscript in the army of Napoleon the First. He was an active participant in many of the exciting events of that bloody period (1790-93) and was, at one time, the president of a Jacobin club.*

At the suggestion of Mr. Foster, the late Francis Sales, for many years instructor of French and Spanish in Harvard College, was induced to come to the United States, with Mr. Foster, in 1792. The first pair of Merino sheep imported into this country, was brought here by Mr. Foster in the same year,† and by so doing he risked the ship in which he brought them. He also brought several valuable paintings, one of which, called " Rebecca at the Well," was afterward presented to the Boston Athenæum, where it now is.

---

* He first met Mlle. Perron in an humble garb assumed by her to escape persecutions, to which at that time all the wealthier classes of society were exposed. Her father, proprietor of valuable estates in Normandy, had fled from the fury of the "Red Republicans," leaving his daughter in charge of one of his tenants, in whom he placed confidence she would escape observation. Mr. Foster, who at once penetrated her disguise was attracted by her beauty and loveliness of character, and the acquaintance ripened into mutual regard. When her guardian discovered the interest she betrayed for the young American, he revealed her identity, imploring him to desist from attentions which, if noticed, might subject them all to serious consequences. He, of course, felt bound to acquiesce in the prudence of this course. But, not long after, her father returning before the popular agitation had subsided, his chateau was attacked by the Republicans. Mr. Foster rendered such efficient service in successfully defending it, that all further objection was removed, and they were married. Long after the death of his wife, Mr. Foster erected, on the borders of Spot Pond, in Cambridge, a handsome stone mansion, beautifully situated, which he said, in material and arrangement, resembled, as nearly as prevailing modes of construction permitted, the chateau of his wife's parents in Normandy. (Thomas C. Amory, N. E. H. G. R. XXV., p. 47.)

†These sheep were purchased of Mr. Foster by Elkanah Watson, the celebrated agricultural writer, who gave "an exhibition under the lofty elm tree, on the public square in Pittsfield, Mass., of my two merino sheep." Thus was initiated the first agricultural fairs in the country. The wool of the two sheep referred to, was manufactured into cloth with great pains, and far excelled any woollen fabric that had yet appeared in America. It was spoken of in the papers of the day, and samples of it were exhibited in the principal cities. In bringing them over Mr. Foster violated a law of Spain, more than a thousand years old, prohibiting the exportation of Merino sheep under a penalty of hard labor in the mines for life. It was not until 1807, during the war between

While in France he met with a singular adventure in which he came near losing his life. He had taken up his abode at Morlaix, near the English channel, where spies from England frequently came. One of these persons landed here, and having made himself acquainted with the place and the people, learned that an American gentleman resided at Morlaix by the name of William Foster, and he immediately resolved to assume his name. Soon after, as Mr. Foster was travelling a short distance from his home, he was accosted by the police and inquiry was made as to his name; he replied innocently, "My name is William Foster." He was taken before the authorities and questioned: what is remarkable, he had exchange on the same house in England known to be in the possession of the spy. At that time spies were promptly dealt with, and Mr. Foster was placed in a disagreeable situation. His protestations and statements were of no avail, but recollecting that a M. Moreau, a lawyer and brother of General Moreau, was attending to some legal business in that neighborhood, he referred the mayor to him. M. Moreau was introduced, and being interrogated replied that the person under trial was his brother-in-law! This settled the question and Mr. Foster was liberated. M. Moreau had married Mrs. Foster's sister. Mr. Foster was in business in Bordeaux for several years in partnership with a Scotch gentleman named Davidson, under the firm of Davidson and Foster.

He returned to Boston with his wife and two children in 1807. His wife died some years since; his two daughters survive him;[*] one of them, Fanny H., married Henry J. Tudor, Esq.,[†] of Boston. Mr. Foster spoke and wrote French, Spanish and Italian equally as well as his own language, and was frequently called into court to translate and explain difficult and obscure passages in said languages. He translated a complicated specification of forty pages, from the Eng-

---

France and Spain, that the American Consul at Lisbon, Hon. Wm. Jarvis, was able to purchase 3500 confiscated sheep and send them to his farm at Weathersfield, Vt.

[*] This was written in 1863.

[†] CHARLES STEWART PARNELL (b. 1846; d. 1891) was the son of Henry and Delia Tudor (Stewart) Parnell. His mother was the daughter of Admiral Charles Stewart, U. S. N., and of Delia, daughter of Frederic Tudor, Esq., of Boston. Miss Stewart was a great favorite with President Andrew Jackson, who, at her request (endorsed by Hon. William Foster), appointed her cousin, James Foster (see p. 68) a cadet at the U. S. Naval School. Her son, Charles

lish into the French, from Prof. Treadwell, respecting his improvement on cannon. He had to coin many of the words, as they were not to be found in any French dictionary. When the specification was received in France, it was perfectly understood, but the wonder was expressed that the mechanical terms known only to those interested in such pursuits should be so faithfully given by an American, especially where words and terms had to be manufactured by the translator. Mr. Foster was a prominent politician in the Democratic party and was a State Senator from Suffolk county in 1834. He wrote articles frequently in the *Transcript* and *Courier* under the *nom de plume* of " Franklin." It is a matter of great regret that he did not write his autobiography. It would have been exceedingly interesting and romantic. He could probably have given us some light, as well as dark shades in his touches on the history of the French Revolution. (N. E. Hist. Gen. Register, XVIII., p. 368.)

Stewart Parnell, was born at Avondale, County Wicklow, Ireland, in 1846; educated at Magdalen College, Cambridge, Eng.; entered public life as High Sheriff of Wicklow (1874), was elected M. P. (1875), and became an acknowledged leader, brilliant orator and successful legislator. In 1878 he was elected President of the Home Rule Confederation, in 1879 secured the repeal of the laws permitting flogging as a punishment, and initiated measures to reform the relations between landlords and tenants. While at the height of his prosperity certain disclosures, regarding his private life, caused a great sensation and ruined his career. He died, after a brief illness, at Brighton, Eng., Oct. 6, 1891.

SPANISH MERINO RAM—1792.

Montgomery.

ONTGOMERY is the name of a family of which existing records place the origin in the North of France, in the ninth century.* Its history leads us up from the present, through an unbroken succession of ten centuries in length, to the first known of the name, Roger de Montgomerie, who was " Count of Montgomerie before the coming of Rollo " in 912. A native of Neustria himself, his ancestors were probably, for many generations back, natives of that province which, when conquered by the Northmen, was known as Normandy.

Duke Rollo, in his descent upon France, with his army composed of the various nations of the North, and his seizure of one of her fairest provinces, did not supplant the native lords, in their possessions, by his own chiefs in every case. The Montgomerys retained their hereditary possessions ; and identifying themselves with the new and vigorous government of their native province, in a few generations became allied to the ducal house.

Count Roger, who accompanied Duke William in his victorious invasion of England, had gone so far in his attachment to the descendants of the strangers of a century and a half before, as to lose sight of his own French ancestry, and claimed for himself a common ancestry with them. He designated himself

---

* In the following resumé of the history of this family, the Editor has made copious extracts from "A Genealogical History of the Family of Montgomery, compiled by Thomas Harrison Montgomery, Philadelphia, 1863," an acknowledged authority. The full account of Rear Admiral JOHN BERRIEN MONTGOMERY, U. S. N., and his descendants is, however, published for the first time.

Century Magazine. Copyright—1890

JOHN BERRIEN MONTGOMERY,
REAR ADMIRAL U. S. N.

as "Northmanus Northmanoram," but for all practical purposes Roger was a Frenchman of the Frenchmen, though he might not like to own it. This ancestral reminiscence must have resulted from some peculiar fancy : no Montgomery possessed or transmitted any memorials of his Norman progenitors.

The earlier generations of the Montgomerys took their surname from the early appanage of the family, the County of Montgomery. This custom was common with all families dating back to that era, family names with but few exceptions having a local derivation. The County of Montgomery is situated in the Pays d'Auge and consists of several baronies and of about one hundred and fifty fiefs and arrière fiefs, dependent on the bailiwicks of Argentam, Caen, Alençon, and the Vicounty of Trau.

The derivation of the name of Montgomery can be but a matter of conjecture. It is suggested, however, by a writer who has made the derivation of proper names a study, to be a corruption of the Latin " Mons Gomeris," Gomer's Mount. Gomer (the son of Japhet) being the hereditary name of the Gauls. There was more than one locality in Europe bearing this designation. Eustace in his "Classical Tour," mentions that not far from Loretto in Italy is a lofty hill called " Monte Gomero," which was the ancient "cumerium promontorium ;" and it is quite possible that a locality bearing a similar designation in Neustria, embraced within the hereditary estates of one family, should have conferred its name on its lords. This view of its derivation is confirmed by the name Mons Gomerici, being equally with Montgomery, applied by the English to the town in Wales subsequently named after Roger de Montgomerie, whose property it had become. The spelling of the name has been various : *Montgommeri* and *Mundegumbrie*, were the most frequently used by the earlier generations ; but later, *Montgomerie* was employed altogether until within a century, when many of the branches substituted *Montgomery* for that having the terminal of *ie*. The first of the name, with whom contemporary annalists make us acquainted, was :

Births, Marriages and Deaths.

1 **Roger de Montgomerie** who, according to William, the monk of Jumieges, was "Count of Montgomerie before the coming of Rollo" in 912. William of Jumieges, in speaking of Roger's descendant, Hugh de Montgomerie (the father of Roger de Montgomerie who accompanied William the Conqueror) says he was the "son of William de Montgomerie, which William was the son of Roger, who was son of Roger, son of another Roger, Count of Montgomerie, before the coming of Rollo." This would place the birth of the last named at about the middle of the ninth century; at a time when France was rent and torn by the ambition of Charlemagne's descendants, each struggling against the other for the possession of the great empire their ancestor had left to his children. . . .

5 **Roger** (de Montgomerie) Count of Montgomerie and Viscount d'Eymes in Normandy, and subsequently Earl of Shrewsbury, Arundel and Chichester, in England, the eldest son of Count Hugh, was one of the most powerful and influential nobles at William's court.

But little is known of Roger's history prior to the year 1048, the date of his first marriage. He married (1048) Mabel, daughter and heiress of William de Talons, Count of Belesme and Alençon, whose large estates he succeeded to in 1070. The monkish chronicles of the time give Mabel a not very enviable character; in their estimation "she was a wicked, unnatural and cruel woman"; "haughty, worldly-minded, crafty and a babbler." Her cruelties at last brought upon her a violent death.

Roger's marriage, into a violent and turbulent family, brought him in connection with some severe family feuds. Owing to his large estates, inherited, as well as acquired by marriage, together with his relationship with the ducal house of Normandy, his position in the counsels of William was a very influential one; and in his after connection with the history of England, he proved himself no less a statesman than he showed himself a bold and successful soldier. He accompanied William in his great expedition, and at the battle of Hastings, October 14, 1066, that event which so changed the face of England and turned the current of its history, Roger commanded the advance division of the Norman army.

Robert Wace in his "Roman de Rou," which is reputed to be the best contemporary account of this great battle, speaks of "William who sat on his war horse, and who called out Rogier, whom they call de Montgomeri. 'I rely much on you' said he: 'lead your men thitherward, and attack them from that side. William, the son of Osbur, the seneschal, a right good vassal, shall go with you, and help in the attack, and you shall have the men of Boilogne and Poix, and all my soldiers. Alain Fergant and Aimeri shall attack on the other side; they shall lead the Poiterins and the Bretons, and all the barons of Maine; and I with my own great men, my friends and kindred, will fight in the middle throng when the battle shall be the hottest.'" And the chronicler relates the following incident of Roger's valor and skill.

"The Normans were playing their part well, when an English knight came rushing up, having in his company one hundred men, furnished with various arms. He wielded a northern hatchet, with the blade a full foot long, and was well armed after his manner, being tall, bold and of noble carriage. In the front of the battle, where the Normans thronged most, he came bounding on swifter than the stag, many Normans falling before him and his company. He rushed straight upon a Norman who was armed and riding upon a war horse and tried with his hatchet of steel to cleave his helmet, but the blow miscarried, and the sharp blade glanced down before the saddle bow, driving through the horse's neck down to the ground, so that both horse and master fell together to the earth. I know not whether the Englishman struck another blow: but the Normans who saw the stroke were astonished and about to abandon the assault, when Rogier de Montgomeri came riding up, with his lance set and heeding not the long-handled axe, which the Englishman wielded aloft, struck him down and left him stretched upon the ground. Then Rogier cried out, 'Frenchmen, strike! the day is ours!'"

In the division of the English territories which William made among his followers, Roger de Montgomerie was munificently rewarded by the Conqueror, who first advanced him to the Earldom of Chichester and Arundel and soon afterward to that of Shrewsbury. His possessions lay in perhaps the most turbulent portion of the kingdom, and his life seemed to be mainly spent in defending it against the frequent incursions of the Welsh.

At Shrewsbury, about 1085, Roger built a castle on an eminence and for that purpose pulled down about fifty houses. He also repaired the castle of Arundel, which was famous in the time of the Saxons for its extent "being a mile in compass." He also built the castle of Bridgenorth and Ludlow castle, the scene of "Comus," and enclosed the town of Ludlow with a wall. Sir Robert Douglas says that Roger "had most extensive landed possessions." His endowments to religious bodies were exceedingly generous. He founded several abbeys in England and several religious houses in Normandy.

Upon the death of the Conqueror, Roger and his sons became involved in an unsuccessful movement to place Robert, the eldest son of William, upon the throne. After this Roger turned his attention entirely to religious matters, and, when well advanced in years, entered into holy orders and was shorn a monk of the Abbey of St. Peter and St. Paul (his own foundation) where he spent the remaining years of his life and was there buried upon his death, July 27, 1094. The Earl of Shrewsbury had, by his wife Mabel, nine children, viz.: ROBERT, HUGH, ROGER, PHILIP, ARNULPH,* MAUD, MABEL and SYBILLE.

6 Arnulph (or Arnaud de Montgomerie), sometimes called Earl of Pembroke, was the fifth son of Roger de Montgomerie, Earl of Shrewsbury and Arundel. After his father's death and the assumption of the crown, on the death of William Rufus, by Henry I., he joined his brothers in resistance to the assumption and with them was banished the kingdom. He crossed over to Ireland (1100) to obtain succor for Duke Robert's cause. He

---

*Sometimes called Earl of Pembroke, the ancestor of the present male line of the family.

subsequently "sent Gerald, his steward, to Marckhardt or Murtagh O'Brien, King of Munster, desiring his daughter LAFRACOTH in marriage, which was easily granted." In right of his wife he subsequently aspired to get possession of her father's kingdom. During the invasion of Ireland by Magnus, King of Norway, the Irish called on the Normans for aid. Arnulph responded with his auxiliaries and repelled Magnus; later "the Irish, tasting blood, attempted to murder the Normans. Arnulph's wife was captured by her father's followers but Arnulph escaped and returned to Normandy. In the year 1118, Arnulph joined the Duke of Anjou in aiding the inhabitants of Alençon in a successful resistance to the oppression of Stephen, Count of Mortain." In 1119 Arnulph returned to Ireland, was apparently reconciled to his father-in-law, and was re-united to his wife; but, it is related that "on the morrow of his new nuptials, after a banquet, he fell into a sleep from which he never awoke." Arnulph left an only son, PHILIP.

7 **Philip** (de Montgomerie) was born in 1101 at Pembroke. He is next heard from in Scotland with the Earl of Huntingdon, afterward David I. of Scotland. Here he appears to have been called the Welshman or "Cymbricus," an evidence of his birthplace having been in Wales. He obtained a "fair inheritance in Renfrewshire," and married, about 1120, Lady MARGARET DUNBAR, daughter of Cospatrie, second Earl of Dunbar and March. As the manor and castle of Thorntoun came into the possession of the family at this period, it came, in all probability, as Lady Margaret s dower. It is situated about three and a half miles from Dunbar, and immediately opposite Innerwick Castle, divided only by a ravine, through which a stream flows, where the Montgomeries had early possessions. Philip de Montgomerie left two sons, ROBERT and HUGH.

8 **Robert** (de Montgomerie, or Mundegumberie, as it was sometimes written) "succeeded his father in his lands of Thorntoun of Innerwick and was granted the estate of Eaglesham,* which forms the

---

* A church having existed here from a remote period, a probable derivation is from Eaglais (Gaelic) a church, and the Saxon term for a hamlet. Thus Eaglesham signifies the church hamlet, according to a Scottish phrase still in use, the Kirktoun. (Gazetteer of Scotland.)

parish of that name in Renfrew. This estate, which was the first of any extent, and for two centuries the chief possession of the Scottish family of Montgomery, has remained their property undiminished for the period of seven hundred years." " Robert " was called in Gaelic " Mac Cymbrie " or son of the Welshman. Who he married is not known, but he was succeeded by his son JOHN.

9 **Sir John** (de Montgomerie) " Miles " of Eaglesham, who married HELEN, daughter of Robert de Kent of Innerwick, with whom he obtained a portion of her father's estate. This appears by a charter, on the division of his lands, to which among others, his son Sir Alan, is a witness, about 1190. Sir John left three sons: ALAN, ROBERT and WILLIAM.

10 **Sir Alan** (de Montgomerie) of Eaglesham, " Miles," so designated in the chartulary of Kelso and upon many documents witnessed by him 1204–31. It is not known who his wife was, but dying before 1234, he left three sons, ROBERT, JOHN and HENRY.

11 **Sir Robert** (de Montgomerie) " Miles " of Eaglesham succeeded his father and became on the death of his kinsman WILLIAM, Count of Ponthim and Montgomerie, the Chief of the Montgomeries. His name appears on several charters of land issued by the High Steward of Scotland in 1240–48. Dying, without issue, before 1261, he was succeeded by his brother.

12 **Sir John** (de Montgomerie) of Eaglesham. " It is not unreasonable to suppose that Sir John was in the army raised by Alexander III., to meet the Norwegians under their King, Haco, whom he defeated on their landing in the Bay of Ayr, at the famous battle of Largs, in August, 1263. So much was feared from these marauders that the whole available strength of the country was put in requisition. Sir John died about 1285, leaving five children: JOHN, MURTHAW, ALAN, THOMAS and a daughter who married Archibald Mure of Rowallan, who was slain at Berwick (1298).

13 **Sir John** (de Montgomerie) of Eaglesham and Eastwood, is designated "del Conte de Lanark," in Peynne's collections, the lordship of Eaglesham and Eastwood, as well as the whole of Renfrewshire, being then in Lanarkshire. He was one of the Great Barons of Scotland, summoned to appear at Berwick, in

1291, and was afterwards, with many of his countrymen, obliged to swear fealty to Edward I., it is said, although his name does not appear on the "Ragman's Roll" as do those of two of his brothers. As soon as Bruce asserted his claim to the Scottish throne, Sir John joined his standard. He married JANET, daughter of John Erskine of Erskine and had three children: ALEXANDER, ———, and MARJORY.

14 **Sir Alexander** (de Montgomerie) of Eaglesham and Eastwood, is designated in a charter by David II. as "Alexander de Montgomery de Elisham, filius, Johannis de Montgomery." In the year 1358 he was one of the barons despatched to England to treat for the release of their captive sovereign, and, on the 24th of October of that year, he had letters of permission to pass through England on his way abroad, accompanied by a retinue of sixty horse and foot. Sir Alexander married a daughter of William, first Earl of Douglas, by whom he had a son JOHN.

15 **Sir John** (de Montgomerie) of Eaglesham and Eastwood and afterwards of Eglinton and Ardrossan, was the son of Sir Alexander, whom he succeeded about the year 1388. "He married in 1361, ELIZABETH, the daughter and heiress of Sir Hugh Eglinton of Eglinton,* and by her obtained the large possessions of that family on the death of her father, which occurred about 1374. Sir John quartered with his own the Eglinton arms, which were " gules, three rings *or*, gemmed *azure*."

Sir John de Montgomerie greatly distinguished himself at the battle of Otterbourne, where James, Earl of Douglas, his uncle, was slain. Hugh, the eldest son of Sir John, lost his life there ; as the ballad has it :

> Sir Hugh was slain, Sir John maintained
> The honor of the day ;
> And with him brought the victory
> And Percy's son away.

The spear and pennon of Percy were carried along with the body of the gallant Sir Hugh to Edinburgh Castle, and the tro-

---

* The *Eglinton*, whose name furnishes a title to a branch of Sir John de Montgomerie's descendants, was a family of much antiquity in Scotland ; " Eglinton " is a large and valuable estate of 1700 acres lying within the parish

phies still remain in possession of the Eglinton House. It is said that when the Duke of Northumberland requested their restoration, the late Earl of Eglinton replied, "There is as good lea land here as any at Chevy Chace, let Percy come and take them." Sir John died 1398, leaving four sons, HUGH, JOHN, ALEXANDER and HUGH (2d).

16 Sir John (de Montgomerie), "Dominus Ejusdem, or of that Ilk," which title shows he was the male heir and chief of the French house of Montgomerie. In 1402 he became one of the chiefs of the Scotch army which invaded England, and was taken prisoner at the disastrous battle of Halidon Hill. He married MARGARET, daughter of Sir Robert Maxwell of Caerlaverock (ancestor of the Earls of Nithsdale) and dying, previous to November 1429, left three sons and three daughters, viz.: ALEXANDER, ROBERT, HUGH, ANNE, JANET and ISABEL.

17 Alexander (de Montgomerie), the first Lord Montgomerie, succeeded his father about 1429. He had charters under the Great Seal of a large number of lands, 1430-50, was distinguished for his loyalty to James I., and his successor, and was a member of the Privy Council. Lord Montgomery married MARGARET, daughter of Sir Thomas Boyd of Kilmarnock, and had four sons and four daughters: ALEXANDER, GEORGE, JOHN, THOMAS,* MARGARET,† ELIZABETH, JANET, and AGNES. John's son Robert went to France in 1480. His grandson GABRIEL, Count

---

of Kilwinning, county of Ayr. The castle of Eglinton was in 1526 burnt by the Cuninghames. The present one is comparatively a modern building. The second castle (that built probably after 1526) was a strong, but rude and incommodious, edifice, and was taken down by Hugh Montgomerie, the twelfth Earl of Eglinton, who erected on its site the present building "which is an extensive and solid one, in the castellated form, and was finished in 1802." The former earls had done much to improve the property and beautify the grounds, but this earl spared no cost in making it one of the most delightful in the west of Scotland.

* Became Rector of the University of Glasgow and was known as "Parson of Eaglesham."

† Margaret married John, Earl of Lennox, Lord Darnley, from whom descended Lord Darnley, father of James VI.

de Montgomerie, accidentally, caused the death of Henri II. of France, at a tournament, in 1559. On the occasion of a grand festival in honor of the marriage of one of the royal family, the King having vanquished several noble antagonists, challenged the Count of Montgomery to break a lance with him. They met in full array, in the presence of the noblest assemblage in France, and, on the first tilt, a fragment of the lance held by the Count struck the King in the left eye, at the moment when the sudden shock had moved the visor of his helmet, and he fell mortally wounded. Upon this awful mishap, the Count retired first to Normandy and then into England, filled with the deepest grief. He became a convert to Protestantism and returned to France, joined Admiral Coligny and the Huguenot cause, and for that was finally brought to the scaffold in 1576.

18 **Alexander** (de Montgomerie) Master of Montgomerie, died in 1452, before his father. It was during his lifetime that there sprang up the feud between the Cuninghames and the Montgomeries, which lasted for nearly a century. The King, James II., conferred (1448) upon the Master of Montgomery "the heritable Bailliarry of Cuninghame," causing great dissatisfaction to the family of Glencairn, relations of the house of Eglinton. Alexander married ELIZABETH, daughter of Sir Adam Hepburn of Hailles (from whom descended James, Earl of Bothwell) and, by her, left three sons, ALEXANDER, ROBERT, and HUGH.

19 **Alexander** (second Lord Montgomerie) succeeded his grandfather in his estates and honors. He married CATHARINE, daughter of Gilbert, first Lord Kennedy, and had three sons and a daughter. He died prior to the year 1484. He had HUGH, JAMES, JOHN, HELEN.

20 Hugh (third Lord Montgomerie) was, subsequently, the first Earl of Eglinton, having been created by James IV. in 1508. He was concerned in the revolt of all the barons against James III. in 1487, which resulted in the death of that king, as he fled from the battle of Sauchie, and the accession of his son to the throne, June 11, 1488. In the following year he was made a member of the Privy Council and was in great favor with James IV., who created him Earl of Eglinton and granted him the Constabulary of Rothesay. He was one of the lords to whom the tuition of James V., when in his minority, was entrusted by the Duke of Albany, the Governor, and in 1536 was, with the Earl of Huntley, appointed joint governor of Scotland by James, when he went to France for his bride, the Princess Magdalene. During Lord Hugh's lifetime the Montgomerie-Cuninghame feud broke out with violence. Frequently encounters took place between representatives of the rival families, and several lives were lost. In revenge for the murder of Cuninghame of Waerstoun, by the Montgomeries, it is said that the Cuninghames under William, Master of Glencairn, made a furious inroad upon the possessions of the former and burned Eglinton Castle in 1526. The Earl married Lady HELEN, daughter of Colin, first Earl of Argyll, by whom he had six sons and eight daughters. He died November, 1545, and was succeeded by his grandson, his two older sons predeceasing him. His children were ALEXANDER, JOHN,* NEIL, WILLIAM, HUGH, ROBERT, MARGARET, MARJORY, MAUDE, ISABEL, ELIZABETH, AGNES, JANET and CATHARINE.

---

*JOHN was father of Hugh, the second Earl of Eglinton, whose son HUGH, the third Earl, was a warm supporter of Mary, Queen of Scots. The fourth Earl, Hugh, fell a victim to the Cuninghame-Montgomery vendetta, being shot and killed in the town of Stewarton, April 12, 1586, by a party under the leadership of his kinsman, John, brother of the Earl of Glencairn. His son Hugh was the fifth Earl and last of that title of the male line of the family. Foreseeing that he would die without issue, he made a resignation of his earldom dated at Seton, July 27–Aug. 1, 1611, and obtained a new grant of it under the great seal, settling the title and estates upon Sir Alexander Seton of Foulstrather (the son of his Aunt Margaret, Countess of Winton) and heirs male of his body ; which failing, Thomas and John Seton and their heirs male ; whom all failing, to his own nearest and lawful heirs male whatsoever, bearing name and arms of

21 **Sir Neil** (Montgomerie) of Lainshaw* was the third son of the first Earl of Eglinton. He married MARGARET, daughter of Quintin Mure, Laird of Skeldon, by whom he got the lands of Skeldon, Hollow Chapel, etc. He lost his life in a fight with Lord Boyd's son and his adherents in the streets of Irvine, June 1547. His death was warmly resented by the Montgomeries, and the Master of Boyd is said to have gone abroad for a time to avoid their vengeance. The matter was eventually compromised by the rival clans, which action culminated in permanent friendship.† Sir Neil had two sons and three daughters: JOHN, NEIL, CHRISTIAN, ELIZABETH and HELEN.

22 **Sir Neil** (Montgomerie) of Lainshaw, succeeded his father and married JEAN, daughter and eventually heiress of John, fourth and last, Lord Lyle. By this marriage the Lyle estates came into possession of the Montgomeries, but the title was not as-

Montgomerie. This action of the Earl was to the prejudice of his cousin, Sir Neil Montgomerie of Lainshaw, who was the heir male. Upon the death of the Earl (1612) Sir Alexander Seton assumed the title and arms of Montgomerie, but King James VI. would not permit him to use the title until two years later. Upon the extinction of the first line of Earls of Eglinton, the succession of the family was carried on by the descendants of SIR NEIL MONTGOMERIE of Lainshaw. John's brother, Hugh, was killed at the battle of Pinkie, 1547. Robert became Bishop of Argyle, 1557.

* Lainshaw, which gave a designation to several of the later generations of Montgomeries, is situated in the parish of Stewarton, County of Ayr, Scotland. "On the estate is Lainshaw Castle. It consists of a large square tower, with a lesser one of a different style and a number of buildings of more modern date connecting them together and a large and elegant modern addition." "It was the inheritance of the predecessors of the Scots' Kings," and was on that account frequently called "Stewartstoun Castell."

† A contract was signed with Sir Neil's son by which the Boyds were "to appear in the toune of Irvine, in quhat manner the saidis Neile pleisses to devyis, at the mercat croce or kirk of the said toune . . . and in plane audience of the people, thair upon thair knees, with reverence, as efferis, sall unfenzeitlie ask God forgifness for the saidis offence . . . sall offir to the said Neile ane naikit swoirde be ye poynt, in taikin of thair repentance fra the boddom o' their hartis . . . and sall content and pay to the saidis Neile Mungumry the soume of auchtene hundre and fourty merkis moneye. . . ."

sumed by Sir Neil or his son, simply the Lyle arms (Lyle and Marr quarterly). By his wife Lady Jean, he had three sons of whom the eldest, NEIL succeeded.

23 **Sir Neil** (Montgomerie) of Lainshaw, as heir-male to the title and honors of the fifth Earl of Eglinton, should have succeeded to them on that nobleman's death in 1613, but they went with his estates, by the new grant of November, 1611, to the Earl's cousin. On that Earl's death, however, Sir Neil succeeded to the lineal male representation of the family, an honor which is in the line of Sir Neil's descendants to this day. He married ELIZABETH, daughter of John Cuninghame of Aitel, whose great-grandfather, Alexander Cuninghame, was of the Glencairn family. This branch of the Cuninghames were active participants in all the feuds of their family. Sir Neil died before 1613, leaving six children—NEIL,* WILLIAM, JAMES,† JOHN, MARIOT and another daughter.‡

24 **William** (Montgomerie) of Brigend,§ was the second son of the last Sir Neil Montgomerie. He married JEAN MONTGOMERIE the heiress of Brigend, in 1602, who was a daughter of John Montgomerie, the son and heir of the late James Montgomerie.‖ Mention of William Montgomerie of Brigend is found, in testamentary and other documents, as late as the year 1652; but he died prior to 1658. He had four sons: JOHN, WILLIAM, JAMES and HUGH.

---

* Neil Montgomerie of Lainshaw married about 1601 Marion, daughter of Sir William Mure of Rowallan, and died before 1625.

† Minister of Dunlop.

‡ Who married Graham of Gengar.

§ Brigend (or Bridgend, as formerly spelt) is in the Parish of Maybole, Ayrshire, and situated immediately on the banks of the river Doon, about one-fourth of a mile below, and on the opposite side to Alloway Kirkyard. It was known as Nether Auchindraine, previously to the building (in the year 1466) of the "Old Bridge of Doon" so celebrated in "Tam O'Shanter." Abercrummie, who wrote prior to the Revolution, speaks of it as "a pretty dwelling, surrounded also with gardens, orchards, and parks," but of this pretty dwelling scarcely a vestige now remains.

‖ To what branch of the family this James belonged, does not appear.

25 John (Montgomerie,* called the younger) of Brigend ; he had not that full designation, having predeceased his father. In 1620 he married ELIZABETH, daughter of Thomas Baxter of Shrinston and by her left two sons : HUGH and JAMES. His grandson, William, brought over to America the marriage settlement of John and Elizabeth, and a portion of it is still preserved by his descendants.

26 Hugh (Montgomerie,) of Brigend, succeeded to his grandfather subsequently to the year 1652 ; and on the death of John Montgomerie of Lainshaw (about 1655) became as his heir male, the chief of the family. In 1647, 1654 and 1671, his name appears in certain deeds as possessed of certain lands and baronies. He married in 1653 KATHARINE, second daughter of Sir William Scott of Clerkington,† by whom he had two sons and two daughters.‡ Hugh had inherited a valuable property but lost the greater part of it some years before his death, which occured May 6, 1710, at the age of eighty. To what this change in his affairs was attributable, cannot now be certainly ascertained ; but it is more than probable that his religious belief § was in a great degree the cause of his misfortunes ; as many families in that part of Scotland, holding similar views with his, had been ruined in estate for their opinions' sake. To this may be added pecuniary embarrassments, arising as well from his indulgent disposition as from a want of proper knowledge

---

* In a document recorded at Irvine, Aug. 1, 1626, he is described as "William Montgomerie's eldest lawful son and heir apparent."

† Sir William Scott of Clerkington was the eldest son of Laurence Scott of Clerkington, of the Buccleuch family, a person of distinction in the time of Charles I., a Clerk to the Privy Council and one of the principal Clerks of Session, and whose possessions in Edinburghshire were very extensive.

‡ The marriage settlement of this couple is still in existence in a fair state of preservation ; it is a roll measuring seven and a half feet in length.

§ What creed of dissent he embraced cannot now be known. That he was a strong Nonconformist, and suffered, temporally, in consequence can well be inferred from his connections and associations. If names were proof of kin, his mother could claim relationship with the most eminent Nonconformist divine of the seventeenth century ; and his wife's family, the Scotts, were many of them strong dissenters.

of business affairs. A large sum of money had been loaned his kinsman, the Earl of Loudoun,* which was retained on different pretenses, until many years after his death. In 1692 Hugh and his son, William Montgomerie, disposed of their estate to their cousin, John Montgomerie of Beoch,† in deeds recorded at Ayr, Dec. 1, 1692. They even parted with their seats in the Kirk and the Brigend burial place in Alloway Kirkyard. Hugh resided after that date with his younger son, James, while the eldest, William, had already in contemplation the removal of his family to America. Hugh Montgomerie, by his wife Katharine, had: WILLIAM, JAMES,‡ MARGARET, CATHARINE and ELIZABETH.

27 **William** (of Brigend) eldest son of Hugh, married Jan. 8, 1684, in Edinburgh, ISABEL, daughter of Robert Burnet of Lethintie, Aberdeenshire, of the family of the Leys Burnets of which was Gilbert Burnet, Bishop of Salisbury. Robert Burnet§ was

---

* It appears that in 1700 this sum amounted to £5906. 1s. 8d. (Scots). The third Earl of Loudoun was son of Lady Margaret Montgomerie, daughter of the sixth Earl of Eglinton. He died 1731.

† John Montgomerie of Beoch was the son of Hugh the younger and nephew of William of Brigend and married Jean, daughter of George Montgomerie of Broomlands. He died 1714, when his son James obtained leave, from the magistrates, to bury his father "the Laird of Brigend" in Alloway Kirkyard and have the bell rung.

‡ James Montgomerie was a merchant in Glasgow. With a numerous family depending upon him and sharing his father Hugh's misfortunes, he was only in moderate circumstances. He had six sons and two daughters, of whom Margaret married Robert Maxwell of Arkland. Mr. Maxwell corresponded with his wife's cousins in America, and his letters have been preserved.

§ Robert Burnett of Lethintie married a sister of Alexander Forbes of Ballogie. He was a member of the Society of Friends, and for his persistency and constancy in his religious views often suffered at the hands of those in authority. On March 12, 1676, he, among others, was arrested at a "conventicle" in Aberdeen, and removed to the Tolbooth ; where, after three months' imprisonment, he and his companions were brought to trial, when each was "fined, in one-fourth of their respective valued rents, for their own keeping conventicles, and an eighth part of the same for withdrawing from the public worship." He died in 1714 and was buried at Crosswicks, N. J.

extensively concerned in the Quaker settlement of New Jersey, and became one of the proprietors of that province; and it appears that his daughter went with him to America but was sent back, to complete her education, to Scotland, where she was married. Her acquaintance with the new country, as well as her father's large interests there, led William Montgomerie, eventually, to move his family from Ayrshire, and make a new home for his children in the colonies of America. In 1692 he had joined with his father in disposing of the estate of Brigend to his cousin, John Montgomerie of Beoch, and in 1701–1702 crossed the ocean with his young family, and settled on Doctor's Creek, in Monmouth county, East Jersey. " Eglinton "—the name of this estate—is situated about two miles from Allentown. The original house is not now standing; the present brick mansion was erected partly on its site, prior to the Revolutionary War, and was built of bricks made on the property. William purchased 500 acres of land of his father-in-law (deed dated May 20, 1706), and settled upon it.*

There is every evidence to show that William was a member of the Society of Friends, and after he came to this country that he brought his family up in their faith. That he was so before leaving Scotland, seems to be disproved by the circumstance of the promptness with which he had his children baptized. His sons married Friends, and so did his grandson James; and there is reason to believe he is buried where so many of his descendants lie, in the Old Meeting Ground at Crosswicks, in Burlington county, from which Eglinton was about four miles distant. He lived subsequently to the year 1721, but the precise date of his death is not known.

William and Isabel Montgomerie had seven children: ROBERT,† ANNA, ELIZABETH, WILLIAM, JAMES, ALEXANDER and JANE,

---

* This original tract has been much added to by the succeeding generations, both from purchase and by inheritance from their cousins, John and William Burnett, the nephews of Isabel Montgomerie. The last one of the name who held this property was the late Robert Montgomery of Eglinton; and it is now (1863) divided among the children of his daughter, the late Mrs. S. C. Newell; the mansion-house being the property of his daughter Lucy, and the residence of Mr. Bennington Gill, Mrs. Newell's son-in-law.

† Robert Montgomerie of Eglinton was born in 1687. He married in 1709.

28 **James** (Montgomerie) of Upper Freehold, was the third son of William of Brigend.* He was born on his father's estate in Ayrshire and in his youth accompanied his father to East Jersey. His will, in which he gives himself the above designation, is dated April 12, 1756; in it he mentions his wife MARY and his children as follows: ROBERT, ALEXANDER, JAMES, WILLIAM and BURNET.

29 **Alexander** (the second son of James) was born in 1735 and married EUNIA WEST of Eatontown, N. J. He resided in Allentown, where he died, July 14, 1798, and was buried by the side of his wife who died, March 18, 1796, aged 63. They had five children: LUCY,** MARTHA,† THOMAS WEST, ROBERT,‡ and SARAH.§

30 **Thomas West** (Alexander,[29] James,[28] William,[27] Hugh,[26] John.[25] William,[24] Neil[23]) ‖ was born July 1764, and married (1788) MARY, daughter of the Hon. John[2] Berrien ¶ of Rocky Sarah Stacy of Burlington, N. J. He died in 1768. He was the last of his line to use the terminal *rie* in writing his name, his son was the first to substitute the terminal *ry*.

* William, second son of William of Brigend, was the father of Major William Montgomery (b. Philada. 1750) who served in the N. J. Line in the Revolution and was the father of William Montgomery of New Orleans, who was an officer under Gen. Jackson during the invasion of Louisiana by the British.

** Lucy m. Samuel Quay of Allentown, and d. 1815.

† Martha m. Dr. Jeremiah Woolsey.

‡ Robert died young.

§ Sarah b. 1777; m. 18c5, John Johnston of Poplar Grove, N. J.

‖ The last Sir Neil Montgomerie, who died 1613.

¶ Judge Berrien[2] (b. Nov. 19, 1711; d. April 22, 1722) was the son of Cornelius Jansen Berrien, of Huguenot descent, who settled at Flatbush, L. I., in 1669 and d. Newtown, 1687. He married Margaret, daughter of John Eaton of Eatontown, N. J., a wealthy English Friend, who marrying Joanna Wardell, a member of the Church of England, was only saved from being "read out of meeting" by saying he regretted his wife was not a Friend. Judge Berrien's only other daughter, Eliza, m. Nathaniel Lawrence, son of Captain Thomas Lawrence of "Don't give up the ship" fame, and after his death in 1797 she m. his cousin John Lawrence (son of William Lawrence of

Hill, one of the Justices of the Supreme Court of the Province of New Jersey. Her brother Samuel Berrien married Ann Hepburn, grand-daughter of Robert Montgomery the first, of Eglinton. Dr. Montgomery was admitted to the practice of medicine, Nov. 6, 1787, after which he went to Paris and there remained two or three years pursuing his medical studies. On his return he practised his profession for many years in Allentown, in Princeton, and in the city of New York, until his death Jan. 12, 1820. He was interred in Trinity Churchyard.

They had:

I. MARGARET EATON, b. 1788 ; m. 1809 (1st) Samuel Riker of N. Y., and (2d) John R. Shaw, Purser, U. S. N., and had : Anne Deborah Randall (who married Rt. Rev'd William H. Odenheimer, Bishop of New Jersey), Montgomery Porter and Archibald.

II. MARIA S., b. 1790; m. Horatio Eaton, her cousin, and had : Maria Louise (who married John A. Welles of Detroit)

New York). His eldest son John Berrien[3] m. Margaret, daughter of Capt. John Macpherson of Philadelphia, whose son John was an aide-de-camp to Gen. Montgomery, by whose side he fell at Quebec. They removed to Georgia in 1775 and had John[4] Macpherson Berrien (1781–1856) who became Member of Congress (1820), U. S. Senator from Georgia (1825, 1841, 1847) and Attorney-General of the United States (1829–31). It was at Judge John[2] Berrien's residence at Rocky Hill that Gen. Washington made his headquarters when in that section during the Revolution. The tail piece on page 121, illustrates one of a pair of card tables presented by Washington to Judge Berrien and now (1891) in the possession of his great-grand-daughter, Mrs. Delia (Montgomery) Foster of Boston.

Rocky Hill, Somerset County, N. J., is about three miles from Princeton. The Berrien house is located on elevated ground about a quarter of a mile east of the river on the right hand of the road as it ascends from Rocky Hill village to the top of the hill towards Kingston. It is still standing, in much the same condition that it was, in the days of the Revolution, excepting that a veranda which formerly extended along the entire south side of the building has since been demolished. The room occupied by Washington, as his headquarters and office, remains just as he left it, and is kept open for inspection by visitors. It was in this room that he received committees, members of Congress, and other dignitaries, and it was in this room that he wrote his Farewell Address to the Army.

and Theodore Horatio. Some years subsequent to Mr. Eaton's death she married William Inman, Commodore U. S. N., and had Eliza Montgomery (who married Francis B. Odenheimer of Phila.), Mary Berrien and William Taylor.

III. ALEXANDER MAXWELL, M.D., b. Dec. 2, 1792; m. May 17, 1821, Phoebe, daughter of Aaron Hassert of New Brunswick, and had Letitia and Thomas Berrien (b. May 19, 1825; d. July 29, 1827). He was Actg. Surgeon's Mate on the frigate *Essex* in Porter's fight off the harbor of Valparaiso, March 28, 1814. He was commissioned Asst. Surgeon July 16, 1814, and Surgeon May 7, 1825. After much sea service he was ordered to the command of the Naval Asylum at Brooklyn, where he died, Jan. 3, 1838.

31. IV. JOHN BERRIEN, b. Allentown, N. J., Nov. 17, 1794; m. 1821, Mary Henry; d. Carlisle, Pa., March 25, 1873.

V. JULIA, b. March 19, 1797; m. January 27, 1825, William M. Biddle of Philadelphia, and had: Lydia Spencer (b. Nov. 1825; m. Feb. 7, 1850, William D. Smith, U. S. Army; d. Detroit, Nov. 11, 1855), Thomas Montgomery (b. July 9, 1827), Edward McFunn (b. Aug. 27, 1832), Mary Montgomery (b. Oct. 10, 1824; m. Oct. 18, 1855, De Garmo Whiting of Detroit), William M. (b. Feb. 13, 1837, Major 4th Penna. Cavalry, severely wounded near Richmond, June, 1862), Julia Montgomery (b. July 14, 1840).

VI. NATHANIEL LAWRENCE, b. Dec. 9, 1800. He entered the American Navy as Midshipman, Dec. 17, 1810. Was in the action of the *President* with the *Belvidere*, June 23, 1812, where he lost an arm. He was aide-de-camp to Commodore McDonough at his victory on Lake Champlain, Sept. 11, 1814, where he was again wounded. For his gallant services he was promoted to be Lieutenant, Dec. 9, 1814, the youngest officer ever thus commissioned. After many years of active service, he died in the West Indies, of yellow fever, July 30, 1824. He married (1821) Miss Colton of New York, but had no children.

VII. ELIZA LAWRENCE, b. May 19, 1804; m. 1821, Samuel A.

McCoskry, D. D. (afterward Bishop of Michigan ; d. 1887), and had Mary Berrien (m. Stephen K. Stanton, and had Alexandrine M., Samuel McC., Henry F., Lawrence M. [m. Gertrude Blake Hill], and Stephen B.)

31 **John Berrien**[31] (Thomas W.,[30] Alexander,[29] James,[28] William,[27] Hugh,[26] John,[25] William,[24] Neil[23]) was born at Allentown, N. J., November 17, 1794, educated there, and upon the outbreak of war with Great Britain received (June 4, 1812) a warrant as Midshipman in the U. S. Navy. He served with distinction under Commodore Perry and in several affairs on Lake Erie, received a sword of honor and a share in the thanks of Congress, at the close of hostilities. Midshipman Montgomery was actively engaged (1815) in punishing pirates in the Mediterranean under Commodore Decatur. Promoted Lieutenant (April 1, 1818), he was stationed on the African coast until 1820, when he was ordered to the *Erie*, and for several years served in the Mediterranean. In 1835 he became Executive Officer of the famous frigate *Constitution*, and was promoted Commander, December 9, 1839. In 1844, Commander Montgomery was appointed to command the new sloop of war *Portsmouth*, 22 guns, and during the cruise of three years and seven months which ensued, took possession of and permanently established the flag of the U. S. at San Francisco, Sonoma, New Helvetia and Santa Clara, Upper California, maintained the blockade of Mazatlan, Mexico, and in March and April, 1847, hoisted the first U. S. flags at Cape St. Lucas, San José and La Paz, Lower California, which ports were held until the close of the war. In October, 1847, in company with the frigate *Congress*, he bombarded and captured the fortified town and port of Guaymas, Gulf of California. His admirable conduct of the blockade of Mazatlan won him the thanks of the British government. In April, 1849, Commander Montgomery was ordered to the Washington Navy Yard as Executive Officer. He was promoted Captain, January 6, 1853, and in 1857 was assigned to the command of the new steam frigate *Roanoke*. In April, 1859, he was ordered to command the Pacific station, hoisting his flag on the U. S. steam corvette *Lancaster*. Captain Montgomery was relieved as Flag Officer, January 2, 1862, and ordered to take charge of the Charlestown Navy Yard, one of the most important supply stations of the service. He was pro-

moted Commodore July 16, 1862, transferred to the command of the Washington Yard December, 31, 1863, and remained there until October 13, 1865. He was promoted Rear Admiral, July 25, 1866, and at his own request was placed on waiting orders September 1, 1869. After a brilliant public career of fifty years (he was retired from active sea service, December 21, 1861), he died at Carlisle, Pa., March 25, 1873.*

Admiral Montgomery married ———, 1821, MARY† (b. July 9, 1801), daughter of William Henry,‡ of New York.

They had:

I. WILLIAM HENRY, b. ———, 1820. Entered the U. S. Navy as Midshipman, Dec. 21, 1837, became a Passed Midshipman June 29, 1843, and while serving on the Pacific coast on his father's ship, the *Portsmouth*, was sent (Dec. 1846) in charge of an expedition up the Sacramento River, from which none of the officers or crew ever returned. His brother, JOHN ELLIOTT, was one of the party. (See App. " Patriot, Officer and Gentleman.")

II. JULIA MARIA, b. ———. 1821 ; m. April 23, 1851, David N. Mahon, M. D., of Carlisle, Pa. and had: Annie Duncan§ (b. April 12, 1853), John Montgomery (b. Aug. 15, 1854).

III. DELIA HENRY, b. ———, March 6, 1823; m. (1) July 18, 1843, James Foster, U. S. N., and had: Mary (b. March 15,

---

* For sketch of his life see App., " Patriot, Officer and Gentleman."

† One of Mrs. Montgomery's sisters, DELIA, (b. April 22, 1806; d. 1879) m. Captain William Stout of the American merchant service, who retired from the sea (about 1862) with a handsome fortune. Another sister, HARRIET ELIZA (b. September 16, 1808 ; d. ———) m. David S. Edwards, Surgeon, U. S. N. (See App., " One of the Old Navy.")

‡ Who m. February 23, 1800, Delia, (b. March 18, 1784 ; d. October 4, 1839) daughter of Jonathan Harned, (b. Woodbridge, N. J., August 8, 1756 ; m. May 9, 1782, Mary Cotteral and had ten children) the son of Nathaniel Harned, a large landed proprietor in New Jersey, who was read out of Friends' Meeting for taking up arms in the Revolutionary War. Mr. Henry's father, William,[1] came to America from Belfast about 1780. William,[2] d. June 12, 1811, aged 45.

§ Married ———, Lieut. E. P. Wood, U. S. N.

1846; d. Feb. 14, 1849), Elinor Frances* (b. April 3. 1847). Mrs. Foster m. (2) Sept 16, 1849, Andrew Foster of Boston† and had: Julia Montgomery (b. Feb. 27, 1851 ; d. May 3, 1852), Andrew (b. Sept. 5, 1856) and Kate McCrea (b. Dec. 21, 1860).

IV. JOHN ELLIOTT, b. ———, 1830; d. ———, 1846.‡

V. HENRY EDWARDS, b. ———, 1831 ; d. in infancy.

VI. DAVID EDWARDS, b. ———, 1835 ; m. ———; d. at Phila.

VII. SAMUEL LAWRENCE WARD, b. ———, 1836; d. ——— 1857.

VIII. MARY HENRY, b. ———, 1839.

IX. HELEN VREDENBERGH, b. ———, 1844. ,

*Married Gen. T. F. Rodenbough, U. S. A. (See "FOSTER" and "RODENBOUGH.")

† Brother of Passed Midshipman James Foster, U. S. N. (See "FOSTER.")

‡ Lost while on an expedition up the Sacramento River, California (see William Henry Montgomery, p. 120).

☞ ERRATUM.—*Date of Admiral Montgomery's marriage* (p. 120) *should read* 1819-20.

WASHINGTON-BERRIEN CARD TABLE.

[See Note, p. 117.]

ARMS OF MONTGOMERY.

The actual arms of the Montgomeries of Lainshaw [later of Brigend], Male Representatives of the family in France, Scotland, Ireland, England and America. Blazoned as follows: ARMS : Quarterly : 1st and 4th : quarterly-quartered : 1st and 4th : azure, a band between six-cross crosslets fitchée or, for MAZ : 2d and 3d : gules, a fret or, for LYLE. Second and third grand quarters : Argent, on a fess azure three stars of the first, for MURE of Skeldon. On an escutcheon of pretense, quarterly, 1st and 4th : azure three fleurs-de-lis or, for MONTGOMERY : 2d and 3d : gules, three annulets or, stoned azure, for EGLINTON. CRESTS · I. A female figure proper, anciently attired azure, holding in the dexter hand an anchor or, and in the sinister the head of a savage couped of the first, for MONTGOMERY. II. A cock or, crested gules, for LYLE. SUPPORTERS : two female figures, or angels proper. [The ancient supporters of the Montgomeries before the accession of the Setons.]

—*Curio Mag.*, March, 1887.

Patriot, Officer and Gentleman.

JOHN BERRIEN MONTGOMERY was born at Allentown, N. J., November 17, 1794, the second son of Thomas West Montgomery, M. D., of New York, who died in that city in 1820, aged 56 years. Dr. Montgomery's grandfather, James Montgomerie, of "Upper Freehold," came to America with his father, William, of Brigend, from Ayrshire, Scotland, in 1701-1702, and settled on Doctor's Creek, in Monmouth county, New Jersey. Eglinton, the name of this estate, is situated about two miles from Allentown.

The subject of this sketch derived his Christian name from his maternal grandfather, Hon. John Berrien, one of the Justices of the Supreme Court of New Jersey, at whose residence—Rocky Hill—Washington wrote his farewell address to the Army, and was a frequent guest. Judge Berrien's second daughter married Nathaniel Lawrence, who was Attorney-General of New York from 1792 to 1795. Descended from a race of warriors, it was natural that young Montgomery, together with his brothers Alexander and Nathaniel, should enter the Navy just as this country was on the verge of war with England.

On the 4th of June, 1812, John Berrien Montgomery was appointed a Midshipman, proceeded with the first draft of men from New York to Sackett's Harbor, Lake Ontario, and served successively on the *Hamilton*, *Madison* and *General Pike*. He participated Nov. 10th in an unsuccessful attack upon Kingston, U. C., with the view of cutting out the enemy's flag-ship, the *Royal George*; on April 27, 1813, he assisted at the capture of Little York (Toronto) and May 27th of Fort George and Newark. He volunteered August 4th, 1813, with seven officers and one hundred seamen, for service on Lake Erie, under Commodore Perry, joined the *Niagara*, and took part in the naval engagement (Sept. 10th) which resulted in the capture of the British squadron, for which service he received a sword of honor and shared in the thanks of Congress.

Midshipman Montgomery was present during the blockade and attack (August 4th, 1814) on Macinac, Lake Huron, where the enemy was repulsed with considerable loss. On the 18th of same month he assisted to destroy a block-house and a British gun-brig. During the next six weeks he was employed in protecting the communications between Fort Erie and the hospitals at Buffalo, and in the transportation of troops between the two shores of Lake Erie, remaining in that region, actively employed, during the remainder of the campaign, when he returned to New York, late in February, 1815, in time to witness the general illumination of the city in honor of peace.

In March, 1815, he was ordered to the sloop-of-war *Ontario*, at Baltimore, and sailed, on the ensuing May, in the first squadron under Commodore Decatur for Algiers. Arriving in the Mediterranean, the young midshipman had an early opportunity of meeting the Algerians upon their own ground, taking part in the capture of one of their frigates (50 guns), a brig (20 guns), and in the blockade of the port of Algiers, until the close of the war in July, 1815. He remained on the Mediterranean station until 1817, returning in August to Norfolk, Va., but was immediately ordered to the sloop-of-war *Hornet*, then fitting for sea at New York. In February, 1818, he was transferred to the *Cyane*, and April 1, 1818, was promoted Lieutenant. During the next three years Lieut. Montgomery was cruising upon the coast of Africa, returning to the United States in December, 1820. Almost at once he was ordered to the *Erie*, in which vessel he served during an uneventful period until her return from the Mediterranean in November, 1826, when he was detached and granted a well-deserved leave of absence, the first in fourteen years of continuous sea service. During 1828-29 he was employed on recruiting service at Chambersburg, Pa., and in 1830 was ordered to the West Indies as executive officer of the *Peacock;* off Havana he fell in with the flagship *Erie*, and was transferred to that vessel as executive officer; subsequently commanding her during a cruise in the Gulf and on the coast of Mexico. Upon his return to Pensacola, July, 1831, Lieut. Montgomery was relieved from command of the *Erie*, and ordered as Flag Lieutenant to the *Natchez*, returning in her to Norfolk, Va., August, 1831, and was once more detached on leave. From January, 1833, to February, 1835, he was on recruiting service in Philadelphia and New York. At the latter date he was ordered as executive officer to the frigate *Constitution*, at Boston, which vessel sailed March 2d, for New York, and thence on the 15th for Havre, France, to convey our Minister, Mr. Livingston, to the United States during the Indemnity agitation. He was ordered to command the receiving ship *Columbus* at Boston, March, 1837; detached in April, 1839, and promoted Commander, December 9, 1839. From May, 1841 to February, 1844, he was stationed at Boston on recruiting service. In October, 1844, Commander Montgomery was ordered to command the new sloop-of-war *Portsmouth*,* then fitting for sea at Portsmouth, N. H. He sailed from Norfolk, Va., in the following January, for the Pacific where he was destined to render memorable service in connection with the acquisition of California,† and during the war with Mexico. A recent and important contribution to the history of that period, is from the pen of Professor Josiah Royce of Harvard University, as follows : ‡

CALIFORNIANA.

" There have lately been put into my hands, by the Editor of the *Century*, certain original documents of decided importance for the history of the seizure of California. I have been asked to examine these and to summarize a portion of their contents, a thing which I the more readily do because they serve to set in a clearer light than heretofore the honorable conduct of an officer whose part in the seizure of California was a difficult and delicate one, and who himself did his duty so well and so modestly that he has, in the past, altogether escaped the celebrity that has fallen to the lot of other persons surely not more deserving. This officer, Commander (afterward Rear-Admiral) John B. Montgomery, was in 1846 in command of the United States ship *Portsmouth*. His ship visited California in 1845 ; returned in October to the southern Mexican coast ; was at Mazatlan October 16, 1845, and at Guaymas December 2 ; and returned again to California, under Sloat's orders, in the spring of 1846. The purpose of her coming was to inquire into the alarming reports that had gone south-

---

* The U. S. S. *Portsmouth* was built at Portsmouth, N. H., in 1843. She carried 22 guns and 210 men ; 1022 tons displacement ; length 151.10 feet ; beam 38.1 ; hold 17.2 ; and cost $170,586.

† The name " California " first occurred in a novel entitled " Las Sergas de Esplandian " published in 1510, and was first given to that State by Bernal Diaz Costello, who served under Cortez, who writes in his memoirs of the voyage " from Santa Cruz to California." The Bay of San Francisco was discovered in 1769 by several French savants who came there to see the transit of Venus : they perished of malarial fever near Point St. Lucas. (*Records, Cal. Hist. Soc.*)

‡ *Century Magazine*, March, 1891.

ward concerning the quarrel of March between Frémont and Castro. She reached Monterey towards the end of April, later passing on to San Francisco; and she lay in the harbor of San Francisco until after the raising of the American flag at that port on July 9, a date two days later than the seizure of Monterey.* Montgomery's stay at San Francisco thus covered the entire time of the Bear Flag episode. From him Captain Frémont obtained, through Lieutenant Gillespie, supplies to enable him 'to continue his explorations,' and to accomplish his other peaceful duties during that now famous affair. To him, in fact, Captain Frémont also wrote, as he himself declares in his letter to Senator Benton of July 25, 1846 (see Frémont's 'Memoirs,' p. 546), 'describing to him fully my position and intentions, in order that he might not unwittingly commit himself in affording me other than such assistance as his instructions would authorize him naturally to offer an officer charged with an important public duty; or, in fine, to any citizen of the United States.' To Montgomery, also, General Vallejo appealed, by messenger, after the Bear Flag men had made the general their prisoner. From Montgomery, Castro demanded an account of what the Bear Flag meant, and of what part the United States Government had therein; and meanwhile the Bear Flag men themselves were begging him for counsel and encouragement; and every officer on board the *Portsmouth* was longing for the coming of Sloat and for the end of this tedious attitude of neutrality. In this trying position Montgomery kept his head and did his duty with a firmness that the documents before me set in a very clear light. These documents are, (1) extracts from Montgomery's private diary; (2) copies of the official correspondence of the commander, with letters to and from Larkin, Frémont, Castro, Gillespie, and others. Of these letters some have previously been known, through the papers of Consul Larkin, and otherwise. Several are also printed in Frémont's 'Memoirs,' although the aforesaid letter of Captain Frémont to Montgomery, 'describing to him fully my position and intentions,' has been, as I believe, heretofore unknown, and furnishes the most characteristic and

*[Commodore Sloat had dispatched a messenger to Montgomery informing him of his intention to raise the American flag at Monterey, and directing him to do the same in the northern parts of the province around the bay of San Francisco. This was done under a salute of 21 guns from the *Portsmouth*. The plaza was subsequently named " Portsmouth Square," and the principal street was christened " Montgomery Street." EDITOR.]

interesting addition to our previous knowledge that is contained among these papers.

"There is space here for only a very brief account of the substance of the extracts from Montgomery's diary. The earlier extracts concern the visit to California in 1845. At Monterey, Montgomery interviewed Consul Larkin and 'learned from him that American interests were perfectly secure, and little probability of their being interrupted in any way unless by a war with Mexico.' There was indeed some talk between the two concerning the supposed English designs upon California, and Larkin told Montgomery of a reported subsidy that was to be paid by England to Mexico for the support of the new troops that were to be sent to California. These rumors, to be sure, have long been known to students of this period of California history. It is interesting to find that both Larkin and Montgomery, at the moment, believed them; although there is indeed little evidence for their truth, and although Montgomery learned of no very authoritative source for them.

"In October, Montgomery, then at Acapulco, notes the failure of the Mexican plan to send troops to California, a failure which he attributes to 'the supineness of the Government and want of funds.' It is certain that whatever the English intrigues of those days may have been with regard to California, one in vain looks for any decisive movement of any sort resulting from them. On April 23, 1846, Montgomery, then just arrived at Monterey, received information from Larkin 'that the commercial and other interests of the United States continued safe, having experienced no interruption or annoyance since our visit in October last.' As the quarrel of March between Frémont and Castro was now a matter of very recent history, and as Montgomery had come especially to find out about it, one reads this statement with some surprise, but finds the explanation in words which follow a little later, in the same entry of the diary, after a brief statement of the nature of the March quarrel itself: 'It is here well understood that no real attack upon the camp of Captain Frémont was contemplated by General Castro when he directed this movement, but that it was done with the view only of furnishing materials for forming a high-sounding, flaming despatch to the central government of Mexico.' 'Mr. Larkin informed me,' continues Montgomery, 'that the unsettled condition of California seems to point to a necessity, and naturally produces in the public mind an expectation, of a speedy political change of some kind ; and that the feeling is rife that California is soon to be governed by England or the United States, predilections being divided.' The diary adds that, in Larkin's opinion, the native and Mexican population of the country would find a 'change under either' England or the United States acceptable,' and that if the war with Mexico should come to pass there would be no great trouble in securing the prize for our own flag. On April 29, Montgomery is ' informed by the consul that General Castro is troubled with suspicions of collusion between Captain Frémont and myself, and supposes that I have sent for him to return to Monterey.' On May 4, Lieutenants Bartlett and Wilson having returned from an excursion into the interior, tell Montgomery of their pleasant reception, and say that both American residents in the vicinity of San José, and ' many of the most intelligent Mexicans and Californians,' ' express openly their desire ' for the coming of our flag, and ' fearlessly speak of it ' as an event 'which is near at hand.' Montgomery himself adds the expression of his belief in the growing chances of an easy occupation of the land. His own social relations with Castro continued good during all this time. May 9, he attended a large picnic given by Castro himself, and May 15, Castro was a guest at a ball given on shore by the wardroom officers of the *Portsmouth*. Castro's military preparations, which still continued, are correctly interpreted by Montgomery as having, in the main, relation to the feud between the Commandante General and Governor Pio Pico. Rumors of Frémont's expected return continued.

" We now come, however, to more exciting events. June 7 finds Montgomery in San Francisco Bay. Gillespie has just arrived, on his return from the north, bringing a requisition from Captain Frémont for supplies. Frémont himself has come back to the Sacramento Valley. His party is 'nearly destitute,' as appears from the letter written by Gillespie, and copied in the 'Correspondence' which accompanies the diary. Gillespie's mission to the bay, and his success in getting supplies for Frémont from Montgomery, have always been known matters of our history. It is also known, from a letter summarized in my ' California ' (p. 106), that Gillespie represented to non-official residents at the bay that the purpose of Frémont, in asking for supplies, was solely to equip his party for setting out at once on his return overland. It has, however, never before been absolutely sure that Montgomery received no hint from Gillespie of Frémont's real intentions in asking for this aid. H. H. Bancroft, in Vol. V. of his 'California,' p. 127, can only say: 'I know of no reason to suppose that Montgomery was informed by Gillespie of the revolutionary project on foot.' The present papers, both diary and correspondence, put it beyond doubt that Montgomery had *no* notion of the coming outbreak. He honored in perfectly good faith the topographical engineer's requisition for necessary supplies for his scientific expedition, and on June 11 despatched the ship's launch with the desired stores. On the way up the river, on the very first day of the launch's journey, Gillespie heard of the capture of Arce's horses by the settlers, an act with which, as is known, the Bear Flag affair was begun. A hastily pencilled note from him (here copied) gave the first information to Montgomery of what was afoot; but Gillespie had no intention of revealing, as yet, Frémont's connection with the undertaking. In the postscript to his note Gillespie writes: 'I am of the opinion that the settlers have obtained decided proof of Castro's intention to have their crops burned to warrant the course they have pursued. The bearer hereof says he heard a messenger to Captain Sutter state that they had acted under advice from Captain Frémont. If such is the fact, which I very much doubt, there is positive cause for hostility on the part of the settlers.' In his diary Montgomery now gives, between the 15th and the 18th of June, an interesting account of his earliest relations with the Sonoma insurgents and with their opponents. These four days were very full of news and excitement. Montgomery fully believed the settlers to be acting upon their own responsibility. His private sympathies were altogether with them. They were his countrymen, newcomers in a distant land, exposed to hardship, and now, as he thought, threatened with oppression. He believed, naturally enough, the reports which were freely circulated as to Castro's designs against them, although he knew too much to regard Castro as a very formidable foe to anybody. But meanwhile he valued the honor of his flag, and he knew the duties of a neutral. He could sympathize with the insurgents; but he could not give them aid. With an indignation which must seem to us quite pathetic, he defended Frémont, as a fellow-officer under the flag, from the fierce accusations of Castro, who wrote from Santa Clara on June 17 demanding from the commander an explanation of Frémont's conduct. Castro pointed out that the captain of the surveying expedition, 'without the formalities established among civilized nations,' had invaded the country and seized Sonoma. Montgomery replied (June 18), in a tone of absolute assurance, that Fremont's expedition was solely scientific in its aims, and that it was 'in no manner whatever, either by authority of the United States Government or otherwise, connected with the political movement of residents of the country at Sonoma.' For Castro to assert that such a connection existed was, so Montgomery retorted, ' to impugn the integrity of the United States Government.' It was his turn, he suggested to demand explanations when his flag was by implication thus dishonored. But alas for Montgomery's sincere and genuine indignation on behalf of his brother officer ! Ten days later, June 28, the diary mentions a second visit of Gillespie, bringing the news that Frémont had openly joined the Bears, and was in pursuit of Torre in the San Rafael region. 'This course of Captain Frémont,' says Montgomery in his private diary, ' renders my position as a neutral peculiarly delicate and difficult. Having avowed not only my own but Captain Frémont's entire neutrality and non-interference in the existing difficulties in the country, it can scarcely be supposed, under the circumstances, that I shall be regarded as having spoken in good faith and sincerity.' In fact, as one sees, Montgomery learned that, under certain circumstances, one may expose his country's honor to only the more reproach by chivalrously offering his own honor in defense of his brethren in the service.

"The mission of Lieutenant Misroon, whom Montgomery despatched to Sonoma as neutral and mediator, occupies considerable place in these records ; as do also other well-known public incidents of those days. But there remain still two important topics upon which these documents give significant testimony. With the mention of these I must close :

"First: It has always been doubtful, I believe, when the first news of the actual hostilities on the Rio Grande reached Frémont. What we have known, heretofore, is that Sloat at Mazatlan was informed of the beginning of active hostilities by a message that reached him May 17, and that a letter, which he at once wrote to Larkin, reached Monterey by the *Cyane* on June 19, nearly a week after the seizure of Sonoma. Up to this time Frèmont himself had avoided an open union with the Bears. He had taken charge of Vallejo and the other prisoners first taken. But he had remained quiet. Yet, on the 21st, he was already making preparations to leave

Sutter's Fort with his party, and on the 25th he reached Sonoma. It is, of course, interesting to learn whether the openness of Frémont's hostile proceedings, from this time forth, could have been due to any fresh assurance that actual war was under way on the Atlantic coast. Professor William Carey Jones, in an article recently written in defense of Frémont's conduct during the early part of the seizure of California,* has endeavored to make probable an earlier date for Frémont's knowledge of the hostilities on the Rio Grande than has generally been supposed likely. The present documents do not bear out his view. It appears that, on June 20, both Larkin himself and Captain Mervine, of the *Cyane*, wrote to Montgomery from Monterey. Their two letters, written the day after the *Cyane's* arrival, together inform Montgomery that Sloat is on his way northward, and without directly mentioning the outbreak of hostilities, speak of 'important news,' that 'cannot be revealed,' but of whose nature Montgomery shall before long be 'apprised.' This guarded tone was very tormenting to Montgomery, whose neutral position was daily growing more intolerable. As late as June 26 he still believed Frémont to be as neutral in conduct as himself, and so on the latter day he wrote to Frémont, transmitting the contents of Larkin's letter, as being the whole of his news. This letter, with other despatches, was sent to Frémont at Sutter's Fort, under care of Lieutenant Bartlett. When Bartlett reached the fort Frémont was already with the Bears. The letter, therefore, went on to Sonoma, and was acknowledged by Frémont as late as July 5 as something new, and, as regards the facts about Sloat, very interesting. When one adds that Montgomery, writing on July 2 to Mervine, and begging for more information, says emphatically: 'We have been completely cut off from all information from below [*i. e.*, from Mexico] since the 1st of April last' [*i. e.*, since Montgomery's own departure from the South], one sees the great improbability that, before July 1, any one north of Monterey knew more than the little that Larkin and Mervine chose to reveal to Montgomery, and to one or two other of Larkin's confidants. And this little did *not* include information of the actual hostilities.

---

* See " Proceedings of the California Historical Association," Vol. I., p. 1. Professor Jones' somewhat original interpretation of the relations between Montgomery and Frémont is almost entirely set aside by these new documents.

"The second and final matter of which I spoke above is contained in the text of Frémont's letter to Montgomery, written upon the reception of the supplies brought by the launch. The letter is dated 'New Helvetia,' June 16, and taken in connection with all the circumstances of the moment, it forms one of the most interesting confessions that Frémont ever chose to make of his position at the moment of his entrance upon hostilities. It will be remembered that, according to Frémont's own statement to Benton, this letter was to 'describe fully' his own 'position and intentions;' that it was written especially for the guidance of Montgomery, who had just shown the greatest willingness to aid the leader of the scientific exploration by every means in his power; that it was prepared after the settlers had begun, under Frémont's advice, their movement for independence; and finally, that it was written but a very few days before Frémont started to join the Bears at Sonoma. The moment was a critical one. Frémont has since asserted that he acted upon special instructions. In his 'Memoirs' (p. 520) he speaks of this very time as the one when he decided 'that it was,' as he says, 'for me rather to govern events than to be governed by them.' Under these circumstances, to write to Montgomery, as follows, is to furnish the best possible comment upon one's own conduct. The sentence italicized in the following copy of this letter has in Montgomery's record but one word italicized, viz.: the word *active* in the phrase 'such active and precautionary measures.' I print it thus, here, in order that it may be set side by side in the curious reader's mind with other and later accounts that General Frémont has given of his instructions. Otherwise the letter appears unchanged.

NEW HELVETIA, CALIFORNIA,
June 16, 1846.

SIR: I had the gratification to receive, on the 6th, your letter of the 3d inst.; and the farther gratification to receive yesterday, by the hands of Lieutenant Hunter, your favor of the 10th conveying to me assurances of your disposition to do anything, within the scope of your instructions, to facilitate the public service in which I am engaged. In acknowledging the receipt of the stores with which you have supplied us, I beg you to receive the earnest thanks of myself and party for the prompt and active kindness, which we are all in a condition fully to appreciate. My time to-day has been so constantly engrossed that I could make no opportunity to write, and as it is now nearly midnight you will permit me to refer you to Lieutenant Hunter for an account of the condition of the country, which will doubtless have much interest to you. The people here have made some movements with the view of establishing a settled and stable government, which may give security to their persons and property. This evening I was interrupted in a note to yourself by the arrival of General Vallejo and other officers, who had been taken prisoners and insisted upon surrendering to me. The people and authorities of the country persist in connecting with me every movement of the foreigners, and I am hourly in expectation of the approach of General Castro. My position has consequently become a difficult one. The unexpected hostility which has been exercised towards us, on the part of the military authorities of California, has entirely deranged the plan of our survey and frustrated my intention of examining the Colorado of the Gulf of California, which was one of the principal objects of this expedition. The suffering to which my party would be unavoidably exposed at this advanced period of the year, by deprivation of water during intervals of three and four days, renders any movement in that direction impracticable.

It is therefore my present intention to abandon the farther prosecution of our exploration and proceed immediately across the mountainous country to the eastward in the direction of the head-waters of the Arkansas River, and thence to the frontier of Missouri, where I expect to arrive early in September. In order to recruit my animals and arrange my equipage for a long journey, I shall necessarily be compelled to remain here until about the 1st of July. In the meantime should anything be attempted against me, I cannot, consistently with my own feelings and respect for the national character of the duty in which I am engaged, permit a repetition of the recent insults we have received from General Castro. If, therefore, any hostile movements are made in this direction, I will most assuredly meet or anticipate them; and with such intentions I am regulating my conduct to the people here. *The nature of my instructions and the peaceful nature of our operations do not contemplate any active hostility on my part even in the event of war between the two countries; and therefore, although I am resolved to take such active and precautionary measures as I shall judge necessary for our safety, I am not authorized to ask from you any other than such assistance as, without incurring yourself unusual responsibility, you would feel at liberty to afford me.* Such an emergency could not have been anticipated in any instructions; but, between Indians on the one hand and a hostile people on the other, I trust that our government will not severely censure any efforts to which we may be driven in defense of our lives and character.

In this condition of things I can only then urgently request that you will remain with the *Portsmouth* in the Bay of San Francisco, where your presence will operate strongly to check proceedings against us; and I would feel much more security in my position should you judge it advisable to keep open a communication with me by means of your boats. In this way you would receive the earliest information, and you might possibly spare us the aid of one of your surgeons, in

case of accident here. Repeating my thanks for the assistance you have rendered us, and regretting my inability to visit you on board the *Portsmouth*, I am, sir, very respectfully,
Your obedient servant,
(Signed)   J. C. FRÉMONT,
Bt. Capt. Topl. Engineers, U. S. Army.
CAPT. JNO. B. MONTGOMERY,
U. S. Ship *Portsmouth*,
BAY OF SAN FRANCISCO, CALIFORNIA.

" The italicized sentence excludes the possibility that Frémont's instructions had the warlike nature which he has since attributed to them. In those days his only intent was to pretend that he was in danger from Castro. These papers also contain the record of Montgomery's admirable conduct of the later blockade of Mazatlan, an affair which yet further tried his skill and his excellent discretion."

While lying in the harbor soon after the seizure of California, Commander Montgomery met with a terrible bereavement. His sons were serving near him at the time: WILLIAM HENRY, twenty-six years of age, was a passed midshipman and acting master of the U. S. Sloop *Warren*, and JOHN ELLIOTT, aged sixteen, was his father's secretary.

On Thursday, Dec. 13, 1846, the launch belonging to the *Warren* (then in the harbor with the *Portsmouth*) left the fleet for the purpose of carrying funds and supplies to Fort Sacramento (Sutter's). The launch was under charge of Passed Midshipman William Montgomery with Midshipman Daniel C. Hugenin of the *Portsmouth* (as pilot), Elliott Montgomery and a crew of nine men: Coxswain, George Rodman, Anthony Sylvester, Alexander McDonald, Samuel Turner, Samuel Lane, Milton Ladd, John W. Dowd, Gilman Hilton and Lawson Lee. After an absence of seventeen days fears were entertained for the safety of the party and a thorough and protracted but unavailing search was made up the San Joaquin and Sacramento rivers. For some time it was thought that the boat had capsized in the squall, but many years after the gray-haired father was called to the bed-side of a dying sailor, who confessed that he had taken part in a mutiny and murder of the officers, and that the crew, after scuttling the boat and dividing their plunder, had separated.

The most important service of Montgomery's life was his management of the blockade of the port of Mazatlan, Mexico, February-March, 1847. This proved to be a difficult and delicate matter, as the

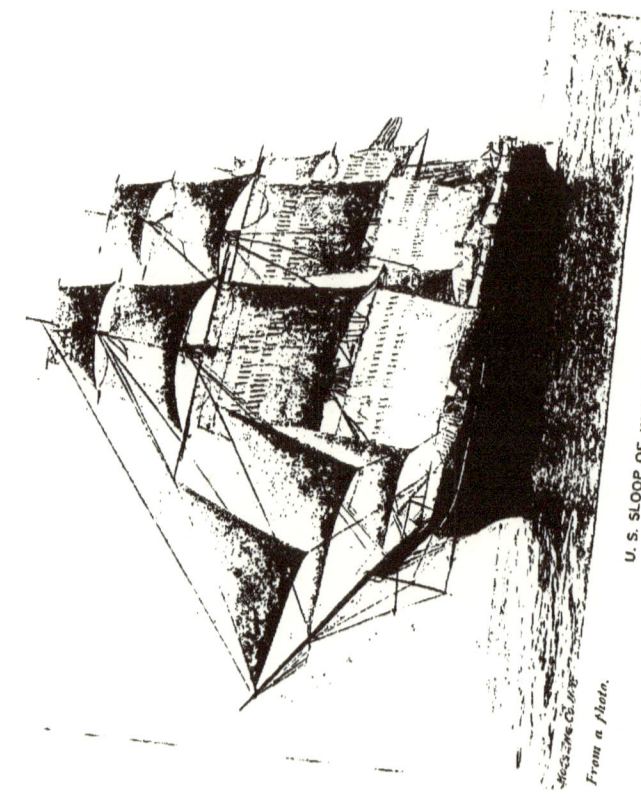
U. S. SLOOP OF WAR "PORTSMOUTH."
From a photo.

following from his report to the "Commander-in-Chief of the Naval Forces of the U. S. in the Pacific," shows. He wrote to that officer that "the blockade of Mazatlan was effectually maintained by the *Portsmouth* for nearly six weeks, although generally opposed and protested against on the ground of illegality, and the service was not relinquished until I had satisfactorily secured the means of communicating Commodore Stockton's orders to Lieutenant-Commander Turner as directed, and the low state of my provisions admonished me of the necessity of immediate attention to duties assigned me on this coast. I think it proper, sir, with the view of averting from others the serious embarrassments through which I deemed it my imperative duty (in obedience to specific orders) to persevere in maintaining the recent blockade of Mazatlan, to apprise you that unless commencing *de novo* by proclamation, any attempt to re-establish a blockade of one or more ports, short of all named in Commodore Stockton's proclamation of August last, will be strenuously opposed by the representatives of neutral powers. Nothing but the amicable forbearance and courtesy of Sir Baldwin Walker, of H. B. M. Frigate *Constance* (such as could only with safety have been exercised by a superior to a very inferior force) prevented a serious difficulty (possibly collision between our ships) growing out of conflicting orders respecting the blockade."

The British government was so much impressed with the firm but reasonable treatment of the interests of neutrals by the American Commander at Mazatlan, that the following handsome recognition of Montgomery's official conduct by Lord Palmerston was transmitted to him through the Departments of State (of which James Buchanan * was the head) and of the Navy (then presided over by J. Y. Mason †).

(No .4). FOREIGN OFFICE.
June 30, 1847,

Sir :—Captain Sir Baldwin Walker, commanding Her Majesty's Ship *Constance*, on the west coast of Mexico, has mentioned in his reports in very favorable terms the kind and considerate manner in which Captain Montgomery of the United States Frigate *Portsmouth* has conducted himself toward neutral vessels whilst he has been employed in blockading the Port of Mazatlan, and I have to desire that you will take an opportunity of conveying to the United States Secretary of State the acknowledgments of Her Majesty's Government for Captain Montgomery's courteous treatment of British subjects upon this occasion. I am, etc., etc.,
J. F. CRAMPTON, ESQ. PALMERSTON.

---

* Afterward President of the United States.
† One of the principals in the Mason-Slidell affair (1861).

In April, 1849, Commander Montgomery was ordered to the Washington Navy Yard as executive officer. Promoted to Captain January 5, 1853. In April, 1857, ordered to command the new steam frigate *Roanoke*, at Norfolk, Va., and sailing thence to Aspinwall, returned in August, same year, to New York, with 250 of Walker's filibusters; thence proceeded to Boston, where the ship, requiring repairs, went out of commission. From this time to January, 1858, on shore duty. Captain Montgomery was ordered April, 1859, to command the Pacific Squadron, and to hoist his flag on the steam corvette *Lancaster*, at Philadelphia, sailing in June for his destination. While upon this duty it was his fortune to revisit the scene of his service in 1846-1848, and, everywhere, he appears to have been received with sincere gratification. Noticing the arrival of the *Lancaster* at Mazatlan, a correspondent of a New York journal wrote: " The little harbor of Mazatlan has been honored for the first time since the Mexican War by the presence of a commodore or flag officer. Flag officer Montgomery is the first of his rank in our service who has indicated any interest in the commercial importance of the port. The *Lancaster*, Captain Rudd, arrived on the evening of the 28th ult. Salutes were exchanged the following day. The Governor and all the officials of the State visited the ship on the 30th, at the invitation of the Consul, and during the afternoon the ship continued crowded with a delighted and wondering multitude. The flag officer returned the visit of the Governor on the 31st, at the Government House, where he was received with the greatest possible demonstrations of respect and with full military honors. Nothing could have exceeded the delicacy of the reception and the marked personal respect which was shown to him on all sides. It is said that no such demonstration was ever witnessed in Mazatlan. The *Lancaster* leaves to-day on a short visit to Guaymas, but will return to this port in about twenty days, and thence proceed to Acapulco, Panama, etc."

While at Panama in October, 1860, a young officer of our fleet was arrested near the British consulate by a guard from H. B. M. ship *Clio*, Captain Miller, stationed there for the protection of the consulate (during recent local disturbances). Although almost instantly released by the officer of the English guard, the matter came to the ears of Captain Montgomery, who took prompt measures to resent the outrage, and demanded an apology and the instant cessation of all interference with citizens of the United States in their passage through the public streets of the city. The British commander called upon Captain Montgomery and tendered a satisfactory apology "for the error of his subordinate."

When the late war opened Captain Montgomery personally assured himself of the status of his officers by assembling them upon the flagship in Panama Bay and causing the prescribed oath of allegiance to be administered with the most impressive solemnity, setting the example in his own person. Only one officer in the entire squadron—then the largest afloat—declined to take it. Many, supposed to be wavering, were confirmed in their fealty, a result largely due to the energy and patriotic action of the flag officer. Not long after, in the regular correspondence of the New York *Tribune* from Washington appeared the following:

"In a crisis like the present, when the Army and the Navy have exhibited so many apostate sons, it is cheering to find such loyalty to the Union as is indicated by the following extract from a private letter of Commodore Montgomery, Flag Officer of the Pacific squadron. . . . As a patriot, an officer and a gentleman he is *sans peur, sans reproche et sans tache*. He says: 'I honestly believe, under an all-wise Providence, that great and permanent good to the Union under our present glorious Constitution will result from our present agitation. I glory in the patriotic course pursued by Major Anderson. For my own part, knowing and having acknowledged no obligation but that which I solemnly swore to the Constitution and Union nearly fifty years ago, it would, indeed, be humiliating to be now reduced to the position of being a citizen of a seceding section of our country; and while two stars and stripes of our proud flag shall be found together I shall adhere to it with my whole heart, affection and devotion. I have great hopes in the wisdom, patriotism and strong sense of Mr. Lincoln, who may, by an all-wise Providence, have been reared for the present crisis in our own history. *That the Union will endure and arise from her present difficulties in greater strength and permanency—I will say, in greater glory than ever—I fully believe.*'"

Captain Montgomery (having been placed on the Retired List, Dec. 21, 1861, by operation of law) was relieved Jan. 2, 1862, from command of the Pacific squadron by Captain Bell, taking with him, as reported: "the best wishes of the entire native and foreign population, and of every officer and sailor in the fleet, to all of whom he has endeared himself by his kind and courteous manners, his moderation and good sound sense."

In May, following, he was ordered to command the Navy-Yard at Boston, Mass., where he continued to render very important services in fitting out vessels, and preparing and forwarding material of war for the immense navy which the Government was compelled to improvise for the emergency. Here Commodore Montgomery (promoted July 16, 1862) was able to display his administrative ability and talent for organization to the fullest extent. He personally supervised all the details of that important station, and applied himself, with all the indomitable energy, perseverance and devotion to duty of his nature, to the interests of the service. Day and night, with sleepless activity, he was to be found at his office; and if perchance he sought an hour's rest it was with the injunction to awaken him upon the receipt of any official papers, in order that he might determine their importance. He demonstrated that duty at a "yard," in time of war, might well be the most important, the most arduous, the most "active" service in the world. Relieved December 31, 1863, by Rear-Admiral Stringham, he assumed command of the Navy-Yard at Washington, where he exhibited the same zeal, tempered with discretion, which was so characteristic of the man, and on the 13th of October, 1865, he once more relinquished his command, with the satisfaction of knowing that his administration had been highly approved by his official superiors and honorable to himself. Public opinion again spoke kindly of him, asserting that "since the establishment of this yard in the year 1804, there never has been a commanding officer here who secured so large a share of high appreciation as John B. Montgomery."

After remaining upon "waiting orders" for a short time, he was ordered, July 10, 1866, to command the naval station at Sackett's Harbor, New York, and on the 25th of the same month was promoted to the grade of Rear-Admiral. He remained in the enjoyment of the society of his immediate family, and near the scene of his early exploits on the lakes under Perry and Elliott until September 1, 1869, when he was placed on waiting orders at his own request. Having recently lost his wife, Admiral Montgomery selected Carlisle, Pennsylvania, as his residence, where, surrounded by his children and many kind friends, after a public service of more than sixty years, the gallant and venerable sailor passed the rest of his life. He died, at that place, March 25, 1873, aged seventy-eight years, five months and twenty-three days. We have given an epitome of the public life of a distinguished officer, and have said but little of the private virtues of this good man. This memoir may be fitly closed with an extract from the funeral sermon delivered by the Rev. C. P. Wing, D.D., who was intimate with the late Admiral during his residence at Carlisle :

"Much as we admired and loved him before, we now see him with a fullness and vividness we never appreciated while he lingered with us. He has been gathered into the celestial garner in his full ripeness. Even friends who are never ready to give up those who are dear to them must concede that the shock of corn was fully matured when it was gathered. As a faithful citizen and public servant, he had passed through all the gradations of honor which belonged to his chosen profession. It is as a man and a Christian that we shall most remember him. In these respects he appears greatest, and evidently was most anxious to excel. The honors of a nation depend much upon the accident of circumstances, but one's manhood and religious character are essential to himself, and sure to meet with the most affectionate and permanent recognition. These were the objects of his most constant study, his prayers and his exertions ; and no one could have had intercourse with him, even for a few moment only, without being struck with his courteous bearing and his high moral culture. Without ostentation or self-assertion, as all who possess such qualities are apt to be, his opinions on every subject were deliberately formed, quite decisive and cautiously expressed. Invariably respectful toward the rights and views of all around him, his politeness was a marked feature of his character, and never forsook him when most worn down by exhaustion or by pain. Justice and kindness—qualities not always found to go together—were in him happily blended. His intellect was cultivated by extensive reading and study, and his heart was watched over and controlled by the most scrupulous conscientiousness ; and yet it was to the Word of God recorded in the Scriptures that he gave the most implicit and child-like submission, and there he sought his highest wisdom. He never appears to have been in the least affected by those speculations which have been directed against the inspiration of the Bible, for having once decided that God's Word was the sole foundation of his hopes, he found no occasion to re-open the question of its authority. He spent much time, habitually and for many years, in reading that sacred volume, and never seemed to tire of its precious consolations. This admirable character could not indeed have been formed on weaker natural endowments; but it was grace that gave to them their development and added a delightful charm."

A reminiscence of his cruise on the Pacific coast, in 1847, was thus related by the Rev. Dr. Woodbridge in an address, delivered before the California Bible Society, in March, 1875 : " But a short time afterwards that noble, glorious gentleman, Captain Montgomery, came here in his sloop-of-war, *Portsmouth*. He went ashore and inquired for the means of grace. Nothing of the kind to be found. 'Well,' said he, 'I will be preacher; I will perform these duties; we will have services every Sunday.' And they did, month after month; and the noble Captain stayed here and proclaimed the truth and read the Word of God, and taught the people the way of salvation. And oftentimes when I go down through that magnificent thoroughfare called by his name and look at those stately edifices, I seem to see them founded on the prayers of that great and good man, who dared to stand up in San Francisco and regularly and constantly present the Word of God to the people."

One of the Old Navy.

DAVID SHELTON EDWARDS, M.D., Surgeon and Medical Director, U. S. Navy, who was fifth in descent from John[1] Edwards (b. England, 1662; m. Mary Hanford, and d. Pequannock, Conn., 1744), departed this life on Wednesday, March 18, 1874, at his residence, Chestnut Hill, near Bridgeport, Conn. He was born at Trumbull, Conn., June 21, 1794, graduated at Yale in 1814, and after practising medicine for a short time in New Haven, was appointed an assistant surgeon in the Navy July 30, 1818, and ordered to the U. S. S. *Alert*. He was transferred to the frigate *Congress* in 1820 ; served in the China sea, and the same year was on duty at Manilla when it was visited by the Asiatic cholera. In 1821, while attached to the U. S. S. *Grampus*, in an engagement with pirates off the coast of Cuba, in which five sail were destroyed, he was severely wounded. He was attached to the *Fulton* in 1823 ; to the *Erie* for the Mediterranean, in September of same year; to the *Nonsuch* in 1824. Promoted surgeon May 6, 1825, and in 1826 ordered to the *Boston* for a four years' cruise. On duty at the Cholera Hospital, Navy-Yard, Brooklyn, 1832; Navy-Yard, Pensacola, 1834; U. S. S. *St. Louis*, 1836. Commissioned fleet surgeon and attached to the West Gulf squadron June, 1837; Navy-Yard, Washington, 1839; steamer *Fulton*, 1841; *North Carolina*, 1843. During the Mexican War, in 1847, Surgeon Edwards was attached to the Army, and accompanied General Scott through the campaign which terminated with the capture of the City of Mexico, as medical director of Quitman's Division; was present at the affairs of the National Bridge, Santa Fé, Fres Rios, and at the battles of Contreras, Cherubusco, and City of Mexico. Appointed fleet surgeon, West India squadron, 1849; Navy-Yard, Washington, 1854; Pacific squadron, 1857. During the late war he was stationed at the Naval Rendezvous, New Bedford, Mass. In 1869 he was appointed president of the Naval Medical Board of Examination and member of the Naval Retiring Board, continuing upon that duty until the spring of 1873. On the 3d of March, 1871, he had attained the relative rank of commodore on the retired list, after a total service of fifty-four years and five months. Such in brief is the record of an exceptionably noble life—a record of faithful, meritorious, and gallant service performed—whether in the din of battle or the deadly quiet of a cholera hospital—with unvarying skill and devotion to duty; without fear and without reproach. In private life Doctor Edwards was no less admirable. Pure and blameless in his daily walk; charitable beyond measure; devoted to his friends and generous to his enemies; simple-hearted and devout in religious faith; a long career of usefulness is fitly ended by "the death of the righteous." He married, November 22, 1830, Harriet Eliza, daughter of William Henry,* Esq., of New York, and had : William Stout (b. September 19, 1831 ; m. April 29, 1865, Lucy Beebe, and had : William B., Martha Lucy and Georgia) and Harriet Summers (b. September 13, 1833 ; m. September 29, 1859, W. G. Waller, and had : Elizabeth, William E., Mary G., and Harriet Henry ; d. ———).

The following documents throw light upon the history of the War with Mexico as well as show the fidelity with which Dr. Edwards performed the unusual duties assigned him :

I.

NATIONAL PALACE, City of Mexico,
Major Gen. JOHN. A. QUITMAN,   Sept. 17, 1847.
   Comdg. 4 Div., U. S. Army.

SIR : The important battles of the 12th, 13th and 14th instant at Chapultepec and before the City of Mexico, in which the 4 Div. under y^r command bore so

* See Note (p. 120)—"MONTGOMERY."

gallant and distinguished a part, seems to require that the unremitted exertions of the Medical Officers of y^r Division (all of whom were under the fire of the enemy's guns) should be represented to the General, who being at the head of the column had not the opportunity of witnessing the untiring care and attention given to the wounded of our several corps as well as to the wounded of the enemy who came under our care. On the morning of the 12th when the battle commenced, a location for the wounded was selected not far from the battery of the lamented Capt. Drum, as a suitable place for collecting and attending the wounded. Surg. McMillan, 2d Pa. Vol., Dr. Bower and myself were in attendance unceasingly. During the cannonade of the 12th but few were wounded ; but on the 13th, between 9 and 10 o'clock, when the assault was ordered and the engagement became general, many wounded were soon collected ; others when wounded were visited on the field. Surgeons Clark, Holstead and McSherry of our Div. were in the field at various points. After 11 o'clock when the Castle of Chapultepec was stormed, Dr. McSherry repaired to that point to assist the Surg. Gen., Dr. Lawson, in attending the numerous wounded collected there. During the attack upon Chapultepec and the City of Mexico, every medical officer was more or less under fire—all performed well the duties assigned them, every thought and action seemed devoted to the relief of the wounded. At the point where I was located, not less than 100 of the wounded came under our care and received constant and immediate surgical aid by day and by night. . . . I now attended to the sepulture of many of our gallant soldiers who had fallen at Chapultepec during the morning of the 14th, among whom was my lamented friend, Major Twiggs of the Marines, who, receiving an escopette ball in his chest, fell while rallying his men for the charge, and was buried near the place where he fell. On the 15th we prepared to remove the sick and wounded to the Hospitals. I found Gen. Shields suffering from a severe and dangerous wound of the left arm, aggravated by his exertions and exposure at the head of his column during the whole of the battle.

In the distribution of the honors which attach to the gallant 4th Div. of the Army, it is hoped the Medical Corps will not be forgotten, having shared in the exposures during the march and in battles, and having made every exertion whenever duty called to relieve and save the unfortunate. A list of the killed and wounded will be given when perfected.

Respectfully,
D. S. EDWARDS,
Surgeon U. S. Navy and Med. Director 4th Division.

II.

VERA CRUZ, November 18, 1847.

Upon parting from my worthy friend, David S. Edwards, surgeon in the Navy, I think it due to him to state that he joined my command—the 4th or

Volunteer Division, at the City of Puebla, Mexico, on the 6th of August last as surgeon of the Marine Regiment under Lieut.-Colonel Watson. Being senior surgeon in the Division, he assumed and performed the duties of medical director of my Division until he was relieved from duty on the last of October. I take great pleasure in stating that, during all the campaign in the City of Mexico Dr. Edwards distinguished himself for his zealous, active and efficient discharge of his arduous and responsible duties.

T. A. QUITMAN,
Maj. Gen. U. S. Army, late Comdg. Vol. Div.

III.

STEAMER *Peytona*, Dec. 2, 1847.

To Dr. D. S. EDWARDS,
U. S. Navy.

SIR: Near the close of a journey from the City of Mexico to our respective homes, we cannot refrain from expressing our sincere thanks to you (as well for those who have left us as for ourselves) for your voluntary attendance upon the sick and wounded of the Army. Your professional services upon the afflicted soldiers upon the transport steamer *Alabama*, during a tempestuous voyage from Vera Cruz to New Orleans, were characterized by unremitting labor and kindness and tendered under circumstances which call for more than this formal expression of our feelings.

You have endeared yourself to many a soldier's heart, and in parting with you allow us to say that none can appreciate more highly your professional and social qualities than your friends.

JNO. GARLAND, Bvt. Col. U. S. N.
T. P. ANDREWS, Col. Voltigeurs, U.S.
GEO. W. MORGAN, Col. 15th Infantry.
JULIAN MAY, U. S. Army.
GEO. THOM, Lt. Top. Engineers.
T. P. MOORE, Lt.-Col. 3d Dragoons.
WARD B. BURNETT, Col. N. Y. Vols.
F. D. CALLENDER, 1st Lt. Ordnance.
O. E. EDWARDS, Capt. U. S. Voltigeurs.
THOS. W. SWEENEY, Lt. N. Y. Vols.
AND. F. MCREYNOLDS, Capt. 3d Dragoons.
JAS. D. POTTER, 2d Lt. U. S. Vols. N. Y.
G. DYCKMAN, Major, U. S. Vols. of N. Y.
J. I. BRODHEAD, 1st Lt. and Adjt. 15th Infantry.
WM. H. IRWIN. Capt. 11th Infantry.

THE SHIP THAT SAILED.*

BY WILLIAM WINTER.

I.

WHITE sail upon the ocean's verge,
    Just crimsoned by the setting sun,
Thou hast thy port beyond the surge,
    Thy happy homeward course to run,
And wingèd hope, with heart of fire,
To gain the bliss of thy desire.

I watch thee till the sombre sky
    Has darkly veiled the lucent plain ;
My thoughts, like homeless spirits, fly
    Behind thee o'er the glimmering main.
Thy prow will kiss a golden strand,
But they can never come to land.

And if they could, the fanes are black
    Where once I bent the reverent knee ;
No shrine would send an answer back,
    No sacred altar blaze for me,
No holy bell, with silver toll,
Declare the ransom of my soul.

'Tis equal darkness, here or there ;
    For nothing that this world can give
Could now the ravaged past repair,
    Or win the precious dead to live !
Life's crumbling ashes quench its flame,
And every place is now the same.

II.

Thou idol of my constant heart,
    Thou child of perfect love and light,
That sudden from my side didst part
    And vanish on the sea of night,
Through whatsoever tempests blow
My weary soul with thine would go !

---

* These verses (from *Harper's Monthly*, Feb., 1890) fitly express the father's emotions upon the loss of his sons (p. 134).

Say, if thy spirit yet have speech,
  What port lies hid within the pall,
What shore death's gloomy billows reach,
  Or if they reach no shore at all !
One word—one little word—to tell
That thou art safe and all is well !

The anchors of my earthly fate,
  As they were cast so must they cling ;
And naught is now to do but wait
  The sweet release that time will bring,
When all these mortal fetters break
For one last voyage that I must make.

Say that across the shuddering dark—
  And whisper that the hour is near—
Thy hand will guide my shattered bark,
  Till Mercy's radiant coasts appear ;
That I shall clasp thee to my breast,
And know once more the name of rest.

"OLD IRONSIDES."

Rodenbough.

ODENBOUGH, variously spelled RODENBACH, RODENBOCK or RODENBOUGH, is a name of German origin signifying "red brook." An influential family by the name of RODENBACH flourished in Silesia in the XV century.

The names of RODENBERG, RODENBURG and RODENBORCH of Dutch origin may be found in the Colonial Records of the State of New York. In the year 1649, Lucas Rodenborch (also spelled Rodenburg) was Vice Director at Curaçoa to whom consignments of American products were made from New Amsterdam. He married Catrine Roeloffse (daughter of the celebrated Anneke Bogardus Jansse) and died in 1656. The early settlement of New Haven, Connecticut, was, under the Dutch rule, known as "Rodenbergh."* On an early map (Notin, 1689) of the New England coast the name of the present Sandy Hook, New York Harbor, is inscribed "Pointe Rodenberg."

The earliest records at hand show that the first of the name of RODENBOUGH in America settled, about the year 1738–39, in what is now Lebanon, Hunterdon County, New Jersey.

"From 1682 to 1776 Pennsylvania was the central point of emigration to America from Germany, France and Switzerland.

---

* All the villages settled by the English, from New Holland or Cape Cod unto Stamford, within the Dutch limits, amount to about thirty, and may be estimated at nearly 5000 persons capable of bearing arms. Among the whole of them the RODENBERGH or NEW HAVEN is the principal. It has a Governor, contains about 1340 families and is a province or market of New England. This place was begun eleven years ago in 1638. (*Colonial History of New York.* V. 1, 286.)

Penn's liberal views and the illiberal course of the government of New York toward the Germans induced many to come to this Province. During the first twenty years (1682-1702) comparatively few Germans arrived—not above two hundred families: they located principally near Germantown.* From 1702 to 1727 nearly 50,000 Germans and other Protestants emigrated to America. In 1705 a number of German Reformed residing near Wolfenbüttel and Halberstadt, fled from religious persecution to Neuwied, a town of Rhenish Prussia, where they remained some time and then went to Holland, from which they took ship (1707) bound for New York. The vessel was, by reason of adverse winds, carried into the Delaware Bay. Determined, however, to reach their destination, her passengers took the overland route from Philadelphia to New York. On entering the fertile valleys in "Nova Cæsaria"—now New Jersey—which is drained by the meandering Musconetcong, the Passaic and their tributaries, and having reached a goodly land, they resolved to remain in what is now known as the German Valley of Hunterdon County."† These men were principally farmers, of whom Governor Thomas said, in 1738, "This Province has been for some years the asylum of the distressed Protestants of the Palatinate and other parts of Germany; and I believe it may truthfully be said that the present flourishing condition of it is in a

* All male persons above the age of sixteen did repeat and subscribe their names or made their mark to the following declaration: "We subscribers, natives and late inhabitants of the Palatinate upon the Rhine and places adjacent, having transported ourselves and families into this Province of Pennsylvania, a colony subject to the crown of Great Britain, in hope and expectation of finding a retreat and peaceable settlement therein, Do solemnly promise and engage that we will be faithful and bear true allegiance to his present Majesty, King George the Second and his successors, Kings of Great Britain, and will be faithful to the proprietor of this Province; and that we will demean ourselves peaceably to all his said Majesty's subjects, and strictly observe and conform to the Laws of England and of this Province, to the utmost of our power and the best of our understanding."

† Rupp's "Thirty thousand Names of German, etc., Immigrants, 1727-1776."

great measure owing to the industry of these people ; it is not altogether the fertility of the soil but the numbers and industry of the people that makes a country flourish." *

Among those who crossed the ocean to avoid religious persecution was HEINRICH RODENBOUGH, a native of the Palatinate, who arrived at Philadelphia, Sept. 9, 1738, in the ship *Glasgow*, Walter Sterling, master, from Rotterdam. He settled in the region just described where he found among the neighbors many of his countrymen. Here, after much hard work, he established a modest homestead, accumulated a few acres, a flock or two of sheep and a due proportion of horses and cattle. Fourteen years after his arrival in New Jersey Heinrich was joined by JOHN PETER RODENBOUGH, his brother. Of the other members of the family, at this date, we are without definite information. The first of whose children there is a family record was :

Births, Marriages and Deaths.

1 **John**[2] (supposed to have been the son of Heinrich[1]) and to have been born in Bethlehem Township, Hunterdon County, N. J., about 1740. He married (1763) ELIZABETH, daughter of ————, and died April, 1788. Letters of administration upon his estate were granted to his wife and son John. JOHN[2] and ELIZABETH RODENBOUGH had : ELIJAH, ADAM, PETER, JOHN, HENRY, HERBERT and WILLIAM.

2 **Henry**[3] (John,[2] Heinrich[1]) was born near Bethlehem, N. J., July 29, 1768. He was brought up to the life of a farmer, and succeeded to the homestead upon his father's death. He was a faithful disciple of Calvin and became a "Ruling Elder" of the Presbyterian Church. He died at Bethlehem, N. J., Nov. 17, 1836. HENRY[3] RODENBOUGH married (1) June, 1790, ANN YOUNG (d. Sept. 1793) and had :

1. JOHN, b. March 18, 1791 ; m. ————; d. ————.

HENRY RODENBOUGH married (2) Aug. 26, 1795, MARGARET

---

* *Colonial Records*, IV. 315.

BROWN (b. Nov. 7, 1774; d. New Hampton, N. J., Aug. 15, 1864). They had:

4.
- II. CHARLES, b. Oct. 1, 1797; m. May 16, 1836, Emily Cauffman; d. Easton, Pa., Aug. 26, 1872.
- III. JAMES, b. July 18, 1800; d. Oct. 1, 1802.
- IV. ANN, b. March 6, 1803; d. Oct. 12, 1804.

5. V. RACHEL, b. July 30, 1805; m. Joseph King; d. Oct. 12, 1866.
6. VI. ELIZABETH, b. June 4, 1808; m. Aug. 29, 1834, Ebenezer Wolverton; d. June 15, 1853.
7. VII. ELIJAH, b, March 11, 1811; m. July, 1840, Elizabeth Anderson; d. Aug. 18, 1862.

VIII. ELISHA, b. May 22, 1814; d, Aug. 21, 1819.

8. IX. SAMUEL LEIGH, b. May 25, 1817; m. (1) Oct. 1, 1851, Clara Ann Shatwell; (2) Nov. 16, 1869, Mary Elizabeth Rinek; d. Easton, Pa., Nov. 28, 1885.

3 **Herbert**[3] (John,[2] Heinrich[1]) was born in Hunterdon County, N. J., about 1769. He married, Oct. 19, 1793, Ann Dils, and died at ——— on ———.

They had: JOHN HOCKENBERRY, (b. Aug. 1, 1785; m. May, 1804, Sarah Smith; d. Canton, Ill., May 1, 1865) HENRY, HERBERT, MORRIS, MARGARET, ANN, SARAH and ELIZABETH.

4 **Charles**[4] (Henry,[3] John,[2] Heinrich[1]) was born at Bethlehem, Hunterdon County, N. J., October 1, 1797. He was naturally studious and while at home made the most of his moderate educational advantages. The life of a farmer was not attractive to him, and at the age of twenty-one he accepted a clerkship with a merchant and mill-owner in Greenwich, Warren County, N. J., with whom he subsequently entered into partnership. In 1825 and in 1834 he made flying trips to the South for the benefit of his health, at the same time adding to his information regarding the industrial and commercial growth of the country. In 1830 he entered into the coal, iron and lumber business at Phillipsburg, N. J., and Easton, Pa. (first in partnership with George W. Housel and William Muirheid, and later with his brother, Samuel Leigh, and his son, Joseph Swift) ; during this

period in connection with John Stewart, Esq., he established a rolling mill and wire manufactory at South Easton, a successful enterprise from which he withdrew in 1853; it is said that the first telegraph wire was made at this mill. In 1868 Mr. Rodenbough retired from active business with an ample fortune. He had no political aspirations, and the few offices held by him were unsolicited. He was the first President of the Lehigh Water Company, a Director of the Easton Bank and President of the Board of Trustees of the Presbyterian Church. To an unblemished integrity, high business attainments and respect for law and order, were joined a practical interest in religious and educational matters, and a broad but undemonstrative charity. Charles Rodenbough died at Easton, Pa., August 26, 1872.

He married at Christ Church, Philadelphia, May 16, 1836, (by Rev. John W. James *) EMILY, daughter of Laurence Cauffman, Esq., of that city.

They had :

10.   I. THEOPHILUS FRANCIS, b. Easton, Pa., Nov. 5, 1838; m. Sept. 1, 1868, Elinor Frances, daughter of James Foster, U. S. N.

11.   II. JOSEPH KINNERSLEY SWIFT, b. Easton, Pa., Dec. 24, 1841; m. Oct. 5, 1865, Emily Holt, daughter of Russell S. Chidsey, Esq., of Easton, Pa.

5 **Rachel**[4] (Henry,[3] John,[2] Heinrich[1]) was born near Bethlehem, Hunterdon County, N. J., July 24, 1805. She married JOSEPH KING, and died Oct. 12, 1866: he died July 20, 1874.

JOSEPH and RACHEL (Rodenbough) KING had :

I. MARGARET RODENBOUGH, b. March 5, 1837; d. March 29, 1874.

---

* Mr. James was Asst. Minister of Christ Church for four years preceding his decease, and was elected Rector July 21, 1826, on the death of Bishop White. On the north wall of Christ Church there is a mural tablet with the following inscription : "In memory of the Reverend JOHN WALLER JAMES Rector of this Church who died Aug. 14, 1836, aged 31 years. ' I wish to say to the dear people of my charge, Remember the words I spake unto you while I was yet alive. The same truths make me happy in the prospect of death and heaven.' "

II. EMILY RODENBOUGH, b. July 13, 1844; d. Dec. 17, 1874.

III. SAMUEL, b, ——— ; m,———,

6 **Elizabeth**[4] (Henry,[3] John,[2] Heinrich[1]) was born in Bethlehem Township, Hunterdon County, June 4, 1808. She married Aug. 29, 1834, EBENEZER WOLVERTON, (b. Aug. 17, 1807; d. Union Township, Hunterdon County, N. J., Sept. 5. 1891) and died at the above place June 17, 1853.

EBENEZER and ELIZABETH (Rodenbough) WOLVERTON had :

I. CHARLES, b. ——— ; m.——— Mary Bowlby.

II. HENRY, b. April 28, 1839; served during War for the Union in Co. B, 41st N. J. Vols.; d. Belle Plain, Va., April 8, 1863.

III. JONATHAN, b. ——— ; m. ———.

IV. ELISHA, b. ——— ; m. Martha Lunger.

V. ANN ELIZABETH, b, ———; m. Joseph Sherer, and had one daughter.

VI. CHESTER, b. Bethlehem, N. J., Dec. 17, 1850; m. Oct. 25, 1875, Mary M. Hoffman, and had: Thomas C. (b. Aug., 1876) and Edwin R. (b. ———). Mr. Wolverton was a member of the N. J. Legislature (187-).

VII. BENJAMIN, b. ———, 1853; m. ——— Scott, and had one son.

7 **Elijah**[4] (Henry,[3] John,[2] Heinrich[1]) was born in Bethlehem Township, Hunterdon County, N. J., March 11, 1811. He married, July, 1840, ELIZABETH ANDERSON, and died at Bethlehem, N. J., Aug. 18, 1862.

They had :

I. STEWART, b. Sept. 1, 1844 ; m. Sept. 29, 1869, Anna Sherman, and had : Charles (b. May 12, 1871).

II. GEORGE, b. Dec. 6, 1846.

III. SAMUEL LEIGH, b. Oct. 15, 1850; m. ——— Bowlby, and had : William (b.———).

8 **Samuel Leigh**[4] (Henry,[3] John,[2] Heinrich[1]) was born at Bethlehem, Hunterdon County, N. J., May 25, 1817. He removed to Easton, Pa., soon after attaining his majority, and, in partner-

ship with his brother Charles, was actively engaged in mercantile pursuits from 1844 to 1869, when on account of failing health he retired from business. He married (1st) Oct. 1, 1851, CLARA ANN SHATWELL, of Manchester, England, who died at Easton, Pa., June 6, 1868, aged 37, and was buried in Easton Cemetery.

They had:

I. STANLEY LEIGH, b. Easton, Pa., Oct. 12, 1853.
II. ADA VICKERS, b. Easton, Pa., Aug. 28, 1857.
III. HATTIE GROVE, b. Easton, Pa., Nov. 29, 1859; m. Dec. 19, 1882, Joseph H. Evans, of Easton ; d. Jersey City, Jan. 31, 1891, and was buried in Easton Cemetery.
IV. CLARA ANN, b. Easton, Pa., March 14, 1862: m. Nov. 20, 1890, Joseph R. Hixson, of Elizabeth, N. J.
V. LUCY FISHER, b. Easton, Pa., Nov. 14, 1864.

Mr. RODENBOUGH married (2d) Nov. 16, 1869, MARY ELIZABETH RINEK, of Easton, Pa., and had:

VI. EMILY CHIDSEY, b. Easton, Pa., Dec. 22, 1870.

SAMUEL LEIGH RODENBOUGH died at Easton, Pa., Nov. 28, 1885, and was buried in the Easton Cemetery.

9 **John Hockenberry**[4] (Herbert,[3] John,[2] Heinrich[1]) was born at ———, Aug. 1, 1785. Educated in village school and became a farmer. He married, May ———, 1804, SARAH SMITH of Hunterdon County, N. J., and died at Canton, Ill., May 1, 1865.

They had:

I. GEORGE SMITH, b. Bethlehem, N. J., Sept. 25, 1805; m. July 28, 1825, Elizabeth Jackson, of Clinton, N. J., and had 12 children.
II. HERBERT, b. Bethlehem, N. J., Nov. 30, 1806; m. Feb. 11, 1826, Margaret Smith, of Lebanon, N. J.
III. ELIZABETH, b. Bethlehem, N. J., June 24, 1808; m. Oct. 22, 1825, Daniel Jones, of Lebanon, N. J.
IV. REBECCA, b. Lebanon, N. J., July 30, 1810; m. Jan. 1, 1829, Henry M. Hammer, of Dryden, N. Y.
V. MARY, b. Lebanon, N. J., Jan. 24, 1813; m. Feb. 22, 1840, John Sellard.

12.   VI. HENRY SMITH, b. Bethlehem, N. J., Dec. 8, 1814; m. Dec. 26, 1840, Elizabeth Keely, of Montgomery County, Pa.
VII. JOSIAH, b. Lebanon, N. J., Feb. 16, 1817; m. Nov. 13, 1839, Mary McElroy, of Warren County, N. J.
VIII. SARAH ANN, b. Lebanon, N. J., May 4, 1820; m. April 18, 1837, Wesley McClary; d. Philadelphia, April 4, 1866.
IX. JOHN CALVIN, b. Lebanon, N. J., Dec. 4, 1821; m. Nov. 2, 1841, Letty Ann Apgar, of Bethlehem, and had 2 children.
X. SUSAN MARTHA, b. Lebanon, N. J., May 3, 1823; m. ———, James Hedden, of Hunterdon County, N. J.; d. ———.
XI. EUPHEMIA MILLER, b. Lebanon, N. J., April 29, 1825; m. Nov. 30, 1845, Nathaniel Wright, of Clinton, N. J., and had 5 children.
XII. DORCAS ADALINE, b. Dryden, N. J., Jan. 29, 1827; m. July 6, 1850, John Allen Todd, of Somerset County, N. J., and had 6 children.
XIII. LYDIA CAROLINE, b. Clinton, N. J., Jan. 12, 1832; m. March 5, 1857, Robert Curry Snyder, of Canton, Ill., and had 2 children.

10 **Theophilus Francis**[5] (Charles,[4] Henry,[3] John,[2] Heinrich [1]) was born at Easton, Pa., Nov. 5, 1838. He attended private schools, had special tutors and took a course of mathematics and English literature at Lafayette College (1856-57). Upon the outbreak of the War for the Union, President Lincoln (at the request of the Hon. Andrew H. Reeder) appointed him (March 27, 1861) a Second Lieutenant in the Second U. S. Dragoons. He served (1861-62) as Post Adjutant and Quartermaster U.S. Cavalry School of Practice, Carlisle, Pa., and with his regiment in all the campaigns of the Army of the Potomac (1862-64). Promoted First Lieutenant (1861) and Captain (July 17, 1862); he was slightly wounded and had two horses shot under him at Beverly Ford, Va. (June 9, 1863), the great cavalry fight in which nearly 20,000 Union and Confederate cavalry crossed sabres. He commanded his regiment at Gettysburg, having two horses killed during that campaign; was severely wounded at Trevillian Station, Va. (June 11, 1864), and, while in command of his regiment, lost his right arm and had his horse killed at the battle of "The

Opequan," Va. (Sept. 19, 1864). Upon the recommendation of General Sheridan he was granted leave of absence, from the Regular Army, to accept the Colonelcy of the 18th Pennsylvania Cavalry, and (July, 1865), by direction of the President was specially assigned, with the rank of Brigadier-General, to command a brigade (consisting of regulars and volunteers) and the District of Clarksburg, W. V. He was honorably mustered out of the volunteer service, October 31, 1865. He served during the winter of 1865 as Inspector General " U. S. Forces in Kansas and the Territories " with headquarters at Fort Leavenworth, and later, with the 2d Cavalry at Fort Ellsworth, Ks. Upon the reoranization of the Army he was appointed Major (July 28, 1866) of the new 42d U. S. Infantry, commanding it and the posts of Plattsburg and Madison Barracks, N. Y. (1866-69); also serving on various boards—for the selection of a magazine gun, the examination of officers, and the investigation of the case of the first colored cadet at West Point. He received brevets to the rank of Brigadier-General U. S. Army, "for gallant and meritorious services" at the battles, respectively, of "Trevillian Station," "the Opequan," "Todd's Tavern" and "Cold Harbor," Va., and was, at his own request, retired from active service, Dec. 15, 1870, " with the full rank (colonel of cavalry) of the command held when wounded." In recommending this officer for his highest brevet, General Sheridan wrote to the War Department as follows: "Colonel Rodenbough was one of the most gallant and valuable young officers, under my command, in the Cavalry Corps, Army of the Potomac. He was constantly in the field with his regiment, the 2d U. S. Cavalry (a portion of the time in command of it), from the spring of '62 up to the time of his being wounded whilst gallantly leading his regiment at the battle of the Opequan, September 19, 1864."*

---

* MILITARY COMMISSIONS: Second Lieut. 2d U. S. Dragoons, March 27, 1861; First Lieut. May 14, 1861; Capt. 2d U. S. Cavalry, July 17, 1862; Colonel 18th Penna. Vol. Cav., April 29, 1865; Major 42d U. S. Infantry, July 28, 1866. BREVETED as follows: MAJOR, "battles of Trevillian Station and Opequan, Va."; Lieut.-Colonel, U. S. A., "during the War"; Colonel, U. S. A., "battle of Todd's Tavern, Va."; Brigadier-General, U. S. V., "during the War"; Brigadier-General, U. S. A., "battle of Cold Harbor, Va."; Asst. Inspector-General, S. N. Y. (1879-82)

He married, Sept. 1, 1868 (at the Church of the Incarnation, N. Y. City, by Rt. Rev. W. H. Odenheimer, D.D., Bishop of New Jersey, assisted by the Rector, Rev. Henry Montgomery, D.D.), ELINOR FRANCES, daughter of Passed Midshipman James Foster,* U. S. N., and granddaughter of the late Rear Admiral John Berrien Montgomery, U. S. N., and had:

I. MARY MCCULLAGH, b. Detroit, Mich., Jan. 7, 1870; d. New York, Feb. 11, 1872.

II. JAMES FOSTER, b. Washington, D. C., Aug. 7, 1871; educated at Dr. Callisen's Academy, N. Y. City, St. Austin's School, Staten Island, and by special tutors. Is engaged (1891) as a member of Civil Engineer Corps of Lehigh Valley R. R. Co. (Pennsylvania.)

III. NINA, b. New York, Oct. 8, 1874; educated at St. Mary's

BATTLES. 1862: "New Bridge," Va. (May 2); "Manassas" or "Second Bull Run" (Aug. 29-30). 1863: "Stoneman Raid" (April 23-30); "Beverly Ford" (June 9)—slightly wounded; "Aldie" (June 17); "Middleburg" (June 18); "Upperville" (June 27); "Gettysburg," Pa. (July 1-3); "Williamsport" (July 6); "Boonesboro'," Md. (July 8); "Funkstown" July 10); "Falling Waters" (July 14); "Manassas Gap," Va. (July 21); "Brandy Station" (Aug. 1-2); "Culpeper C. H." (Sept. 13); "Bristoe Station" (Oct. —). 1864: "The Furnaces" (May 6); "Todd's Tavern" (May 8); "Ground Squirrel Bridge" (May 10); "Yellow Tavern" (May 11); "Meadow Bridge" (May 12); "Hawes' Shop" (May 28); "Old Church" (May 30); "Cold Harbor" (May 31-June 1); "Trevillian Station" (June 11-12)—severely wounded; "Winchester" or "the Opequan" (Sept. 19)—severely wounded.

OCCUPATION AFTER RETIREMENT: Deputy Governor U. S. Soldiers' Home, Washington, D. C. (1870-71); General Eastern Agent, Pullman Car Co. (1872-73); Associate Editor *Army and Navy Journal* (1876-77); Corresponding Secretary, Society Army of the Potomac (1878); Secretary and Editor of the *Journal* (1878-90) and Vice-President (1891-3) Military Service Institution of the United States; Chief of the Bureau of Elections, City of New York (1890-2); author of several essays, sketches and the following books: "From Everglade to Cañon with the Second Dragoons" (1875); "Afghanistan or the Anglo-Russian Dispute" (1882); "Uncle Sam's Medal of Honor" (1887); "The Bravest Five Hundred of 'Sixty-one" (1891), and "Autumn Leaves from Family Trees" (1891).

* See "FOSTER."

P. E. School (1881), Miss Comstock's Seminary (1888–89) in New York City, and at Bishopthorpe School, Bethlehem, Pa. (1890–91).

11 **Joseph Kinnersley Swift**[5] (Charles,[4] Henry,[3] John,[2] Heinrich[1]) was born at Easton, Pa., Dec. 24, 1841. He was educated at private schools, and at an early age entered the counting room of Rodenbough and Brother, of Easton, Pa., and Phillipsburg, N. J. In 1862, his health being impaired by confinement in an office, he joined a party of civil engineers and assisted in the survey and construction of a part of the Lehigh Valley Railroad. In 1865 he became a member of the firm of Rodenbough Brother and Son, wholesale dealers in iron, coal and provisions (a business house founded by his father in 1832), from which he withdrew (upon the dissolution of the firm) in ——. He was a member of the " Easton Grays," P. N. G., became a Director of the Easton Bank (1882), Easton Cemetery, Northampton Mutual Fire Insurance Co., Easton Trust Co., President of the "Crypt" and Pomfret Clubs, Trustee of St. Luke's Hospital, Bethlehem, Pa., and is (1891) President of the Lehigh Water Company. Possessing an inherited taste for the mechanic arts, together with conservative but progressive business methods, personal tact and great energy, Mr. Rodenbough has been conspicuously connected with the improvement of his native town. He was one of the pioneers in promoting the development of the northern section of that city, particularly in the establishment and extension of the Paxinosa Improvement Company, of which he is (1891) President and General Manager.

He married, October 5, 1865 (by Rev. C. H. Edgar, D.D.), EMILY HARRIET, third daughter of Russell S. Chidsey, Esq., of Easton, Pa. (See "CHIDSEY.")

They had:

  I. CHARLES RUSSELL, b. Easton, Pa., June 26, 1867; entered Lafayette College (class of 1888), taking Latin scientific course; became (1891) a manufacturer; m. April 15, 1891, Lillian H. Seitz, of Easton, Pa.

  II. ALBERT CHURCHMAN, b. Easton, Pa., July 4, 1870; educated at Easton High School and graduated at Lafayette College (1892).

III. FRANCES JOSEPHINE, b. Easton, Pa., Feb. 25, 1875; educated at Miss Porter's School, Farmington, Conn. (1891-)

12 **Henry Smith**[5] (John H.,[4] Herbert,[3] John,[2] Heinrich[1]) was born at Bethlehem, N. J., June 24, 1808. He was educated at common schools and at Lafayette College (1840). After teaching school for a season, he was duly ordained a minister of the Gospel and, for forty-five years, was the pastor of the Providence Presbyterian Church at Trappe, Pa. He married, Dec. 26, 1840, ELIZABETH KEELY of Montgomery County, Pa. (b. Nov. 3, 1815). He died at Norristown, Pa., May 3, 1890.

They had:

13. I. THEODORE FRELINGHUYSEN, b. Sept. 14, 1844; m. Sept. 14, 1863; d. Norristown, Pa., Feb. 27, 1885.

II. ADELIA, b. March 18, 1847.

III. WILLIE CRAWFORD, b. May 17, 1850; d. July 19, 1851.

IV. JOHN NER, b. Sept. 11, 1852; d. Dec. 30, 1862.

V. ELIZABETH ANN, b. Sept. 9, 1855; d. Aug. 2, 1856.

VI. HANNAH CRAWFORD, b. June 16, 1857; d. Dec. 24, 1862.

13 **Theodore Frelinghuysen**[6] (Henry S.,[5] John H.,[4] Herbert,[3] John,[2] Heinrich[1]) was born at Trappe, Pa., Sept. 14, 1844. He was educated by his father, and taught school for a short time; Deputy Recorder of Deeds, Norristown, Pa. (1872-78); bookseller and stationer (1878-84); Clerk of Council 1883-84, and Adjutant 51st Regiment, Penna. National Guard (1877). He was also a good musician, a member of Curtis Lodge 239, I. O. O. F., of Consonance Chamber, O. K. F., and a citizen "whose sterling integrity won for him universal esteem." He married, Sept. 14, 1863, MARGARETTA SMITH SHEPPS (b. Germany, Dec. 19, 1835), and died at Norristown, Feb. 27, 1885.

They had: JOHN NER (b. Norristown, Pa., July 10, 1864; d. Aug. 11, 1864), HENRY SHEPPS (b. Norristown, Pa., Dec. 14, 1868), and GEORGE SMITH (b. Norristown, Pa., Feb. 21, 1871).

Easton to New Orleans in 1825.

THE following extracts from the Diary of CHARLES RODENBOUGH* of Easton, Pa., are interesting as indicating the primitive travelling facilities of the time and the impressions of a young American tourist in search of health and information.

Nov. 8, 1825.—At 12 o'clock left Bidlemansville, embarked on a Durham boat, for Trenton, and descended the Delaware twenty-seven miles.

Nov. 9.—Arrived at Trenton in time to secure passage on the steamboat to Philadelphia, where I landed at half past 5 P. M.

Nov. 15.—Having yesterday secured a seat in the mail stage for Pittsburgh, was awakened this morning at three o'clock to occupy it; got up with some unwillingness, as I had been to the circus, with C. I. Ihrie, the preceding evening. Although I left it at half past nine, it was nearly twelve o'clock before I got to sleep, in consequence of being obliged to overhaul my trunks and repack them after I came in from the circus. The performance was good. Upon taking my seat this morning, I found the company to consist of two gentlemen and two German ladies and their children ; all five unable to speak or understand a single word of English, and ourselves quite as ignorant of the German,—really a cheering prospect for a day's ride of 100 miles! This, however, made no difference to the driver, for as soon as the old town-clock had counted four he drove us off at the rate of five miles per hour, and, ere the sun had gilded the east, we found ourselves fifteen miles from the city. Four o'clock found us dining in Lancaster, 64 miles from where we started, and eleven o'clock of the same evening set us down in Harrisburg, one hundred miles from Philadelphia; sleepy and tired and as ignorant of the German language as we were in the morning, notwithstanding the children kept up a constant chattering, sometimes singing, sometimes crying.

Nov. 16.—Left Harrisburg this morning at 8 o'clock, crossed the Susquehannah River on a bridge about a mile in length. The town is beautifully situated on its eastern bank in the midst of an extensive plain, has a number of handsome buildings, among which is the

---
* See page 149.

by Emily Kauffman Rodowich.

I left it at half past nine, it
leep, in consequence of being
k them after I came in from
Upon taking my seat this
of two gentlemen and two
c an ble to speak or under-
... as ignorant of the
... side or 100 miles!
... soon as the
... of five
... and our-
... dining, in
... lock of the
... miles from
... language
... kept up a
... in ...
... ck, ... ssed the
... ngth. The town
... s of an extensive
... among which is the

EASTON, PA., IN 1825-35.

From a water-color drawing, by Emily Cauffman Rodenbough.

Capitol, built of brick, on a very commanding eminence near the river; the town, in size, is very like Easton. After passing through Carlisle and Shippensburg (the first a very handsome town nearly as large as Harrisburg, with better buildings, the last much smaller and in no way interesting) I arrived at Chambersburg, a distance of fifty miles, the last thirty-two of which I was the only and lonely passenger. The appearance of the country, through which the road passes, is very like that between Easton and Bethlehem.

Nov. 17.—Was called, at 3 o'clock this morning, to take my seat in the stage; after my baggage was in, and I was ready to start, inquired for my cloak; it was not to be found, the servant who took charge of it, when I came, could give no account of it. I directed him to inform the landlord of my determination not to leave until my cloak, or another as good, was produced. He made his appearance soon after and found that one of his boarders was absent, and in all probability had made a mistake and had taken my cloak instead of his own. As there appeared to be one without an owner, I proposed taking that for mine, to which he eventually consented. Fortunately it was rather better than my own, so that I had no reason to regret the change. When I got in the stage found myself the only passenger. The first ten miles was through a dreary country with here and there a solitary cabin in the bushes; being dark and very cloudy added to the general gloom, and several times induced me to think of mail robbers, and, at the same time, lay my hand involuntarily upon my pistol-belt to know how I was prepared for an attack of that kind, and finally prevailed so far as to make me think of a place of safety for my pocketbook; having some room in my boot-leg, I slipped it in and carried it there all day. Daylight brought the stage to the foot of the mountain, the ascent of which is four miles, and the descent as long; from the top I had one of the finest views I ever beheld; the perpendicular height of this mountain cannot be less than twelve hundred feet above the adjoining plain, on the eastern side upon which the town of Chambersburg is situated. It has about the same amount of population that Easton has, though much more the characteristics of a city; such, for instance, as those of a town-clock, and a night watch who parade the streets as regularly as those of Philadelphia. Soon after daylight this morning, the loneliness of my situation was relieved by the addition of two gentlemen from Nashville, in the State of Tennessee, who were returning to that place; in consequence of which I think myself fortunate, as they will travel my route at least 600 miles. I rode fifty miles this day over a very hilly country to a small town called Bedford, where I arrived about dark and had the satisfaction to find good accommodations; after being furnished with a good supper and while sitting round the fire in our room, we were gratified with a few tunes on the piano, by the landlord's daughter, in an adjoining room.

Nov. 18.—We were called to take our seats in the stage at three o'clock this morning, found it snowing and blowing and very cold withal; rode twenty miles to breakfast on the top of the Allegheny Mountains—after which continued our journey over the hills and through the storm, fifty miles further, to Greensburgh, making seventy miles this day; the whole of which was performed over a road of constant hills, some of which were three miles from bottom to top; arriving between 8 and 9 o'clock.

Nov. 19.—We took our departure this morning at 4 o'clock. Rode twelve miles to breakfast, soon after which we passed the ever memorable battle ground, on which General Braddock was defeated and killed by the Indians, about twelve miles south of Pittsburgh; at which city we had the pleasure of finding ourselves safely landed, at 12 o'clock, after a rough ride of 300 miles, from Philadelphia, performed in four and a half days. Took lodgings at the Mansion House, kept by Col. Ramsay. During the afternoon took occasion to view the town, and present one of my introductory letters, which made me acquainted with a gentleman who, among other civilities, gave me an invitation to go to Church with him to-morrow, it being Sunday. Found the town just what you supposed New Orleans was, namely, very smoky and of course very dirty, occasioned by the exclusive use of stove coal for fire, the cheapness of which recommending it in all cases where fire is necessary; the coal delivered at the doors of the inhabitants being but 3 cents per bushel and 16 bushels are considered equal to a cord of oak wood. On account of the great quantity consumed, there is a constant fall of dust in the street; it is in appearance very much like lampblack and gives to the inhabitants, who are exposed in the street, a blacksmith's complexion.

Nov. 20.—At 11 o'clock this morning my new acquaintance called according to promise and took me to Church; when returning said he would call again after dinner—he did so, and went with me to hear an Episcopalian, who gave us as fine a sermon as I have ever heard de-

livered. During the day was made acquainted with Mrs. McKnight
(that is the wife of my friend), with whom I returned from Church and
took tea as well as spent the evening very pleasantly.

Nov. 21.—This day I visited the penitentiary, now building on the
north side of the Allegheny River, in company with Mrs. McKnight
and some ladies of her acquaintance. It is handsomely situated in the
midst of a large plain about three hundred yards from the river, and
when completed will be an elegant stone structure. Its form is that
of a circle of one hundred yards diameter—the height about 25 feet,
built of freestone; it is intended for solitary confinement, i. e., each cul-
prit will have an apartment to himself; these apartments are built of
stone also, and arranged around the inside of the circular wall, ten
feet square inside, seven feet high, the top being a stone arch. In the
centre of this little room is a large iron ring fastened in the floor for
the purpose of chaining the prisoner. In crossing from Pittsburgh to
this building we passed over the Allegheny bridge, the length of
which is nearly half a mile and the height about fifty feet above the
water. It is covered like the Easton Bridge, and has a footway on
each side of the carriage passage with a partition between which pro-
tects the foot passenger from all dust of the wagons. On our return to the city this evening, when descending a steep hill, Miss B.,
and another lady, attempted to run down, in doing which Miss B.
had the misfortune to come against a tree, by which she injured her
breast and hand very much; it had like to have made our walk
quite an adventure. Miss B. is from Germantown, near Philadelphia.
She says Mr. Rodney is very popular in that place.

Nov. 22, 23 were devoted to the examination of the nail and glass
factories; of the latter there is none more extensive in the United
States, nor any whose ware has a higher reputation, than this one. I
saw some of the most beautiful specimens of cut glass that I have
ever witnessed. I visited a paper mill also, the extent of which may
be judged of when I say there were one hundred and twenty hands
employed, among which were many females and small boys.

Nov. 24.—The forenoon of this day was spent in preparations for
my journey to Cincinnati, to which place I am now convinced I shall
be obliged to travel by stage, the distance 300 miles. Accordingly, at
one o'clock this afternoon, I left this city in the mail stage for Washington, Penn., the company consisting of eleven passengers, four of
whom are bound South, one to New Orleans.

Nov. 25.—After a rough ride of 27 miles, eight o'clock last evening set us down in Washington—a neat village, many of the buildings are of brick. It is situated on the National road near the western boundary of Pennsylvania. After three hours' disturbed sleep was called, at one o'clock this morning, to take my seat in the stage for Wheeling in Virginia, distance 30 miles, which we rode in six hours and before breakfast; after that necessary ceremony was performed we crossed the Ohio River in a ferry-boat propelled by two horses; found the river very low and about twice the width of the Delaware. Rode 25 miles in the State of Ohio to Fair-view—an insignificant little place with two taverns and not much else.

Nov. 26.—Took my seat in the stage this morning at three o'clock; found a fine frosty moonlight morning; rode 57 miles this day to Zanesville on the Muskingum River, an active, well-built, little town of about one thousand inhabitants. A neat brick Court-house is among the public buildings, and there are a number of handsome dwellings built by the citizens.

Nov. 27.—Sunday. This morning I was permitted to take my breakfast before leaving. At nine o'clock we set off for Lancaster, distant 30 miles, where we arrived about dark. During the day we were gratified with specimens of the Ohio ladies and gentlemen in their Sunday attire, as many of them were going to and returning from Church. In the afternoon I walked on before the stage; while ascending a hill before I was overtaken, I came to a log meeting-house situated in the woods, in which were a congregation listening attentively to a zealous speaker. I had but a few minutes to hear before the stage came up—but long enough to be reminded of times gone by.

Nov. 28.—After getting an excellent supper last night and sleeping four hours, we resumed our seats in the mail stage. It being moonlight, I had an opportunity to see the principal street, the buildings upon which are good, a large proportion of them are of brick, and the place has as much the appearance of comfort as any small town through which I have passed. Went eighteen miles, to Circleville, for breakfast; this is a county town, with a Court-house, jail, etc., and the usual number of inns and stores; remarkable for nothing but the remains of extensive ancient fortifications. Immediately after leaving this place we crossed the Scioto River, a stream much like the Lehigh in size but not so rapid. Our road from here to another county town (30 miles from Circleville) where we arrived soon after sundown, lay through a most beautiful country, being the whole distance and as far as the eye could reach, on either hand, as level as the surface of a lake on a summer morning

Nov. 29.—Having but twenty-two miles to travel this day, we were permitted to breakfast before we set off. Found the face of the country very similar to that through which we passed yesterday, occasionally finding the tall forest invaded by the hardy back-woods man whose residence and mode of living are rather romantic—though to me not at all enviable. Imagine an opening about the size of a small garden, (made in the midst of an overgrown forest where trees are like church steeples in height, and like hogsheads in the circumference) and in the centre of this spot a building, ten or twelve feet square, composed of round logs fastened at the corners, laid up to the height of a man's head, covered with split boards on which large poles are placed to prevent the wind from carrying them off; to one end of this cabin is attached a chimney made by short logs, being laid up like a pig-pen, and plastered inside with mud, a square hole cut through the logs of the main fabric for a fireplace; in the front another similar hole for a door, with a blanket hanging in the same to keep out the wind. Then another building situated on one side of the clearing constructed in the same way and of the same material as those of the dwelling, for a stable and barn,—and you will have a tolerably good idea of the usual improvements of a first settler in this, or in fact, of almost any other part of the western country. Notwithstanding, however, the forbidding appearance of this establishment, the traveller will find much of comfort and more of real hospitality reigning within—for the truth of which I can vouch. In the course of this day we passed through an extensive prairie or naturally clear country, upon which there has never been known any timber. They occur, frequently, in travelling through this country. At three o'clock we arrived at Wilmington, another county town and the end of this day's journey; found the place much crowded in consequence of this being Court week. After dinner I stepped into the Court-house to observe the appearance and manners of the natives, of which I found a great concourse, and of course as great a variety. Upon entering the Court-room, I was forcibly reminded of the Court held at Templeton, described in the "Pioneers;" the judges, the lawyers, the audience and the interior of the Court-house, as well as everything connected with it, seemed to be an exact counterpart of that described by Cooper; the effect was so like as almost to induce me to look round for Natty Bumppo, (Leather Stocking), and last, though not least, the interesting " Elisabeth."

Nov. 30.—This morning we took our departure at three o'clock—had not gone far before it became very dark and soon after began to rain; about daybreak we crossed the Miami River, at this time an inconsiderable stream, tho' in certain seasons a large river. Eight o'clock found the stage at Lebanon, a small town—but some good buildings—where we breakfasted, having come 17 miles. After eating and changing horses, we continued our journey 35 miles to Cincinnati, where we arrived in six days from Pittsburgh—considerably fatigued.

Dec. 1.—Found me snugly quartered at Colonel Mack's Hotel, the accommodations at which are of the Philadelphia stamp, and of course draw many visitors—regular boarders as well as travellers—the number of both, I suppose, might be nearly 80 at dinner to-day. Having been favored by a friend in Philadelphia, with a letter of introduction to Mr. Neff, an extensive merchant of this city, I took occasion to present it this morning, and found him extremely polite and attentive in giving me all the information in his possession relative to the subjects upon which I inquired. After learning that a steamboat would leave here to-morrow for Louisville, at the falls of the Ohio River, I devoted the remainder of the day to the examination of the town and its improvements, with which found myself quite satisfied, it being equal to the printed descriptions circulated through the country, which nine times out of ten, are much too highly colored, and consequently liable to give the stranger a very erroneous impression. The style of building is very neat and principally of brick, the town is laid out in squares like Philadelphia, and in fact the whole appearance of the place is so like it, that a stranger, transported from one to the other in his sleep would, upon waking, hardly suspect the change of situations—that is as far as this place goes, it being in extent about one-eighth of that of Philadelphia, or about 14,000 souls. The building of steamboats is going on here this winter very extensively. I saw ten or twelve new ones nearly finished, many of them of the first order. Its public buildings are not numerous yet, among them however are several neat Churches and a beautiful Court-house; the society of the place has the reputation of being very good.

Dec. 2.—After supping with, and spending an evening very pleasantly, at my new acquaintances, I returned to my lodgings at ten o'clock last night with some regret that the nature of business renders a longer stay in this town impracticable; while walking with Mr. N. from his store to his house, he informed me that he had not been long keeping house (having been lately married), his furniture was not all received from Philadelphia, and at the same time requested that the absence of it might be excused. Upon entering his parlour, however, I found that, at least, very handsomely if not elegantly furnished; among other articles a very amiable wife was not least attractive. This morning was spent in making arrangements to continue my journey on board the steamboat, which got under way about 10 o'clock and proceeded down the Ohio River at the rate of six miles per hour. The width of the river between the banks varies from a half to one mile—but being very low at this time, is of course much narrower—and at this season of the year presents to the eye of a traveller very little that is interesting. At intervals of three or four miles he sees perhaps a small opening in the tall forest that is to be seen growing up on the rich bottoms and valleys of this noble river, and here and there a little village starting up, as it were, out of the stumps. In the course of this afternoon we passed the residence of General Harrison—of Indian War memory—situated near the bank of the river; buildings of brick and neat in appearance.

Dec. 3.—Some time in the night a part of our machinery failed, and we were obliged, in consequence, to cast anchor in the middle of the river and there to remain all day for repairs.

Dec. 4.—When I awoke this morning, I found we were again in motion and about 12 o'clock arrived at Zanesville, in Kentucky, a very active place nearly as large as Easton—The buildings larger and mostly of brick, situated at the falls of the Ohio, 150 miles below Cincinnati and 330 from the Mississippi, following the course of the Ohio River. Here our worst foreboding was realized as regarded our mode of conveyance to the mouth of the Ohio; finding the water too low for steamboat navigation, myself and seven others engaged two carriages with four horses each, to carry us to the mouth of Cumberland River, 250 miles from this place.

Dec. 5.—I spent this day in viewing the town and steamboats at the landing, many of them very fine ones; altogether not less than ten or twelve were waiting for high water.

Dec. 6.—About one o'clock, this day, we took our seats in the carriages for the mouth of Cumberland, four in each; the four of us who had travelled in company for the last 400 miles, filled one, and four strangers the other; went 23 miles, through a level but new country, and stopped for the night.

Dec. 7.—Rose early this morning and drove on over a very hilly country, without any improvements, till twelve o'clock, for our breakfast; great complaints at the length of the road as well as anxiety for breakfast; after hurrying the landlord, we were permitted to sit down to a purely Kentucky meal; our bread was made of corn meal coarsely ground, and not sifted, mixed with water, baked in round cakes about the size of a dinner plate and two inches thick. With this we had liver and beefsteak fried to a crisp, strong coffee without cream, and no butter.

Dec. 8.—This morning we discovered that we might secure a better breakfast than we had yesterday, and accordingly took it before we departed, and before sunrise were on the way; rode about 40 miles and halted for the night. Soon after dark it commenced to rain; retired not without apprehension for the comfort of to-morrow's ride.

Dec. 9.—Quite surprised this morning to find it clear and rather cold; drove 35 miles this day, during which we passed through "Bowling Green," a little village of about 100 houses, and halted at sundown in "Shaker-town," inhabited and owned, together with the adjoining country, entirely by the Shakers (no doubt you recollect the description given of this singular and infatuated people by the author of "Redwood"). They have a community here of about 800 persons and these all grown or nearly so. Their creed not allowing them to marry, they have no children of their own; the men and women occupy different apartments for sleeping, calling each other Sister and Brother; many of their habits resemble those of the Moravians—particularly in neatness and regularity; everything goes on like clockwork, it is all "yea," "yea" and "nay," "nay," with them. They are building two very large and beautiful brick houses for the accommodation of themselves in two families, a Sister's House and Brother's House. The supper and breakfast reminded me of New Jersey living. Supposing the opportunity a good one, I requested mush and milk to be put on the supper table, which, with an excellent apple pie made it seem like my late home.

Dec. 10.—This day we rode near forty miles, the weather quite cold, country thinly settled but with good roads. In order to pass away the time, as fast and pleasantly as possible, each contributed what he could by relating what he had heard and seen on his course through this "Vale of Tears." One of my companions was from near Albany, going to close some unfinished business in Louisiana, where he had spent ten years of his life; a second was a merchant now established at Memphis, a little village on the banks of the Mississippi in the State of Tennessee, but who had spent several years in the service of his country among the Indians; the third was also a merchant of the same place but younger than either of the others, and of course had not so much to regale us with, but being quite intelligent and having experienced some adventures, he excited, occasionally, our attention. I recollect one instance in particular: being the son of General Winchester, who was in command during the late War, he was taken into the service when about sixteen years of age, and underwent many hardships for one so young; he said that at the encampment of the American Army on the river Raisin, near Detroit, he became acquainted with a French girl, of about the same age as himself, who soon succeeded in gaining a place in his affections. The quarters of his father, the General, being at the house of the French girl's father, gave him frequent opportunities to indulge his partiality for the company of the daughter; but, "the course of true love never runs smooth," for the Americans were attacked at their encampment in the night by a superior force of British and Indians, whose bullets on the roof of the Frenchman's house were the first indication of danger to our young soldier. His first thought was of his fair one (this he declared to us himself, it is not my invention) and flew directly to her chamber, knowing where she slept, but when he burst in, what was his disappointment to find it deserted by her whom he wished to serve; she having, as he supposed, taken the alarm sooner than himself, and fled from her window—whither, he was never able to learn, nor her fate; but that of her father was certain, as he soon after saw his lifeless body lying on the ground near his former dwelling; the conflict soon became sharp and he found it necessary to look out for his own safety. The fortune of the day made him a prisoner, and wounded his father; this you will say, and say truly, is a long story and badly told.

Dec. 11.—Our road this day carried us through Hopkinsonville, a considerable village; rode 20 miles before breakfast and 20 after, which brought us to Princeton, a poor looking little town, though in a fine looking country; the tavern at which we stopped is a huge brick castle with an empty inside.

Dec. 12.—When we arose this morning found the snow had fallen three inches deep during the night; got a cup of coffee and drove 12 miles for our breakfast; having had corn bread for supper last night we thought ourselves happy when we saw miserable buckwheat cakes on the table this morning. Thirteen miles after breakfast brought us to Salem, a little town of about 50 houses, where we were glad to put up for the night, it being dark and most intolerably cold. After an excellent supper we retired for the night. This was the first place where we were annoyed by gambling.

Dec. 13.—After securing a very good breakfast we set off at nine o'clock, and, riding and walking 15 miles up and down hill, we found ourselves at the mouth of Cumberland River, 60 miles from the Mississippi. We decided upon rowing down the Ohio in a small boat which we soon bought and stored with two days' provisions, and at dark found ourselves five miles down the Ohio River; got lodging on a steamboat that was lying at the shore.

Dec. 14.—The coldness of my feet compelled me to rise early this morning and sunrise found us all on board our little bark, taking tours, by twos, of half an hour each; it being very cold, it was with difficulty that we kept ourselves from freezing; enjoyed our situation very much until after sunset, when it first occurred to us that we might have to take up our lodging, by a fire, on the bank of the river for the night, as we could not see any house. We of course looked out in good earnest for a light on the shore, and after rowing half an hour discovered, to our great joy, a log cabin on the bank, where we landed. Having come 30 miles this day, we were all much fatigued by rowing, and were very glad to get a place before the fire to lie down on the floor of the rudest cabin you ever saw inhabited.

Dec. 15.—Loud complaints were common this morning when we attempted to rise, on account of stiff joints; took breakfast and embarked on board our boat, and at three o'clock this afternoon arrived where we expected to meet a steamboat, but to our great disappointment there was none there.

Dec. 16.—Having now arrived within six miles of the Mississippi we supposed it would not be long before we should have the sight of a steamboat, and to avoid loss of time took passage on board of a "keel boat" that was going down the Mississippi, knowing that we could exchange our mode of conveyance whenever a steamboat might overtake us; in two hours we arrived at the Mississippi and found it so full of ice as to prevent our entering it.

Dec. 18.—After being ice bound, for two days, we, this morning, determined to venture out and try it. After arranging our force as necessity required, we launched forth into the stream and soon found ourselves employed, some in rowing and some in pushing off large cakes of ice by which we were now surrounded on all sides; a prospect anything but pleasing, as we were liable to be forced upon the snags, of which there was any quantity, and if we were, our fate was almost certain destruction. After navigating our boat ten or twelve miles, in a state of constant anxiety, and being much fatigued, it was deemed advisable to land, which was effected with great difficulty and some murmuring, there being a number in favor of continuing under way. Having landed on the Missouri shore, many of us took the opportunity of setting feet on its prolific soil and, thereby, enabling us to say we had been in the "State of Missouri." After ranging about through the forest until we were satisfied, we returned to the boat and found we had two, first-rate, flute performers among our number, who regaled us after supper with some excellent music. While the table was clearing off, I found that cards was to be the order of the evening; for of fifteen of us there were but two besides myself that did not play. Having been together two or three days, I have ascertained that our company consists of four Frenchmen, one doctor, one lawyer and a dozen merchants—with three married ladies and one spinster, children, servants, etc., etc.

Dec. 19.—This day we made but three or four miles, having headwind, as well as ice, to contend with. The banks of the river look very wild, not even a cabin for many miles, nothing but a close forest, growing to the edge of the bank, which is generally 50 feet high and yet is often overflown; and, when that happens, the water extends many miles from the river, as the banks are higher at the water than any other place.

Dec. 22.—The last two days were passed as the two preceding, gaining only 10 to 12 miles each day, with great exertion, the passengers taking turns at the oars—with the exception of three or four lazy fellows who always have some trifling excuse. This evening there was some dissatisfaction on account of our captain refusing to land at sundown; it got so high that one of the passengers struck the captain and threatened to throw him overboard if he did not permit the pilot to land immediately; the passengers seemed to have command of the boat, for the pilot was obliged to land agreeably to their wishes.

Dec. 28.—The last six days have passed as those last described with the exception of having no ice to contend with for the last two—in consequence of which we made 25 or 30 miles each day. Last night we landed at an Indian encampment of some half a dozen families; we went to see them and found that they were picking cotton for a planter—their condition and appearance were miserable indeed; one of our company, the son of General Winchester, was able to converse with them, in their own language, which made our visit more interesting. This morning found us at Memphis, a little town that has lately sprung up and promises to become a place of some consequence. We have now been out on the Mississippi 10 or 12 days, and have run but 250 miles to this place and have yet 750 to New Orleans. About 4 o'clock we were gratified with the welcome sight of a steamboat, a few miles behind us, and in fifteen minutes had the pleasure of being taken off our uncomfortable as well as tedious boat by the steamboat *Magnet*, Captain Bickworth. We were so much pleased that we could not eat our supper; we now have a prospect of arriving at the end of our journey in the course of four or five days.

Dec. 30.—Yesterday we ran 100 miles; this day it has been snowing and blowing incessantly, notwithstanding which we shall run over a hundred miles from daylight to dark; we find ourselves very much crowded, there being about 40 cabin passengers and only twenty beds; of course we, who came on board last, fare worst. Having some acquaintance with the clerk I succeeded in getting a settee, upon which, rolled up in my cloak, I reposed in wakefulness, during the greater part of the night while some less fortunate are obliged to take their rest on the floor.

Dec. 31.—This day we passed the wreck of a steamboat that a few days since, on her way up the river, ran against a snag and sank in a few minutes; no lives lost. It has been quite cold all day.

Jan. 1, 1826.—This morning introduces us to a new year, whether happy or otherwise, time alone can determine; be that as it may, allow me to wish you a new year of happiness and disappointments few. At 10 o'clock we arrived at Natchez, a handsome town on the banks of the river, 300 miles above New Orleans. Its situation is beautiful and in appearance healthy, but it has just recovered from the yellow fever, which has raged here for many weeks this season, and been more fatal than at New Orleans.

Jan. 3.—This morning at 8 o'clock we discovered the city and in one hour afterwards were landed alongside of this celebrated place, so long the object of our anxiety.

Jan. 14.—I have now been here ten days, during which I have presented my letters of introduction and collected necessary information to enable me to decide that there is no commercial inducement to remain here all winter; my letters being, fortunately, to some of the most respectable merchants in this city, I have had a good opportunity to make enquiry; from all I have been able to collect I am convinced that my time will be of more service at the North, in the spring, than here, and have, therefore, concluded to take passage for New York in the brig *Ave Maria*, Captain Wood.

EASTON, PA., IN 1825.

"A Mother in Israel."*

THERE are lives, unnoticed by the many, with little to the general eye that is remarkable in them, that yet are full of precious fruits. There are lives, whose stream scarce disturbed by a ripple seems almost motionless, that bear refreshing and enriching influences wherever they touch. There are lives, the tenor of whose way is quiet, even, calm, simple, noiseless, that give forth to the attentive ear strains of sweetest melody, lessons which speak of the love of heaven. The life of Mrs. Charles Rodenbough, now at rest, was such an one. Undemonstrative and retiring, to appreciate her worth one had need to know her well and nearly; and one, who so knew her, will bear such respect to the memory of her modest, shrinking disposition as to make his words few, and free from a praise that would offend her living.

EMILY CAUFFMAN RODENBOUGH, daughter of Laurence and Sarah Shewell Cauffman, was born at Philadelphia, on May 6, 1806; she was baptized in the Roman communion, but confirmed by the Right Rev. Dr. Onderdonk, Bishop of the Protestant Episcopal Church in Pennsylvania, at Christ Church, Philadelphia. In the same parish church, on May 16, 1836, her marriage with Charles Rodenbough was solemnized, by the Rev. John Waller James. Her married life and the days of her widowhood were mainly passed in the Borough of Easton, where, on Monday of last week, the 11th of December, 1876, after a brief but distressing illness, surrounded by her devoted family, she departed this life to enter upon her life eternal.

Mrs. Rodenbough was a devoted and earnest member of Trinity Church in this borough. From her earliest years she had learned to love its holy ways, its blessed services and its sacred seasons.

She lived in Jesus, and now she rests in Him. He, only, knows how hardly she attained, and through what troubles was made perfect. But we have seen, and can testify, that her daily course amongst us here was beautiful with the loves and graces of a Christly character, and her life abounded with the new works of the Gospel—the works that spring out of a lively faith. Her nature was wondrously cheerful and cheering. Her sympathy was ever fresh and full and true. Was any sick?—her heart ached for all their pains. Was any troubled?

---

* Obituary, *Free Press*, Easton, Pa., Dec. 18, 1876.

—her spirit, too, was vexed until they found relief. Her constant rule—the law of her heart—seemed, to rejoice with them that did rejoice, and to weep with them that wept. Many were the needy whom her shy bounty relieved, many the afflicted whom her tender kindness cheered. It was not in her to wait for the necessitous to press their wants upon her; she would seek out the needy cause, and in all her giving was seen the delicacy of the Christian lady. We doubt not that her prayers and her alms have gone up for a memorial before God, and now she finds the treasures which she had laid up in heaven. Singularly esteemed by all who called her *friend*—cherished with deep affection by her kindred—she filled, as few can excel, all the natural relations of life; and now, all her earthly labors past, she enters upon the work of those ministering spirits, who delighting to do God's will, excel in strength, and "circle His throne, rejoicing."

For we have a good hope; nay, we have a blessed assurance—that she died in the Lord. Absent from us, she is present with Him, which is far better. So let her rest, on whose fresh grave we would cast a garland twined with flowers that tell of a love which never shall decay. When Christ, who is our life, shall appear, then shall she also appear with Him in glory. Yet we love to dwell upon the sweetness of her memory. It blossoms, as the seed of her glorified body is planted in the bosom of the earth. "Precious in the sight of the Lord is the death of His saints." God grant that the remembrance of her life may be powerful with those who loved her, calling them to forsake the sin she hated, to follow her in the path she trod, to the rest where she has gone!

MEMORIAL FONT—TRINITY CHURCH, EASTON, PA.
(Mary McCullagh Rodenbough—p. 155.)

Shewell.

HEWELL, a name of Saxon origin, is derived from "sha," a small wood or thicket, and "well," a fountain or spring. Walter Shewell, the founder of the American branch of the family, always spelled the name "Shawell."

In the history of the Shewells certain hereditary peculiarities are noted. Among the men, large and vigorous physique, great tenacity and directness of purpose, unswerving integrity, strong affections and simple tastes, among the women, delicate constitutions, amiable manners, generous hands and warm hearts. In religious matters decidedly non-conformist—Quakers in England, Baptists in America: they have excelled as preachers, magistrates, soldiers, merchants and farmers.

In the year 1722, there arrived, at Philadelphia, three young Englishmen: Walter, Robert and Thomas Shewell. The first two settled in Pennsylvania, the other went to Maryland. Robert Shewell bought timber lands, put up saw mills, became a builder and owner of ships and a shipping merchant, principally in the West India trade; Walter bought land from the Penns in Bucks County, where he became a farmer and magistrate.

Births, Marriages and Deaths.

PART I.—WALTER SHEWELL'S LINE.

1 **Walter Shewell**[1] was born near the village of Painswick, Gloucestershire, England, 1702. In company with his brothers, Robert[1] and Thomas,[1] he came to Philadelphia June 7, 1722. Possessing some means, he purchased, from the Penn Estate, a tract of land in New Britain township, Bucks Co., Pa., near

From an old painting—1775

Doylestown. He married in ———— 1731, MARY KIMBER of Cecil Co., Maryland. She died at Painswick Hall, Bucks Co., Pa., Dec. 29, 1790, aged 88 years 10 months 9 days. WALTER SHEWELL[1] died at the same place, Oct. 23, 1795.*

They had :

I. WALTER, b. ————, Feb 22, 1732 ; d. Aug. 13, 1822.*

2. II. ROBERT, b. New Britain, Pa., Jan. 27, 1740 ; m. Jan. 15, 1764 ; d. Dec. 28, 1825.

III. THOMAS, b. ———— ; d.

IV. ELIZABETH, b.———— ; m. Williams ; d.————.

2 Robert[2](Walter[1]) was born in New Britain township, Bucks Co., Pa., Jan 27, 1740. He received a fair education and a good business training. In 1764, he became engaged in the West India trade, as a partner, in the firm of Oldman & Shewell.† He retired from business and returned to Bucks Co. in 1769, completing Painswick Hall the following year.† On the 15th of Jan., 1764, ROBERT SHEWELL[2] was married to SARAH, daughter of RICHARD SALLOWS of Philadelphia.‡ The ceremony was performed by the Rev. Morgan Edwards, in presence of Mr. and Mrs. William Masters,§ Mr. and Mrs. Stephen Shewell, Mr. and Mrs. Abraham Bickley, Mr. Joseph Shewell, Miss Elizabeth Shewell (afterward the wife of Benjamin West, P. R. A.), Miss

---

* See App. "Reminiscences of Painswick Hall."

† See App. "Reminiscences of Painswick Hall," and "An Ancestor's Letter-Book."

‡ RICHARD SALLOWS was born at Eastbarshold, in the County of Suffolk, England, Nov. 4, 1694, and died at Philadelphia, Sept. 30, 1741. He married SARAH STONE (b. St. Clement's Lane, Lombard St., London, Eng., March 16, 1704) and had SARAH (b. Phila., April 2, 1741, and bapt. by Rev. Morgan Edwards, June 11, 1762) who married ROBERT SHEWELL as above.

§ WILLIAM MASTERS was the grandson of Thomas Masters (who came from Bermuda to Philadelphia in 1687 and became one of its wealthiest citizens: Mayor 1708 and Provincial Councillor 1720–23. His estate at one time extended from the Delaware River to Broad Street) and married Sarah, daughter of Evan Morgan (and sister of Mrs. Buckridge Sims) who died May 18, 1768, aged 28. William Masters died Aug. 5, 1788, aged 53 years. Sybilla, the wife of Thomas Masters, received in 1715 the first patent granted by the Crown to an American, " for cleaning and curing the Indian corn grown in the Colonies."

Polly Bickley and Isaac Hunt, Esq. (the father of Leigh Hunt). ROBERT SHEWELL[2] died at Painswick Hall, Dec. 28, 1825. SARAH SALLOWS SHEWELL died at the same place, Aug. 15, 1804, aged 63 years.* They had :

3.   I. SALLOWS, b. Phila., Sept. 14, 1765; m. M. McIlhenny, Dec. 6, 1794; d. March 28, 1824.

    II. JOHN KIMBER, b. Phila., Oct. 26, 1767; d. Frederick, Md., Oct. 8, 1793.

4.   III. JULIANA, b. April 5, 1769; m. May 16, 1793. James Dunlap.

5.   IV. NATHANIEL, b. Painswick Hall, Nov. 22, 1770; m. Feb. 3, 1796, Cynthia Fell; d. Painswick, April 6, 1860.

6.   V. ROBERT, b. Painswick Hall, June 20. 1772; m. Mch. 30, 1796, Sarah Dickinson ; d. Feb. 4, 1819.

7.   VI. ELIZABETH, b. Painswick Hall, June 20, 1772 (4.30 P. M.); m. Apl. 23, 1796, Samuel Currie; d. June 29, 1822.

8.   VII. THOMAS, b. Painswick Hall, July 13, 1774 ; m. (1st) Mch. 10, 1802, Sarah Linington ; (2d) Jan. 12, 1822, Hannah Brown; (3d) Mch. 1, 1831, Augusta Anderson ; d. Mch. 23, 1848.

    VIII. SARAH FALCONER, b. Painswick Hall, Nov. 26, 1776; m. April 23, 1796, Laurence Cauffman†; d. Phila. Mch. 26, 1856.

3 Sallows[3] (Robert,[2] Walter[1]) was born in Philadelphia. Pa., Sept. 14, 1765. He was married at Phila. Dec. 6, 1794 (by Rev. D. Green), to MARIA MCILHENNY. He died at Painswick Hall, March 28, 1824.

They had : JULIA, WILLIAM and MARY.

---

*On the 15th inst., much lamented by her numerous offspring and friends, MRS. SARAH SHEWELL, aged 62, wife of Robert Shewell, Esquire, of Bucks County. In early youth she became a member of the Baptist Church, and continued through life a firm believer in the Christian religion, which supported her to bear with pious resignation a lingering illness. It may be truly said, she walked through the dark valley of death's dismal shade, and feared no ill, but rested in full hope of a blessed immortality. (Poulson's *Am. Daily Advertiser*, Sept. 10, 1804.)

† See " CAUFFMAN."

4 **Juliana**[3] (Robert,[2] Walter[1]) was born at Phila., April 5, 1769. She married May 16, 1793 (at Neshaminy Baptist Ch.), JAMES DUNLAP* of Philadelphia.

JAMES and JULIANA (Shewell) DUNLAP had:

9.
   I. SALLOWS, b. Doylestown, Pa., April 16, 1794; m. March 14, 1816, Susan Bispham; d. Phila., Jan. 5, 1872.
   II. HAZLETT, b. Phila., June 26, 1796; d. Jan. 7, 1815.
   III. SARAH, b. Phila., Aug. 30, 1798.
   IV. JULIA, b. Phila., Jan. 3, 1801.
   V. MARY, b. Phila., June 25, 1803.

10.
   VI. ANN, b. Phila., Nov. 10, 1805; m. April 14, 1825, W. S. Hendrie, M. D.; d. Doylestown, Pa., July 30, 1857.
   VII. WILLIAM, b. Phila., Aug. 22, 1807; d. Phila. ———.

5 **Nathaniel**[4] (Robert,[2] Walter,[1]) was born at Painswick Hall, Bucks Co., Pa., Nov. 22, 1770.* He received a good common school education, and in early life devoted himself to farming and the management of his father's estate. He took some interest in politics and was elected High Sheriff of Bucks County, Pa., 1800-1803; Member of Assembly of the State, 1805-6-7; County Commissioner, 1817; and was a Trustee of Union Academy of Doylestown, 1804. He married Feb. 3, 1796, CYNTHIA FELL.

NATHANIEL SHEWELL died at Painswick Hall, April 6, 1860.†

---

*See App. " Reminiscences of Painswick Hall."

† " By reference to the obituary department of this paper it will be seen that NATHANIEL SHEWELL, Esq., has closed his long life of a score of years beyond the time allotted to man. He died, we believe, on the spot where he was born some years before this country threw off her allegiance to a foreign power. He was, in many respects, a remarkable man and connected, in the storehouse of his memory, the history of the past with the present. Mr. Shewell throughout his life was an active, vigorous, high-minded, honorable man, generous and social in his nature—warm in his friendships—honest and upright in his dealings. He held sundry positions of public usefulness, in all of which stations, we believe, his duties were discharged with fidelity and satisfaction to the public. He was always, of late years, fond of recurring in conversation to the scenes and experiences of his early and middle life—and was able to relate, from personal knowledge, many interesting facts known to his contemporaries only by tradition. His mental

His wife died February 14, 1848. They had:

 I. THOMAS, b. July 3, 1797; d. ———.

11. II. CHARLES, b. Doylestown, Pa., Mch. 9, 1799; m. Oct. 25, 1838, Jane Wallace; d. Jan. 13, 1883.

 III. MARGARET, b. Doylestown, Pa., Sept. 3, 1801; d. Painswick Hall, March 3, 1879.

 IV. SARAH, b. Doylestown, Pa., May 5, 1805; d. Painswick Hall, Aug. 26, 1880.

 V. HANNAH, b. Doylestown, Pa., July 6, 1807.

 VI. JOSEPH, b. Doylestown, Pa., Aug. 2, 1810; d. Painswick Hall, June 2, 1883.

 VII. JANE, b. Doylestown, Pa., Oct. 15, 1812; d. November 19, 1885.

 VIII. CYNTHIA, b. Doylestown, Pa., March 23, 1814; d. Painswick Hall, April 7, 1875.

 IX. SUSAN DUNLAP, b. Painswick Hall, March 23, 1817.

 X. MARY, b. Painswick Hall, July 15, 1820.

6 Robert[3] (Robert,[2] Walter[1]) was born at Painswick Hall, Bucks Co., Pa., June 20, 1772 (a twin child with Elizabeth[3]). He was married at Philadelphia, March 30, 1796 (by Rev. Thomas Ustick) to SARAH DICKINSON of New York. He died at ———, Feb. 4, 1819, and was buried in New Britain churchyard. His widow married Governor Robinson, of Vermont, and died at Bennington, Vt., Aug. 9, 1854.

ROBERT and SARAH D. SHEWELL had:

12. I. JOHN KIMBER, b. Painswick Hall, March 20, 1801; m. ——— 1821, Rachel Bouden; d. ———, 1846.

---

faculties were preserved, till recently, in a remarkable degree, but he finally yielded to the corroding hand of time, and, with his physical nature worn out, quietly passed away. Mr. Shewell took an active part in politics, and was associated with the Democratic party until Henry Clay became a candidate for the Presidency, when his admiration for that distinguished statesman led him away, and he became and remained an ardent Whig, while that party had an existence."—*Newcastle Valley*, April 16, 1860.

II. WALTER DICKINSON, b. Phila., March 20, 1803; m. July 21, 1825, Sarah Naylor of ——— (no children).

13. III. GEORGE STUART, b. Phila., Aug. 20, 1804; m. April 26, 1827, Ann Thomas.

IV. LOUISE, b. Phila., Dec. 3, 1805; d. Bennington, Vt., Dec. 15, 1878.

14. V. EDWARD STONE, b. Phila., July 1, 1807; m. ———, Susan A. Mann.

7 Elizabeth[3] (Robert,[2] Walter[1]) was born at Painswick Hall, Bucks Co., Pa., June 20, 1772, 4.30 P.M. (a twin child with Robert[3]). Married at Painswick Hall (by Rev. W. White) April 23, 1796, to SAMUEL CURRIE.*

She died at Painswick Hall, June 29, 1822; he died Nov. 26, 1860, aged 91. They were interred in the Baptist churchyard, New Britain, Bucks County, Pa.

SAMUEL and ELIZABETH (Shewell) CURRIE had:

15. I. HARRIET SHEWELL, b. Painswick, Jan. 20, 1797; m. Capt. R. M. Donnaldson,† of Phila., Jan. 31, 1832.

---

* See App., "Reminiscences of Painswick Hall."

†JOHN DONNALDSON (the father of Captain Richard Donnaldson) was born in Philadelphia, March 11, 1754. He was the first person elected a member of the cavalry troop known as "The Light Horse of the City of Philadelphia," afterward the "First Troop, Philadelphia City Cavalry" formed in 1774. He served with the Troop during the Revolution and was one of the twelve gentlemen who aided Adjutant-General Read in reconnoitring the enemy before the battle of Princeton, at which the Troop acted (about Trenton) as body-guard to Gen. Washington, and "distinguished himself, in an eminent degree, taking a score of prisoners" (see Memoirs of Gen. Wilkinson I, 133). He continued in active service until Jan. 23, 1777, when the Commander-in-Chief tendered the members of the Troop commissions in the Continental Army, as a reward for their gallantry. He was present in the field during part of 1778-79, subscribed £2000 toward the National Bank established in Philadelphia, 1780, for the purpose of supplying the Army with provisions, and thereafter filled a number of civil offices of trust. He was Registrar-General (1789-93) and Comptroller-General (1794-1801) of Pennsylvania. He was a vestryman of the United Prot. Epis. Churches of Christ Church and St. Peter's in Philadelphia. He died there Dec. 29, 1831.

16.
   II. ELIZA GRAEME, b. May 24, 1800; m. Rev. S. Aaron, April 20, 1833; d. Mount Holly, N. J., Nov. 25, 1870.
   III. MARY SHEWELL, b. May 24, 1802; m. David Tyson of Abingdon, Pa., Oct. 6, 1835; d. March 10, 1847.
   IV. LOUISA, b. Sept. 16, 1805; d. Jan. 1, 1806.
   V. LAUGHLIN, b. Jan. 2. 1807; m. ———, and had a son Arthur; d. Scioto Co., Ohio, Jan. 8, 1843.

17.
   VI. THOMAS SHEWELL, b. Painswick, July 24, 1809; m. Sept. 9, 1835, Hannah Wyner Evans of Trenton, N. J.; d. Portsmouth, O., June 19, 1869.

8 Thomas[3] (Robert,[2] Walter[1]) was born at Painswick Hall, Bucks Co., Pa., July 13, 1774. He was educated at private schools and, at the age of eighteen, came to Philadelphia and engaged in mercantile pursuits. In 1796 he took a voyage for the benefit of his health to the West Indies. From thence he went to England and entered the house of Bonsfield & Co., of London (extensive woollen staplers and army contractors). After a satisfactory business engagement, of three years, he returned to America. While in London he made many friends and enjoyed the social opportunities afforded at the house of his kinswoman, Mrs. Benjamin West, whose husband was afterward President of the Royal Academy. He again in 1803, engaged in business as a merchant, in Philadelphia, was for many years one of the Board of Managers of the House of Refuge, and after an honorable career retired to private life in 1832. THOMAS SHEWELL[3] was married three times. His first wife (b. March 10, 1784; m. March 10, 1802) was SARAH B. LININGTON, a granddaughter of Dr. George de Benneville,* of Bristol township, near Germantown, Pa. She died Feb. 11, 1819. His second wife (m. Jan. 12, 1822) was HANNAH BROWN, who died July 26, 1828. His third wife (m. March 31, 1831) was AUGUSTA ANDERSON, who died June 12, 1861, leaving no issue.

THOMAS SHEWELL[3] died at Philadelphia, March 23, 1848, and was buried in the family ground at Branchtown, Pa.†

By his first wife (SARAH B. LININGTON) he had:

---
* See App., " The Founder of a Creed."
† See App., " Reminiscences of Painswick Hall."

18.   I. MARY LININGTON, b. ———, June 5, 1805; m. Nov. 17, 1829, Daniel May Keim.
      II. DANIEL LININGTON, b. ———, Oct. 9, 1806; d. Dec. 11, 1806.
19.   III. LININGTON DANIEL, b. ———, Jan. 1, 1808; m. March 10, 1831, Martha Roberts; d. Jan. 24, 1873.
      IV. THOMAS, b. ———, Sept. 3, 1809; d. Oct. 26, 1809.
20.   V. THOMAS FASSITT, b. Phila., Dec. 26, 1810.
21.   VI. ESTHER DE BENNEVILLE, b. Jan. 23, 1814; m. Oct. 15, 1833, John E. Young; d. Feb. 21, 1855.
      VII. EDWARD GRANVILLE, b. Phila., Dec. 21, 1815; d. Rockland, Del., Aug. 31, 1845.

By his second wife (HANNAH BROWN) he had:

22.   VIII. JOSEPH BROWN, b. Oct. 22, 1822; m. Oct. 1, 1845, Kate Backus; d. Jan., 1864.
      IX. JAMES WORTH, b. ———, 1824; d. ———, 1832.
      X. HENRY, b. ———, 1826.
      XI. SARAH LININGTON, b. ———, 1827; d. New Britain, Bucks Co., Pa., 1829.

9 Sallows Dunlap[4] (Juliana (Dunlap), Robert,[2] Walter[1]) was born at Doylestown, April 16, 1794. He was married March 14, 1816, to SUSAN BISPHAM,* of Morristown, N. J. (by Robert Wharton, Mayor of Philadelphia). Susan Bispham Dunlap died at Philadelphia, Sept. 1, 1880.

SALLOWS and SUSAN (Bispham) DUNLAP had:

      I. JOSEPH BISPHAM, b. Phila., May 1, 1817; grad. Univ. Pa., as M.D.; m. Nov. 10, 1842, Lydia J. Strader of Sussex, N. J.; d. Norristown, Pa. July 21, 1871.
23.   II. ROBERT SHEWELL, b. Phila., July 19, 1818; m. Dec. 5, 1843, Sarah Oat; d. Phila. Sept, 29, 1870.
24.   III. JAMES HENDRIE, b. Phila., June 2, 1820; m. June 29, 1848, Elizabeth Bennett; d. Nov. 30, 1876.

---

* SUSAN BISPHAM (b. Dec. 2, 1794) dau. of Joseph and Susanna Pearson Bispham was descended from Joshua Bispham, of Lancashire, Eng., of a Quaker family tracing its lineage to A. D. 1100. ("Bispham Family"— W. Bispham, N. Y., 1890.)

25.   IV. JULIANA, b. Phila., March 23, 1822; m. Oct. 27, 1846, Benj. M. Dusenbery; d. Nov. 30, 1876.
26.   V. SUSAN BISPHAM, b. Phila., May 19, 1824; m. June 16, 1852, William C. Newell.
27.   VI. SARAH CAUFFMAN, b. Phila., Dec. 13, 1825; m. Oct. 28, 1851, John Todhunter Sill.
      VII. JOSEPHINE TUCKER BISPHAM, b. Phila., Oct. 21, 1827; m. Norristown, Pa., Nov. 22, 1865, William Riehla Lownes, who d. Oct. 16, 1882. Mrs. Lownes d. Clifton Heights, Del. Co., Pa., Jan. 2, 1879.

10 **Ann Dunlap**[4] (Juliana[3] (Dunlap), Robert,[2] Walter[1]) was born at ———, Nov. 10, 1805. Married at Philadelphia, April 14, 1825 (by Rev. William Engles), WILLIAM SCOTT HENDRIE, M.D., of Bucks Co., Pa. Died at Doylestown, Pa., July 30, 1857.
   WILLIAM SCOTT and ANN (Dunlap) HENDRIE had:
   I. JOSEPH JOHN, b. Hilltown, Pa. ———; d. Hilltown.
28.   II. JULIA DUNLAP, b. Hilltown, Pa., Dec. 7, 1828; m. Doylestown, Pa., Dec. 26, 1848, E. M. Lloyd.
29.   III. JOSEPHINE, b. Hilltown, Pa., June 19, 1831; m. Doylestown, Pa., C. S. Widdifield, M.D.
30.   IV. JAMES DUNLAP, b. Hilltown, Pa., Sept. 25, 1833.
31.   V. WILLIAM SCOTT, b. Hilltown, Pa., Oct. 25, 1835; m. Doylestown, Pa., Nov. 6, 1862, M. L. Morton; d. Holmesburgh, July 10, 1881.

11 **Charles**[4] (Nathaniel,[3] Robert,[2] Walter[1]) was born at Doylestown, Pa., March 9, 1799. He was educated at the Academy in his native town and, in 1814, removed to Painswick Hall, and thereafter made it his residence. On Oct. 25, 1838, he married JANE, daughter of Robert Wallace, of the township of Warwick. He preferred the life of a farmer to a more stirring avocation, and was highly respected for his sterling qualities of heart and head. He died at Painswick Hall, Jan. 13, 1883. Jane Wallace Shewell died, April 18, 1874. They had: REBECCA WALLACE (b. Painswick Hall, Nov. 7, 1839; m. July 14, 1870, J. W. McDowell), JULIA (b. Painswick Hall, Dec. 2, 1841; d. March 11, 1875), MARY W. (b. Painswick Hall, March 25, 1844).

12 John Kimber[4] (Robert,[3] Robert,[2] Walter[1]) was born at Painswick Hall, Bucks County, Pa., March 20, 1801. He removed to Philadelphia, and although, nominally, a "business man," was noted as an amateur sportsman and angler. He was one of the original owners of the Fish House at Red Bank, N. J., on the Shrewsbury. He was also a magnificent skater and, for a long time, held the championship of Philadelphia. JOHN KIMBER SHEWELL married ——— 1821, RACHEL BOUDEN of Philadelphia. He died in 1846; she died Dec. 26, 1870. They had:

32. I. ANNA LOUISA, b. ———; m. Oct. 11, 1838, A. R. Johnson.
33. II. GEORGE EDWARD, b. ———; m. Jan. 6, 1855, Sarah Parkin.
34. IV. EMILY CAUFFMAN, b. Nov. 19, 1829; m. Feb. 19, 1856, F. Theo. Fisher.
35. III. WALTER DICKINSON, b. Feb. 22, 1828; m. July 31, 1851, Emma Miller.

13 George Stuart[4] (Robert,[3] Robert,[2] Walter[1]) was born at Philadelphia, August 20, 1804. He married April 26, 1827, ANN THOMAS, of Bucks County, Pa., where she was born July 10, 1806. Mrs. Shewell died in St. Louis, Mo., March 19, 1880. In memory of her pious life, a beautiful chapel, erected at Block Island, R. I., by visitors to that summer resort (mainly through the exertions and liberality of her daughter, Mrs. John N. Bofinger) was named "Saint-Ann's-by-the Sea." It was consecrated July 27, 1890, with impressive ceremonies by the Rt. Rev'd. Thomas M. Clark, D.D., Bishop of Rhode Island. GEORGE STUART and ANN (Thomas) SHEWELL had:

  I. THOMAS THOMAS, b. Phila., March 18, 1829; d. New Orleans, Sept. 22, 1854.

  II. LAUCHLIN CURRIE, b. Phila., Nov. 3, 1832; d. Phila., May 5, 1835.

36. III. LOUISE, b. Phila., Nov. 1, 1835; m, May, 1852, R. F. Coningham, of St. Louis.

  IV. ELIZA, b. Phila., March 25, 1837; d. Phila., April 27, 1838.

  V. MARY ELIZABETH, b. Phila., June 24, 1841; m. July 13, 1857, John N. Bofinger, of St. Louis.

184   *AUTUMN LEAVES FROM FAMILY TREES.*

     VI. AUGUSTA, b. St. Louis, Mo., Dec. 20, 1844; m. April 27, 1885, William H. Beach, of St. Louis.
37. VII. GEORGE STUART, b. St. Louis, Dec. 18, 1845; m. Feb. 22, 1883, Ida L. Phillips, of Oglethorpe Co., Ga.
     VIII. RACHEL, b. St. Louis, July 21, 1847; d. St. Louis, Aug. 17, 1847.

14 Edward Stone (Robert,[3] Robert,[2] Walter[1]) was born at Phila., July 1, 1807. He married in Boston, Mass., Nov. 27, 1834, ADELINE SUSAN MANN, and died Portsmouth, O., Oct. 29, 1854.

     They had:
38. I. MARIE ISABEL, b. Phila., April 4, 1836; m. ———.
     II. ROBERT A., b. Portsmouth, O., Dec. 11, 1839; d. Portsmouth, O., June, 1841.
     III. LOWELL ACKERMAN, b. Dec. 5, 1842; d. Cinn., O., June 21, 1853.
     IV. EDWARD DAVIS, b. Oct. 19, 1845; d. Aug, 10, 1846.
39. V. FREDERICK SEYMOUR, b. Cinn., O., Sept. 5, 1848; m. Oct. 5, 1871, Susan C. Slocum; d. Hinsdale, Ills., Nov. 29, 1875.

15 Harriet Shewell Currie[4] (Elizabeth,[3] (Currie) Robert,[2] Walter[1]) was born at Painswick Hall, Bucks Co., Pa., Jan. 20, 1797. Married (by Rev. Samuel Aaron of Doylestown) Jan. 31, 1832, to Captain RICHARD MARTIN DONNALDSON of Philadelphia. They resided at the Donnaldson homestead, "Green Farm," Bucks County, Pa. Capt. Donnaldson died April 24, 1873, aged 86 years; Mrs. Donnaldson died Oct. 4, 1882; they were buried in New Britain (Baptist) Churchyard.

     RICHARD and HARRIET (Currie) DONNALDSON had:
     I. HELEN, b. "Green Farm," Jan. 5, 1834.
     II. JOHN, b. "Green Farm." Feb. 9, 1836; d. Aug. 27, 1836.
40. III. EDWARD MILNOR, b. "Green Farm," March 4, 1837; m. Dec. 9, 1834, Annie Stagner of Montgomery Co., Pa.

16 Eliza Graeme Currie[4] (Elizabeth,[3] (Currie) Robert,[2] Walter[1]) was born at Painswick Hall, Pa., May 24, 1800. Married April 20, 1833, Rev. SAMUEL AARON of the Baptist Church at New Britain, Pa. She died at Mount Holly, N. J., Nov. 23, 1870.

SAMUEL and ELIZA (Currie) AARON had: JOHN (b. Burlington, N. J., Jan. 18, 1834; d. Burlington, N. J., April 26, 1836), MARY (b. Burlington, N. J., March 12, 1836; d. Mt. Holly, N. J., March 24, 1888), EMILIA (b. Burlington, N. J., Dec. 13, 1837), and LOUISA (b. Burlington, N. J., July 10, 1840).

17 **Thomas Shewell Currie**[4] (Elizabeth[3] (Currie), Robert,[2] Walter[1]) was born at Painswick Hall, Bucks County, Pa., July 24, 1809. He was educated at Doylestown and at an early age entered, as a clerk, his uncle Thomas Shewell's countinghouse in Philadelphia. He married in that city, Sept. 9, 1835, HANNAH WYNER, daughter of Lewis Evans of Trenton, N. J., and in August, 1836 removed to Portsmouth, Ohio, where he was engaged in business for many years, and died June 19, 1869.

THOMAS SHEWELL and HANNAH W. E. CURRIE had :*

I. MARGARET A. B., b. Dec. 12, 1836; m. July 1, 1856, Joseph S. Patterson of Steubenville, O.; d. March 26, 1879. They had: Hannah K., b. March 28, 1857; d. Oct. 5, 1862; Thomas Currie, b. July 26, 1859 (m. Ida Showers).

II. MARY ELIZABETH, b. Sept. 16, 1838; m. May 27, 1857, Giles Gilbert, and had two children.

III. SAMUEL AUGUSTUS, b. Oct. 16, 1840; served as Captain, "A" 33d O. V. I. 1861-62; d. Shelbyville, Tenn., April 16, 1862, "from disease contracted in the line of duty."

IV. LEWIS EVAN, b. Nov. 24, 1845; merchant, and Recorder, Scioto County, O.; d. March 14, 1873.

V. HANNAH EVELINE, b. Nov. 29, 1849; m. April 6, 1869, Charles E. James of Jackson, O. (who served gallantly during the War for the Union, 36th O. V. I.; severely wounded Sept. 19, 1864, at "the Opequan," Winchester, Va.; since Clerk of County Court and Mayor). They have a son Ripley Currie, b. Sept. 13, 1870.

18 **Mary Linington**[4] (Thomas,[3] Robert,[2] Walter[1]) was born at Philadelphia, June 5, 1805. She married, Nov. 17, 1829, DANIEL MAY KEIM of Reading, Pa., who died Feb. 12, 1868.

DANIEL M. and MARY L. (Shewell) KEIM had :

---
* All born at Portsmouth, O.

THOMAS SHEWELL (b. Jan. 3, 1834; d. Nov. 9, 1867), JOSEPH DE BENNEVILLE (b. Nov. 26, 1835; m. April 17, 1868, Lillie Paxson and had 5 children), ESTHER DE BENNEVILLE (b. Nov. 15, 1837; m. June 20, 1870, James P. Wood; d. Jan. 24, 1874), AUGUSTA SHEWELL (b. Sept. 6, 1840), MARY SHEWELL (b. Dec. 1, 1843; m. Jan. 22, 1884, Francis Abbott), and ANNETTA FABER (b. Dec. 29, 1845; d. Dec. 20, 1860).

19 **Linington Daniel**[4] (Thomas,[3] Robert,[2] Walter[1]) was born at Philadelphia, Jan. 1, 1808. He was educated at Bordeaux, France, and became a merchant and importer.

He married at ———, March 10, 1831, MARTHA RAKESTRAW ROBERTS of Philadelphia (who died April 14, 1871, aged 59 years).

LININGTON DANIEL SHEWELL died, at sea, on board S. S. *Adriatic*, Jan. 24, 1873, having completed his one hundredth trans-Atlantic voyage. The following mention was made in an English newspaper at the time:

" Just a month ago the writer of this paragraph had occasion to go to the Lancashire and Yorkshire Station to meet a train. While there a number of town councillors and other prominent citizens gathered together, and the inquiry was made, ' What has brought you here ? ' ' Well, we have come to bid Mr. Shewell good-bye ; he is just off to America.' Mr. Shewell was partner in a large house in Philadelphia. He had lived in Bradford as the representative of that house for many years, and was well known in the Bradford trade, and was highly esteemed by a numerous circle in Bradford society. He was a man of fine presence, and as he walked the streets men stood to look at him. He sailed from Liverpool in the *Adriatic* on the 16th January, but he did not reach his native land. He was seized with paralysis, on the passage, from which he partially recovered ; but a second shock came from which he never rallied. After some hours of unconsciousness he died on the 24th January. Anticipating his end, he requested the doctors to place him with his face towards America, for he said, ' I cannot die with my back toward the country I so dearly loved.' His body was kept on shipboard, and on the ship arriving in port was conveyed to Philadelphia, where it was piously interred by a large concourse of sorrowing friends."

LININGTON D. and MARTHA R. SHEWELL had:
  I. ROBERTS, b. Phila., Dec. 16, 1831.
41. II. LININGTON ROBERTS, b. Phila., Jan. 20, 1833; m. ———.
42. III. SARAH LININGTON, b. Phila., Nov. 2, 1835; m. J. B. Conard.
43. IV. THOMAS ROBERTS, b. Phila., Oct. 18, 1836; m. Nov. 7, 1867, Laura W. Davis.
44. V. DE BENNEVILLE BROWN, b. Phila., Sept. 1, 1838; d. Bellevue Hospital, N. Y., July 26, 1862.
  VI. MARY ROBERTS, b. Phila., Aug. 13, 1841; d. May 29, 1867.
  VII. JULIA CHURCHMAN, b. Phila., Nov. 18, 1843; m. July 10, 1865, to ———; d. April 30, 1882.
  VIII. CHARLES AUGUSTE FIOT, b. Phila., April 23, 1846; d. March 3, 1867.
  IX. MARTHA ROBERTS, b. Phila., June 8, 1848.
  X. OLIVER FULLER, b. Phila., July 11, 1851; d. April 27, 1873.
  XI. ESTHER BROWN, b. Phila., May 11, 1857.

20 **Thomas Fassitt**[4] (Thomas,[3] Robert,[2] Walter[1]) was born in Philadelphia, Dec. 26, 1810. He was educated at the grammar school of the University of Pennsylvania. Entered his father's counting house early in life and remained there until April, 1830, when he accepted a confidential clerical position with Geo. Wildes & Co., Bankers, in London. He returned to Philadelphia in 1831, and, in partnership with his brother Linington, succeeded to his father's business. In the first month of its existence the new firm met with a share of the financial disaster which followed the failure of the U. S. Bank, and lost a handsome fortune. Mr. SHEWELL was, for many years thereafter, a commission merchant in Philadelphia, finally retiring from business in 1885. He has (1891) long resided at Bristol, Pa. His literary tastes and excellent memory have enabled him to make valuable genealogical and biographical contributions to this work. Thomas Fassitt Shewell never married.

21 **Esther de Benneville**[4] (Thomas,[3] Robert,[2] Walter[1]) was born ———, June 23, 1814. She was married Oct. 15, 1833, to JOHN E. YOUNG, of ———, and died Feb. 21, 1855.

JOHN E. and ESTHER DE B. (Shewell) YOUNG had:

I. MARY, b. Rockland, Del., Feb. 24, 1837; m. Feb. 7, 1860, William Wilson; d. Dec. 21, 1875.

II. FANNY G., b. March 23, 1839; m. Dec. 10, 1873, Horatio B. Beattie.

III. ALFRED F., b. Feb. 28, 1842; m. June 17, 1871, Clara F. Pote.

IV. SARAH LININGTON, b. March 26, 1842; d. May 3, 1843.

V. CORA DE BENNEVILLE, b. Jan. 24, 1844; d. March 30, 1845.

VI. HENRY DUPONT, b. Nov. 17, 1845; m. June, 1873, Sarah V. Hoguet; d. Mar. 25, 1878.

VII. KATE ROWE, b. June 6, 1848; d. Dec. 31, 1852.

JOHN EVANS YOUNG was U. S. Consul at Curaçoa, where he died, July 11, 1850.

22 Joseph Brown[4] (Thomas[3] Robert,[2] Walter[1]) was born at Philadelphia, Oct. 13, 1822. He entered mercantile life in 1840 and became a member of the firm of Tustin and Shewell, 1849-1860. In 1862 he volunteered in defense of his State as a member of the "Corn Exchange Regiment." He was a member of the Masonic Order. He married, Oct. 1, 1850, CATHARINE CLEMENS, dau. of Fred. R. Backus, and had: EDITH (b. ———; m. George Meiggs; d———), KATE (b. ———; m. Prof. James Patterson), HELEN (b. ———; m. William Breck), and ALICE.

JOSEPH B. SHEWELL died in Germantown, Pa., Jan. 23, 1864.

23 Robert Shewell Dunlap[5] (Sallows[4] (Dunlap), Juliana,[3] Robert,[2] Walter[1]) was born at Phila., July 19, 1818. He married SARAH OAT, of Phila., Dec. 5, 1843, and died in that city Sept. 29, 1870.

They had:

I. HELEN, b. ———, Aug. 6, 1845.

II. ANNA ROE, b. ———, July 30, 1847; d. Sept. 19, 1847.

45. III. JOSEPHINE AUGUSTA, b. ———, Aug. 17, 1848; m. D. W. Hunt, May 22, 1879.

24 James Hendrie Dunlap[5] (Sallows[4] (Dunlap), Juliana,[3] Robert,[2] Walter[1]) was born at Phila., June 2, 1820; married, June 29, 1848, ELIZABETH BENNETT, of Phila.

They had:
46.   I. SALLOWS, b. Phila., July 1, 1849; m. Feb. 1, 1883, CECILIA M. BERWIND.
     II. EMILY, b. Phila., Nov. 24, 1851; d. Phila., Jan. 28, 1854.
    III. ELLA, b. Phila., June 5, 1854.
     IV. WILLIAM B., b. Phila., Jan. 1, 1858; d. Aug. 28, 1879.
      V. CAROLINE WAY, b. Phila., Feb. 2, 1862.

25 **Juliana Dunlap**[5] (Sallows[4] (Dunlap), Juliana,[3] Robert,[2] Walter[1]) was born at Phila., March 23, 1822. Married at Phila., Oct. 27, 1846, BENJAMIN MEREDITH DUSENBERY, of New Hampton, N. J. (b. March 1, 1820). Died "Thanksgiving Day," Nov. 30, 1876.

BENJAMIN M. and JULIANA D. DUSENBERY had:
  I. JULIA, b. Phila., Oct. 8, 1848.
 II. HENRY, b. Phila., July 14, 1850; d. Phila., Nov. 3, 1853.
III. SUSAN DUNLAP, b. Phila., May 25, 1852; d. Phila., Aug. 19, 1853.
 IV. BENJAMIN MEREDITH, b. Phila., March 10, 1855; m. June 27, 1883, Carrie H. Joy, and had: Henry (b. March 31, 1884). Mary Gertrude (b. March 23, 1885).
  V. FLORENCE, b. Phila., Sept. 18, 1860; m. April 2, 1884, John Parker Van Dyke, and had: Harold Meredith (b. May 13, 1885).
 VI. JOSEPHINE, b. Phila., July 31, 1862; d. Phila. Aug. 16, 1862.
VII. SARAH DUNLAP, b. Phila., Sept. 20, 1863; m. Oct. 14, 1885, Charles Henry Woodruff, Jr.

26 **Susan Bispham Dunlap**[5] (Sallows[4] (Dunlap), Juliana,[3] Robert,[2] Walter[1]) was born at Phila., May 19, 1824. Married at Philadelphia, June 16, 1862, WILLIAM C. NEWELL, who died at Haddonfield, N. J., June 27, 1865.

WILLIAM C. and SUSAN B. D. NEWELL had:
      I. SUSAN DUNLAP, b. Phila., April 15, 1853; m. Oct. 15, 1879, James Hendrie Lloyd, M.D., of Phila., Pa.
47. II. WILLIAM C., b. Phila., Oct. 23, 1856; m. April 27, 1880, Sarah R. Harvey, of Doylestown, Pa.

III. REBECCA WOODSIDE, b. Phila., Feb. 28, 1862 ; m. ———, Grellet Collins and had Dorothy, b. Dec. 30, 1889.

27 **Sarah Cauffman Dunlap**[5] (Sallows,[4] (Dunlap), Juliana,[3] Robert,[2] Walter[1]) was born at Phila., Dec. 13, 1825. Married at Phila., Oct. 28, 1851, JOHN TODHUNTER SILL, who was born at Phila., Aug. 1, 1828, and died at sea, on board S. S. *Atlantic*, Capt. West, off Holyhead, Wales, Nov. 11, 1855, and was buried at " Laurel Hill," Phila.

JOHN T. and SARAH C. D. SILL had : JOSEPH (b. Phila., Nov. 21, 1852; d. Phila., Nov. 7, 1857). HAROLD MONTGOMERY (b. Phila., April 15, 1854; m. Germantown, Pa., Oct. 10, 1877, Pauline Wiener—b. May 26, 1855).

28 **Julia Dunlap Hendrie**[5] (Ann[4] (Hendrie), Juliana,[3] (Dunlap) Robert,[2] Walter[1]) was born at Hilltown, Bucks Co., Pa., Dec. 7, 1828. Married at Doylestown, Pa., Dec. 26, 1848, (by Rev. S. M. Andrews) E. MORRIS LLOYD of Doylestown.

E. MORRIS and JULIA D. H. LLOYD had :

48. I. HENRY ALBERT, b. Doylestown, Pa., Nov. 12, 1849.
49. II. JAMES HENDRIE, b. Doylestown, Pa., Dec. 1, 1853.

29 **Josephine Hendrie**[5] (Ann,[4] (Hendrie) Juliana[3] (Dunlap), Robert,[2] Walter[1]) was born at Hilltown, Bucks Co., Pa., June 19, 1831. Married Doylestown, Pa., Sept. 6, 1855 (by Rev. S. M. Andrews), CASPAR S. WIDDIFIELD, M.D., of Bucks Co., Pa.

CASPAR S. and JOSEPHINE H. WIDDIFIELD had : WILLIAM SCOTT HENDRIE (b. June 2, 1858).

30 **James Dunlap Hendrie**[5] (Ann[4] (Hendrie), Juliana[3] (Dunlap), Robert,[2] Walter[1]) was born at Hilltown, Bucks Co., Pa., Sept. 25, 1833. He was educated at Philadelphia and was graduated M. D. University of Pennsylvania. He served during the War for the Union, 1861-65 as Regimental Quartermaster 104 Pa. Vols. and was badly wounded in one arm at the battle of Fair Oaks, Va.

31 **William Scott Hendrie**[5] (Ann[4] (Hendrie), Juliana[3] (Dunlap) Robert,[2] Walter[1]) was born at Hilltown, Bucks Co., Pa., Oct. 25, 1835. He was educated at Philadelphia and was graduated

A. B., A. M., and M. D., University of Penna. He served as an Asst. Surgeon U. S. Vols., during the War for the Union, 1861-65. Married at Doylestown, Pa., Nov. 6, 1862, M. LOUISE MORTON. He died at Holmesburg, Pa., July 10, 1881. They had: ANITA (b. Holmesburg, Pa., Nov. 9, 1863).

32 **Anna Louisa**[5] (John K.,[4] Robert,[3] Robert,[2] Walter[1]) was born at———. She married, Oct. 11, 1838, ALEXANDER R. JOHNSON of Philadelphia, who died there Dec. 1, 1868. They had: CATHARINE ELIZABETH (b. Phila., Aug. 29, 1839; m. June 15, 1859, William R. Gibson, since Deputy Paymaster-General U.S. Army; d. Albuquerque, N. M., Nov. 25, 1860), ALEXINA LOUISA (b.——— Sept. 26, 1841; m. Oct. 12, 1859, Edwin K. Birch; d. Germantown, Pa., Nov. 1, 1874), GEORGIANA (b.———, Dec. 3, 1843; m. Oct. 26, 1865, John A. Kinsler), RACHEL EMMA (b. ———, Dec. 14, 1845), SARAH (b. ———, April 30, 1849; d. Phila., April 28, 1885), ALEXANDER SHEWELL (b.——— May 10, 1851; d. Phila., Jan. 17, 1881), RICHARD ASHURST (b.——— Nov. 20, 1854; m. Jan. 10, 1887, Caroline Strong), MATILDA WINTER (b. ——— Feb. 14, 1857 ; m. Nov. 5, 1879, T. Ellwood Potts), GEORGE EDWARD (b. ——— July 29, 1860; m. July 19, 1883).

33 **George Edward**[5] (John K.,[4] Robert,[3] Robert,[2] Walter[1]) was born at Philadelphia, Pa., ———. He married Jan. 6, 1855, SARAH PARKIN of Philadelphia. They had: CLARA PARKIN (b. Phila., April 22, 1858; m. Dec. 11, 1878, Monroe R. Collins, Jr., of St. Louis, Mo., and had Clara Monroe Shewell, b. July 15, 1880, and Robert Eli, b. April 29, 1886), WALTER DICKINSON (b. Phila., March 8, 1860 ; m. ———), and HORACE NEWTON (b. Phila., Feb. 9, 1862 ; m. ———).

34 **Emily Cauffman**[5] (John K.,[4] Robert,[3] Robert,[2] Walter[1]) was born Nov. 19, 1829. She married Feb. 19, 1856, F. THEODORE FISHER of ——— and had : MARY B. (b. Feb. 14, 1857 ; m. Nov. 12, 1886, James L. Dillon, and had : Florence Hazel, b. Nov. 12, 1887, and Theo. Fisher, b. Dec. 19, 1890), FLORENCE (b. Aug. 6, 1865 ; d. July 14, 1866), THEODORE (b. June 15, 1867 ; d. Feb. 11, 1868), CHRISTIAN FREDERICK (b. Dec. 22, 1869), and CLARENCE STANLEY (b. Aug. 17, 1876).

35 **Walter Dickinson**[5] (John K.,[4] Robert,[3] Robert,[2] Walter[1]) was born at Philadelphia, Feb. 22, 1828. He married, July 31, 1851, EMMA MILLER of Philadelphia, who was born July 13, 1833, and died Feb. 22, 1883. They had: MARY P. (b. April 11, 1853; m. April 17, 1882, W. H. Butler of Brooklyn, N. Y.), CHARLES T. (b. August 22, 1856; m. May 2, 1882, Cora Libby of St. Louis, Mo.), and KATIE M. (b. Jan. 3, 1858).

36 **Louise**[5] (George Stuart,[4] Robert,[3] Robert,[2] Walter[1]) was born at Philadelphia, Nov. 1, 1835, and married in May 1852, R. F. CONINGHAM, of St. Louis. She died Sept. 1, 1856. They had: ANNA (b. St. Louis, Sept. 1, 1854), and MIRIAM (b. St. Louis, July 11, 1856).

37 **George Stuart**[5] (George Stuart,[4] Robert,[3] Robert,[2] Walter[1]) was born at St. Louis, Mo., Dec. 18, 1845. He married (at Athens, Ga.) Feb. 22, 1883, IDA L. PHILLIPS of Oglethorpe Co., Ga. They had: MARY B. (b. Athens, Ga., April 25, 1884), HELENE (b. Athens, Ga., Oct. 9, 1886), and GEORGE STUART (b. Athens, Oct. 5, 1888).

38 **Marie Isabel**[5] (Edward S.,[4] Robert,[3] Robert,[2] Walter[1]) was born at Philadelphia, Pa., April 4, 1836. She married at Cincinnati, O., June 23, 1857, CHARLES R. ELLIS of Brooklyn, N. Y. CHARLES R. and MARIE I. S. ELLIS had: ADALINE ISABEL, (b. May 24, 1859; d. Oct. 31, 1879), WILLIAM H. ALLEN (b. June 25, 1861), RICHMOND (b. Aug. 14, 1863), and TERESA NEUVILLE (b. March 13, 1872; d. Aug. 2, 1872).

39 **Frederick Seymour**[5] (Edward S.,[4] Robert,[3] Robert,[2] Walter[1]) was born at Cincinnati, O., Sept. 5, 1848. He married, Oct. 5, 1871, SUSAN CLARK SLOCUM of Brooklyn, N. Y. They had: ROBERT EDWARD (b. ——— Sept. 10, 1872; d. Dec. 21, 1872), and FREDERICK SEYMOUR (b. Hinsdale, Ill., Dec. 30, 1875). He died Hinsdale, Ill., Nov. 29, 1875.

40 **Edward Milnor Donnaldson**[5] (Harriet S.[4] (Donnaldson), Elizabeth[3] (Currie), Robert,[2] Walter[1]) was born at "Green Farm," March 4, 1837. Married Dec. 29, 1864, ANNIE STAGNER of Montgomery county, Pa. He resides (1891) at "Green Farm," the family homestead since 1770, an estate of 167 acres

lying partly in Montgomery county and part in Bucks county, Pa. They had: SARAH (b. "Green Farm," July 21, 1866), RACHEL (b. " Green Farm," Jan. 24, 1872), and HELEN (b. "Green Farm," Dec. 6, 1874).

41 Linington Roberts[5] (Linington D.,[4] Thomas,[3] Robert,[2] Walter[1]) was born at Philadelphia, January 20, 1833. Although educated for a commercial career, he early evinced a strong inclination toward the stage as a profession, and made his first appearance, in a minor part, at the old Chestnut Street theatre, Philadelphia, May 10, 1852. His decided talent attracted public attention; he became a favorite in his native city 1855-56, and in Richmond, 1856-57. In 1858 he appeared in New York and was chosen to support Charlotte Cushman in a starring tour throughout the Union. In 1863 he was engaged as "leading man " at the Boston Museum and for five years held that responsible position, winning great popularity. In 1869 Mr. Shewell accepted the management of the Boston Theatre, then the largest but one in the country, performing the duties of the position with much success for a number of years. For some time he has been known as a playwright and has written a number of successful melodramas. "Scholarly without pedantry and urbane without affectation, Mr. Shewell has now seen professional service as manager and actor, for nearly a quarter of a century : and though still too young to make applicable the remark that 'Age cannot wither him,' the warmth of his receptions, whenever he performs, makes it certain that custom has not staled 'his infinite variety.' " *

Mr. Shewell married (1st) June 17, 1856, HENRIETTA M. WILKES, and had: HENRI LININGTON (b. ——— ; d. Aug. ——— 1857).

Mr. Shewell married (2d) Oct. 11, 1860, ROSE SKERRETT, and had : EDWARD GRANVILLE (b. ——— ; d. ———).

Mr. Shewell married (3d) Dec. 17, 1878, OLIVIA G. RAND, and had : EMMA DE BENNEVILLE (b. ———).

42 Sarah Linington[5] (Linington D.,[4] Thomas,[3] Robert,[2] Walter[1])

---

* Boston Transcript, June 2, 1876.

was born at Philadelphia, Nov. 2, 1835. She married ———;
JOSEPH B. CONARD of Buffalo, N. Y.

43 **Thomas Roberts**[5] (Linington D.,[4] Thomas,[3] Robert,[2] Walter[1]) was born at Philadelphia, Oct. 18, 1836.

He married Nov. 7, 1867, LAURA WOOD DAVIS of Brookline, Mass., and had:

 I. MARTHA ROBERTS, b. ———, Jan. 9, 1869.
 II. MARY SHANNON, b. ———, Nov. 2, 1870; d. ———, July 9, 1876.
 III. LAURA DAVIS, b. ———, July 5, 1875; d. ———, May 18, 1876.
 IV. JULIA ABBOT, b. ———, Aug. 19, 1877.
 V. ROBERT LININGTON, b. ———, Sept. 8, 1879.

LAURA WOOD, wife of Thomas R. Shewell[5] died at Brookline, Mass., May 26, 1889, aged 44 years.

44 **De Benneville Brown**[5] (Linington D.,[4] Thomas,[3] Robert,[2] Walter[1]) was born at Philadelphia, Sept. 1, 1838. At the outbreak of the War for the Union he enlisted in the ——— Pa. Vol Infantry ("Baxter Fire Zouaves") and served until severely wounded at Savage Station, Va. ("Seven Days' Battles"), falling into the hands of the enemy and being imprisoned for a month in Libby Prison. Upon his exchange he was taken North, suffered amputation of his leg and died from wounds and exposure at Bellevue Hospital, New York City, on July 26, 1862.

45 **Josephine Augusta Dunlap**[6] (Robert S.,[5] Sallows[4] (Dunlap), Juliana,[3] Robert,[2] Walter[1]) was born in Philada., Aug. 17, 1848. Married at Philada., May 22, 1879, to DAVID W. HUNT.

DAVID W. and JOSEPHINE A. D. HUNT had: HELEN DUNLAP (b. April 9, 1881), MARIAN WILHELMINA (b. May 15, 1883), and VIDA JOSEPHINE (b. June 25, 1889).

46 **Sallows Dunlap**[6] (James H.,[5] Sallows[4] (Dunlap), Juliana,[3] Robert,[2] Walter[1]) was born at Phila., July 1, 1849. Educated at public and private schools. He married at Phila., Feb. 1, 1883, CECILIA M. BERWIND.

They had: BERWIND SALLOWS (b. Phila. Oct. 3, 1885; d.

Phila., Dec. 1, 1887), CHARLES E. (b. Phila., Dec. 3, 1888), and MARGARET E. (b. Phila., Sept. 22, 1890).

47 **William Clayton Newell**[6] (Susan B,[5] Sallows[4] (Dunlap), Juliana,[3] Robert,[2] Walter[1]) was born at Phila., Oct. 23, 1856. He married, April 27, 1880, SARAH R. HARVEY, of Doylestown, Penn. They had: GEORGE HARVEY (b. Phila., June 24, 1881 ; d. July 28, 1881) , WILLIAM CLAYTON (b. Phila., Sept. 16, 1883), EDWARD HARVEY (b. Phila., Sept. 24, 1885) , LOUIS HENRY FIELD (b. Phila., Nov. 16, 1887) and MARIE LOUISE (b. Phila., April 4, 1890).

48 **Henry Albert Lloyd**[6] (Julia D. H.[5] (Lloyd), Ann[4] (Dunlap), Juliana,[3] Robert,[2] Walter[1]) was born at Doylestown, Pa., Nov. 12, 1849. He was educated at Princeton College and was graduated with degrees of A. B. (1869) and A. M. (1872.) He was admitted to the Bar in 1871, and married at Detroit, Mich., Nov. 8, 1871, CORNELIA POLHEMUS VOORHEES, of Princeton, N. J. He removed to St. Louis, Mo., in 1884 and was (1891) Assistant Secretary, Wabash Railway Co.

HENRY A. and CORNELIA P. V. LLOYD had : MARTIN VOORHEES (b. Phila., Sept. 20, 1872), JULIA MORRIS (b. Doylestown, Pa., April 12, 1876), HENRY DUNLAP (b. Doylestown, Pa., Jan. 4, 1878) ; ERNEST MORRIS (b. Doylestown, Pa., Feb. 19, 1880, and ARCHIBALD TALMAGE (b. St. Louis, Mo., Aug. 1885; d. July, 1886).

49 **James Hendrie Lloyd**[6] (Julia Dunlap[5] (Hendrie) Ann[4] (Dunlap), Juliana,[3] Robert,[2] Walter[1]) was born at Doylestown, Pa., Dec. 1, 1853. Educated at Princeton College, where he was graduated with degrees of A. B. (1873) and A. M. (1876), and at the University of Pennsylvania (1878) as M. D. He married at Haddonfield, N. J., Oct. 15, 1879, SUSAN DUNLAP NEWELL, of Phila. (See 26.) They had: MARION (b. Phila., Aug. 18, 1880), JAMES PAUL (b. Phila., Dec. 2, 1881), WILLIAM HENDRIE (b. Phila., Feb. 26, 1885, and VIRGINIA GROSHOLZ (b. Phila., Nov. 28, 1890).

PART II.—ROBERT SHEWELL'S LINE.

1. **Robert Shewell**[1] (brother of Walter[1]) came to Philadelphia from Gloucestershire, Eng., in 1722. (See " SHEWELL.")

He married ——, ELIZABETH BARTON of Bucks Co., Pa.,*
and had:

2.   I. STEPHEN, b. Phila., Jan. 29, 1727; m. Elizabeth Fordham; d. Dec. ——, 1809.
3. II. JOSEPH, b. Phila., Jan. 14, 1728; m. April 22, 1765, Esther Kinnersley; d. Nov. 4, 1784.
4. III. MARY, b. Phila., Feb. 7, 1731; m. Sept. 28, 1758, Abraham Bickley, Jr.; d. ——.
   IV. WILLIAM, b. Phila., Jan. 11, 1733; d. unm.
    V. ELIZABETH, b. Phila., Sept. 20, 1741; m. Sept. 7, 1765 (at "St. Martin-in-the-fields," London, Eng.) Benjamin West;† d. London, Dec. 6, 1817. They had Raphael Lamar and Benjamin.
   VI. ROBERT, b. Phila., ——; m. ——, Boyer of Maryland.

2 Stephen[2] (Robert[1]) was born at Philadelphia, Pa., Jan. 29, 1727. He was educated there and became a successful merchant.‡ He married ——, 17—, ELIZABETH FORDHAM of ——, (b. 1731; d. Oct. 10, 1794) and died at Phila., Dec. ——, 1809.

They had:

  I. ELIZABETH, b. ——, 1751; unmarried; d. June 7, 1810.
 II. MARY, b. ——; m. June 17, 1767, Isaac Hunt § of Phila.; d. ——. They had Isaac, John and James Leigh.
III. HANNAH, b. April 7, 1773; m. Feb. 2, 1794, Benj. Gibbs; d. April 3, 1856.

---

* "Robert Shewell and Elizabeth his wife bp. by Jenkins Jones at Pennipeck and rec'd in ye next day by laying on of hands." (Records of Pennipeck Ch. 1727.)

† See App. "An Elopement by Proxy" and "Benjamin West's Funeral."

‡ See App. "He Sent out his Argosies."

§ ISAAC HUNT (father of Leigh Hunt and son of Rev. Isaac Hunt, Rector of St Michael's, Bridgetown, Barb.) was b. Barbadoes, W. I., 1751; d. London, Eng., 1809. He was sent to Philadelphia to be educated; grad. University of Penn. (1765). Being an aggressive loyalist he was imprisoned in Phila. (1776) but escaped to England, was ordained to the ministry, and became tutor to the Hon. Mr. Leigh, the nephew of the Duke of Chandos. Some years before his death he became a Unitarian. He was the author of several political and religious essays.

IV. FRANCES, b. ———; m. Joseph Beddome Smith; d. ———.
They had a dau. (who m. —— Bye and had 5 children).

5.   V. LYDIA, b. —— 1776; m. —— 1793, John Lorraine (d. 1817);
d. Burlington, Iowa, 1865.

VI. STEPHEN, b. ———; unmarried; d. at sea.

VII. JOSEPH, b. ———; m. ———; d. at sea.

3 Joseph² (Robert¹) was born at Philadelphia, Pa., Jan. 14, 1728. He was educated in that city and became a member of the firm of Stephen and Joseph Shewell, shipping and importing merchants of Philadelphia (about 1760–75). He married, April 22, 1765, ESTHER* (b. Nov. 13, 1740), daughter of Professor Ebenezer Kinnersley of Philadelphia,† (Professor of Oratory and Belle Lettres, Coll. of Philada.) and died at Philadelphia, Nov. 4, 1784.
They had:

    I. SARAH, b. March 8, 1767; d. (unmarried) 1822.

    II. BENJAMIN, b. July 7, 1770, became owner and commander of ship *Manchester* and d. (unmarried) Liverpool, Eng., 1798.

6.   III. ELIZABETH, b. March 30, 1772; m. Oct. 12, 1791, Edward Swift; d. March 9, 1850.

4 Mary² (Robert,¹) was born at Philadelphia, Pa., Feb. 7, 1731. She married, Sept. 28, 1758, ABRAHAM BICKLEY, JR‡., and died at ———.

ABRAHAM and MARY (Shewell) BICKLEY had seven children: MARGUERITE, LYDIA, HANNAH, ELIZABETH, ISAAC, ABRAHAM and ROBERT, who all died unmarried.

5 Lydia³ (Stephen,² Robert¹) was born at Philadelphia, in 1776, married at ———, on ———, 1793, JOHN LORRAINE, and died at Burlington, Iowa, on Jan. 12, 1865. He died at ———, on ———, 1817.

---

*ESTHER KINNERSLEY, daughter of Rev. E. Kinnersley and Sarah Duffield, his wife, was b. Phila., Nov. 13, 1740, and d. May 19, 1773.

† See App. "Franklin to Kinnersley."

‡ ABRAHAM BICKLEY, SR., was a prominent merchant and citizen of Philadelphia and a member of the House of Representatives of the Province of Pennsylvania, 1708–9, 1717, 1721, 1724, 1725.

JOHN and LYDIA (Shewell) LORRAINE had :
  I. ELIZABETH, b. Germantown, Pa., 1795 ; m. Joseph Swift of Easton ; d. Easton, Pa., May, 1872.
  II. MARTHA, b. Germantown, 1797 ; d. unm. Burlington, Ia., Sept. 8, 1878.
  III. HANNAH, b. Germantown, 1804 ; died young.
  IV. MARY, b. Germantown, 1806 ; d. Easton, Pa., 1832.
  V. LYDIA, b. Germantown, 1807 ; d. Germantown, Nov. 21, 1809.
  VI. FRANCES, b. Germantown, 1809 ; d. Germantown, 1849.
  VII. JOSEPHINE, b. Germantown, 1810 ; m. Chas. Hendrie of Burlington, Iowa (no children) ; d. Jan. 27, 1881.
  VIII. OCTAVIA, b. Germantown, 1811 ; m. (about 1849) Lyman Cook of Burlington, Iowa, and had : Henry Trevor* (b. 1847 ; d. 1887) and Mary Frances† (b. Oct. 14, 1850 ; d. Easton, Pa., 1856.
7. IX. JOHN SHEWELL, b. Germantown, July 29, 1812 ; m, Dec. 5, 1845, Virginia L. Litle of Galena, Ill. ; d. St. Louis, Mo., March 30, 1886.
  X. STEPHEN SHEWELL, b. Germantown, July, 1814 ; m. (1850) Marcia Moulton‡ of Galena, Ill. ; d. ———, Aug. 1863 : had Eugene (d. young), Josephine (b. 1855 ; m. Wallace Campbell and had 4 children), Walter (d. young), and Susan (b. 1864 ; m. Chas. Ransom of Chicago).

6 Elizabeth[3] (Joseph,[2] Robert[1]) was born at Philadelphia, March 30, 1772.

She married, ———, Oct. 12, 1791, EDWARD SWIFT,§ of Moreland, Pa., and died at Philadelphia, March 9, 1850.

---

* HENRY TREVOR COOK, m. Lizzie, dau. of C. W. Hempstead, of Chicago and had : Margery and Lorraine.

† MARY FRANCES COOK, m. Thos. Hedge of Burlington, Ia., and had : Thomas, Lyman, Anna and Henry Lorraine.

‡ MARCIA MOULTON LORRAINE, m. (2d.) Chas. W. Hempstead, of Chicago (who d. ———).

§ EDWARD SWIFT, son of John Swift, of Moreland, Pa., and Phœbe Comly, his wife. Born Oct. 4, 1736 ; m. Feb. 21, 1764 ; died Dec. 29, 1813. Phœbe Comly was a descendant of Henry and Jean Comly, who came from England with William Penn in 1682. She was born Feb. 15, 1737; died Dec. 26, 1813.

EDWARD and ELIZABETH (Shewell) SWIFT had:
  I. JOHN, b. Nov. 17, 1792; d. Sept. ———, 1799.
  II. JOSEPH KINNERSLEY, b. March 10, 1795; grad. at ———, ( ) and became a physician; m. Elizabeth Shewell Lorraine (who d. 1872); d. Easton, Pa. April 9, 1871.
  III. SARAH, b. Jan. 10, 1797; d. Jan. 14, 1813.
  IV. MARY, b. Dec. 21, 1799; m. Nov. 26, 1817, Caleb Boutcher; d. March 30, 1842. They had: Elizabeth Swift, Edward Swift, Charles Swift and Caroline Swift (who m. Edward Hart Green, April 22, 1863, and died Jan. 25, 1880. They had John Traill, Charles Boutcher, Edward Hart and Juliette Hart).
  V. SAMUEL, b. Jan. 3, 1801; m. ———. Mary Thompson; d. Aug. 3, 1864. They had Catharine, Joseph Kinnersley, Henry (who m. Julia Stockdale, and had: Henry, Louise and Marguerite), Robert Bickley, Mary (who m. C. W. Taylor and had: Samuel Swift, William and Julia Brock)* and Samuel.
  VI. CAROLINE, b. Mar. 22, 1803; m. ———, John Trump; d. Sept 1835. They had: Frances Caroline† and Charles.
8 VII. EDWARD, b. Jan. 15, 1805; m. Mar. 18, 1832, Hannah Robeson; d. Nov. 6, 1869.
  VIII. JOHN, b. Mar. 15, 1808; m. May 6, 1834, Jane Galloway Swift; d. Mar. 10, 1872.
9 IX. CHARLES, b. May 30, 1810: m. (1) Mar. 22, 1833, Mary Sheetz; (2) Oct. 31, 1848, Mary Mattes; (3) Dec. 7, 1854, Emily A. Schott.
  X. HENRY, b. Mar. 6, 1814; d. April 4, 1829.

7 **John Shewell Lorraine** (Lydia,[3] Stephen,[2] Robert[1]) was born at Germantown, July 19, 1812. He married Dec. 5, 1844, VIRGINIA L. LITLE of Galena, Ills., and died in St. Louis, Mo., March 30, 1886, and was buried at Galena.

* JULIA BROCK TAYLOR m. Edmond Harrison and had two children.
† FRANCES C. TRUMP m. Edmond G. Harrison and had: Robert, Charles (who m. Laura Curtis), Caroline, Mary R. (who m. Dr. Edwin S. Huntsman), William Emslie, Alice Kinnersley, Lillian Middleton, Francis and Theodora Herbert.

They had:

I. LYDIA, b. ———, Aug. 1845; d. July 29, 1855.
II. MARY, b. ———, 1847; d. ———, 1847.
III. CELESTINE FRANCES, b. Sept. 19, 1848; m. Feb. 9, 1875, W. P. Hazard, of St. Louis, and had: Lorraine (b. Nov. 5, 1876; died April 4, 1877), William Evan (b. April 19, 1878), Virginia Laura Lorraine (b. Oct. 24, 1880), and Stanton Leigh Hunt (b. June 13, 1885).
IV. FRANK, b. Sept. 14, 1850; d. 1851.
V. MADISON J., b. Sept. 15, 1853; m. Dec. 5, 1877, Caroline V. Conklin, of Galena, Ill,, and had Claude (b. Jan., 1878; d. April, 1879), Grant (b. June, 1879), Percy (b. Nov. 1880), and Litle (b. June 10, 1885; d. 1887).
VI. CLAUDE LITLE, b. July, 1857; d. Sept. 20, 1865.
VII. JOHN SHEWELL, b. Feb. 23, 1863.
VIII. MAUDE HELEN, b. Galena, Ill., May 2, 1867; m. Oct. 8, 1891, Beauregard Lorraine, of Richmond, Va.

8 Edward[4] (Elizabeth[3] (Swift), Joseph,[2] Robert[1]) was born at ———, Jan. 15, 1805. He was educated at ———, and graduated and received degree of M. D. at University of Penna. He married Mar. 18, 1832, HANNAH ROBESON, of Bustleton, and died at Easton, Pa., Nov. 6, 1869.

They had:

I. EDWARD, b. Feb. 19, 1833; d. Bustleton, Pa., April 7, 1834.
II. SARAH, b. Easton, Pa., Aug. 16, 1834.
III. JOHN, b. Easton, Pa., June 3, 1836; m. Aug. 11, 1869, Gabriella Du Pont Breck,, of Scranton, Pa.; d. Oct. 31, 1880. They had: William Breck (b. June 23, 1871; d. April 23, 1872), Edward (b. 1873), Charles Du Pont Breck (b. Aug. 25, 1875), George Breck (b. July 15, 1877; d. Aug. 1, 1878) and Amelia Elizabeth (b. Feb. 1, 1880).
IV. JOSEPH ROBESON, b. Easton, Pa., July 31, 1838; d. March 30, 1839.
V. BEATES ROBESON, b. Easton, Pa., Feb. 1, 1840; m. Sept. 18, 1867, Mary Araminta Mercein, of Jersey City, N. J. They had: Stanbury Mercein (b. Feb. 26, 1870; d. Nov.

29, 1872), Edward Robeson (b. Dec. 15, 1871; d. Jan. 13, 1872), Helen Mercein (b. April 16, 1873; d. Aug. 3, 1873), Louise Mercein (b. Sept. 1, 1874), James Mercein (b. Jan. 7, 1876; d. Jan. 7, 1876), Robeson Kinnersley (b. Dec. 30, 1877), and Francis Bacon (b. March 6, 1880).

VI. EDWARD CLEMENT, b. Easton, Pa., Jan. 30, 1842. Graduated at University of Pennsylvania (186-), and took degree of M. D.

VII. CHARLES KINNERSLEY, b. Easton, Pa., July 30, 1846; m. Oct. 18, 1887, Sarah Pollock, of Easton. They had: Douglas Pollock (b. Oct. 10, 1888; d. June 9, 1889) and Clement Kinnersley (b. ———, 1890).

VIII. HENRY, b. Easton, Pa., Sept. 21, 1848; m. Oct. 4, 1875, Matilda A. Hays, of Pittsburg. He was ordained to the Protestant Episcopal ministry (———), served as missionary among the Indians (———), and was appointed Post Chaplain U. S. Army, Jan. 21, 1887. They had: Henry Thomas (b. Aug. 31, 1876) and Francis Joseph (b. Nov. 15, 1878).

9 Charles[4] (Elizabeth[3] (Swift), Joseph,[2] Robert[1]) was born at the Homestead, Moreland Township, Pa., May 30, 1810. He married (1) March 18, 1832, MARY ANNA, daughter of the Rev. George Sheetz of Sandyford, Pa. (who died Oakland Falls, Mo., March 29, 1846).

They had:

I. GEORGE, b. Sandyford, Pa., July 4, 1833; m. Nov. 24, 1859, Frances A. Gardner. They had: Charles F.* (b. Oct. 24, 1860), George Joseph (b. July 4, 1862), Emila Eliza (b. Jan. 29, 1864), Mary Frances (b. Feb. 1, 1869), and Jane (b. Aug. 22, 1872).

II. ANNA, b. Easton, Pa., July 31, 1835; m. Aug. 3, 1857, Horatio Hubbard Hayden. They had: Martha May (b. July 18, 1858), Charles Edward (b. Mch. 17, 1860), Sarah Sill b. Feb. 28, 1862), Horatio Hubbard (b. Nov. 26, 1864), Anna Gabrielle (b. June 18, 1869), Mary Gertrude (b. Sept. 20, 1873), Eugene Capelle (b. Aug. 29, 1876), and Evelyn Shewell (b. May 10, 1881).

*Married, July 3, 1889, LETTY BINDWELL of Streator, Ill.

III. CHARLES, b. South Easton, Pa., Jan. 31, 1837; m. (1) Aug. 14, 1862, Mary G. Green (who d. March 20, 1875); (2) Nov. 3, 1886, Mary C. Hopkins. He had by first wife, Frederick Ellis* (b. May 19, 1863), William Green (b. Mch. 3 1865), Mary Anna (b. Mch. 10, 1871), and Arthur Woodruff (b. Feb. 12, 1873).

IV. FREDERICK, b. South Easton, Pa., June 8, 1839; m. (1) Sept. 4, 1867, Deborah Fletcher (who d. Troy, N. Y., Nov. 12, 1871); (2) Sept. 20, 1874, Catharine Mitchell. By first wife, one child (died June 7, 1871).

V. JOHN HENRY, b. Oakland, Mo., Aug. 20, 1842; d. near Henderson, Ky., June 14, 1846.

VI. EUGENE CAPELLE, b. Oakland, Mo., April 20, 1844; m. Oct. ———, 1871, Sarah Carman; d. Petersburg, Ill., Jan. 3, 1882. They had: Eugene Lee (b. July 22, 1873), William Frederick (b. Jan. 15, 1874), Hayden (b. Feb. 17, 1876), and Roy Wright (b. April 18, 1880).

VII. MARY, b. Oakland, Mo., March 13, 1846; m. Jan. 12, 1875, George A. Stearns (who d. Nov. 30, 1877). They had: Willard Dickerson (b. Oct. 18, 1875), and Georgia Anna (b. Sept. 3, 1877).

CHARLES SWIFT[1] married (2d) Oct. 31, 1848, MARY GERTRUDE MATTES, (by Rev. P. L. Jaques) of Easton, Pa. (who died at Easton, Oct. 14, 1853).

They had:

VIII. KATHARINE MATTES, b. Easton, Pa., Jan. 1, 1850; d. ———.

IX. ELIZABETH SHEWELL, b. Scranton, Pa., Jan. 30, 1852; d. Easton, Pa., Jan. 16, 1853.

CHARLES SWIFT[1] married (3d) Dec. 7, 1854, EMILY A. SCHOTT of Kingston, Pa.

They had:

X. EDWARD SCHOTT, b. Scranton, Pa., Oct. 16, 1855; m. Oct. 21, 1886, Janet Everts, and had: Lawrence Dudley (b. Feb. 29, 1888).

---

* Married, Nov. 15, 1888, ELIZABETH BROWN of Shelby Co., Mo., and had Penelope Swift, b. Hunnewell, Mo., Sept. 12, 1889.

An Ancestor's Letter Book.*

I.—TO BUCKRIDGE SIMS, ESQ., PHILA.

KINGSTON, JAMAICA, May 29, 1766. After a very pleasant and agreeable passage of nineteen days from our capes, am once more arrived to Kingston, but at the same time, am sorry to say, to but indifferent marketts; and they have been so, for some time past, owing to such vast quantities coming from Maryland and Virginia. On the 19th and 20th we had great rejoicing and illuminations, on account of the happy news of the Stamp Act being repealed, and nothing was drank but long life to the great patriot, Mr. Pitt, and the glorious North Americans. I will assure you, my friend, that America has got great honour by their noble spirit in opposing that infernal act.†

Let me beg you will take good care of my dear wife, committed

---

*From a letter book containing copies of mercantile correspondence, in the handwriting and over the signature of Robert Shewell,² a few extracts of more or less interest are selected. Mr. Shewell was a member of the firm of Oldman and Shewell, commission merchants, in Philadelphia and the West Indies, 1765-67.

† The stamps were embossed on a coarse bluish paper and bore the device of the English rose, crowned, surrounded by the motto of the Garter. At the left of the crown was the letter "A." Above was the word "America" and below, the value. On the face of the stamp at the right might be seen an oblong space, showing where a piece of lead or tin was inserted, by which the stamp was attached to the document, passing through them both, and covered behind by a counterstamp, somewhat smaller, bearing the device of a crown and the cypher G. R. This counterstamp was printed on similar but usually white paper.

FACSIMILES OF BRITISH STAMPS.

to your charge on my departure, for should any accident happen to me before my return, I know of no friend on earth I could put more confidence in than yourself to discharge that trust. My love to my sister, and may God bless you with a lovely boy and girl against my return, the former with its father's disposition, and the latter inheriting its mother's virtues, is the sincere prayer of, dear Sims,* yours affectionately, ROBT. SHEWELL.

II.—TO EDWARD SPENCE, ESQ., ST. LUCIA.

Kingston, June 28, 1766.—I am very glad to find your friends and relations are so willing for you to pay your addresses to the pretty, sensible and, what is still more endearing, the virtuous Miss Ay—Sh—, who I am certain is capable of making my friend completely happy, and I am confirmed by some conversation that passed between her honoured father and myself that you may have her for asking for; so you may see there is nothing wanting but your presence to complete matters. I will assure you have a good friend in Mrs. Shewell, who, you may depend, will render you all the services in her power. I shall write Mr. Shippen by Hardcastle, who will sail for Philadelphia in about two weeks time, and it's my opinion you had much better write to the old gentleman, and I will inclose it in mine. . . .

III.—TO DOCTOR JOHN KEARSLEY, PHILA.

Kingston, August 6, 1766.—I received a letter from Mrs. Shewell some time since, wherein she informed me that you desired I might purchase on your account a quantity of Jesuits' Bark, but as it has been a very scarce article, could not find any but what was in the Apothecaries hands, and they asked 15/ P. lb.; a few days ago I found one scaroom which was partly ingaged, but as the doctor it was for

---

\# BUCKRIDGE SIMS was Lieutenant "Independent Company of Foot" in Phila., 1756, comprising among its members Robert Barclay, William Bingham, Thomas Cadwallader and Samuel McCall. (Pa. Mag. Vol. IV, p. 350.) He died at Phila. Sept. 27, 1799, aged 78, and was buried by the side of his wife in Christ Churchyard. His wife was Elizabeth, third daughter of Evan Morgan of Phila., whose sister married William Masters (see Robert[2] Shewell). Mrs. Sims died May 30th, 1798, aged 57 ; the following is engraved upon her tombstone : " And left her disconsolate Husband to mourn her loss, in humble hope that he shall hereafter meet her again in a better world where sin and sorrow will be no more."

did not want the whole, he spared me the one-half at the same price he gave for it ; so, after having the opinion of three doctors of my acquaintance who assured me of its being good, I purchased it for you and have shipped it on board the ship *Rachel*, William Hardcastle, master. It amounts to £30. 6. 6, this currency, which makes £34. 4. 6 your currency. . . Let me beg you will take good care of my dear family. A vessel arrived here the other day in a very short passage from London, and brings us account of this port being made free for all nations, which, if true, will be the means of making money, once more, plenty in this flourishing city. . .

IV.—TO MR. JOHN JARMAN, KINGSTON.

Philadelphia, Jan. 15, 1767.—Dear Sir: I have now the pleasure to acquaint you of my safe arrival after a pleasant and agreeable passage of twenty-seven days; I had the supreme happiness to find my dear little family in good health. My fever continued many days after I left your place, but, thank God, I am now pretty well recovered. As you know, my friend, there is nothing like good nursing, which I have not wanted, since my arrival, with my dear Sally. . . .

V.—TO MESSRS. S. AND J. SHEWELL, PHILA.

Brig. Ann, off Cape Henlopen, April 21, 1767.—I have just time to acquaint you of my getting safe on board the Brig at Rudy Island, tho' with some difficulty, as it blew exceeding hard the day I left town. I am of the opinion the Brig will do very well as she is stiff and sails well. I beg you will render Sally any little service she may want at moving, as I have nobody else can depend on but yourselves. I have made bold to appoint your S. S. Ex. and Guardian for my dear wife and child, for fear any accident should happen me on my passage, or before my return, and should that be the case, let me intreat you to take them under your fatherly care, as I forgot to mention it before my departure from home. Please to make an apology to your families for not taking leave of them in form, as I found that task too severe to undertake.

VI.—TO MR. S. OLDMAN, ST. LUCIA.

Kingston, Jamaica, May 23, 1767.—I take this opportunity to acquaint you of my safe arrival once more to this place, after a passage of twenty-eight days from our Capes; tho' I had the pleasure of receiving both yours and our friend Spence's letters before my departure from home, and he has nothing to fear with respect to his love affair with the amiable Miss A. S., as I have made such intercession with her good parents that they assured me from the character I gave of my friend, that if it proved agreeable to the young lady, that their consent should not be wanting, and even promised that they would use their interest in his behalf. I left a letter for Spence with my wife, who has promised me she will introduce him to his charmer, and will render him all the services in her power. I make no doubt but you'll see her out with him next fall.* . . .

VII.—TO BUCKRIDGE SIMS, ESQ., PHILA.

Kingston, July 6, 1767.—I arrived here the 26th of May after a long and tedious passage of twenty-eight days from the Capes, and in good health; and, since, have disposed of the greatest part the cargo, I brought, to a very good advantage. I am now indeavouring to settle my old affairs, that I may, as soon as possible, transport my body where my whole soul and affections dwell; when I shall again injoy what I now contemplate as my greatest happiness,—the conversation of a real friend in whose company disappointments lose their weight and pleasures receive their greatest addition.

I am obliged for the pleasing account you gave me of my dear wife and family, which I had the happiness of having confirmed under her own hand, forwarded by you, for which I return you my hearty thanks.

I am exceeding sorry our poor sister Masters is in such a bad state of health, and I sincerely wish she may receive the wished for relief from Doctors Bond and Water; tho' should it not turn out so, and the Almighty should think her ripe for Heaven, we ought not repine at his divine dispensation, but rather say, " Not my will but Thine be done." I pray most sincerely we may all be prepared for Heaven as well as she, let her go when she will, and my dear friend, we ought all of us indeavour to make as good a provision as possible against the coming of that great and awfull day of the Lord, . . . as we must all inevitably see it one time or other. It is with concern I observe what you relate of our great and mighty wheat merchants, not so much on their own account as the consequence that must attend the community

---

* " Edward Spence and Abigail Shippen m. Sept 26, 1767." (" Marriages in Penn."—*Pa. Archives*, V. 2, p. 273.)

in general by so severe a shock, in which I am sorry to find you will be such a considerable loser, and can heartily sympathize with you on the occasion, having so often experienced things of that kind.

I am happy to learn my dear sister is so much better than when I left you, and sincerely hope that your fears, which I well know, to be founded on your unbounded love, and that she will live long to make you happy as a father as well as a husband, and sooth your cares in this weary Wild.

VIII.—TO MR. JAMES DICK, JAMAICA.

Philadelphia, Feb. 3, 1768.—There is nothing stirring amongst us except that of an Indian War, which is generally thought will be very soon, as there have been numbers of Indians lately murdered by some of the back inhabitants, which has inraged the poor savage much; especially as the government did not take that notice they ought, in calling the blood-thirsty villains to account. I am in hopes they will very soon, as there is a number of the Indians come down, as our Assembly is now sitting and one of them this day informed me they had this matter under their consideration, and that they were determined to bring them all to justice. . .

IX.—TO MR. THOMAS DENNIE, KINGSTON, JAMAICA.

Philadelphia, Feb. 3, 1768.—I imagine you are accusing me of a breach of promise, but had I not been disappointed in sending my letter, you would have heard from me long before this. Your little boys are both in good health, and Mr. Kenersley* who is one of the Masters in the College, assures me Harry will make as fine a youth as ever was turned of the school, as he is uncommonly assiduous in his study; Bob being so young and wild, is not yet admitted into the College, as they take none there that can't read, but I make no doubt but time will make as clever a fellow of him as master Harry.

I have imployed a limner, most recommended for his art in portrait painting, to take both their faces, and I hope the likeness may be answerable to the merit he claims in that way. They are to be done by the time I sail for your place, which will be sometime in April, and shall bring them myself. . .

---

* Kinnersley (?).

X.—TO CAPT. NATHANIEL FALCONER, LONDON.*

Philadelphia, Nov. 7, 1768.—Dear Sir: I should esteem it a particular favour if you would call at the Navy Pay Office and learn how Sally's brother James Stone's account stands with the Crown. He was either Surgeon or Surgeon's mate on board His Majesty's Ship of War the *Levant*, Wm. Tucker, Esq., Commander. I have letters from him dated in St. Christopher's, March 17, 1761, from on board this ship; he was also at the taking of Martinico, but falling sick there he changed ships with the Doctor of the Sloop of War the *Zephyr* in order to go to England for his health; but he died two days after his arrival in Portsmouth: if there should be anything worth while we can get the requisites made out to send by you, the next voyage, to recover it, and any expenses you may be at in examining the office shall be repaid with thanks. I forgot, in my directions about my gun, to beg you to get a thing (I cannot tell what they call it) to prevent its going off half-cocked. Your wife is in good health, as also all friends. Sally presents her kindest respects. . .

XI.—TO WILLIAM JONES, ESQ., KINGSTON.

Philadelphia, June 21, 1769.—I have built a convenient house † in the county of Bucks, about twenty miles from town, a most healthy and pleasant part of the country, and I think it necessary to inform you how we shall be accommodated as to a school, that you may judge whether you would have Neddy to remain with us or to be boarded with some careful person in town. There is at present, very near where we shall be settled, a master who teaches reading, writing and arithmetick very well, and we are in expectations, in a short time, of one who has had his education in our College, to keep an Academy within half a mile of us. I am informed he is well qualified for such an undertaking, and as I have some personal acquaintance with him, know him to be a man of a good character and of untainted morals. . .

---

*See letter from Gov. Mifflin addressed " NATHANIEL FALCONER, Master Warden of the Port of Philadelphia" also Member Council of Safety, Phila., July, 1776. (*Penna. Archives*, V. 4, p. 332.)

† " Painswick Hall," New Britain Township, Bucks Co., Pa.

Reminiscences of Painswick Hall.

BY THOMAS FASSITT SHEWELL.*

"AS my father THOMAS SHEWELL,² the next youngest child of Robert and Sarah Shewell to your grandmother Sarah Cauffman, had a firm belief in the benefit of country air, he dispatched us all every Spring to my Aunt Currie; she was living on a farm of 70 acres purchased by my father for her—adjoining Painswick—on the western side of Featherbed Hill and part of the original estate of our great-grandfather Walter Shewell, who settled there in the time of the second Penn, about 1725, and where, to keep us out of mischief, we went to school, kept in 1818, and for some years after, by one Pickering; to this school also came the children of the neighboring families—the Matthews, James, Fitzingers, Dungans, Blacks, *et al.*

"Of our great-grandfather WALTER,¹ I have heard but little, only that he was very like our grandfather in character and appearance. There is a well-authenticated tradition that he took charge of and caused to be buried the body of the famous Indian Chief TAMENEND,† with whom Penn made his treaty of Shakamaxon—a treaty

---

* The letter containing these " Reminiscences " was addressed to the Editor.

† A few words may be devoted to an Indian who achieved so honorable a distinction in the calendar of saints. His name is variously spelled TAMANEN, TAMANEND, TAMANAND, and finally TAMANY. The earliest record of Tamanen is the affix of his mark to a deed, dated the 23d day of the 4th mo., 1683, by which he and Metamequan conveyed to the Proprietary, Penn, a tract of land lying between the creeks Pennypack and Neshaminy, in Bucks County. In 1683 " William Penn visits King Tamany at Perkasie." Long after this the good chief passed away, at a ripe old age, but the memory of his exalted character remained as a priceless treasure among his people, and also, as it appears, among the whites. " When Col. Geo. Morgan of Princeton, N. J., was, about the year 1776, sent by Congress as an agent to the Western Indians, the Delawares conferred on him the name of Tamanend in honour and remembrance of their ancient chief, and as the greatest mark of respect which they could show to that gentleman, who, they said, had the same address, affability, and meekness as their honored chief, and therefore ought to be named after him." " In the Revolutionary War his enthusiastic admirers dubbed him a saint and he was established under the name of St. Tamany, the Patron Saint of America."

which is recorded as never having been broken. The Chief was buried on the rise of Prospect Hill, about three miles from Painswick, (where a spring burst out) with a tree at the head and foot of the grave; when I was a child it was a favorite trysting place for Strephon and Phyllis. One of Tamanend's sons was afterwards buried by his side and two more in New Britain churchyard. But although there is a St. Tammany's Society in Philadelphia and the Tammany Association has been a political power in New York, no effort has been made to preserve the grave or mark the spot where the great friend of the white settlers of the State of Pennsylvania takes his repose.

"The last time I visited it the trees had been cut down and the plow had passed over it—*sic transit gloria mundi!*

> On sunny slope and beechen swell,
> The shadowed light of evening fell ;
> And, where the maple's leaf was brown,
> With soft and silent lapse came down,
> The glory, that the wood receives,
> At sunset, in its brazen leaves.
>
> . . . .
>
> But soon a funeral hymn was heard
> Where the soft breath of evening stirred
> The tall, gray forest ; and a band
> Of stern in heart, and strong in hand,
> Came winding down beside the wave,
> To lay the red chief in his grave.*

"Of course, until his death in the winter of 1823-24, at 84 years our Grandfather, ROBERT,[2] † at Painswick where he resided with

---

His name, as a saint, appeared in almanacs, and his festival was celebrated in many cities with considerable pomp on the first day of May in every year. (Penna. Mag. Hist. Biog. VIII., 204.)

* Longfellow.

† Before I went to sea, few boys were more mischievous than myself; two or three of my companions were much the same—ROBERT SHEWELL, Townsend White, Frank Munny, W. Budden, who was some years older than either of us, S. Hepburn, and Esquire Forman. . . . One day Shewell persuaded me, without much difficulty, to take a very large imported horse belonging to Mr. Gray, a brewer, out of the stable. We rode this horse, without anything but a halter up to Chestnut Hill, where we both had relatives, to buy some fowls upon credit, for we had no money. Upon our return, Shewell, according to agree-

Uncle Nathaniel, was the great source of attraction to us children, who one and all idolized him ; each on entering the house seeking his room at once to greet him with affection and respect. On one occasion of a thunderstorm, when driven into the house by stress of weather, we counted up thirty-two grandchildren surrounding him in a circle at one time. This room was on the ground floor looking towards the meadows, and here he sat during the last years of his life, smoking innumerable cigars with a silver holder or mouthpiece (which I now have in my possession); his feet upon one end of a Franklin stove let into the chimney—which shows the rubbing of his slippers yet. He was upwards of six feet in height, blue eyed and of prominent features, genial and full of anecdote—a perfect gentleman of the old school,—full of consideration for the smallest and weakest of his species. As he lived among a people of only common education, composed mostly of Welsh and Germans—the first high tempered, the last obstinate—and as he delighted in the character of a peacemaker ("Blessed are the peacemakers" being engraven on his tomb as appropriate to his life and habit of mind), he applied for the appointment of magistrate and was thus enabled to settle many disputes. It was fashionable among the young folks intent on matrimony, to go to the Hall to be married by Squire Shewell, and many anecdotes are told of occurrences on those occasions ; as that he was accustomed to assign the marriage fees to his daughters, for a month in turn, for pin money; that, in one case, on departing, the groom put in the Squire's hand something wrapped up in white paper, which was afterwards found to contain a bright, silver "quarter," much to the chagrin of the fair recipient.

"UNCLE WALTER,[2] —who had sold the farm above mentioned to the Curries, retaining about ten acres, on which he had built a cottage—was ten years older than Grandfather and lived very happily with his wife, Aunt Rachel, a lively little black-eyed Dutchwoman, possessing at 84 the elements of former beauty. Uncle Walter had

---

ment, took the horse back to the stable. The Sunday following, we were in the brewhouse yard when one of the porters, who had seen Shewell bring the horse home, caught him and beat him very severely. At this time Shewell was not more than thirteen years of age : I was two years younger. ("Autobiography of Charles Biddle," Vice-President, Supreme Executive Council of Pennsylvania, 1745-1821, Phila., 1883.)

been a man above six feet high and of vigorous frame. A favorite spot with him was under a large mulberry tree, where the children would gather around and listen to his anecdotes. One, I remember, was that when 12 years old (1744) his father had given him a calf that was stunted in its growth, which he played with as a pet and finally harnessed and drove in a species of dogcart. Upon one occasion, going to the store on Iron Hill, about three miles from Painswick, he had to pass the farm of the Blacks at the foot of the hill—then and still famous for its fine grazing qualities, having fine large meadows bordering the road. Seeing the herd near the fence and looking round to know that he was not observed, he unharnessed his bull, and letting down the bars to admit the bull from the herd into the road—retreated to the top of the fence to enjoy, all alone, his bull fight. This incident marks, I think, a curious courage in one so young, arising perhaps from the wild state of the surrounding country, Indians still being about, having encamped on the Painswick farm; our Grandmother Shewell, many years after this event often receiving from them the present of a buck; rewarding them in return with tobacco and the privilege of sleeping upon the floor of the kitchen at Painswick.

"UNCLE SALLOWS[3] was, like the rest, of large frame, and as I remember him of stooping figure. He had been at one time a large merchant in Philadelphia, prominent in the City Council, etc., but failed in business about 1800 and died in 1818.

"UNCLE NATHANIEL[3] was a bluff old man, inheriting from his mother (who was originally a Baptist but was converted to Restorationism by the celebrated Elhanan Winchester, who was her pastor at the First Baptist Church) Restoration views. He seceded from the family church after a particularly hot Baptist sermon. 'D—n him!' said our worthy uncle, 'he said we'd all be damned; I won't go to hear him any more,' and he never did. He was very strong, being able to lift two or three times as much as ordinary men.

"UNCLE JAMES DUNLAP was a contemporary of Uncle Nat's, but possessed a quiet equable disposition which nothing could disturb. It accounted in a great measure for his good health and long life. He was also vigorous, but of thin physique, and told me, three weeks before his death at the age of 94, that when young men he 'and Nat could run and jump over a string suspended six feet from the ground between two posts and kept in place by two stones.'

"UNCLE ROBERT[2] was a twin with Aunt Elizabeth, and married a very handsome woman, Miss Dickinson. When walking together they attracted universal attention for their distinguished appearance. He died when comparatively young.

"UNCLE SAMUEL CURRIE was amiable but extremely deaf. He was somewhat of a wag, and amused us frequently by remarking after a hearty meal, ' Excuse me, children, I have no appetite.'

"My father THOMAS[3] was the youngest son of my grandfather Robert. He was very delicate in constitution, remaining so until his death in 1848 at seventy-four. He spent three years in England, 1797–99. Shortly after his return he married Miss Linington, the granddaughter of Dr. Geo. de Benneville, Sr., of a French Huguenot family ; she was a beautiful woman, who was of great aid in encouraging him in his early struggles in business. He was very successful in establishing a name and credit in this city that was almost unexampled, so that 25 years after his death an old Philadelphian speaking of the merchants of his day 'whose names had a perfume about them,' first mentioned that of Thomas Shewell. He was genial and pleasant in his manner, very shrewd in thought and constantly sought as an adviser in delicate matters of business and family. He was tall but slender in person with prominent features. He was gifted with a quick perception of the humorous in life, and, like his father, full of anecdote. Like him, too, he was a peacemaker, and was often engaged in quieting the angry passions of men—in which his shrewdness as a business man gave him great influence.

" He was for many years a director of the House of Refuge ; he had personal care of 8 or 10 boys (as is one of the rules of the house) and on his tri-weekly visits filled his pockets with cake and apples to reward those, among them, the Superintendent reported most deserving. In his walks about the city—which he indulged in, daily, after his retirement, to the extent of 10 or 12 miles—he often met ' his boys '; who would hail him by name and on asking who they were would be referred to their residence at the Refuge and his kindness to them there.

" My recollections of my numerous Aunts are without exception delightful. Of AUNT CURRIE, the most gentle, ever ready to comfort us in our childish trials and never, even when we were mischievous, had she an angry word for any. She was still more loveable—if that were possible—than AUNT SALLY—your grandmother; for the last named had a more spirited nature. AUNT CYNTHIA (Uncle Nat's wife) was also noted for her amiability and the quiet influence she possessed over her impulsive but stern husband. AUNT JULIA DUNLAP died before my time. AUNT BETSY and AUNT SALLY CAUFFMAN I remember well: they were both ladies of refinement and socially esteemed. Indeed this seems to have been characteristic of all the women of the family, MRS. WEST, a simple hearted country girl of Bucks County, becoming a cherished friend of Queen Charlotte and with her niece, MRS. HUNT (the mother of Leigh Hunt), was received everywhere at the English Court. Others became wives of some of the principal landholders along the Delaware, as the Gordons, Lardners, Bickleys, Bouchers, etc."

The Founder of a Creed.

ON Thursday, June 12, 1890, the attention of Universalists, all over the United States, was centred upon a unique observance conducted near the time-honored settlement of Oley, in Berks County, a few miles from Reading, Pa. In an old mansion near that village the one hundred and fifty-fifth anniversary of the founding of Universalism in America, by Dr. George de Benneville, was celebrated. Representative Universalists from all the strongholds of that belief, on that day, made a pilgrimage of love and affection to the home built in 1745 by De Benneville, the real founder and first teacher, in this country, of the gospel of Universal Restoration as it is now received.

Readers of ecclesiastical history, particularly in New England, are disposed to ascribe the credit of planting that creed in the new world to the Rev. John Murray, who achieved great prominence and success while identified with Universalist missionary work in New England during the Revolutionary war. But Murray did not set foot on the New Jersey shore until 1770, and did not settle in Gloucester, Mass. (erroneously regarded as the American cradle of Universalism), until 1779; whereas De Benneville came hither from Europe as early as 1741, and preached here the new dispensation, unremittingly, until 1755, and subsequently in Germantown and Milestone, Pa., until his death, in 1793.

De Benneville's home is an old and picturesque stone mansion, two stories high, situated in a delightful hollow and surrounded by stately trees. Though built in 1745, it is still in an excellent state of preservation. It was designed to serve the double purpose of a residence and a church. When De Benneville first settled in Oley he was received most cordially by the Moravians, who had a monastic house at Bethlehem and a mission school just two miles distant from Oley line, nine miles from Reading. In the mission school De Benneville preached regularly until growing differences of creed between himself and the Moravians led them to close their doors against him. That was in 1745. De Benneville at once set to work with the aid of Jean Bertolette of France, whose daughter he had recently married, to rear a substantial mansion, of his own, wherein he could preach at will. The second or upper story, which was originally reached through a door, directly over the main entrance below, by a long flight of steps leading up on the outside, he constructed as a hall for holding meetings, with a seating capacity for fifty people. The steps are not there now, but otherwise the appearance of the building is practically unchanged. A spring of living water gushes from a rock in the cellar and flows out at one corner. In this spring of running water, to him a mystic symbol of spiritual purity, De Benneville baptized his converts. Here he was wont, Sabbath after Sabbath, to gather his friends and neighbors about him and preach to them what is now the accepted Universalist creed. With such quaint memories clustering around it and such historical associations investing it, the old De Benneville mansion is bound in time to become a centre of interest to every Universalist in the land.

De Benneville's labors exercised a most potent influence over his contemporaries, and upon the development of spirituality among the Colonies. His time was evenly divided between the practice of medicine, in which he possessed considerable skill, and in preaching, for which he never accepted compensation. Until prevented by extreme age, it was his custom to perform a journey, twice each year, through Pennsylvania, Maryland and Virginia, preaching among the weaker churches. William Penn had thrown open the State of Pennsylvania for the purpose of trying "the holy experiment," as he styled it, of toleration of all religions; and here French Huguenots, Dutch Mennonites, German Mystics of all shades of belief, and Roman Catholics as well, received a welcome of honest friendship. De Benneville cared little for superficial distinctions of creed, and moved with equal ease among all the various denominations, the Dunkers, Moravians, Lutherans, Mennonites, Separatists, Reformed, and Schwenkfelders. These various sects, however, were more closely allied then than now, and among them all De Benneville discovered a marked readiness to accept the doctrine of Universalism.

De Benneville's life and experiences were stranger than fiction. His mother was of the noble Granville family of England, and bore to her husband nine children in five years after marriage, having twins four years successively. She died at De Benneville's birth. The father was a French refugee attached to the Court of King William III. After the death of his mother, Queen Anne herself provided the infant De Benneville with a nurse and personally superintended his early education. At the age of twelve he was sent to sea, to learn navigation, in a war vessel belonging to a little fleet bound for the coast of Barbary. On his return to England he was stricken with a fainting fit, during which he had a vision of himself as a firebrand in hell. On coming to himself he cried out: "I am damned!" This incident determined the trend of his future life. He became melancholy and continued so for fifteen months. At the end of that time, as he himself records, he was awakened out of a sleep and heard a voice within him which pronounced upon him a sentence of condemnation. Then, as he relates, he "heard the Saviour's universal voice, which penetrated through him with divine power, saying: 'Take courage, my son, thy sins are forgiven thee.'" He became a convert and began to preach the doctrine of repentance. He was arrested for preaching in the markets and on the streets and imprisoned. Some of his companions were hanged. De Benneville himself was sentenced to be beheaded, but, through the intervention of Queen Anne, he was pardoned by Louis XV. After that he removed to Germany, where he had as acquaintances "a company of gentry, who dwelt together near Siegen, some of whom were married, but only dwelt together as brethren and sisters," and engaged in literary pursuits and religious contemplation.

In Holland he underwent his most extraordinary experience, which resulted in his openly expounding the creed of Universalism. He fell into a wasting disorder. He felt himself die by degrees, and was regarded as dead, by his friends, for forty-two hours. He saw them prepare his body for burial and inclose it in a coffin. During the interval he had one of the most remarkable visions on record. In spirit he visited the abodes of the dead, both the wicked and the good. He relates this experience, in detail, in a little volume written by his own hand in French, an English edition of which was published in Philadelphia under the title of "A True and Remarkable Account of the Life and Trance of Dr. George De Benneville, Late of Germantown, Pennsylvania. Including What He Heard and Saw During a Trance of Forty-two Hours, Both in the Regions of Happiness and Misery." Only two or three copies of this little book are now extant. One is in possession of the Congressional Library at Washington, and is pronounced by Librarian Spofford to be, in a commercial sense, worth double its weight in gold. The Rev. Elhanan Winchester, an eminent divine of his day, says, regarding the revelations of the book in his preface: "I bless God that I was ever acquainted with Dr. George de Benneville, for such a humble, pious, loving man I have scarcely ever seen in my pilgrimage through life. 'I have no doubt of this revelation myself." In the latter pages of the book De Benneville relates his experiences during the trance. Occult mysteries, things hidden from the wise and prudent, are there set forth with a vividness of conception and strength of coloring that recall the works of Virgil and Dante in the same line. He says:

"I felt myself die by degrees. Exactly at midnight I was separated from the body and saw the people occupied in washing it, according to the custom of the country. Immediately I was drawn up as in a cloud, and beheld great wonders where I passed, impossible to be written or expressed. I quickly came to a place which appeared to my eyes as a level plane, so extensive that my sight was not able to reach its limits, filled with all sorts of fruit trees. In this plane I found I had two guardians, one at my right hand and the other at my left, exceeding beautiful beyond expression. They had wings and resembled angels, and had shining bodies and white garments. One took his place at my right hand. Immediately we were lifted up in the air, and some time after we

arrived in a dark and obscure place where nothing but weeping and lamentation and anguish could be understood. . . . I was conducted into each of the seven habitations of the damned. After we had passed through we were lifted up some distance from the place where we reposed ourselves. A messenger was sent to us who said: 'My dear Sir and my dear brother, the most Holy Trinity order that you shall proclaim to the people of the world a universal Gospel.' . . . A glorious multitude approached. The glory caused us to fall down. . . . After they had passed us we were lifted up, and arrived in the places of the seven habitations of the damned. We could perceive no more darkness. Then all the heavenly hosts shouted with one voice: 'An eternal and everlasting deliverance. An eternal and everlasting restoration!' Presently we passed again through the seven habitations of the damned, and a multitude were delivered from each. Many thrones, palaces, temples, and buildings were erected in all parts, with fruit trees intermingled and rivers of pleasure gliding along through the celestial land. . . . Then my guardian touched me and reconducted me to the house from whence I came; where I perceived the people assembled, and, discovering my body in the coffin, I was reunited with the same, and found myself lodged within my earthly tabernacle; and, coming to myself, I knew Brother Marsey and many others, who gave me an account of my being twenty-five hours in the coffin, which altogether made forty-two hours. To me this seemed so many years."

ABOU BEN ADHEM.

BY LEIGH HUNT.

ABOU BEN ADHEM (may his tribe increase!)
Awoke one night from a deep dream of peace,
And saw, within the moonlight in his room,
Making it rich, and like a lily in bloom,
An angel writing in a book of gold:
Exceeding peace had made Ben Adhem bold,
And to the presence in the room he said,
"What writest thou?"—The vision raised its head,
And with a look made of all sweet accord,
Answered, "The names of those who love the Lord."
"And is mine one?" said Abou, "Nay, not so,'
Replied the angel. Abou spoke more low,
But cheerly still: and said " I pray thee then,
Write me as one that loves his fellow-men."
The Angel wrote, and vanished. The next night
It came again with a great wakening light,
And showed the names whom love of God had blessed,
And lo! Ben Adhem's name led all the rest.

Anglo=American Notes.

I. "BLOOD IS THICKER THAN WATER."

THOMAS FASSITT SHEWELL, ESQ., of Bristol, Pa., contributes the following account of certain curious incidents bearing upon his name and family.*

" With regard to the Shewells in England, my brother, Linington, had an interesting experience about the year 1825. While in Liverpool he stopped at the 'Albion.' Upon arriving he ordered his trunk to his room. To his surprise a trunk, not his own, but bearing the name of 'Shewell,' plainly marked, was brought up. He was about ringing for the porter when that worthy made his appearance, accompanied by a fine looking man of about 45, who came to claim the trunk. Of course, they entered into conversation, and after spending a few hours together, separated—not, however, until Linington had promised to visit the stranger's father, Joseph Shewell, at Colchester, some forty miles south of London, and one of the oldest towns in England. Subsequently, Linington finding himself in London, with a day to spare, went to Colchester and called upon Mr. Joseph Shewell, whose family at home comprised a wife and three daughters. The names of these ladies were those in use in our family, as 'Sarah,' 'Mary,' etc.; and of the men, 'Joseph,' 'Thomas,' 'Robert,' 'Charles,' showing a common origin.

"Mr. Shewell was a hale and venerable man, of upwards of 80, and entertained Linington with hearty hospitality during his short stay. After pressing his guest to remain some days with them, Mr. Shewell said: 'In England we observe the old saying, "Welcome the coming, speed the parting."' Linington understood that the family came from a neighboring county, but was not able, then, to identify it with ours in Gloucestershire.

" In 1831, during a visit to Scarboro', England, I, too, had a curious adventure similar to the foregoing. At this famous seaside resort I went, as is customary, to register my name at the Library for a month. A few evenings after, while sitting on a bench on the Parade, waching the passers-by, a gentleman and lady came up and took a seat beside me. I did not notice them particularly, excepting that the lady had a sprightly, dark eye, full of intelligence. Shortly after, her

---
* Letter to the Editor, dated May 14, 1876.

companion addressed me and—first apologizing for doing so—asked me if my name was 'Shewell'; I said it was. He then said his wife's name was also 'Shewell,' and that, in looking over the Register, she had been surprised at seeing the name of her brother (as she supposed) written as he wrote it, and wondered he had not been to see her. We then entered into conversation about our family. The gentleman was a clergyman from Derbyshire, named Richards (or Richardson). His wife was the daughter of Sir John Shewell, of Berks (or Wiltshire), who had, I think, three sons and one or two daughters. I spoke of a Captain Shewell of the Army, who had shot himself at Edinboro' recently; it proved to be the brother of Mrs. Richardson, and her husband subsequently gave me the particulars of the sad story. Captain Shewell had been engaged to the daughter of a wealthy baronet—rather against her parents' wishes. All, however, seemed bright to the lovers when there came a cloud ; his letters remained unanswered; a rumor reached him that his *fiancée* was to marry another. Anguished in mind, without asking for leave of absence, as he expected to be absent but a few hours, he posted down to Yorkshire only to learn that the rumor was true. He returned immediately, but met with unavoidable detentions by the way, and found on his arrival at Edinboro'—his station—that he was in arrest for absence without leave. In his chagrin, disappointment and madness he blew out his brains.

" Referring to the hero (not then fledged) of Balaclava,* I found he was another brother."

II.—A KINSWOMAN'S LEAFLET.

The following letter from Miss Ann Shewell was received in 1876 by the compiler of this book. It contains some information of family interest :

London, Oct 25.—Dear Sir : Your letter addressed some months since to my late father, Joseph Shewell, has come into my hands. It arrived in Colchester some time after his decease and when the family had left the place. I am sorry that I can neither give, myself, or inform you how to obtain the particulars of our family pedigree which you are so desirous of possessing. I well remember Mr. Linington D. Shewell's visit to our house, and have a letter he wrote to my father previously, in which he refers to your ancestor Walter Shewell, but

---
* See " A Balaclava Hero."

the date of his death that *he gives* (1712) is 20 years earlier than the year you name as the time of his arrival in America. Be this as it may, we fully believe that our family sprung from the same house, but I know of no means of tracing the connecting link.

Although I have not a complete genealogical register, I can give you a few particulars of my ancestry that may be of some interest and may, also, be some clue to *your* earlier history.

My father's great-grandfather, Edward Shewell, was the owner of a sugar plantation in the Bermuda Islands. He married Elizabeth, daughter of Thomas Gray, of Whitechapel, London, May 19th, 1725. His son Edward, the only child of his 5 children of whom I have any account, was my father's grandfather, and married Sarah Bird of London, 5th May, 1751 ; of S. Bird's parentage there seems no record ; of their children, 8 in number, only 3 were married, leaving any descendants, viz.: Thomas, Ann and Edward.

Thomas, born June 2d, 1754, my father's father, married Ann, daughter of Elizabeth and John Talwin. John Talwin was a surgeon at Royston, in Cambridgeshire. They had 9 children, all of whom are now deceased except my Uncle Edward Shewell, who resides not far from Kingston, in Canada West. He has the title of Captain having joined the Army in his young days, but has long since retired from it and follows the occupation of a farmer; he has been twice married and has a large family. The other members of my father's family, with one exception, belonged to the Society of Friends. My dear father and his elder brother John Talwin were preachers in that body. Nearly all the family arrived to length of days. My father had completed 90 years when he died in Sept. last year, and my Uncle Edward in Canada will be 89 if he lives till next Christmas Day. Ann, my father's aunt, married a Thomas Brewster, of London ; I think they had one son, Richard, who died single, and one daughter, Sarah Shewell, also unmarried : she still survives at an advanced age.

Edward, my father's uncle, was born Dec. 9th, 1765, died 1838, was twice married and had a very large family. His widow is still living at ———, in Sussex. The late Colonel Fred. Geo. Shewell and the George Maunsell Shewell were his sons.

We long dwelt under the impression that the only Shewells in this country were the descendants of our family, but of late years we have discovered that there are a few bearing this name, in Gloucestershire, in the neighborhood of Painswick.

An Early English Shewell.

"MR. THOMAS SHEWELL, M.A., of Cambridge University, was born at Coventry, where his father was a reputable citizen. He was scholar to that learned and excellent person, Mr. James Crawford. His first settlement in the ministry was at this place (Lenham Vicarage, Kent) and he was ejected from hence by the Act of Uniformity. He afterwards kept a private school at Leeds in this county. He married a niece of the Rev.. Mr. Thos. Case. After many years he returned to his native city and continued preaching there to the last.

"There was something extraordinary in his death. He had been for some time preaching on the Lord's Day upon the subject of original sin from Rom. v. and had not finished the subject. Coming into the pulpit the Lord's Day before he died, though in perfect health, instead of going on, as was universally expected, with his former discourse, he, to the great surprise of all his auditors, took for his text Rev. xxii., 21 : ' The Grace of our Lord Jesus Christ be with you all. Amen ! ' and preached a most excellent sermon.

"The people were under a very great concern and some were afraid he had a design to leave them and enquired of his daughter whether she knew the occasion of his changing his subject. She told them that, on the Saturday evening, she perceived him walk about in his chamber and he did not come to family prayer at the usual time ; whereupon she went up to him and enquired how he did. He told her he found his thoughts in so great confusion that he could not go on with his subject but must preach, the next day, on something else. However, he appeared to continue very well until Wednesday, which was his lecture day, and went to the meeting-house in perfect health. He prayed as long and consistently as ever, and, having opened his Bible and named his text, he began to falter in the reading of it, and immediately dropped down in the pulpit in an apoplectic fit and was carried into the vestry and never spoke one word after, but died in about two hours, Jan. 19th, 1693. Mr. Tory preached and published his funeral sermon."*

---

* From " The Nonconformists' Memorial, being an account of the ministers who were ejected or silenced after the Restoration, particularly by the Act of Uniformity which took place on Bartholomew Day, Aug. 24, 1662. By Ed. Calamy, D.D. London, 1775."

A Waterloo Survivor.

*What long-enduring hearts could do
In that world's earthquake, Waterloo!* *

EDWARD WARNER SHEWELL, the son of Thomas Shewell, was born in Sussex, England, 1788.

He was commissioned as Ensign of the 35th (Sussex) Regiment of Foot, Aug. 13, 1812: Lieutenant, Dec. 22, 1813. Served at Waterloo, and was placed on "Half Pay" March 25, 1817. Restored to active service as a Lieutenant of the 32d (Cornwall) Regiment of Foot, May 11, 1820, and became Captain, Aug. 29, 1826. He was finally placed on "Half Pay," Nov. 29, 1827.†

Captain Shewell subsequently removed to Canada and settled near Napanee, Ontario. Of the early Shewells he writes in 1877.

"About the year 1780 my great-grandfather, a banker in Lombard Street (London), was induced by the flattering accounts made by the government, offering great grants of land, to emigrate to the West Indies.

" But the climate was so bad that no European could stand it, and nearly all died, the first season, but Edward, John and Thomas, who returned to London penniless. Edward Shewell became a bank clerk, and afterwards made a great fortune, as a stock-broker, and purchased a house on Camberwell Green, near London, where all the family died. Until very lately we never knew what became of the persons who emigrated with William Penn, but there is no doubt they are the same family. As the two countries are so widely divided, we knew but little of them. I am now in my 88th year, but perfectly competent to vouch for the truth of this account. I believe I am the only Waterloo officer remaining in America.

---

* Tennyson.

† This information was obtained from the British Army List and by correspondence with Captain Shewell. (See also " A Kinswoman's Leaflet.")

A Balaclava Hero.

When can their glory fade?
O the wild charge they made!
All the world wondered.
Honor the charge they made!
Honor the Light Brigade,
Noble six hundred.

FREDERICK GEORGE SHEWELL, the son of Edward Shewell, was born in Sussex, England, in 1809. He entered the Army in 1827, and in due time passed through the various grades in his regiment, the 8th (King's Royal Irish Hussars) whose motto is "pristina virtutis memores." He was commissioned as follows: Cornet, 28 August, 1827; Lieutenant, 6 September, 1831; Captain, 28 April, 1837; Major, 23 August, 1844; Lieutenant Colonel, 19 February, 1847 and Colonel, 28 November, 1854. He commanded his regiment at Balaclava, in the Crimea, October 25, 1854, where the Light Brigade of the British Cavalry made the famous charge upon the Russian artillery. Colonel Shewell bore a very distinguished part in this memorable affair, according to the historian Kinglake, from whose "Invasion of the Crimea" we make some extracts.

Later in that campaign, Colonel Shewell was assigned to command a provisional brigade with rank of Brigadier-General. He was finally retired from active service for physical disability and died at home, Sussex, Eng., 18—.

It may be a mere coincidence but certain characteristics of the family, on both sides of the Atlantic, are forcibly illustrated in the following sketch which, in part for that reason and in part for its historical value, is here inserted at some length.

As will be remembered by students of history "the Light Brigade" was commanded by Lord Cardigan. The division, of which it was a part, was commanded by Lord Lucan to whom, by the hands of an aide-de-camp, Captain Nolan, was sent the following order from the commander-in-chief, Lord Raglan:

"Lord Raglan wishes the cavalry to advance rapidly to the front, and try to prevent the enemy carrying away the guns. Troop of horse artillery may accompany. French cavalry is on your left. Immediate."

According to Kinglake:

"As altered by Lord Lucan at the moment of directing the advance, the disposition of the Light Brigade was as follows: The 13th Light Dragoons, commanded by Captain Oldham, and the 17th Lancers, commanded by Captain Morris, were to form the first line; the 11th Hussars, commanded by Colonel Douglas, was ordered to follow in support; and the third line was composed of the 4th Light Dragoons under Lord George Paget, and the 8th Hussars, or rather, one may say, the main portion of it, under Colonel Shewell. Lord Cardigan, as commander of the whole brigade, had to place himself at the head of the first line. The second line, consisting of only one regiment, was commanded by Douglas, its colonel; and the two regiments comprising the third line were in charge of Lord George Paget. Each of these regiments stood extended, in line, two deep."

An old sergeant of Colonel Shewell's regiment (8th Hussars) thus describes the situation at the moment:*

"It was now, I suppose, about nine o'clock, and the morning was clear and bright; in fact, as beautiful a morning as you would wish to see. We could hear the dull boom of the firing, and the shouts of the men, and occasionally, when the smoke lifted, saw here and there flying parties of men, but little more, owing to the nature of the ground, and we were chatting together in groups expecting every moment the order to move—some wondering whether we should have a slap at the Russians or not, and I'm quite sure we all hoped for it. I should say that we had been removed again from the vineyard to the brow of the hill, when we saw our Colonel (Colonel Shewell) galloping up to take the command from Major de Salis (who was also in charge), and, says one of our men, 'Well, I'm d——d if it isn't the Colonel; what do you say to the "Old Woman" now?'

"The fact is, we had left him very ill, as we thought, in his tent, for he had been sadly troubled with gout and sickness, and suffering like the rest of us, besides being old for such exposure—and so, from one thing to another, he had got that name. But he was full of pluck, and when he knew that fighting was going on up he came to us, and we were pleased enough to see him, too.

"I saw, as he passed in front of us, that all at once his face expressed the

---

* See *Colburn's U. S. Magazine.*

greatest surprise and astonishment, and even anger, and, walking on, he broke out with—' What's this? what's this? one, two, four, six, seven men *smoking!* Sergeant !—Sergeant Pickworth !' he calls out.

"And the truth is," continued the narrator very frankly—" for I was one of them—the truth is, we were warming our noses, each with a short black pipe, and thinking no harm of the matter; and, by the bye," he added parenthetically, " I lost mine, for I passed it quietly to poor Jock Miller in my rear, who went in with us into the charge, and was missed, so that I never got back my pipe.

" ' I never heard of such a thing,' the Colonel said, ' and no regiment except an " Irish " regiment would be guilty of it. Sergeant, advance and take these men's names,' and, leaving the sergeant to find us out, though he couldn't discover any, the Colonel passed on, and halted again. All this time I heard strange, dull noises thickening in the air. It might not be quite according to regulation to be smoking, sword in hand, when the charge might be sounded at any moment. Our Colonel was a religious man too, which helped him to his nickname, I dare say, and he imagined, perhaps, we ought to have been thinking of our souls instead of our tobacco pouches and inch of clay.

" He comes up to another now, that hadn't heard what had been said, and sings out—

" ' Sergeant Williams !'

" ' Yes, sir,' replies the sergeant.

" ' Did you not hear what I said about smoking just now?'

" ' I've not lit my pipe yet, sir,' answered the sergeant.

"But ' fall back to the rear,' says the Colonel, ' and take off your belts. Farrier, forward and take them, and—why here's another !—to the rear, fall back. I'll have this breach of discipline punished !' and the men fell out and gave their belts to the farrier ; and I understand that one *was* punished the next day, but Sergeant Williams, who was mounted, but quite unarmed, as he had given up his sword, belt and carbine, went into the charge with us (it came directly), and was killed."

Kinglake's account is continued :

" Although the part of the enemy's line which Lord Cardigan meant to attack lay as yet very distant before him, it was evident, from the position of the flanking batteries betwixt which he must pass, that his brigade would not long be in motion without incurring a heavy fire; and, upon the whole, he seems to have considered that almost from the first his advance was in the nature of a charge. Followed immediately by his first line, and, at a greater distance, by the other regiments of his brigade, Lord Cardigan moved forward at a trot, taking strictly the direction in which his troops before moving had fronted, and making straight down the valley towards the battery which crossed it at the distance of about a mile and a quarter. . .

"Soon the fated advance of the Light Brigade had proceeded so far as to begin to disclose its strange purpose—the purpose of making straight for the far distant battery, which crossed the foot of the valley, by passing for a mile between two Russian forces, and this at such ugly distance from each as to allow of our squadrons going down under a double flanking fire of round-shot, grape, and rifle-balls, without the opportunity of yet doing any manner of harm to their assailants. Then, from the slopes of the Causeway Heights on the one side, and the Fedioukine Hills on the other, the Russian artillery brought its power to bear right and left, with an efficiency every moment increasing ; and large numbers of riflemen on the slopes of the Causeway Heights who had been placed where they were in order to cover the retreat of the Russian battalions, found means to take their part in the work of destroying our horsemen. Whilst Lord Cardigan and his squadrons rode thus under heavy cross-fire, the visible object they had straight before them was the white bank of smoke, from time to time pierced by issues of flame, which marks the site of a battery in action ; for in truth the very goal that had been chosen for our devoted squadrons—a goal rarely before assigned to cavalry—was the front of a battery—the front of that twelve-gun battery, with the main body of the Russian cavalry in rear of it, which crossed the lower end of the valley.

"Lord Cardigan and his first line had come down to within about eighty yards of the mouths of the guns, when the battery delivered a fire from so many of its pieces, at once, as to constitute almost a salvo. Numbers and numbers of saddles were emptied, and along its whole length the line of the 13th Light Dragoons and 17th Lancers was subjected to the rending perturbance that must needs be created in a body of cavalry by every man who falls slain or wounded, by the sinking and the plunging of every horse that is killed or disabled, and again by the wild, piteous intrusion of the riderless charger, appalled by his sudden freedom, coming thus in the midst of a battle, and knowing not whither to rush, unless he can rejoin his old troop, and wedge himself into its ranks. . . .

"Whilst the first line thus moved in advance, it was followed, at a somewhat less pace, by the three regiments which were to act in support. The officers present with these regiments—I take them from left to right—were as follows : With the 8th Hussars (which had only three of its troops present) there rode, besides Colonel Shewell who commanded the regiment, Major de Salis, Captain Tomkinson, Lieutenant Seager (the Adjutant), Lieutenant Clutterbuck, Lieutenant Lord Viscount Fitzgibbon, Lieutenant Phillips, Cornet Heneage, Cornet Clowes and Cornet William Mussenden. . . .

When the 8th Hussars began to encounter the riderless horses dashing back from the first line, there was created some degree of unsteadiness, which showed itself in a spontaneous increase of speed; but this tendency was rigorously checked by the officers, and they brought back the pace of the regiment to a good trot. Of the three officers commanding the three troops, one—namely, Captain Tomkinson—was at this time disabled. Another, Lord Fitzgibbon, was killed; and several men and horses fell; but Lieutenant Seager and Cornet Clowes took the vacant commands, and those of this small and now isolated regiment who had not been yet slain or disabled moved steadily down the valley.

"Throughout their whole course down the valley the officers and the men of the 11th Hussars, the 4th Light Dragoons, and the 8th Hussars never judged themselves to be absolved from the hard task of maintaining their formation, and patiently enduring to see their ranks torn, without having means for the time of even trying to harm their destroyers. These three regiments, moreover, were subjected to another kind of trial from which the first line was exempt; for men not only had (as had had the first line) to see numbers torn out of their ranks, and then close up and pass on, but were also compelled to be witnesses of the havoc that battle had been making with their comrades in front. The ground they had to pass over was thickly strewn with men and horses lying prostrate in death, or from wounds altogether disabling; but these were less painful to see than the maimed officers or soldiers, still able to walk or to crawl, and the charger moving horribly with three of his limbs, whilst dragging the wreck of the fourth, or convulsively laboring to rise from the ground by the power of the fore legs when the quarters had been shattered by round-shot. And, although less distressing to see, the horses which had just lost their riders without being themselves disabled, were formidable disturbers of any regiment which had to encounter them. . . .

"Familiar pulpit reflections concerning man's frail tenure of life

come to have all the air of fresh truths when they are pressed upon
the attention of mortals by the 'ping' of the bullet, by the sighing,
the humming, and at last the 'whang' of the round-shot, by the harsh
'whirr' of the jagged iron fragments thrown abroad from a bursting
shell, by the sound—most abhorred of all those heard in battle—the
sound that issues from the moist plunge of the round-shot when it
buries itself with a 'slosh' in the trunk of a man or a horse. Under
tension of this kind, prolonged for some minutes, the human mind,
without being flurried, may be wrought into so high a state of activity
as to be capable of well-sustained thought; and a man, if he chose,
whilst he rode down the length of this fatal North Valley, could examine and test and criticise—nay, even could change or restore that
armor of the soul, by which he had been accustomed to guard his
serenity in the trials and dangers of life. One of the most gifted of
the officers now acting with the supports was able, whilst descending
the valley, to construct and adopt such a theory of divine governance
as he judged to be the best-fitted for the battle-field. Without having been, hitherto, accustomed to let his thoughts dwell very gravely
on any such subjects of speculation, he now all at once, whilst he
rode, encased himself, body and soul, in the iron creed of the fatalist; and, connecting destiny in his mind with the inferred will of
God, defied any missile to touch him, unless it should come with the
warrant of a providential and foregone decree. As soon as he had
put on this armor of faith, a shot struck one of his holsters without
harming him or his horse; and he was so constituted as to be able to
see in this incident a confirmation of his new fatalist doctrine. Then,
with something of the confidence often shown by other sectarians
not engaged in a cavalry onset, he went on to determine that his,
and his only, was the creed which could keep a man firm in battle.
There, plainly, he erred; and, indeed, there is reason for saying that
it would be ill for our cavalry regiments, if their prowess were really
depèndent upon the adoption of any highly spiritual or philosophic
theory. I imagine that the great body of our cavalry people, whether
officers or men, were borne forward and sustained in their path of
duty by moral forces of another kind—by sense of military obligation, by innate love of fighting and of danger—by the shame of dis-
closing weakness—by pride of nation and of race—by pride of regiment, of squadron, of troop—by personal pride; not least, by the
power of that wheel-going mechanism which assigns to each man his

task, and inclines him to give but short audience to distracting, irrelevant thoughts. . . .

"At the part of the battery which had been entered by these men of the 17th Lancers, the Russian artillerymen were limbering up and making great exertions to carry off their guns, whilst our Lancers, seeing this, began to busy themselves with the task of hindering the withdrawal of the prey and in particular the leftermost portion of them, under the direction of Sergeant O'Hara, were stopping the withdrawal of one of the guns which already had been moved off some paces when a voice was heard calling 'Seventeenth! Seventeenth! this way! this way!' The voice came from Mayow, the officer who held the post of brigade-major. Putting himself at the head of these last, Mayow led them against a body of Russian cavalry which stood halted in rear of the guns. With his handful of Lancers he charged the Russian horsemen and drove them in on their second reserve, pushing forward so far as to be at last some five hundred yards in the rear (Russian rear) of the battery.

"It may well be imagined that, intruding, as he was, with less than a score of horsemen, into the very rear of the Russian position, and dealing with a hostile cavalry which numbered itself by thousands, Mayow was not so enticed by the yielding, nay, fugitive tendency of the squadrons retreating before him, as to forget that the usefulness of the singular venture which had brought him thus far must depend, after all, upon the chance of its being supported. He halted his little band; and whether he caught his earliest glimpse of the truth with his own eyes, or whether he gathered it from the mirthful voices of his Lancers saying something of 'the Busby-bags coming,' or 'the Busby-bags taking it coolly,' he at all events learnt to his joy that exactly at the time when he best could welcome its aid, a fresh English force was at hand. The force seen was only one squadron, but a squadron in beautiful order; and, though halted when first discerned, it presently resumed its advance, and was seen to be now fast approaching.

"The 8th Hussars, we remember, was on the extreme right of the forces advancing in support. Reduced to one-half of its former strength by that triple fire through which it had been passing, but still in excellent order, and maintaining that well-steadied trot which Colonel Shewell had chosen as the pace best adapted for a lengthened advance of this kind, this regiment had continued its advance down the valley, had moved past the now silent battery at a distance of a few horses' lengths from its (proper) left flank, had pressed on beyond it some three or four hundred yards, and by that time had so passed through the jaws of the enemy's position, as to be actually for the moment in a region almost out of harm's way—in the region, if so one may speak, which lies behind the north wind. Colonel Shewell then halted the regiment. Making only now one squadron—and that a very weak one—its remains stood formed up to their front. Colonel Shewell, it seems, had the hope that an order of some kind would presently reach him; and he well might desire to have guidance, for the position into which he had pushed forward his regiment was somewhat a strange one. On three sides—that is, on his front, and on the rising grounds which hemmed in the valley on either flank—Colonel Shewell saw bodies of the enemy's cavalry and infantry; but the Russian forces in front of him, both horse and foot, were in retreat, and numbers of them crowding over the bridges of the aqueduct. Yet nowhere, with the exception of his regiment, now reduced to a very small squadron, could he descry any body of our cavalry in a state of formation, though before him in small knots or groups, or acting as single assailants, he saw a few English horsemen who were pressing the retreat of the enemy, by pursuing and cutting down stragglers.* After continuing this halt during a period which has been reckoned at three, and also at five minutes, Colonel Shewell resumed his advance. These

---

* "I now heard Colonel Shewell's voice, and saw the old man waving his sword on the other side of the guns, as if calling us together, and we got round, or through, the best way we could, and formed in line, every Russian that was at the guns being cut down, and the cavalry that had ventured to come to their help had been driven back, some across the aqueduct, and even to the Tchernaya, but only to renew the charge, for that they would let us return without a trial to stop us was not a likely thing.

"As we were in line, I was just saying, 'Sergeant Riley, you're out of place' (he was on the left and ought to have been on my right), but he did not speak. I looked up at him, his eyes were fixed and staring, and his face was rigid and white as a flagstone. I saw he was dead, though yet seated on his horse, and that too was shocking to think of and look at. I hadn't time to say more, for the Colonel sings out, 'Sergeant! Sergeant! just look there, they are reinforcements,' as a body of Lancers came right upon us, whom I took to be our own, the 17th, and the Sergeant shouts out, 'By ——, they're Russsians!'" (A "Survivor."—*Colburn's U. S. Magazine.*)

remains of the 8th Hussars formed the small but still well ordered squadron, which we saw coming down towards the spot where Mayow had checked the pursuit, and halted his small group of Lancers. . .

"Towards our centre, we had no troops at all in a state of formation; but on our extreme right, as we know, the 8th Hussars, now reduced to a strength of about fifty-five, and commanded by Colonel Shewell, was advancing towards the group under Mayow. The event proved that this group of fifteen under Mayow was still in a state of coherence which rendered it capable of acting with military efficiency in concert with other troops, and it may therefore be said that Colonel Shewell (who was senior to Mayow) had under his orders a force of about seventy sabres. . .

"Upon descrying the English squadron, which had come down, as we saw, in the direction of his right rear, Mayow hastened to join it, and was presently in contact with the squadron, which represented the 8th Hussars. It appeared that Colonel Shewell, the commander of the 8th Hussars, had not been killed or disabled; and, Mayow being now once more in the presence of an officer senior to himself, the temporary command which the chances of battle had cast upon him, came at once to an end.

"The fifteen men whom Mayow had brought with him were ranged on the left of the 8th Hussars; and this little addition brought up Colonel Shewell's strength to about seventy. The panic which was driving from the field the whole bulk of the enemy's horse plainly did not extend to the Russian infantry on the eastern part of the Causeway Heights; for looking back towards their then right rear, our Hussars at this time were able to see the grey battalions still holding their ground, in good order. Nor was this all; for presently the glances cast back in nearly the same direction disclosed some new comers. Three squadrons of Russian Lancers were seen issuing from behind one of the spurs of the Causeway Heights and descending into the valley. Another instant, and this body of Lancers was wheeling into line, and forming a front towards the Russian rear, thus interposing itself as a bar between the English and their line of retreat.

"At the moment when Colonel Mayow joined the 8th Hussars, Colonel Shewell had asked him, 'where Lord Cardigan was'; and Mayow having replied that he did not know, it resulted that Colonel Shewell, as the senior officer present, became charged with the duty of determining how the emergency should be met by the troops within reach of his orders. It does not, however, appear that there was much scope for doubt. After an almost momentary consultation with the senior officers present, including Colonel Mayow and Major de Salis, Colonel Shewell gave the word, ' Right about wheel !' and the squadron, with its adjunct of fifteen Lancers, came round at once with the neatness of well-practised troops on parade. Colonel Shewell and Major de Salis put themselves in the front, and Lieutenant Seager commanded the one squadron into which, as we saw, the remains of the 8th Hussars had been fused. Mayow led the small band of Lancers which had attached itself to the Hussars. The seventy horsemen rode straight at the fluttering line of gay lances which the enemy was then in the very act of forming.* The three Russian squadrons thus wheeling into line were at a distance from Shewell of something less than 300 yards, and the two leading squadrons had already established their line, but the third squadron was still in process of wheeling. Once more in this singular battle of horsemen, our people had before them a body of cavalry which passively awaited the charge. With his seventy against three hundred, Shewell needed some such counterbalancing advantage as that ; but he might have lost his occasion if he had been wanting in that swiftness of decision which is one of the main conditions of excellence in a cavalry officer, for it was to be inferred that upon the completion of the manœuvre by their third squadron, the Russians would charge down on our people. Colonel Shewell proved equal to the occasion. He lost not one moment. He was a man whose mind had received a deep impress from some of the contents of the Bible ; but those who might differ from his opinions still recognized in him a man of high honor who extended the authority of conscience to the performance of military duties ; and it has not been found in practice that a piety strictly founded on the Holy

---

* " ' Keep together, men,' cried the Colonel—ah ! he did show himself a *man*, ill, laid up as he had been, and I'm sure fitter then to be in his tent that day, but he was too plucky—' keep together,' he said, ' and death or glory ! but we'll ride them down !' and slap into them we went again, cutting, parrying, slashing right and left, and then the flank batteries opened, and the riflemen picked us off, and the firing grew hotter, the smoke thicker and denser, while the Russians in blind fury were killing their own men, as well as ours, as if they didn't care who they hit, so long as they could hit at all—nor what they sacrificed, so long as they could sacrifice *us*—and they didn't often miss, I can tell you."—(" A Survivor."—*Colburn's U. S. Mag.*)

Testaments (taken fairly, the one with the other) has any such softening tendency as to unfit a man for the task of fierce, bodily conflict. One of Shewell's companions in arms—a man well entitled to deliver a judgment on the merits of his lost comrade—has said of him, 'I knew the man with whom I had to deal—I knew that I was dealing with one of the most honorable, the most gallant, the most conscientious, the most single-minded men it has ever been my good fortune to meet with.'

"As in the battles of old times, so now, and not for the first time, this day, he who was the chief on one side singled out for his special foe the man who seemed chief on the other. Shewell had not the advantage of being highly skilled as a swordsman, and being conscious of his deficiency in this respect, he asked himself how best he could act. The result was that he determined to rely upon the power which can be exerted by sheer impact. He resolved that whilst charging at the head of his little band of horsemen, he would single out the Russian officer whom he perceived to be the leader of the opposing force, and endeavor to overthrow him by the shock of a heavy concussion. To do this, the more effectively, he discarded the lessons of the riding school, clenched a rein in each hand, got his head somewhat down; and, as though he were going at a leap which his horse, unless forced, might refuse, drove full at the Russian chief. The assailant came on so swift, so resolute, and, if so one may speak, with such a conscientious exactness of aim that, for the Russian officer who sat in his saddle under the disadvantage of having to await the onset, there remained no alternative at the last moment but either to move a little aside or else be run down, without mercy, by this straightforward, pious Hussar. As was only natural, the charger of the Russian officer shrank aside to avoid the shock; and Shewell, still driving straight on, with all his momentum unchecked, broke through the two ranks of the Lancers. He was well followed by his seventy horsemen. Upon their close approach some of the Russian Lancers turned and made off; but the rest stood their ground and received the shock prepared for them.* By that shock, however, they were broken and

---

* "We seemed already to have cut and hacked our way through thousands, and were going at it once more, as if we meant to ride down the whole Russian army, with the old Colonel ahead of us, and through showers of grape, and canister, and Minié balls, we were fairly cutting our way as a man would *cut*

overthrown. It is true that in the moment of the impact, or in the moments immediately following, men had, some of them, a fleeting opportunity for the use of the sword or the lance, and one at least of our Hussars received a great number of slight wounds from the enemy's spearheads; but the clash was brief. The whole of these three Russian squadrons were quickly in retreat, a part of them going back into the fold betwixt the Causeway Heights, from which just before they had issued, whilst the rest fled across to the Fedioukine Hills; and there is reason for inferring that these last attached themselves to the other three squadrons of their regiment which had been posted, as we saw, on the northern side of the valley. After having thus conquered their way through the body of Lancers opposed to them, Colonel Shewell and those who had followed him in his victorious charge could see a good way up the valley; but their eyes searched in vain for an English force advancing to their support; and, in truth, the very attempt which Jeropkine's Lancers had just been making went far to show that no English succors were near; for it is evident that the endeavor to cut off our horsemen by showing a front towards the Russian rear would never have been made by troops which were able to see a red squadron coming down to the support of their comrades. Therefore, having now cut open a retreat not only for themselves, but also for such of the other remnants of the Light Brigade as might be near enough to seize the occasion, Shewell's regiment and the men who had joined it continued to pursue the direction in which they had charged, in other words, to retire. Colonel Shewell, it seems, did not judge that the condition of things was such as to warrant any attempt at the usual operation of governing a retreat by fronting from time to time with a portion of the force; and those who remained of the seventy had only to withdraw up the valley with such speed as they could.

"Upon counting the brigade, it appeared that the force, which numbered 673 horsemen when it went into action, had been reduced to a mounted strength of 195; and there was one regiment, it seems, namely, the 13th Light Dragoons, which, after the charge, mustered only ten mounted troopers. From a later examination it resulted

---

through a thick-set-hedge with a bill-hook! A regular avalanche of cavalry had burst around us, thinking, no doubt, that where we had got to we *ought* to remain, having done quite enough for one morning, and we were quite of a different mind." ("A Survivor."—*Colburn's U. S. Mag.*)

that, in officers and men killed and wounded, the brigade had suffered losses to the number of 247, of whom 113 had been killed and 134 wounded; and that (including 43 horses shot as unserviceable on account of their wounds) the brigade had 475 horses killed, besides having 42 others wounded.

"In the 8th Hussars, Lieutenant Lord Fitzgibbon was killed, and Lieutenant Clutterbuck, Lieutenant Seager, and Cornet Clowes were wounded. Of the ten officers who went into action with the regiment, Colonel Shewell and Cornet Heneage were the only two of whom it could be said that both they and their chargers were unstricken.

"The well-known criticism delivered by General Bosquet was sound and generous. He said of the charge, 'It is splendid; but it is not war.' He spoke with a most exact justice; but already the progress of time has been changing the relative significance of that glory and that fault which his terse comment threw into contrast. What were once the impassioned desires of the great nations of the West for the humbling of the Czar are now as cold as the ashes which remind men of flames extinguished; and our people can cease from deploring the errors which marred a battle, yet refuse to forget an achievement which those very errors provoked. Therefore, the perversity which sent our squadrons to their doom is only, after all, the mortal part of the story. Half forgotten already, the origin of the 'Light Cavalry Charge' is fading away out of sight. Its splendor remains. And splendor like this is something more than the mere outward adornment which graces the life of a nation. It is strength —strength other than that of mere riches, and other than that of gross numbers—strength carried by proud descent from one generation to another—strength awaiting the trials that are to come."

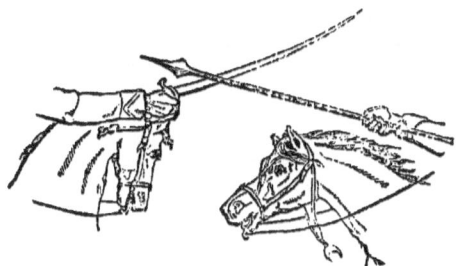

CAPTAIN SWORD AND CAPTAIN PEN.*

I.

HOW CAPTAIN SWORD MARCHED TO WAR.

CAPTAIN SWORD got up one day
   Over the hills to march away,
Over the hills and through the towns ;
They heard him coming across the downs,
Stepping in music and thunder sweet,
Which his drums sent before him into the street,
And lo ! 'twas a beautiful sight in the sun ;
For first came his foot, all marching like one,
With tranquil faces, and bristling steel,
And the flag full of honor as though it could feel,
And the officers gentle, the sword that hold
'Gainst the shoulder heavy with tumbling gold,
And the massy tread, that in passing is heard,
Though the drums and the music say never a word.

And then came his horse, a clustering sound,
Of shapely potency, forward bound,
Glossy black steeds, and riders tall,
Rank after rank, each looking like all,
Midst moving repose and a threatening charm,
With mortal sharpness at each right arm,
And hues that painters and ladies love,
And ever the small flag blush'd above.

And ever and anon the kettle-drums beat
Hasty power midst order meet ;
And ever and anon the drums and fifes
Came like motion's voice and life's ;
Or unto the golden grandeurs fell
Of deeper instruments, mingling well,
Burdens of beauty for winds to bear ;
And the cymbals kiss'd in the shining air,
And the trumpets their visible voices rear'd,
Each looking forth with its tapestried beard,
Bidding the heavens and earth make way
For Captain Sword and his battle array.

   .   .   .   .   .

---

* By Leigh Hunt.

II.

Through fair and through foul went Captain Sword,
Pacer of highway and piercer of ford,
Steady of face in rain and sun,
He and his merry men, all as one ;
Till they came to a place, where in battle array
Stood thousands of faces firm as they,
Waiting to see which could best maintain
Bloody argument, lords of pain ;
And down the throats of their fellow-men
Thrust the draught never drunk again.

. . . .

Death for death ! The storm begins :
Rush the drums in a torrent of dins ;
Crash the muskets, gash the swords ;
Shoes grow red in a thousand fords ;
Now for the flint, and the cartridge bite ;
Darkly gathers the breath of the fight.
Salt to the palate, and stinging to sight ;
Muskets were pointed they scarce know where ;
No matter: Murder is cluttering there.
Reel the hollows : close up ! close up !
Death feeds thick, and his food is his cup.

. . . . .

No time to be "breather of thoughtful breath "
Has the giver and taker of dreadful death.
See where comes the horse-tempest again,
Visible earthquake, bloody of mane !
Part are upon us, with edges of pain ;
Part burst, riderless, over the plain,
Crashing their spurs, and twice slaying the slain.

. . . . .

Victory ! victory ! Man flies man ;
Cannibal patience hath done what it can,
Carved and been carved, drunk the drinkers down,
And now there is one that hath won the crown ;—
One pale visage stands lord of the board—
Joy to the trumpets of Captain Sword !

III.

OF THE BALL THAT WAS GIVEN.

But Captain Sword was a man among men,
And he hath become their playmate again ;
Boot, nor sword, nor stern look hath he,
But holdeth the hand of a fair ladye,
And floweth the dance a palace within,
Half the night, to a golden din,
Midst lights in windows, and love in eyes,
And a constant feeling of sweet surprise ;
And ever the look of Captain Sword
Is the look that's thank'd, and the look that's adored.

There was the country-dance, small of taste ;
And the waltz, that loveth the lady's waist ;
And the gallopade, strange agreeable tramp,
Made of a scrape, a hobble and stamp ;
And the high-stepping minuet, face to face,
(Mutual worship of conscious grace)
And all the shapes in which beauty goes
Weaving motion with blithe repose.

And then a table a feast display'd,
Like a garden of light without a shade,
All of gold, and flowers, and sweets,
With wines of old church-lands, and sylvan meats
Food that maketh the heart feel choice ;
Yet all the face of the feast, and the voice,
And heart, still turned to the head of the board ;
Forever the look of Captain Sword
Is the look that's thank'd, and the look that's adored.

Well content was Captain Sword ;
At his feet all wealth was pour'd ;
On his head all glory set ;
For his ease all comfort met ;
And around him seem'd entwined
All the arms of womankind.

IV.

THE BATTLE-FIELD AT NIGHT.

'Tis a wild night out of doors :
The wind is mad upon the moors,

And comes into the rocking town,
Stabbing all things, up and down,
And then there is a weeping rain
Huddling 'gainst the window pane,
And good men bless themselves in bed :
The mother brings her infant's head
Closer, with a joy like tears,
And thinks of angels in her prayers ;
She sleeps, with his small hand in hers.

Two loving women, lingering yet
Ere the fire is out, are met,
Talking sweetly, time-beguiling,
One of her bridegroom, one her child,
The bridegroom he. They have received
Happy letters, more believed
For public news, and feel the bliss
The heavenlier on a night like this.
They think him housed, they think him blest,
Curtained in the cove of rest,
Danger distant, all good near ;
Why hath their " Goodnight " a tear?

Behold him ! By a ditch he lies
Clutching the wet earth, his eyes
Beginning to be mad. In vain
His tongue still thirsts to lick the rain,
That mocked but now his homeward tears ,
And ever and anon he rears
His legs and knees with all their strength,
And then as strongly thrusts at length,
Raised, or stretched, he cannot bear
The wound that girds him, weltering there :
And " Water ! " he cries, with moonward stare.

.   .   .   .   .

A shriek !—Great God ! what superhuman
Peal was that ? Not man, nor woman,
Nor twenty madmen, crushed, could wreak
Their soul in such a ponderous shriek.
Dumbly, for an instant, stares
The field : and creep men's dying hairs.

Two noble steeds lay side by side,
One cropped the meek grass ere it died;
Pang-struck it struck t'other, already torn,
And out of its bowels that shriek was born.

Sneereth the trumpet, and stampeth the drum,
And again Captain Sword in his pride doth come;
He passeth the field where his friends lie lorn,
Feeding the flowers and the feeding corn,
Where under the sunshine cold they lie,
And he hasteth a tear from his cold grey eye.
Small thinking is his but of work to be done,
And onward he marcheth, using the sun:
He slayeth, he wasteth, he spouteth his fires
On babes at the bosom, and bed-rid sires;
He bursteth pale cities through smoke and through yell
And bringeth behind him, hot-blooded, his hell.
Then the weak door is barred and the soul all sore,
And hand-wringing helplessness paceth the floor,
And the lover is slain, and the parents are nigh—

Oh God! let me breathe, and look up at thy sky!
Good is as hundreds, evil as one;
Round about goeth the golden sun.

V.

HOW CAPTAIN SWORD BECAME INFIRM.

But to win at the game, whose moves are death;
It maketh a man draw too proud a breath:
And to see his force taken for reason and right,
It tendeth to unsettle his reason quite.
Never did chief of the line of Sword
Keep his wits whole at that drunken board.
He taketh the size, and the roar, and fate,
Of the field of his action, for soul as great.
He smiteth and stunneth the cheek of mankind,
And saith, "Lo! I rule both body and mind."

Captain Sword, like a witless thing,
Of all under heaven must needs be a king,
King of kings, and lord of lords,
Swayer of souls as well as of swords,
Ruler of speech, and through speech, of thought;
And hence to his brain was a madness brought.

He madden'd in East, he madden'd in West,
Fiercer for sights of men's unrest,
Fiercer for talk, amongst awful men,
Of their new mighty leader, Captain Pen,
A conqueror strange, who sat in his home
Like the wizard that plagued the ships of Rome,
Noiseless, showless, dealing no death
But victories, winged, went forth from his breath.

Three thousand miles across the waves
Did Captain Sword cry, bidding souls be slaves :*
Three thousand miles did the echo return
With a laugh and a blow made his old cheeks burn.

. . . . .

'Twas painful to see his extravagant way ;
But heart ne'er so bold, and hand ne'er so strong,
What are they when truth and the wits go wrong?

VI.

Now tidings of Captain Sword and his state
Were brought to the ears of Pen the Great,
Who rose and said, " His time is come."
And he sent him, but not by sound of drum,
Nor trumpet, nor other hasty breath,
Hot with questions of life and death,
But only a letter calm and mild ;
And Captain Sword he read it, and smiled,
And said, half in scorn, and nothing in fear,
(Though his wits seem'd restor'd by a danger near,
For brave was he ever) " Let Captain Pen
Bring at his back a million men,
And I'll talk with his wisdom, and not till then."
Then replied to his messenger Captain Pen,
" I'll bring at my back a *world* of men."

. . . . .

'Twas only for many-soul'd Captain Pen
To make a world of swordless men.

---

* America, 1776.

"Who Sent Out His Argosies."

STEPHEN SHEWELL, eldest son of Robert[1] and nephew of Walter[1] is thus described in "The Autobiography of Leigh Hunt,"[*] from which the following extract is made.

"My grandfather by my mother's side was Stephen Shewell of Philadelphia, who sent out his 'argosies.' His mother was a Quaker and he himself, I believe, descended from a Quaker stock. He had ships trading to England, Holland and the West Indies, and used to put his sons and nephews in them as captains,[†] probably to save charges; for in everything but stocking his cellars with provisions he was penurious.[‡] For sausages and 'botargoes' (first

---

[*] JAMES HENRY LEIGH HUNT (b. Southgate, England, Oct. 19, 1784, d. Putney, Aug. 26, 1859) was the son of Isaac Hunt and Mary, daughter of Stephen Shewell of Philadelphia. He was one of the most delightful of English essayists and miscellaneous writers, and remarkable for his connection with the most eminent literati of his time. He was educated at Christ's Hospital, was a clerk in the War Office (1807-8), editor of a radical newspaper, the Examiner, and was imprisoned for two years for publishing a libel upon the Prince Regent. Subsequently he wrote many essays and poems marked by brilliance of thought and grace of diction, and also became a play-wright. In 1850 he wrote his "Autobiography." Having become reduced in fortune, he in 1844 accepted an annuity from the family of his old friend the poet Shelley, and in 1847 the British government settled upon him a civil list pension of £200.

[†] " I had this voyage (1764) four masters of ships, passengers: Captains Green, Shewell, and two of the name of Welsh: . . . "There were a good many duels fought at this time in the Bay. Captain Shewell was wounded in the breast by one Brockholst, of New York, and the celebrated Arnold (Benedict), who was here at that time, fought and wounded one of the Baymen. It was said that Arnold frightened his antagonist, who had agreed that he should fix the distance, by naming five yards. They were more turbulent at this time in the Bay than I had ever known them before." (Autobiog. of Charles Biddle, Vice Prest. Supreme Executive Council of Penna., 1745-1821, Phila., 1883.)

[‡] STEPHEN SHEWELL was capable of generous impulses as shown in his provision for his daughter, the wife of Isaac and mother of Leigh, when left be-

authors, perhaps, of the jaundice in our blood) Friar John would have commended him. As Chaucer says:

" 'It snewed, in his house, of meat and drink.'

" My grandmother's maiden name was Bickley. Her family came from Buckinghamshire. The coat-of-arms are three half moons, which I happen to recollect because of a tradition we had that an honorable augmentation was made to them of three wheat-sheaves, in reward of some gallant achievement performed in cutting off a convoy of provisions by Sir William Bickley, a partisan of the House of Orange who was made a banneret. My grandmother was an open-hearted, cheerful woman, of a good healthy blood and as generous as her husband was otherwise. The family consisted of five daughters and two sons. One of the daughters died unmarried : the three surviving ones were lately wives and mothers in Philadelphia. They and their husbands, agreeably to the American law of equal division, were in receipt of a pretty prɛ erty in lands and houses ; our due share of which some inadvertence on our parts seems to have forfeited. I confess I have often wished at the close of a day's work that people were not so excessively delicate on legal points and so afraid of hurting the feelings of others by supposing it possible for them to want a little of their grandfather's money. But I believe I ought to blush while I say this, and I do. One of my uncles died in England, a mild, excellent creature, more fit for solitude than the sea. The other, my uncle Stephen, a fine, handsome fellow of great good nature and gallantry, was never heard of after leaving the port of Philadelphia for the West Indies. He had a practice of crowding too much sail, which is supposed to have been his destruction. They said he did it 'to get back to his ladies.'

" My uncle was the means of saving his namesake, my brother Stephen, from a singular destiny. Some Indians who came into the city to traffic, had been observed to notice my brother a good deal. It is supposed they saw in his tall, lithe person, dark face and long black hair a resemblance to themselves. One day they enticed him from my grandfather's house in Front street and taking him to the Delaware, which was close by, were carrying him off across the river

---

hind upon her husband's flight. Stephen supported Isaac Hunt's family for some time, and upon their departure to join the Reverend refugee, presented them with transportation to London and a purse of £500. (T. F. R.)

when his uncle descried them and gave the alarm. His threats induced them to come back; otherwise it is thought they intended to carry him into their own quarter and bring him up as an Indian; so that instead of a rare character of another sort—an attorney who would rather compound a quarrel for his clients than get rich by it—he might have had for a client the Great Buffalo, Bloody Bear, or some such grim personage. I will indulge myself with the liberty of observing in this place, that with great diversity of character among us, with strong points of dispute even among ourselves, and with the usual amount, though not perhaps exactly the like nature, of infirmities common to other people—some of us may be with greater—we have all been persons who inherited the power of making sacrifices for the sake of a principle.

"My grandfather, though intimate with Dr. Franklin, was secretly on the British side of the question when the American war broke out. He professed to be neutral and to attend only to business; but his neutrality did not avail him. One of his most valuably laden ships was burnt in the Delaware by the Revolutionists to prevent it getting into the hands of the British; and besides making free with his botargoes they dispatched every now and then a file of soldiers to rifle his house of everything else that could be serviceable; linen, blankets, etc. And this unfortunately was only a taste of what he was to suffer; for emptying his mercantile stores from time to time they paid him with their continental currency, paper money; the depreciation of which was so great as to leave him at the close of the war bankrupt of everything but some houses, which his wife brought him; they amounted to a sufficiency for the family support; and thus, after all his cunning neutralities and his preference of individual to public good, he owed all that he retained to a generous and unsuspecting woman. His saving grace, however, was not on every possible occasion confined to his money. He gave a very strong instance (for him) of his partiality to the British cause, by secreting in his house a gentleman of the name of Slater, who commanded a small armed vessel on the Delaware, and who was not long since residing in London. Mr. Slater had been taken prisoner and confined at some miles distance from Philadelphia. He contrived to make his escape and astonished my grandfather's family by appearing before them, at night, drenched in the rain which descends in torrents in that climate. They secreted him for several months in a room at the top of the house."

The Mother of Leigh Hunt.

MARY SHEWELL, daughter of Stephen Shewell, and niece of Elizabeth Shewell, the wife of Benjamin West, was the mother of Leigh Hunt,* from whose autobiography the following is taken:

"My father took the degree of Master of Arts, both at Philadelphia and New York. When he spoke the farewell oration on leaving college, two young ladies fell in love with him, one of whom he afterwards married. He was fair and handsome, with delicate features, a small aquiline nose and blue eyes. To a graceful address he joined a remarkably fine voice, which he modulated with great effect. It was in reading with this voice, the poets and other classics of England, that he completed the conquest of my mother's heart. He used to spend his evenings in this manner with her and her family—a noble way of courtship: and my grandmother became so hearty in his cause that she succeeded in carrying it against her husband, who wished his daughter to marry a wealthy neighbor. . . .

"At this period (1775) the Revolution broke out: and he entered with so much zeal into the cause of the British government, that besides pleading for the loyalists with great fervor at the bar, he wrote pamphlets equally full of party warmth, which drew on him the popular odium. His fortunes then came to a crisis in America. Early one morning a great concourse of people appeared before his

---

*In personal appearance, Leigh Hunt was tall and straight, while his eyes were black and very brilliant. His hair, early in life, was dark, but as he grew older, changed to pure white. His complexion was dark. His face was intellectual, and withal indicated by its genial expression that he had a great heart. He had to a large degree that power of attracting the affection of others by a winning sympathy and a cordial manner, which he so enthusiastically attributes to his friend Charles Lamb. He was ever thinking, talking, and writing of his friends, always anxious to please them, and his chief enjoyment seems to have been in their companionship. The three salient traits that appear in his works and in his record of himself are amiableness, self-esteem, and a sprightly and almost romantic imagination. To the first he owed his chief happiness in life; the second enabled him to keep up a stout heart against disappointment; the third gave him the power and the will so to write that he has cheered many a weary soul, and filled many a winter evening with entertainment and instruction. His philosophy of life was, to look on the best phase of every subject and circumstance, never to despair, to meet rebuffs with a cheerful countenance,

house. He came out—or was brought. They put him into a cart prepared for the purpose (conceive the anxiety of his wife!) and after parading him about the streets were joined by a party of the revolutionary soldiers with drum and fife. The multitude then went with him to the house of Dr. Kearsley, a staunch Tory, who shut up the windows and endeavored to prevent their getting in. The Doctor had his hand pierced by a bayonet as it entered between the shutters behind which he had planted himself. He was dragged out and put into the cart all over blood; but he lost none of his intrepidity, for he answered their reproaches and outrage with vehement reprehensions; and by the way of retaliation on the 'Rogue's March,' struck up 'God Save the King.' My father gave way as little as the Doctor. He would say nothing that was dictated to him, nor renounce a single opinion, but on the other hand, he maintained a tranquil air, and endeavored to persuade his companion not to add to their irritation. This was to no purpose. Dr. Kearsley continued infuriate and more than once fainted from loss of blood and the violence of his feelings. The two loyalists narrowly escaped tarring and feathering. A tub of tar which had been set in a conspicuous place in one of the streets for that purpose was overturned by an officer intimate with

---

and to endure misfortune with fortitude, hoping for and living in a better time to come. In this way he survived political persecution and critical denunciation, bore sickness with patience, was melancholy without being misanthropic, was cheerful in the midst of poverty, made a happy home in a prison, and finally died, at a good old age, contented, calm, and looking back with complacency on a varied, but on the whole successful career.

> Thou lofty mirror, Truth, let me be shown
> Such as I am, in body and in mind ;—
> Hair plainly red, retreating now behind ;
> Of stature tall, head bent and looking prone ;
> A meagre body on two stilts of bone ;
> Fair skin, blue eyes, good air, nose well defined,
> Mouth handsome, teeth such as are rare to find,
> And paler in the face than king on throne.
> Now harsh and bitter, pleasant now and mild ;
> A quickly roused yet no malignant foe ;
> My heart, and mind, and self never in tune ;
> Sad for the most part, then in such a flow
> Of spirits, I seem now hero, now buffoon ;—
> Man, art thou great or vile ? Die, and thou'lt know.
> (*Hunt.*)

our family. My father, however, did not escape entirely from personal injury. One of the stones thrown by the mob gave him such a severe blow on the head as not only laid him swooning in the cart, but dimmed his sight for life, so as to oblige him from that time to wear spectacles. At length, after being carried through every street in Philadelphia, the two captives were deposited in the evening in a prison in Market Street. What became of Dr. Kearsley I cannot say.* My father, by means of a large sum of money given to the sentinel who had charge of him, was enabled to escape at midnight. He went immediately on board a ship in the Delaware, that belonged to my grandfather, and was bound for the West Indies. She dropped down the river that same night : and my father went first to Barbadoes and afterward to England, where he settled.†

* " Upon our arrival in the Delaware (May 4, 1775) we heard of the battle of Lexington, and found the whole country preparing for war. Being young and considering my country unjustly persecuted, I was as willing to go to war as any man in America. Perhaps my having little to lose was another reason for my having no objection to it. Talking with my old friend Apsden, I found him as much averse to a war as I was for it ; and this was not surprising, for he is what is called a worldly man, and had much to lose. I never felt the less friendship for him, nor did I ever feel the least resentment against any man in America for being opposed to the Revolution, where he acted from principle. The conduct of our people at this time was not always correct. . . . When Dr. Kearsley and Hunt were afterward carted around the town, I did not feel for them. Kearsley would huzza for the king, notwithstanding his friends begged him to be quiet and that they would take him out of the cart. The Doctor made a shocking appearance—he had declared he would not be taken alive out of his house, and when the mob went there he was sitting in his front parlor with pistols. A young man broke the sash, and several entered and dragged him out of the window. His face and head were much cut. He was prudent enough not to fire, for if he had done so he certainly would have been killed. Captain Shewell, a relation of Hunt's, was anxious to get him out of the cart, and would have attempted it, at all hazards, had I not persuaded him against it ; for it appeared to me that Mr. Hunt was much pleased with his situation. He was going to England, where he thought it would be a recommendation to him, and I believe it was. He was a lawyer when here, but turned clergyman in England and had a living given to him." (*Autobiography of Charles Biddle*, Phila., 1883.)

† Isaac Hunt died in 1809 and was buried in the churchyard in Bishopsgate Street.

"My father and mother took breath in the meantime under the friendly roof of Mr. West, the painter, who had married her aunt. The aunt and niece were much of an age and both fond of books. Mrs. West, indeed, ultimately became a martyr to them; for the physician declared that she lost the use of her limbs by sitting indoors. My mother at that time was a brunette with fine eyes, a tall ladylike person and hair blacker than is seen of English growth. It was supposed that Anglo-Americans already began to exhibit the influence of climate in their appearance. The late Mr. West told me that if he had met myself or any of my brothers in the streets, he should have pronounced, without knowing us, that we were Americans. A likeness has been discovered between us and some of the Indians in his pictures. My mother had no accomplishments but the two best of all, a love of nature and of books. Dr. Franklin offered to teach her the guitar, but she was too bashful to become his pupil. She regretted this afterward, partly no doubt for having missed so illustrious a master. Her first child who died was named after him. .

. . Among the visitors at my grandfather's* house besides Franklin was Thomas Paine, whom I have heard my mother speak of as having a countenance that inspired her with terror. I believe his aspect was not captivating; but most likely his political and religious opinions did it no good in the eyes of the fair loyalist. My mother was diffident of her personal merit but she had great energy of principle. When the troubles broke out and my father took that violent part in favor of the king, a letter was received by her from a person high in authority, stating that if her husband would desist from opposition to the general wishes of the colonists, he should remain in security, but that if he thought fit to do otherwise, he must suffer the consequences which inevitably awaited him. The letter concluded with advising her, as she valued her husband's and family's happiness, to use her influence with him to act accordingly. To this "in the spirit of old Rome and Greece," as one of her sons has proudly and justly observed (I will add of Old England, and, though contrary to our royalist opinions, of New America, too) my mother replied that she knew her husband's mind too well to suppose for a moment that he would so degrade himself; and that the writer of the letter entirely mistook her if he thought her capable of endeavoring to per-

---

* Stephen Shewell.

suade him to an action contrary to the convictions of his heart, whatever the consequences threatened might be. Yet the heart of this excellent woman, strong as it was, was already bending with anxiety for what might occur; and on the day when my father was seized, she fell into a fit of the jaundice, so violent as to affect her ever afterward, and subject a previously fine constitution to every ill that came across it."

A Man Introduced to his Ancestors.*

HAPPENING to read the other evening some observations respecting the geometrical ratio of descent, by which it appears that a man has, *at the twentieth remove, one million forty-eight thousand five hundred and seventy-six ancestors in the lineal degree—grandfathers and grandmothers*—I dropped into a reverie, during which I thought I stood by myself at one end of an immense public place, the other being occupied with a huge motley assembly, whose faces were all turned towards me. I had lost my ordinary sense of individuality, and fancied that my name was Manson.

At this multitudinous gaze, I felt the sort of confusion which is natural to a modest man, and which almost makes us believe that we have been guilty of some crime without knowing it. But what was my astonishment, when a Master of the Ceremonies issued forth, and saluting me by the title of his great-grandson, introduced me to the assembly in the manner and form following:

May it please your Majesties and his Holiness the Pope;

My Lord Cardinal, may it please your most reverend and illustrious Eminence;

May it please your graces, my Lord Dukes;

My Lords, and Ladies, and Lady Abbesses;

Sir Charles, give me leave; Sir Thomas also, Sir John, Sir Nicholas, Sir William, Sir Owen, Sir Hugh, etc.

Right Worshipful the several Courts of Aldermen;

Mesdames the Married Ladies;

Mesdames the Nuns and other Maiden Ladies; Messieurs Manson, Womanson, Jones, Hervey, Smith, Merryweather, Hipkins, Jackson, Johnson, Jephson, Damant, Delavigne, De la Bleterie, Macpherson,

* Leigh Hunt in New Monthly Mag., Oct., 1825.

Scott, O'Bryan, O'Shaughnessy, O'Halloran, Clutterbuck, Brown, White, Black, Lindygreen, Southey, Pip, Trip, Cherdorlaomer (who the devil, thought I, is he?), Morandi, Moroni, Ventura, Mazarin, D'Orsay, Puckering, Pickering, Haddon, Somerset, Kent, Franklin, Hunter, Le Fevre, Le Roi (more French!), Du Val (a highwayman, by all that's gentlemanly!), Howard, Cavendish, Russell, Argentine, Gustafson, Olafson, Bras-de-feu, Sweyn, Hacho and Tycho, Price, Lloyd, Llewellyn, Hanno, Hiram, etc., and all you intermediate gentlemen, reverend and otherwise, with your infinite sons, nephews, uncles, grandfathers, and all kinds of relations;

Then, you, sergeants and corporals, and other pretty fellows;

You footmen there, and coachmen younger than your wigs,—

You gipsies, pedlars, criminals, Botany-Bay men, old Romans, informers, and other vagabonds,—

Gentlemen and ladies, one and all,—

Allow me to introduce to you, your descendant, Mr. Manson.

Mr. Manson, your ANCESTORS.

What a sensation!

I made the most innumerable kind of bow I could think of, and was saluted with a noise like that of a hundred oceans. Presently I was in the midst of the uproar, which became like a fair of the human race.

Dreams pay as little attention to ceremony as the world of which they are supposed to form a part. The gentleman-usher was the only person who retained a regard for it. Pope Innocent himself was but one of the crowd. I saw him elbowed and laughing among a parcel of lawyers. It was the same with the dukes and the princes. One of the kings was familiarly addressed by a lord of the bed-chamber as Tom Wildman; and a little French page had a queen much older than himself by the arm, whom he introduced to me as his daughter. I discerned very plainly my immediate ancestors the Mansons, but could not get near enough to speak to them, by reason of a motley crowd, who, with all imaginable kindness, seemed as if they would have torn me to pieces.

"This is my arm," said one, "as sure as fate;" at the same time seizing me by the wrist. "The Franklin shoulder," cried another. A gay fellow pushing up to me, and giving me a lively shake, exclaimed, "The family mouth, by the Lord Harry! and the eye—there's a bit of my father in the eye." "A very little bit, please your honour," said a gipsy, a real gipsy, thrusting in her brown face : " All the rest's mine, Kitty Lee's, and the eyebrows are Johnny Faw's to a hair." "The right leg is my property, however," returned the beau; "I'll swear to the calf."—"*Mais-but-notta to de autre calf*," added a ludicrous voice, half gruff and half polite, belonging to a fantastic-looking person, whom I found to be a dancing master. I did not care for the gipsy : but to owe my left leg to a dancing master was not quite so pleasant, especially as, like Mr. Brummel's, it happens to be my favorite leg. Besides, I cannot dance. However, the truth must out. My left leg is more of a man's than my right, and yet it certainly originated with Mons. Fauxpas. He came over from France in the train of the Duke of Buckingham. The rest of me went in the same manner. A Catholic priest was rejoiced at the sight of my head of hair, though by no means remarkable but for quantity; but it seems to me he never expected to see it again since he received the tonsure. A little coquette of quality laid claim to my nose, and a more romantic young lady to my chin. I could not say my soul was my own. I was claimed not only by the Mansons, but by a little timid boy, a bold patriot, a moper, a merry-andrew, a coxcomb, a hermit, a voluptuary, a water-drinker, a Greek of the name of Pythias, a free-thinker, a religionist, a bookworm, a simpleton, a beggar, a philosopher, a triumphant cosmopolite, a trembling father, a hack-author, an old soldier dying with harness on his back.

"Well," said I, looking at this agreeable mixture of claimants, "at any rate my vices are not my own."

" And how many virtues? " cried they in stern voice.

"Gentlemen," said I, "if you had waited, you would have seen that I could give up one as well as the other; that is to say, as far as either can be given up by a nature that partakes of ye all. I see very plainly, that all which a descendant no better than myself has to do, is neither to boast of his virtues, nor pretend exemption from his vices, nor be overcome with his misfortunes; but solely to regard the great mixture of all as gathered together in his person, and to try what he can do with it for the honour of those who preceded him, and the good of those that come after."

At this I thought the whole enormous assembly put on a very earnest but affectionate face; which was a fine sight. A noble humanity was in the looks of the best. Tears, not without dignity, stood in the eyes of the worst.

"It is late for me," added I; "I can do little. But I will tell this vision to the younger and stouter; they perhaps may do more."

"Go and tell it," answered the multitude. But the noise was so loud that I awoke, and found my little child crowing in my ear.

CUPID SWALLOWED.*

'OTHER day as I was twining
Roses, for a crown to dine in,
What of all things, 'midst the heap,
Should I light on, fast asleep,
But the little desperate elf,
The tiny traitor, Love himself !
By the wings I pinched him up
Like a bee, and in a cup
Of my wine I plunged and sank him,
And what d'ye think I did ? I drank him.
Faith I thought him dead. Not he !
There he lives with tenfold glee.
And now, this moment, with his wings
I feel him tickling my heartstrings.

---
*Leigh Hunt.

From Harper's Magazine.—Copyright, 1876, by Harper & Brothers.

THE ELOPEMENT.

An Elopement by Proxy.*

SOMETHING more than a hundred years ago, when Philadelphia was little more than a large village, the spacious old-fashioned mansion of Mr. Shewell, which stood in one of the principal streets, was of the aristocratic class of dwellings. He was a proud and hard man, and thought much of the distinction of his family, to say nothing of his wealth. At the time of our narrative, his sister Elizabeth, an orphan, was a member of his family and dependent on him for support. She was never a belle in the brilliant circles of that period, for her beauty was of that soft and touching kind which wins gradually upon the heart rather than that which strikes the sense like that of the more dazzling order. She usually wore her dark brown hair parted in waves over a low white forehead, and her complexion was of that clear paleness which better interprets the varying phases of feeling than a more brilliant color. Her eyes were dark and gray, and

---

* We have been unable to obtain the name of the author of this sketch but append from a letter by Thomas F. Shewell, Esq., of Bristol, Pa., under date of February 17, 1837, the following graphic reminiscence of this incident:

"About the year 1833, Bishop White made his last diocesan visit to the interior of the State, and being entertained at the house of Dr. Joseph Swift, of Easton, was induced during the evening by Mrs. Betsey Swift to give the details of an occurrence happening so long before.

"Mr. West was a native of Delaware County, a gentleman of most genial manners, and very popular in society, both with the ladies and gentlemen; and at length the young merchants belonging to the wealthier families determined to raise a subscription of two thousand dollars to send Mr. West, who was poor, to Italy for two years' study and improvement. Before his departure, however, evidently some love passages had occurred between the young people, for the merchant brother, Stephen Shewell, who was a very proud man, took a violent prejudice against Mr. West, on his sister's account, calling him a 'pauper,' an 'object of charity,' etc.

"West remained two years in Italy, much to his advantage, and was returning through England toward his native country, when the King, having seen some sketches showing a wonderful power of grouping, appointed him his painter. After some time, Mr. West wrote to Miss Shewell that it would be

so shadowed by thick and long lashes that they seemed black in the imperfect light: her small, rosy mouth had a slight compression of the lips that betokened determination and strength of will. The superb curve of her neck and the rounding of her shoulders would have enchanted a statuary. Her nature, too soft and clinging for the *rôle* of leadership in society, had yet a firmness that promised full development whenever called into action through her affections.

She had already come into collision with the iron will of her brother and that in a point which she could not yield. One afternoon there had been words between them, such as should not pass between those so near in blood. Mr. Shewell angrily paced the handsomely furnished parlor where the stormy interview had taken place. His features were marked by strength bordering on hardness, and the heavy frown on his brow did not render them more prepossessing. The young girl was seated in an attitude of deep dejection, and wiped away at intervals the tears that stole silently down her cheeks.

Suddenly Mr. Shewell stopped before her and said, with a sternness his effort to speak mildly could not overcome:

---

impossible for him to return to Philadelphia, but a certain brig was about coming to London, bringing his father to pay him a visit, and if she would accompany him with her maid they would be married as soon as she arrived in London.

"As soon as Mr. Shewell learned of this arrangement he became violently angry, declared that no pauper should marry his sister, and finally locked her up in her room until the vessel should have departed.

"As soon as this state of things became known to those friends of West who had aided him to go to Italy, they determined, in the Bishop's words, that 'Ben should have his wife,' sending to Miss Shewell, by her maid, concealed under her dress, a rope-ladder, with a note saying that they would cause the vessel to drop down to Chester, sixteen miles, to obviate suspicion, and that on a given evening they would have a carriage round the corner at eleven o'clock at night, and if she would use the ladder to reach the ground they would safely convey her to Chester and put her on board the vessel.

"The plan was entirely successful. The lady entered the carriage with two of the gentlemen, while one rode outside with the driver.

"The roads were abominably bad, and the eloping company only reached the vessel at daybreak, and the weary night came to an end. The party safely crossed the ocean, and a long and happy life awaited the married pair.

"During the whole course of the story, the venerable Bishop spoke with

"Once for all I ask, Elizabeth, will you do as I wish?"

"I cannot, brother," she answered, looking up.

He had been urging her to marry a wealthy suitor.

"I have told Mr. ——————— my mind," continued the young girl, encouraged by her brother's silence, "and it is not to his credit that he should apply to you after knowing my feelings."

"Elizabeth," exclaimed Mr. Shewell, with a violence that startled her, "I will know the reason of this obstinacy. Once my wish was law to you."

"And so it is, and so it shall be, in all things right. But I cannot do what duty, virtue, religion, forbid; I cannot utter false vows—"

"No more of this nonsense!" cried the brother. "Your duty is to do as I counsel for your good; your religion is worthless if it teaches disobedience to your natural protector. Mr. ——————— is the husband I have chosen for you."

"But I cannot love him, and therefore I will not marry him," answered the girl firmly.

"Will not?"

"No, brother."

"I'll tell whom you shall *not* marry then!" cried Mr. Shewell, angrily.

---

great animation, and seemed to relish the adventure, saying, 'Ben deserved a good wife, and old as I am I am ready to do it again to serve such worthy people.'

"I believe you are aware that the party consisted of Benjamin Franklin, then about fifty-six years old; Francis Hopkinson, author of 'The Battle of the Kegs' (a humorous ditty of Revolutionary times); and Bishop White. Mr. West became President of the Royal Society, and was noted for his genial character. Both Mr. and Mrs. West were most intimate with the King and Queen, with whom both were great favorites. Mrs. West was the aunt of Mrs. Hunt, the mother of Leigh Hunt, both having been Miss Shewells. My father, the late Thomas Shewell, was in London from 1796 to 1799, and frequently called upon Mrs. West, also attending Mr. West's famous Sunday dinners. One day a tall flunkey brought in a plate carefully covered with a napkin, when Mrs. West remarked to my father, ' You must not laugh, Cousin Tommy, at my attempt to raise some Indian corn in a hot-house. I only succeeded in growing cobs, but I have had them boiled so as to get the perfume.'

"I have thus endeavored to give you the statement as related to me by Dr. Swift, as the story given by the Bishop. Mrs. West was the first cousin of my grandfather, Robert Shewell."

"The beggarly young Quaker on whom you have thrown away your affections. Ha!" as the girl's face flushed the deepest crimson, "it is for *him* you have rejected the excellent offers made to you within the last year. Now, listen, Elizabeth! You are not to see nor speak with that rascal of a painter again! Do you hear me?"

"I do, brother," was the faint reply.

"Give me your word that you will never speak to him again."

"I cannot," she faltered; and a violent burst of tears choked her voice.

"Go to your chamber!" cried the brother. "I'll take care of you, since you will not take care of yourself. Not a word, but go." And as the weeping girl quitted the parlor Mr. Shewell called up the servants and laid his injunctions upon them, one and all, to refuse admittance to "Ben West," should he ever present himself at the door; and on no account to convey to him any communication from their young mistress on the penalty of severe punishment.

Elizabeth retired to her chamber, and wept long over her brother's austerity, wondering who had betrayed to him the closely kept secret of her love. After many conjectures her suspicions fastened on the right person; it was, it could be no other than her rejected suitor, who in the hope of furthering his own views, had informed Mr. Shewell of her interviews and correspondence with the young artist. How she hated him for the mean betrayal! How she longed for the moment to pour out on him the scorn she felt! But her heart was made for gentler emotions than the desire of vengeance, and her thoughts were soon turned to plan how she might effect a reconciliation between her brother and her plighted lover. As it grew toward dusk she arose, put on her cloak and hood, and bidding a faithful negress, a slave, attend her, went to the house of a friend where she had been accustomed of late to meet the youth to whom she had promised her hand.

The lovers met, and parted with lingering pledges of affection and promises of truth—promises that through all changes and chances their faith should be kept inviolate; that no interference should prevent the fulfilment of their vows when fortune removed the barriers that now interposed. They parted to meet no more for long, long years. The boy artist to his toil, as yet unrewarded by fame or gold, to his dreams of a bright future, and cheerful hopes, destined to many a disappointment, ere any goal was won; the maiden to her solitary secluded cherishing of the one dear trust which alone gave life its value; to sorrow and strife and trial, which strengthen and purify faith in the loving heart. It was late before she reached home, and her steps had been watched. The same ungenerous espial had followed her that evening as hitherto; her brother was informed of her interview with the youth he had forbidden her to see, and in his resentment at what he termed her daring disobedience, he resolved on measures which should subdue her spirit to submission. The next day Elizabeth found herself a prisoner in her own apartment. None of the household were allowed to approach the room save the female slave before mentioned; and Mr. Shewell gave notice to his sister that she would be allowed no freedom till she gave the pledge he required— never to hold intercourse with young West. She refused to give the promise, and bore the durance patiently.

Elizabeth Shewell was the daughter of an English gentleman, and had been early left an orphan; she was committed to the care of her wealthy brother, who deemed himself the sole and rightful arbiter of her destiny, and had resolved that she should make an advantageous match. Though not naturally an austere man, he possessed a resolution that nothing could bend; and it never occurred to him that his gentle and yielding sister could offer opposition to his will. When she showed symptoms of having a mind of her own on a subject involving the happiness of her future life, her resistance only strengthened his determination to control her decision. " What does a young girl know about marriage ? " was his mental observation. The conviction that she was incapable of wise judgment justified, in his opinion, the measures he saw fit to adopt, that she might be made happy in spite of herself. The evil of imprudent, unequal marriage was sufficiently obvious to all who had any observation of life; it would be his fault, if he permitted a giddy girl to precipitate herself into ruin. In those times the distinctions of rank were as impassable as in the old world. By such reflections he quieted conscience when the pale, sad face of his sister uttered reproaches keener than words could have conveyed.

Elizabeth found consolation in her forced seclusion, for the faithful negress was the bearer of many a letter between the separated lovers ; and absence was cheered by the sweet assurances contained in those folded treasures. The maiden trusted and hoped on, for her fond and true heart felt itself strong to overcome all things.

At this period the genius of the youthful painter was hardly known beyond his own neighborhood. It was not long, however, before the knowledge that artist power of no common order was hidden in the Quaker lad whose poverty prevented its development, awakened the interest of a few liberal gentlemen in Philadelphia and New York. The productions on which young West had bestowed most labor were purchased by them, and these evidences of his great talent inspired them with a wish to aid him further. His industrious application to the art to which his life had been consecrated with the prayers and blessings of his parents, enabled him in a few months to realize a sum sufficient, as he thought, for a foundation on which to begin the building of his fortunes; and by the advice and assistance of his patrons he determined to go and prosecute his studies at Rome. His spirit longed to breathe in the inspiration of the Eternal City, to rejoice in the creations of the genius of the past. On the successes for which he would strive, too, depended the happiness of the one loved being, for whom he would have sacrificed every other hope and aspiration. Elizabeth shed tears of mingled joy and grief over the farewell letter of her betrothed. In it were portrayed his wishes, his aims, his plans, the warm coloring of youthful hope was shed over his vision of the future, and he claimed her promise of unchangeable love as the guiding star of his life, the solace of his toils. How bright seemed the prospect! and how dimly were discerned the clouds and storms that might soon overshadow it.

In 1760 West sailed for Leghorn, and thence proceeded to Rome, where he arrived in July. To this biography belongs the account of his reception and brilliant success. The maiden of his choice, on his departure, was restored to freedom and society; but she lived only in the hope of reunion with him, in whose rising fortunes she rejoiced, because they brought nearer and nearer the day of their joyful meeting.

Five years passed, and West was established in London. His fame was spread throughout Europe, and sovereigns did honor to his genius. Independence was secured. His desire now was to return to his native country, and claim the hand of her who had remained faithful to him in every change of fortune. Letters from his American friends altered his purpose. They informed him that Mr. Shewell still opposed his marriage with his sister, and that she could not receive him at her own home. A plan was proposed—somewhat romantic, but suited to the exigencies of the case—which had been submitted to Miss Shewell, and met with her approval. The artist's father, Mr. West, was to take the young lady under his protection, and cross the ocean to bring the bride to her husband.

This scene was highly pleasing to the lover, who wished to save his betrothed the pain and mortification the struggle with the will of so near a relative would cause her. He wrote to his friends to signify his glad assent, and to urge Miss Shewell's immediate departure. He wrote also to Elizabeth, describing the life to which he should introduce her, and the impatient anxiety with which he should await her arrival.

All a lover's fond hope and blissful expectations were poured out in his letters, and earnestly he besought her to hasten the hour when their long separation should be ended.

The course of their true love, however, was destined to another interruption. One of the letters, by some unfortunate miscarriage, fell into the wrong hands, and the whole plan of her flight was discovered by her brother. There is reason to believe he forgot the tenderness due his sister in his resentment at what he termed her obstinate disobedience and duplicity toward him. Forgetful that past harshness had justly forfeited her confidence, and that he had no good reason to offer for a refusal to sanction her heart's choice, he aimed to conquer her, as before, by violent measures. Once more the fair girl was condemned to the solitude of her own apartment; her sole companion being the female slave who had always attended her. This injustice aroused the spirit of Elizabeth. In trifles her nature was yielding; but her love for West had become a religion. Her duty to him was felt to be paramount, and she was firm as adamant where principle was concerned. Her resolution was taken. The negress, in the confidence of her young mistress, was the bearer of letters between her and the devoted friends of West who had first concerted the plan of her going to him.

Those friends were Francis—afterward Judge—Hopkinson, Benjamin Franklin, and William White, afterward Bishop of Pennsylvania. The particulars of Miss Shewell's escape were communicated by the Bishop himself to a grand-daughter of Mr. Shewell, a lady of acknowledged literary ability, and distinguished in the society of the town where she resides. She was named after her aunt, Mrs. West.

It was not long before the friends had matured a plan, which they communicated to Elizabeth Shewell. She approved it and promised her co-operation.

It was past midnight, and a vessel at the dock was in readiness to set sail for England, in less than an hour. The preparations had been completed before dusk, and passages engaged for the elder West and a lady who was to be brought on board late that night. At that period the custom of retiring to rest early prevailed. The deep silence that reigned through the city was unbroken by voice or footstep, and the lights had long been extinguished in Mr. Shewell's mansion, as four or five men, wrapped in cloaks, passed cautiously along the street opposite, crossed directly in front of the house, stopped, and looked up, as if they expected a signal from one of the upper windows. All was quite dark; and the faint light of the street lamps, scarcely served to dissipate the gloom in which it was scarcely possible to recognize each other's features.

They had waited but a few minutes when a window above was softly raised, and the outside of a figure might be dimly discerned bending from it, as if seeking to discover who stood below. One of the party threw up a rope, which was caught. A rope ladder was drawn up, and after the lapse of a short time was again lowered. Those below pulled at it forcibly to ascertain that it was securely fastened, and then one ascended to the apartment into which the window opened, and gave his assistance in fastening the ladder more firmly.

It was now the moment for summoning all her energies, and Elizabeth stepped upon the ladder, aided by her companion, the negress having been dismissed at the usual hour for retiring, for her mistress was too generous to involve her in difficulty by making her a party to her elopement. The descent was accomplished in safety, and the trembling girl was received in the arms of those awaiting her, so overcome with fear that she was near fainting, and unable to articulate a reply to the anxious inquiries of her friends. One terror possessed her—the dread that her brother would be awakened by the noise, and intercept them before her escape could be accomplished. She made eager signals that they should be gone, and supported by two of the party, walked forward as rapidly as possible. Her strength might not have held out for a long walk, weakened as she was by alarm and anxiety but a carriage was in waiting at the corner of the next street. Before they reached this the noise of hurried footsteps startled them and the party hastened with their prize into the shadow of a narrow alley. The beating of the poor girl's heart might have been heard as they stood thus concealed and her apprehensions, almost darkened into despair as the irregular footsteps approached. It was only some late wanderers returning home, after perhaps a long revel, unwonted in the city of orderly habits. When the sound of footsteps ceased, the maiden was borne rather than led along by her friends to the carriage, and placed securely within it. One by one they followed her, and the carriage was driven fast to the wharf where the vessel lay in readiness to weigh anchor.

The elder West, the father of Benjamin, received them on the wharf, and welcomed his future daughter. The weeping girl was taken on board, and conducted to the cabin. In silent sympathy to her feelings—natural in a situation so new and embarrassing, the friends stood around her. The ship's crew were busy on deck, and in half an hour all was ready to sail. The signal was made for the departure of those who had escorted the fair passenger, and they took a kindly leave of her, speaking words of encouragement and hope that the future might be all sunshine to one so trustful and so loving. A slight bustle overhead, a noise of cheering, and the vessel was in motion. The danger of discovery was over!

Elizabeth breathed more freely as the bark that bore her to her lover glided over the waters, but she wept still; for tears were the natural vent of the conflicting emotions that oppressed her. She had quitted home and country for ever; she had abandoned him who was nearest in blood, and the friends of her youth, to enter on untried scenes and encounter unknown trials; to meet the cold gaze of strangers, who might judge her conduct harshly; perhaps the scorn of a hard and heartless world! Then came thoughts of the lover who waited her, and she half reproached herself for having lingered over the sacrifices made for him. The moment of their meeting; the bliss that was to repay her for years of hope deferred; the bright and smiling future—it was a sweet anticipation of happiness, but her heart was chilled to think of the dark, cold ocean still rolling between them; the weeks that must pass before the happy moment arrived; the uncertainty that hung over it, and might dash the cup from her lips. She passed the night in the alternations of feeling caused by such reflections; but with the morning came more pleasant thoughts, and the kind assiduity of Mr. West, who strove to cheer her, and pointed out to her admiring observation the many beautiful and brilliant things to be seen in a voyage was not unrewarded. She ceased to weep, and the sunny smiles that animated her face in conversation with him she already regarded as a father, showed a soul susceptible to all that was beautiful in nature, and all that was lovely and amiable in social life.

The voyage was a tedious one, the vessel being delayed by storms and contrary winds. She anchored safe at length in the harbor of Liverpool. Many people were on the wharf, and there was no little commotion—for the arrival of a ship was not so common a thing as now—and the people were eager to hear the news from the colonies, between which and the mother country discontents had already arisen to an alarming height.

Amidst the scene of confusion, the shouting and running to and fro, one young man pressed forward eagerly, making his way through the crowd to the edge of the pier. He was one of the first to spring on board the vessel as she touched the wharf. It was the painter West. His father, whom he had not seen for eight years, had perceived him, and, with an exclamation of joy on his lips, started foward to greet him. The son, unable to speak, waved him aside with his hand, gasping the single word "Elizabeth?" while the eagerness of his pale face expressed the questioning more earnestly than language could have done.

The old Quaker pointed toward the cabin. The young man rushed hither, and in a moment the long-divided lovers were locked in each other's arms.

The elder West had followed his son, and saw the embrace in which both forgot their long years of cruel separation. Again and again the young artist drew back to gaze on his beloved and clasp her again to his full heart.

"Hast thou no welcome, Benjamin, for thy old father?" at length asked the old man, who had stood quietly for some minutes smiling at the joy he witnessed.

"That I have, father!" cried the son; and a warm greeting was given to the venerable parent, who needed no apology for having been at first neglected. The happy party proceeded the same day to London.

On the 2d of September, 1765, the wedding was solemnized in the church of St. Martin-in-the-Fields. The lovely young bride felt that she had done right in sacrificing some natural scruples to bestow her hand on him to whom her faith was pledged. The years that had flown since their parting had added intellectual grace to her girlish

Engraved from the picture A FAMILY GROUP. *by Benjamin West, P.R.A.*

beauty with a touching interest never imparted till sorrow had chastened the gay spirit of youth. As she stood at the altar, the meek light of truth upon her brow—her eyes beaming with the gentle and loving expression habitual to them—all who saw her thought so beautiful a bride had never stood in that sacred place.

Leaflets—Social and Scientific.

I.

ELIZABETH SHEWELL WEST TO ELIZABETH SHEWELL SWIFT.

MY DEAR NIECE:—Your favor of the 20th inst. I have rec'd, and am happy to hear from you that my request to Messrs. Rathbone, Hughes and Duncan has been so practically complied with. What I have said on that subject you will no doubt see in my letter to your sister, with whom I hope there is that affection and communication which ought ever to subsist between those so closely allied, and it is my sincere wish that it may be the determination of both of you ever to resist and counteract the interference of any malicious or impertinent meddler who may endeavor to interrupt it.

I was indeed happy to hear from you that there is an affectionate

---

The picture entitled "A Family Group," which faces this page, has elicited the praises, by no means undeserved, of the distinguished English painter, Leslie, who says : " We undervalue that which costs us little effort, and West while engaged on a small picture of his own family, little thought how much it would surpass in interest many of his more ambitious works. Its subject is the first visit of his father and elder brother to his young wife after the birth of her second child. They are Quakers, and the venerable old man and his eldest son wear their hats according to the custom of their sect. Nothing can be more beautifully conceived than the mother bending over the babe sleeping in her lap. She is wrapped in a white dressing gown, and her eldest son, a boy five years old, is leaning on the arm of her chair. West stands behind his father, with his palette and brushes in his hand, and the silence that reigns over the whole is that of religious meditation. The picture has no excellence of color, but the masses of light and shadow are impressive and simple, and I know not a more original illustration of the often painted subject, the ages of man. Infancy, childhood, youth, middle life and extreme age are beautifully brought together in the quiet chamber of the painter's wife." (*The Art Journal*, 1863.)

intercourse between you and my dear sister Bickley's amiable family. I say amiable for I am told they are truly so; that, perhaps, and the affectionate manner with which they live together may be the cause of Envy in those who might wish to break the Bond by which they seem so firmly united. Will you, my dear Betsey, have the goodness to remember me affectionately to *all* of them, tell them how happy I should be to receive letters from them—I think it possible that Peggy may have some recollection of me, Hannah was once my correspondent, but alas, I know not by what means it was discontinued. Now I have a little plan which, when you have opportunity, I beg that you will communicate to them. You are all Children of my dearest Brother and Sister, and it certainly would be no great task to you, though a high gratification to me, for *one* or *other* of you to write me *two* or *three* a year, as you can determine among yourselves, a kind of general letters of information by which I shall partake of your happiness and feel again that I have some connection with my Native Country. I have heard that you were married—but to hear from yourself that you were united to the best of Husbands, and settled with Parents, who so well supply the place of the Dear ones you have lost, and that you are blessed with three children, whose names at least I know, it is indeed a gratification. I beg that you will present my affectionate regards to Mr. Swift, your Parents and children, that you may be always happy is the sincere wish of your

                 Affectionate Aunt,

London, 14 Newman St.   ELIZABETH WEST.
    Sept. 25, 1793.

    P. S.—This letter will, I hope, be delivered to you by our Cousin, Thomas Shewell. Mr. West writes his good wishes to yourself and family.

                                      II.

ELIZABETH SHEWELL WEST TO ROBERT AND SARAH SHEWELL.

My dear Cousins Robert and Sally:—Altho' I have not heard from either of you, yet I cannot resist the inclination of writing, in hopes it will be a further inducement to you to afford me the pleasing satisfaction of hearing from you. You will no doubt expect that I should say something of your son, my Cousin Thomas, but I am truly sorry to be under the necessity of acknowledging that I have not seen him more than twice or thrice since his arrival here—which is to me the more unaccountable as, knowingly or willingly, we have never given any offense. I have made strict inquiry, and never yet have been able to find his abode, or any connection by which I could trace him, and it has at times made me really unhappy; Mr. Hunt told me a long while ago that he had left London and was gone on a Commercial Scheme into the country; but whether he has returned to America or not, I am totally ignorant.

I have the happiness my d^r Cousins to say that Mr. West and our sons are perfectly well, that my health still fluctuates, tho' I think myself better than I was some years ago—tho' still troubled with Nervous and Billious Complaints—I stay much at home as usual.

As to news, it grieves me to reflect on the deplorable situation the world is in—the Thousands that have perished, and are likely still to fall by the desolating sword,—Oh! God preserve and keep us; I sincerely pray that America may be enabled to preserve her neutrality; but sometimes my fears will prevail.

I have sprained my thumb some time ago, and it is at present so painful that I can scarcely hold the pen, therefore will only beg you will have the goodness to remember me to all your family. Accept yourselves my dearest Love & believe me, most truly, your affect.

ELIZA WEST.

London, 20 July, 1798.

III.

ELIZABETH SHEWELL WEST TO ELIZABETH S. SWIFT.[*]

My dear Mrs. Swift :—I was much concerned to find by your letter of the 7th June that your health as well as your dear little Mary's was in so indifferent a state, but I hope long ere this you are both perfectly recovered. I also rejoice that Mrs. Kinnersley has recovered her health, but you do indeed surprise me by saying that she can read without glasses; that is more than I can say for myself. I began to use glasses too soon—my sight depends greatly on the state of my

---

[*] "On Sunday last about 3 o'clock P. M., the seat of Robert Shewell, Esq., (known by the name of 'Painswick') in Bucks Co., was discovered to be on fire. The family, excepting a few females, were at a meeting a mile distant. Notwithstanding the alacrity with which the inhabitants of the vicinity assembled and their great exertions to extinguish the flames, all the woodwork to the ground floor was consumed, and nothing but the outer walls and household furniture was saved."—(*The Weekly Magazine*, Phila., Saturday, June 2, 1798.)

nerves, which are at times intolerably bad. I have heard with great concern that my Cousin Robt. Shewell's house has been burnt, it must be a considerable loss to him. Did not hear the particulars, but hope there were no lives lost. We have had letters from our son Raphael, he was at G—— and intended making a Tour through the Country. I think his Wife will have suffered considerably from fatigue before they reach Philadelphia, if she performs the journey with him. Mr. West and our son Ben are I hope well. They are at present in the Country. We have had great rejoicing on account of our recent success on the Coast of Holland. Last night the City, etc., were illuminated and every wild demonstration of joy exhibited. For my part I can never rejoice at the destruction of my fellow Creatures. God grant us Peace. That will be matter of joy to all who are not interested in promoting a cruel war. Shall I beg to be remembered to your good Husband and Parents, and believe me, with good wishes for a continuance of your health and happiness,

Ever my dear Niece,
Your Affect.

London, Sept. 5th, 1799. ELIZA WEST.

IV.

FRANKLIN TO KINNERSLEY.[*]

LONDON, July 28, 1759.

Dear Sir:—I received your favor of Sept. 9, and should have answer'd it sooner but delay'd in expectation of procuring for you some Book that describes and explains the uses of the Instruments you are at a loss about. . . . You do not mention the Reasons of your being tired of your Situation in the Academy. And if you had, it would perhaps be out of my Power at this distance to remedy any Inconvenience you suffer or even if I was present. For before I left

---

[*] From the original in the possession of Mrs. Edw'd Huntsman Langhorne, Pa. Ebenezer Kinnersley was a noted scientist and (in 1769) Professor of Oratory and Belle Lettres in the College of Philadelphia (now the University of Pennsylvania) where there is a memorial window in his honor. He was an intimate friend of Benjamin Franklin and was a valuable coadjutor in the then undeveloped field of electrical research. A programme dated " Philadelphia, ————, 1764 " (now in the possession of Dr. Edward Swift, of Easton, Pa.), announced a course of lectures on Electricity under the following and other descriptive heads: " A wire heated by it so as to become red and

Philadelphia, everything to be done in the Academy was privately preconcerted in a Cabal without my Knowledge or Participation and accordingly carried into Execution. The Schemes of Public Parties made it seem requisite to lessen my Influence wherever it could be lessened. The Trustees had reap'd the full Advantage of my Head, Hands, Heart and Purse, in getting through the first Difficulties of the Design, and when they thought they could do without me, they laid me aside. I wish Success to the School nevertheless and am sorry to hear that the whole Number of Scholars does not at present exceed one hundred & forty.

I once thought of advising you to make Trial of your Lectures here and perhaps in the more early Times of Electricity, it might have answered; but now I much doubt it, so great is the general Negligence of everything in the Way of Science that has not Novelty to recommend it. Courses of Experimental Philosophy, formerly so much in Vogue, are now discarded; so that Mr. Domainbray, who is reputed an excellent Lecturer, and has an apparatus that cost nearly £2000, the finest perhaps in the World, can hardly make up an audience in this great City to attend one Course in a Winter.

I wonder your roughening the Glass Globe did not succeed. I have seen Mr. Canton frequently perform his Experiments with the smooth, rough & Tubes, and they answered perfectly, as he describes them in the Transactions. Perhaps you did not use the same Rubbers.

There are some few new Experiments here in Electricity which at present I can only just hint to you. Mr. Symmer has found that a new black Silk Stocking worn 8 or 10 Minutes on a new white one, then both drawn off together, they have, while together, no great signs of Electricity, *i. e.*, they do not much attract the small Cork Balls of Mr. Canton's Box; but being drawn one out of the other,

---

burning hot"; "Metal melted by it on glass and some of the metal incorporated with the substance of the glass"; "A shower of electrified sand rising again as fast as it falls"; "An artificial spider animated by electricity so as to act like a live one"; "A curious machine put in motion by lightning and playing various tunes on eight musical bells." Professor Kinnersley was one of those modest, unselfish students of science, who sometimes sow where others reap. He is entitled to the credit of having been one of the earliest to utilize that wonderful natural force which more than a century after he passed away became the motor of the world.

they puff out to the full Shape of the Leg, affect the Cork Balls at the Distance of 6 Feet and attract one another at the Distance of 18 inches and will cling together; and either of them against a smooth Wall or a Looking Glass, will stick to it some time. Upon Trial, the black Stocking appears to be electris'd negatively, the white one positively. He charges Vials with them as we us'd to do with a Tube. Mr. Delavan has found that several Bodies which conduct when cold, or hot to a certain Degree, will not conduct when in a middle State. Portland Freestone, for Instance, when cold, conducts; heated to a certain degree will not conduct; heated more it conducts again; and as it cools, passes thro' that Degree in which it will not conduct till it becomes cooled.

This, with what you mention of your Cedar Cylinder, makes me think, that possibly a thin Cedar Board, or Board of other Wood, thoroughly dried and heated, might, if coated and electrified, yield a Shock as glass Planes do. As yet I have not try'd it.

But the greatest Discovery in this Way is the Virtue of the *Tourmalin* Stone, brought from *Ceylon* in the Indies, which being heated in boiling Water, becomes strongly Electrical, one side positive, the other negative, without the least Rubbing. They are very rare but I have two of them & long to show you the Experiments.

Billy joins with me in Compliments to you & to good Mrs. Kinnersley & your promising Children.

I am with much Esteem and Affection Dear Sir,
     Your most obedient Servant,
Mr. Kinnersley.   B. FRANKLIN.

A Pennsylvania Loyalist and George III.*

FIRST DAY, OCT. 10, 1784. This morning at 8 'Clock thy son accompanied B. West's wife to the King's Chappel where he had the opportunity of seeing the King and several of the Princesses. They returned before 9 when we were entertained with breakfast, at which we had the Company of Mr.

---

*Samuel Shoemaker was a resident of Philadelphia, a member of the Society of Friends and prominent as a merchant. From 1755 to 1773 he filled various offices in the municipal government of Philadelphia, including that of Mayor, 1769.

Upon the evacuation of the city by the British in 1778 he accompanied the

Poggy the Italian Gent'n, Mr. Trumble,* Mr. W. Farrington,† and West's two sons. About 10 thy son accompanied Farrington, Trumble and West's Eldest son in a Ride through Windsor Forrest having first been with West and I to this Room in the Castle to see a picture of the Lord's Supper, which he had just finished for the King's Chappel. After part of our Company were gone to take their Ride, West informed me that the King had order'd him to attend at his Painting Room in the Castle at one 'Clock, when the King and Queen and some of the Princesses, on their return from Chappel, intended to call to see the Painting of the Lord's Supper which he had just finished, and West told me it would be a very proper time and Opportunity for me to see the King, Queen and the rest of the family as they came from the Chappel, and therefore requested me to accompany him and his Wife and the Italian Gent'n, and walk at the Castle near the Chappel, till service was over, when he must repair to his room to attend the King, and would leave me with his Wife in a proper Station to have a full view of the King and family. Accordingly, a little before one O'Clock, West and his wife, the Italian Gent'n and I, walk'd up to the Castle and there contin'd walking about till the Clock struck One, when we observed one of the Pages coming from the Chappel.

West then said he must leave us : presently after this two Coaches pass'd and went round towards the Door of the Castle leading to West's Room. In these two coaches were the Queen and Princesses ; presently after the King appear'd attended by his Equery only, and walk'd in great haste, *almost ran* to meet the Coaches at the door of the Castle above mentioned, which he reached just as the coaches got

---

Army to New York, whence he sailed in 1783 for England. He was a prominent Royalist, and was distinguished for his zeal on the side of the Crown, in consequence of which he was attainted of treason and his estate confiscated. While in New York he exerted himself for the relief of the Whig prisoners and, by his intercession with the British authorities, numbers of them were liberated and allowed to return to their homes. At the time to which this extract from Mr. Shoemaker's diary refers, he was spending a few days at Windsor with his friend Benjamin West, the artist. (*Pa. Mag Hist. and Biog.* V. 2, p. 35.)

* Col. Jno. Trumbull, afterwards of Washington's Staff and an American portrait painter.

† A noted English landscape artist.

there, as did West's Wife, the Italian Gent'n and I, when we saw the King go to the Door of the Coach in which the Queen was, and heard him say, "*I have got here in time,*" and then handed the Queen out, and up the steps, into the Castle—the Princess Royal, Princess Elizabeth, Princess Mary, and Princess Sophia, with Col. Goldsworthy, the King's Equery, the Hanoverian Resident, and Miss Goldsworthy, sub-Governess to the two young Princesses, followed. They all went into the Castle, when I heard the King say, "tell him to come in;" *but little did I think I was the Person meant,* and West's Wife, the Italian Gent'n, and I were about going off, when West came out of the Castle and told me the King had order'd him to come out and bring me and Mrs. West in. I was quite unprepar'd for this; however, it was now too late to avoid it. The Italian Gent'n now left us and went to walk the Terras, and West and his wife and I went into the Castle and were ushered up to the Room where the King and Royal family were, and there introduc'd. *Flattered and Embarrassed thou may suppose,* on my entering the Room, the King came up close to me, and very graciously said, "Mr. S., you are well known here, everybody knows you," &c. (complimentary w'ch I can't mention) He then turned to the Queen, the Princesses, &c., who stood by and repeated "Mr. S." I then made my bow to the Queen, then to the Princess Royal, to the Princess Eliza, Princesses Mary and Sophia. The Queen and each of the Princesses were pleased to drop a Curtesy, and then the Queen was pleased to ask me one or two Questions: the King and Queen and the four Princesses, the Hanoverian Resident, Col. Goldsworthy, Miss Goldsworthy, West and his Wife and I were all that were in the Room. The King condescended to ask me many questions and repeated my answers to them to the Queen and to the Hanoverian Resident, and when to the latter, I observ'd he spoke it in German, which I understood. Among other Questions the King was pleased to ask me the reason why the Province of Pennsylvania was so much further advanc'd in improvement than the neighboring ones, some of which had been settled so many years earlier. I told his Majesty (thinking it w'd be a kind of Compliment to the Queen's Countrymen) that I thought it might be attributed to the Germans, great numbers of whom had gone over in the early part of the settlement of that Province, as well as since. The King smiled and said, "It may be so, Mr. S., it may in some measure be owing to that, *but I will tell you the true cause,*—the great improvement and flourishing state of Pennsylvania is principally owing to the *Quakers:*" (this was a full return for my compliment to the Queen's Countrymen for whom I observe the King has a great regard). Finding the King so repeatedly mention'd what I had said to the Hanov'n Resident and to the Queen, in German, on the King's asking me a particular question, I took the liberty to answer in German, at which the King seemed pleased, and *with a smile* turned to the Queen and said, " Mr. S. speaks German," and also mentioned it to the Hanoverian Resident, after which the King was pleased to speak to me several times in German. Then the Queen condescended to ask me several questions, one of the last, *whether I had a family.* On my telling her that I was once bless'd with a numerous family, but that it had pleased Providence to remove them all from me, except a Wife and two Sons, this visibly touched the Queen's delicate feelings, so much so that she shed some tears, at which I was *greatly* affected. She is a charming woman, and if not a beauty, her manners and disposition are so pleasing that no Person who has the Opportunity that I have had can avoid being charm'd with the sweetness of her disposition. The Princess Royal is pretty, has a charming Countenance indeed ; the Princess Elizabeth very agreeable, but rather too fat or bulky for her height. Mary and Sophia are pretty, but being so young their looks will alter.

After being graciously indulged with the opportunity of conversing with the King and Queen, and being in the Room with them three-quarters of an hour, they all departed and went to the Queen's House.

I cannot say but I wished some of my violent Countrymen could have such an opportunity as I have had. I think they would be convinced that George the third has not one grain of Tyranny in his Composition, and that he *is* not, he *cannot* be that bloody minded man they have so repeatedly and so illiberally called him. It is impossible; a man of his fine feelings, so good a husband, so kind a Father *cannot be a Tyrant.*

After the Royal family were gone, West and his wife and I return'd to West's house where we were soon join'd by the Italian Gent'n, and those who had been out Riding, and at three O'clock were entertain'd at a genteel Dinner and spent the afternoon and evening together very pleasantly till 11 'Clock when we retir'd to Bed. This happens to be B. West's birthday : he has now enter'd his forty-seventh year. . . .

Napoleon and Benjamin West.*

DURING the short peace of 1802, when Bonaparte was First Consul of the French Republic, the late President of the Royal Academy of England was among the crowd to visit the gay metropolis of France. He was visited by most of the men of rank and literature, among the rest by those ministers who were most in the confidence of the First Consul. Mr. West had determined before his departure from England for some private reasons of his own, to decline any presentation at the Court of St. Cloud, to which he was given to understand he would have been a very welcome visitor. About a week after his arrival in Paris, he was surprised while at breakfast by a visit from one of the directors of the Louvre, with an invitation to be present at the gallery of the institution to inspect some busts which were about to be erected, and to favor the directors with his judgment as to their relative positions. They proceeded to the gallery where Mr. West was soon surrounded by a crowd of artists, all of whom appeared attired in their official costume. A bustle in the ante-chamber seemed to announce some unusual occurrence. In a moment the doors were thrown open and in walked Napoleon in his little cocked hat and simple uniform, followed by a gorgeous suite of generals, the future dukes and viceroys and monarchs of his creation. "Where is the President of the Arts in England?" was the abrupt and immediate interrogatory of the First Consul. The president was instantly saluted with "Well, Mr. West, you would not come to visit me, and therefore I have been obliged to come to visit you, as I should regret your return to England without our being better acquainted." They then proceeded to the Louvre, and when they arrived at the busts intended to be erected that day, Bonaparte paused, folded his arms as he is represented in his statues, and after appearing to contemplate one of them with peculiar thoughtfulness he turned to West—"Mr. West, if I had my choice I would sooner be the original of that bust than any man I have ever heard or read of." "I was burning (said Mr. West relating the anecdote) to tell him that he had it at that moment in his power, by sacrificing his ambition and establishing the liberties of his country, to be the very man." It was the bust of Washington.

---

* From "Niles Register," Aug 25, 1821.

From Harper's Magazine.   Copyright by Harper & Bros.

Benj. West

Benjamin West's Funeral.*

SOON after Mr. West's decease,† a deputation from the Council of the Royal Academy waited upon his sons to apprise them of the intention of that body to attend the remains of their late President to the grave, the King having given his sanction. At half past twelve the Procession moved from Somerset House to St. Paul's Cathedral. It was composed of a number of mounted Constables, Marshals, Cloakmen and Mutes, nearly one hundred carriages drawn by six, four and two horses each, attended by innumerable pages and containing, besides the members of the Academy, representatives of Church and State, the nobility and gentry, and was witnessed with great solemnity by an immense concourse of people. On arriving at

---

* From Galt's "Life of Benjamin West."

† BENJAMIN WEST was born at Springfield, Penn., Oct. 10, 1738, of an old Quaker family which had emigrated from Buckinghamshire, Eng. As a child he evinced artistic genius, and, at the age of 18, settled in Philadelphia as a portrait painter. Subsequently he resided in New York, and in 1760, with the aid of wealthy friends, he went to Rome and after spending three years in Italy, in the study of his art, removed to London, renewed his acquaintance with certain English noblemen and patrons of art, whom he had met in America, and was presented privately to the King by the Archbishop of York. From that moment he was taken under the special patronage of George III. and was (1772) appointed Historical Painter to the Crown. He was the first to take a new departure in the direction of realism, insisting upon depicting the costume actually worn rather than that of the ancients which had, until West instituted a reform, been used in all historical work. He became very popular at Court and being an expert skater, often attracted crowds by his performances on the Serpentine; one elaborate figure being called "The Philadelphia Salute." On the death of Sir Joshua Reynolds (1792) West was elected his successor as President of the Royal Academy of Painting, Sculpture and Architecture, an office which he held for twenty-eight years. At the age of sixty-four he painted one of his largest works, "Christ Healing the Sick," which he had intended for the new Pennsylvania Hospital at Philadelphia. It was exhibited in London to immense crowds and was purchased by the British Institution, for 3000 guineas, with authority to paint a replica for the hospital ; the copy created an equal sensation in Philadelphia, the receipts from its exhibition enabling the Trustees to add thirty beds to the hospital. He died at London, March 10, 1820, and was buried in St. Paul's Cathedral.

the Cathedral the procession was met at the Great Western Gate by the Church dignitaries, the whole preceded by the choir in the following order :

The two junior Vergers,

The Marshals,

The Choir,

Their Almoner,

The Sub Dean and Junior Canons,

The Feathers with Pages and Mutes,

The two Senior Vergers,

Hon. and Rev. Dr. WELLESLEY,

Canon Residentiary and Rev. the Prebendary.

(*Pall Bearers.*)		(*Pall Bearers.*)
EARL OF ABERDEEN,	C O R P S E	Rt. Hon. Sir W. SCOTT.
AMERICAN MINISTER,		Hon. GEO. PHIPPS.
Hon. AUGUSTUS PHIPPS,		Sir GEORGE BEAUMONT,
Sir THOMAS BARING.		Sir ROBT. WILSON.

(*Chief Mourners.*)

RAPHAEL LAMAR WEST, Esq.

BENJAMIN WEST, Esq.

(and)

Mr. BENJAMIN WEST, Jr.

(*followed by*)

Robert Brunning

(*the old servant of deceased.*)

&c.   &c.   &c.

The Bishop of Salisbury

(*as Chaplain Royal Academy.*)

The Academicians

and

Students

and

Private Friends.

Lost Names.

They lived and they were useful ; this we know
    And naught beside ;
No record of their names is left to show
    How soon they died ;
They did their work, and then they passed away,
    An unknown band,
And took their places with the greater host
    In the higher land.

And were they young, or were they growing old,
    Or ill, or well,
Or lived in poverty, or had much gold,
    No one can tell ;
One only thing is known of them, they were
    Faithful and true
Disciples of the Lord, and strong through prayer
    To save and do.

But what avails the gift of empty fame !
    They live to God,
They loved the sweetness of another name,
    And gladly trod
The rugged ways of earth, that they might be
    Helper, or friend,
And in the joy of this their ministry,
    Be spent and spend.

No glory clusters round their names on earth ;
    But in God's heaven
Is kept a book of names of greater worth,
    And there is given
A place for all who did the Master please,
    Although unknown,
And their lost names shine forth in brightest rays
    Before the throne.

Oh, take who will the boon of fading fame!
        But give to me
A place among the workers, though my name
        Forgotten be;
And if within the book of life is found
        My lowly place,
Honor and glory unto God redound
        For all his grace.

Index.

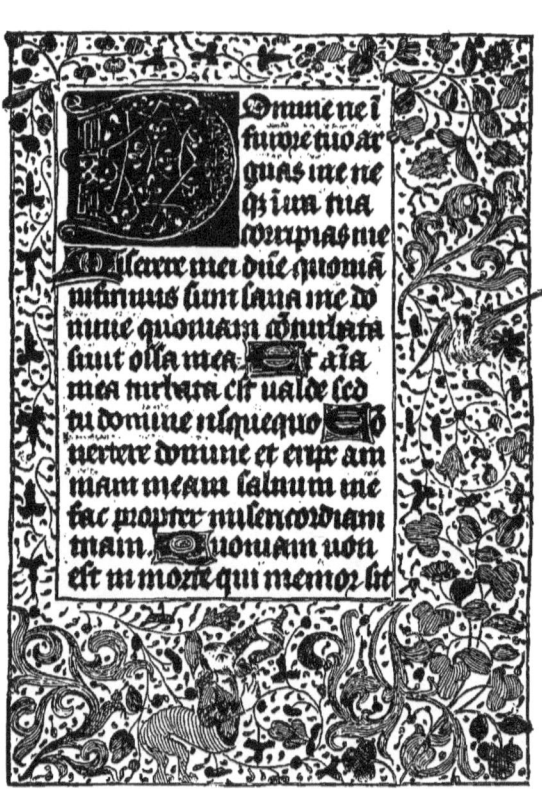

To a Missal of the Thirteenth Century.

(Austin Dobson in *The Century*.)

Missal of the Gothic age,
Missal with the blazoned page,
Whence, O Missal, hither come,
From what dim *scriptorium*?

Whose the name that wrought thee thus,
Ambrose or *Theophilus*,
Bending, through the waning light,
O'er thy vellum scraped and white ;

Weaving, 'twixt thy rubric lines
Sprays and leaves and quaint designs ;
Setting round thy border scrolled
Beds of purple and of gold?

Ah!—a wondering brotherhood,
Doubtless, round that artist stood,
Strewing o'er his careful ways
Little choruses of praise ;

Glad when his deft hand would paint
Strife of *Sathanus* and Saint,
Or in secret coign entwist
Jest of cloister humorist.

Well the worker earned his wage,
Bending o'er the blazoned page !
Tired the hand and tired the wit
Ere the final *Explicit !*

Not as ours the books of old—
Things that steam can stamp and fold ;
Not as ours the books of yore—
Rows of type and nothing more.

Then a book was still a book,
Where a wistful man might look,
Finding something through the whole,
Beating—like a human soul.

In the growth of day by day,
When to labor was to pray,
Surely something vital passed
To the patient page at last ;

Something that one still perceives
Vaguely present in the leaves ;
Something from the worker lent ,
Something mute—but eloquent !

Index.

ARON.
  Eliza, 185.
  Emilia, 185.
  Louisa, 185.
  Mary, 185.
  Samuel, 180-4
bbey St. Peter and St. Paul, 104.
bbott, F., 186.
Abercrummie, 112.
Aberdeen, 114.
  Earl of, 276.
Abingdon, Pa., 180.
Abou, Ben Adhem, 219.
Academy, St. Augustine's, 18.
Acapulco, 127.
A Colonial Indian Fight, 71.
Active, the ship, 61.
Adams.
  John, Mrs., 61.
  John Quincy, 22.
  Samuel, 58.
Adriatic, 55, 186.
Afghanistan or Anglo-Russian Dispute, 155.
A Franco-American Leaf, 62, 86.
African Coast, 119, 124.
Alabama, S., S., 143.
Albany, N. Y., 167.
Albany, Duke of, 72, 110.
Albuquerque, N. M., 191.
Aldie, Va., battle of, 155.
Aldrich.
  Henry, 23.
  Lydia Cloud, 22, 23.
Alert, U. S. S., 140.
Allegheny Mountains, 160.
Allegheny, Pa., Bank, 21.
Allen Frances, 65.
Allentown, N. J., 115, 116, 118, 119, 123.
Alloway Kirk-yard, 112, 114.
Alsace, 13.

American Philosophical Society.
American S. S. Line, 22.
Amherst College, 64.
Amory, Thomas C., 86, 97.
Ancestors, A Man Introduced to, 251.
Ancestor's Letter-Book, 175, 203.
An Elopement by Proxy, 196, 255.
Anderson.
  Augusta, 176, 180.
  Elizabeth, 149.
Andrews, S. M., 190.
  T. P., 143.
Andros Gov., 71.
Anglo-American Notes, 220, 222.
An Impartial Judge, 30.
Anjou, Duke of, 105.
Anne, Queen, 216, 217.
Anson, British brig, 60.
Antietam, battle of, 23.
An Upright Man, 44.
Apgar, Letty Ann, 153.
Appleton, 62.
  Nathaniel, 58.
Apsden, Mr., 249.
Apthorp, John T., 62, 63, 88.
A Quaker Missionary, 51.
Archæology of the United States, 64.
A Relic of Seventy-Six, 93.
Argosies, He sent out his, 196, 244.
Argyll.
  Earl of, 110.
  Lady Helen, 110.
Armstrong.
  Elliot Chidsey, 41.
  Frank Woodin, 41.
  Harry Knox, 41.
  Margaret, 41.
  William H., 39, 40, 41.
  William Russell, 39.
Army and Navy Journal, 155.
Arnold.
  Benedict, 244.
  Mary Barbara, 16.
Art Journal, 265.

Arundel, Castle of, 104.
Athens, Ga., 192.
Atlantic, S. S., 190.
Auburn, Mount.
Ave Maria, brig, 171.
Ayr, Bay of, 106.
Ayrshire (Scot.), 123.
Backus.
  Catharine Clemens, 188.
  F. R., 188.
Balaclava, 10, 221, 225.
Baltimore, Md., 19, 124.
Bancroft, H. H., 129.
Banks.
  John, 57.
  Joseph, Sir, 48.
  Mary, 56, 57.
Baptists, 174.
Barbadoes, 17, 33, 35, 196, 249.
Barclay, Robert, 204.
Baring, Sir Thomas, 276.
Barnard, 63.
Barnes, Lieutenant, 36.
Barrett, 63.
Barron J., 86.
  Lucy, 86.
Bartlett, Lieut., 128.
Barton, Elizabeth, 196.
Batchelder.
  Frank, 62.
  Samuel, 86, 87.
Batchelder House, 58.
Bath, Me., 67.
Battle Creek, Mich., 22.
Battle of the Kegs, 257.
Beach, W. H., 184.
Beatrice, Neb., 41.
Beattie, Horatio B., 186.
Beaumont, Sir George, 276.
Bedford, Pa., 160.
Belvidere, H. B. M. S., 118.
Belle Plain, Va., 151.
Bellevue Hospital, 187, 194.
Bennett, Elizabeth, 181, 188.
Benneville, Geo. de, 180, 213, 215, 219.
Bennington, Vt., 178, 179.
Benton, 132.
Bergen Heights, 40.
Berlin, 65.
Bermuda, 175, 222.
Berrien.

Cornelius Jansen, 116.
  Eliza, 116.
  John, 116, 117, 123.
  John Macpherson, 116.
  Samuel, 116.
Bertolette, Jean, 215.
Berwick, battle of, 106, 107.
Berwind, Cecilia M., 189, 194.
Bethlehem, Pa., 159, 215.
Bethlehem, N. J., 148, 149, 150, 151, 152, 153, 157.
Beverly Ford, Va., battle of, 153.
Bickley.
  Family of, 214.
  Abraham, 175, 176, 196, 197, 214.
  Elizabeth, 197.
  Hannah, 197.
  Isaac, 197.
  Lydia, 197.
  Margaret, 197.
  Mary, 266.
  Robert, 197.
  William, Sir, 235.
Bickworth, Capt., 170.
Biddeford, Eng., 78.
Biddle.
  Charles, 34, 211, 244, 249.
  Edward McFunn, 118.
  Julia Montgomery, 118.
  Lydia Spencer, 118.
  Mary Montgomery, 118.
  Nicholas, 15, 17, 32, 33, 35.
  Thomas Montgomery, 118.
  William, 32.
  William M., 118.
Bidlemansville, Pa., 159.
Bindwell, Letty, 201.
Bingham, W., 204.
Birch, Edwin K., 191.
Bird, Sarah, 222.
Bishopthorpe School, 156.
Bispham.
  Joseph, 181.
  Joshua, 181.
  Susan, 177, 181.
  Susanna Pearson, 181.
Black, family of, 209, 212.
Blackburn, 61.
Blake, J., 34, 36.
Blanchard, Joshua, 59.
Block Island, R. I., 183.
Bloomfield, N. J., 261.

INDEX.   285

Boardman, Eliza, 61.
Bofinger, John N., 183.
Bogert, Mary B., 66, 68.
Bogwell, George, 79.
Bonaparte, N., 274.
Bond, Dr., 30, 206.
Bonsfield & Co., 180.
Boonsboro, Md., battle of, 155.
Bordeaux, 98, 186.
Bosquet, Gen., 237.
Bossenger.
  Ann, 57.
  Mary, 56.
Boston, Mass., 11, 19, 56, 57, 58, 59,
  60, 61, 62, 63, 66, 68, 69, 70, 72,
  80, 82, 83, 88, 98, 124, 125, 184.
  Athenæum, 97.
  Medical College, 65.
  Transcript and Courier, 99, 193.
Bothwell, Earl of, 109.
Bouden, Rachel, 178, 183.
Boutcher.
  Caleb, 199.
  Caroline Swift, 199.
  Charles Swift, 199.
  Edward Swift, 199.
  Elizabeth Swift, 199.
Bowdoin, James, 59.
Bower, Dr., 142.
Bowlby, Mary, 151.
Bowling Green, Ky., 166.
Boyer, Mr., 196.
Brackett.
  Anthony, 79.
  Elizabeth, 17, 19.
  Lieutenant, 71, 74.
  Mary, 17, 26.
  Seth, 79.
Bradbury, 63.
Braddock, Gen., 160.
Bradford, Eng., 186.
Braintree, Mass., 60.
Branchtown, Pa., 180.
Brandy Station, battle of, 155.
Breck.
  Gabriella Du Pont, 200.
Brewster.
  Richard, 222.
  Sarah Shewell, 222.
  Thomas, 222.
Bridgenorth, Castle of, 104.
Brigend, 112, 114, 115.

Brighton, Eng., 98.
Brimmer, Hermain, 59.
Bristoe Station, battle of, 155.
Bristol, Pa., 187. 220, 255.
Bristol, R. I., 20.
British Revenue Stamps, 203.
Broadhead, J. G., 143.
Brookline, Mass., 194.
Brooklyn, N. Y., 66, 67, 192.
Brown.
  Elizabeth, 202.
  Esther, 48.
  Hannah, 176, 180, 181.
  John, 59.
  Margaret, 48, 149.
  William, 48.
Bruce, Robert, 107.
Brunning, Robert, 276.
Bruges, 17, 26.
Buchanan, Prest., 135.
Budden, W., 210.
Buffalo, N. Y., 22, 124, 194.
Bull Run (2d) battle of, 155.
Bunker Hill, 58, 80.
Burlington, N. J., 116, 185.
Burlington, Ia., 197, 198.
Burnet.
  Gilbert, 114.
  Isabel, 114.
  John, 115.
  Ward B., 143.
  Robert, 114.
  William, 115.
Butler, T. H., 192.
Buttler, Edmund, 16.
Butz, Matilda, 39, 40.
Bybury, Pa., 29.
Bye, Mr., 197.
Cabot, Catharine, 62.
Cadiz (Sp.) 96.
Calamy, Edward, 223.
Calcutta, 69.
California, 125.
Callender, F. D., 143.
Callisen's Academy, 155.
Calvin, 148.
Cambridge, Mass., 56, 57, 58, 59, 62,
  63, 64, 65, 79, 81, 82, 83, 86, 87,
  95.
Cambridge University, (Eng.) 40,223.
Campbell, Wallace, 198.
Canada, 72.

INDEX.

Canton, Ill., 149, 152, 153.
Cape St. Lucas, 119.
Cardigan, Lord, 225, 233.
Carlisle, Pa., 118, 138, 139, 153, 159.
Carman, Sarah, 202.
Carr, Matthew, 14.
Carrell.
  Anna Margaret, 21.
  Catharine Josephine, 21.
  Fielding Lucas, 21.
  Henry Carey, 21.
  John, 20, 21.
  Mary Elena, 21.
Carysfort, H. B. M. S., 33, 34.
Casco, Me., 71, 72, 79.
Case, Thomas, 223.
Castine, Baron de, 72.
Castro, Gen., 126, 127, 128, 129, 120, 132, 133.
Cauffman.
  Anna Catharine, 15.
  Anna Mary, 16, 17.
  Ann Theresa, 16.
  Caroline, 18, 21.
  Catharine, 16, 17.
  Emily, 18, 149, 150.
  Emily Hudson, 22, 24.
  Eugene Laurence, 22, 23.
  Frank Guernsey, 22, 24.
  Frieda, 24.
  George, 16.
  Harry Falconer, 22.
  James, 16.
  John, 16, 17.
  Joseph, 15, 17, 25, 30, 33.
  Joseph Theophilus, 12, 13, 14, 15, 16.
  Julia, 18, 50.
  Laurence, 16, 18, 23, 50, 150, 172, 176.
  Margaret, 16.
  Mary Willcox, 18, 23.
  Robert Shewell, 18, 21.
  Sarah, 17, 20.
  Sarah Shewell, 172, 209, 214.
  Stanley Hart, 24.
  Theophilus Francis, 11, 17, 18, 22, 23.
Century Magazine, 125.
Ceort's Eye, 37.
Chadsey, 37.
Chambersburg, Pa., 124, 159.
Champlain, 118.
Chancellor, Dr., 25.
Chandos, Duke of, 196.
Channing, Dr., 68.
Chapel Hill, N. C., 63.
Chapultepec, 142.
Charlemagne, 102.
Charles I., 37, 113.
Charleston S. C., 15, 33, 34, 36.
Charlestown, Mass., 57, 65, 66, 69, 119.
Charlotte, Queen, 214.
Chaucer, 245.
Chedsey, 37.
Chertsey, 37.
Cherubusco, 141.
Chester, Pa., 18, 49, 256.
Chestnut Hill, Conn., 140.
Chevy Chase, 108.
Cheyenne, Wyo., 63.
Chicago, 198.
Chidsey.
  Abigail, 38.
  Abraham, 38.
  Almira, 39.
  Andrew Dwight, 40, 43.
  Ann, 38.
  Anna, 39.
  Anna Eliza, 39, 41.
  Betsey, 39.
  Caleb, 38.
  Charles Francis, 11, 37, 39, 42, 43, 44.
  Daniel, 38.
  Dudley Kirk, 43.
  Ebenezer, 38.
  Edward Hart, 40, 43.
  Eliza Woodin, 39.
  Elizabeth, 37, 38.
  Emily Harriet, 39, 42, 156.
  Emily Heidelberg, 42.
  George Woodin, 39, 40.
  Hannah, 38.
  Harold, 43.
  Harriet, 39.
  Helen Stewart, 43.
  Henry Russell, 39, 40, 43, 44.
  Isaac, 38.
  John, 37, 38.
  John Russell, 43.
  Joseph, 38.
  Kate, 43.

INDEX. 287

Lorinda, 39.
Louis, 38.
Lydia, 38.
Mary, 38.
Morris Dwight, 43.
Myra Louisa, 39, 40.
Russell Smith, 39, 40, 44, 45, 46, 150, 156.
Russell Williams, 42.
Samuel, 38.
Sarah, 38, 39.
Thomas McKeen, 43.
Christ Healing the Sick, 276.
Church.
  Benjamin, 58.
  Capt. 72.
  Martha, 61.
Churches, Atonement, P. E., (Phil.), 24.
Christ, P. E. (Boston), 62.
Christ, P. E. (Cambridge), 23, 31, 82.
Christ, P. E. (Phil.), 23, 24, 155, 172, 179.
Grove, Pres. (Danville, Pa.), 41.
Holy Trinity, P. E. (Phil.), 24.
Incarnation, P. E. (N. Y.), 155.
Neshaminy, Bapt., 177.
Pennypeck Bapt. (Pa.), 196.
Presbyterian (1st) Easton, (Pa.), 44.
Presbyterian (2d) Easton, (Pa.), 44.
St. Ann's by the Sea, P. E. (R. I.)
St. Augustine, R. C. (Phil.), 16.
St. James, P. E. (Gt. Barrington, Mass.), 68.
St. James, P. E. (Phil.), 17.
St. Joseph's, R. C. (Phil.), 14, 15, 16.
St. Luke's P. E. (Germantown, Pa.), 18.
St. Mark's, P. E. (Phil.), 50.
St. Mary's, R. C. (Phil.), 14, 15.
St. Peter's, P. E. (Phil.), 179.
Trinity, P. E. (Easton), 172, 173.
Trinity, P. E. (N. Y.), 117.
Churchman.
  Albert, 50.
  Ann, 49.
  Caleb, 49.
  Dinah, 47.
  Edward, 48, 49, 50.
  Gainer, 48.

  George, 47, 48.
  Hannah, 50.
  Hannah Pierce, 48.
  John, 47, 48, 51.
  Joseph, 48.
  Margaret, 48, 50.
  Margaret Brown, 47, 48.
  Mary, 50.
  Mary Reed, 50.
  Micaijah, 48.
  Mordecai, 48.
  Owen, 49.
  Phœbe, 49.
  Rebecca, 50.
  Rebecca Pierce, 48.
  Robert, 50.
  Sarah, 48.
  Susannah, 47.
Church Row, Cambridge, 86.
Cincinnati, O., 161, 164, 184, 192.
Cincinnati, Society of, 82.
Circleville, O., 162.
Clark.
  Bishop of R. I., 183.
  Surg., 142.
  Thaddeus, 73, 74, 77, 78.
Clarksburg, Va., 154.
Clay, Henry, 23, 178.
Claxton, J. W. 23, 24.
Clerkington (Scot.), 113.
Clifton Heights, Pa., 182.
Clinton, N., J., 151, 153.
Clio, H. B. M. S., 136.
Clock on the Stair, The Old, 20.
Cloice, Thos., 79.
Clowes, Cornet, 229, 237.
Clutterbuck, Lt., 229, 237.
Colburn's Mag., 226, 232, 234.
Colchester, Eng., 220, 221.
Cold Harbor, Va., battle of, 154, 155.
Coligny, Admiral, 109.
Colleges.
  Amherst, 64.
  Brown University, 59.
  Columbia, 41, 68.
  Harvard, 59, 64, 65, 67, 68, 70, 96, 125.
  Lafayette, 21, 40, 41, 42.
  Philada, 197, 208.
  Physicians' and Surgeons' (N. Y.), 42.
  Princeton, 195.

Penna., Univ., of, 195, 196, 200, 201, 268.
Yale, 43, 80.
Collins.
  Clara Monroe Shewell, 191.
  Grellet, 190.
  Monroe, 191.
  Robert Eli, 191.
Colonial Records, 144.
Columbus, U. S. S., 124.
Comly.
  Henry, 198.
  Jane, 198.
  Phœbe, 198.
Comstock Seminary, 156.
Conan, 66.
Conant.
  Agnes, 66.
  Francis O., 66.
  John, 66, 67.
  Lot, 67.
  Margaret, 67.
  Mary, 59, 65, 66, 79.
  Mary Parker, 67.
  Richard, 66, 67.
  Roger, 66, 67.
  Samuel, 67.
Conant, Fort, 66.
Conard, J. B., 187, 194.
Congress, U. S. S., 20, 119, 140.
Coningham.
  Anna Miriam, 192.
  R. F., 192.
Conklin, Caroline, 200.
Connaunt, Alexander, 67.
Connett, 66.
Constance, H. B. M. S., 135.
Constitution, U. S. S., 119, 124.
Contreras, 141.
Cook.
  Henry Trevor, 198.
  Lorraine, 198.
  Lyman, 198.
  Margery, 198.
  Mary Frances, 198.
Cooper.
  Fenimore, 163.
  William, 59.
Copley, 61.
Coppinger, Mr., 62.
Corn, first pat. for curing, 175.
Cornwall, England, 56.

Cortez, 125.
Cotringer, John, 13, 17.
Cotteral, Mary, 120.
Coventry, Eng., 223.
Cowley, the poet, 37.
Craigie.
  Andrew, 58, 82, 83, 85, 87, 93, 94, 95, 96.
  Elizabeth, 57, 58, 59, 82, 83, 84, 85.
  Mary, 57, 59.
Craigie House, 70.
Crampton, J. F., 135.
Cranch, Mrs., 61.
Crawford, James, 223.
Creed, The Founder of a, 215.
Crocker.
  Alsop, 79.
  Edward, 79.
Crosswicks, N. J., 114, 115.
Culpeper, Va., battle of, 155.
Cumberland River, 165, 166, 168.
Cumberland, U. S. S., 120.
Cunninghame.
  Alexander, 112.
  Elizabeth, 112.
  John, 112.
Cupid Swallowed, 254.
Curaçoa, 144, 188.
Curio, the, 57.
Currie.
  Arthur, 180.
  Eliza Graeme, 180.
  Elizabeth, 179, 209, 213, 214.
  Harriet Shewell, 179.
  Laughlin, 180.
  Louisa, 180.
  Mary Shewell, 180.
  Samuel, 176, 179, 213.
  Thomas Shewell, 180, 185.
Curry.
  Hannah, 47.
  Thomas, 47.
Curtis.
  Geo. William, 83.
  Laura, 199.
Cushing, Thomas, 58.
Cushman, Charlotte, 193.
Cutler.
  John, 58, 62, 88.
  Miriam, 58, 62.
Cutting, Nathaniel, 83.
Cyane, U. S. S., 124, 130, 131.

INDEX. 289

Dale.
   Fanny, 42.
   Sarah, 42.
Dana.
   Elizabeth, 59, 60.
   Richard, 59, 60.
Dante, 218.
Danville, Pa., 41.
Darnley, Lord, 108.
Daveis, Chas. S., 61.
David I. (Scot.), 105.
Davidson & Foster, firm of, 98.
Davis.
   Caleb, 58.
   Chas. H., 69.
   Edward Graham, 69.
   Laura, W., 194.
   Sylvanus, 72, 73, 74, 75, 76, 77.
   William, 59.
Decatur, Commodore, 119, 124.
Declaration of Independence, 29.
Dedham, Mass., 63, 64, 65, 66, 67, 96.
Delavan, Mr., 270.
Delaware Capes, 50, 147.
Detroit, Mich., 22, 118, 155, 167, 195.
Dennie.
   Thomas, 207.
   William, 58.
Dick, James, 207.
Dickinson, Sarah, 176, 178, 213.
Dickerman, Hannah, 38.
Dixon, Ill., 23.
Dils, Ann, 149.
Dillon.
   Florence H., 191.
   James L., 191.
   Theo. Fisher, 191.
Doctor's Creek, N. J., 115, 123.
Dodd, Stephen, 37.
Domainbray, Mr., 269.
Donnaldson.
   Edward Milnor, 184.
   Harriet, 184.
   Helen, 184.
   John, 179, 184.
   Richard, M., 179, 184.
Doon River, 112.
   Old bridge of, 112.
Dorchester, Mass., 57, 58.
Dorr.
   Benjamin, 23, 24.

Ebenezer, 59.
Douglas.
   Colonel, 226.
   James, Earl of, 107.
   Robert, Sir, 104.
   William, Earl of, 107.
Doylestown, Pa., 177, 178, 181, 182, 184, 185, 190, 191, 195.
Dow's Seminary, 40.
Dryden, N. Y., 152, 153.
Duché, Parson, 261.
Duffield, Sarah, 197.
Dunbar, Lady Margaret, 105.
Dungan, family of, 209.
Dunkirk, N. Y., 22.
Dunlap.
   Ann, 177.
   Anna Roe, 188.
   Carolina Way, 89.
   Ella, 189.
   Emily, 189.
   Hazlett.
   Helen, 188.
   James, 176, 177, 212.
   James Hendrie, 188.
   Joseph Bispham, 181.
   Josephine Augusta, 188.
   Josephine Tucker Bispham, 182.
   Julia, 177, 214.
   Juliana, 177, 182.
   Mary, 177.
   Robert Shewell, 181, 188.
   Sallows, 177, 181, 189.
   Sarah, 181.
   Sarah Cauffman, 182.
   Susan Bispham, 181, 182.
   William, 181.
Dunn, Capt., 142.
Dusenbery.
   Benjamin, M., 182, 189.
   Florence, 189.
   Henry, 189.
   Josephine, 189.
   Julia, 189.
   Juliana, D., 189.
   Mary Gertrude, 189.
   Sarah Dunlap, 189.
   Susan Dunlap, 189.
Dwight.
   Captain, 57.
   Lucy, 57.
Dyckman, G., 143.

Eaglesham, estate of, 105.
Eastbarshold, Eng., 175.
East Haven, Conn., 37, 38, 39, 40, 43, 44.
Easton, Pa., 11, 21, 30, 39, 40, 41, 42, 43, 44, 45, 53, 49, 150, 151, 152, 153, 156, 158, 208.
Easton to New Orleans, (1825), 158.
Eaton.
  Horatio, 117.
  John, 116.
  Margaret, 116.
  Maria Louise, 117.
  Theodore Horatio, 118.
Eatontown, 116.
Edenton, N. C., 63.
Edinburgh, 17, 25, 28, 29, 221.
  Castle, 108.
Edgar, C. H., 45, 156.
Edward I., 107.
Edwards.
  David S., 120, 140, 143.
  Georgia, 141.
  Harriet S., 141.
  Lucy B., 141.
  Martha L., 141.
  Morgan, 175.
  William S., 141.
Eglinton.
  Castle, 108, 110.
  Earl of, 108, 110, 111, 112, 114.
  Elizabeth, 107.
  Estate of, 107.
  Sir Hugh, 108.
Elizabeth, N. J., 39, 152.
Ellis, C. R., 197.
Ellsworth, Ks., 154.
Elopement by Proxy, 196, 295.
Elms, the Yellow, 85.
Emmettsburg, Md., 17.
Engels, W., 182.
Erie, Fort, 124.
Erie, Lake, 119, 124.
Erie, Pa., 63, 64.
Erie, U. S. S., 69, 119, 124, 140.
Errington, Anna, 66.
Erskine.
  John, 107.
Espy, Prof., 22.
Essex, U. S. S., 118.
Eustis.
  Abraham, 67.

William, 67, 93.
Evans.
  Hannah W., 180, 185.
  Joseph H., 152.
  Lewis, 185.
  Mary Elizabeth, 23.
Everett, Edward, 83.
Everglade to Cañon 155.
Explanatory Note, 12.
Fair American, U. S. S., 33, 34.
Fairfield.
  Mary, 66, 78.
  Daniel, 78.
Fairfield, Conn., 39.
Falconer, N., 208.
Falling Waters, Va., 155.
Falls of Schuylkill, Pa., 24.
Falmouth, Me., 67, 71.
Fanueil, family of, 62.
Fannington, Conn., 157.
Fell, Cynthia, 176, 177.
Fessenden.
  Ellen Lincoln, 68.
  T. A. D., 68.
  William Pitt, 68.
Fisher.
  Christian Stanley, 191.
  Emily C., 191.
  Florence, 191.
  F. Theo., 191.
  Mary B., 191.
  Theo. H., 191.
Fitzgibbon, Lord, 237.
Fitzinger, family of, 209.
Flatbush, L. I., 68.
Fletcher, Deborah, 202.
Forbes, Alex., 114.
Fordham, G., 196.
Forrester, 56.
Forster, 56.
Fort George (Canada), 72.
Fort Loyall, 71, 72.
Foster.
  Andrew, 59, 65, 66, 67, 68, 87, 94, 121.
  Bossenger, 57, 58, 59, 86, 87, 88, 94, 95, 96.
  Caroline Padelford, 62.
  Catharine C., 62.
  Charles Chauncey, 62, 88.
  Charles Francis, 62.
  Charlotte Willis, 62.

INDEX.   291

Conant, 68.
Delia, H. M., 117.
Edith, 70.
Edward, 57, 70.
Elinor Frances, 70, 121.
Elizabeth, 62.
Elizabeth Craigie, 59, 63.
Fanny H., 98.
Fitz Gibbons, 70.
Frances Nelson, 68.
Francis A., 62.
Francis Apthorp, 62, 70.
Francis Charles, 62.
George, 59, 67, 70, 87.
George Craigie, 70.
Grace, 62, 96.
Hannah, 57.
Helen, 68.
Isaac, 57, 93.
James, 59, 66, 68, 87, 98, 120, 121, 150, 155.
James Reginald, 68.
John, 57, 59, 87.
John Francis, 62.
Joseph, 11, 58, 62, 63, 86, 88.
Julia, 67.
Julia Montgomery, 121.
Kate McCrea, 11, 68, 121.
Katharine Borland, 62.
Leonard, 62, 88.
Lydia, 62.
Maria, 63.
Marie H., 61.
Mary, 57, 67, 120.
Mary Conant, 67, 68.
Mary Craigie, 59.
Mary Grace, 62.
Mary Spear, 62.
Millite, 62.
Miriam Cutler, 62.
Sally, 61.
Samuel Conant, 66, 68, 70.
Sarah, 57.
Sarah Lloyd, 62.
Susan Cabot, 62.
Theodore Bogert, 11, 68.
Thomas, 56, 57, 58, 59, 87, 96, 111.
Timothy, 58.
Virginia, 62.
William, 57, 59, 60, 61, 69, 90.
William Leonard, 62.
Fosteriana, 94.

Foster " pedigree," 57, 70.
Fothergill.
  Dr., 28.
  Samuel, 52.
Fox, Charles James, 31.
Foxon, Conn., 39, 44.
Franciscan Order, 14, 15.
Franco-American Leaf, A, 62, 69.
Frankfort, Ky., 21.
Franklin, Dr., 246, 250, 257, 268.
Frederick, Md., 176.
Fredericksburg, Va., 65.
Freehold, N. J., 116.
Fremont, 126, 134.
Fresh Pond, Mass., 69.
Frohock, Theresa Jeannette, 41.
Frontenac, Count, 72, 78.
Fulton, U. S. S., 140, 141.
Funeral of B. West, 275.
Funkstown, Md., 155.
Furnaces, battle of the, 155.
Fussell.
  Bartholomew, 50.
Galena, Ill., 198, 199.
Gallagher, Kate Lee, 20.
Gare, John, 57.
Garland, Col., 143.
Geaubert, Lydia, 62.
Gen. Moultrie, U. S. S., 33, 34, 35.
General Pike, U. S. S., 123.
Geneva, N. Y., 44.
Geneva, Switzerland, 70.
George I., 147.
  III., 270.
Georgia, S. S., 40.
German Society (Phil.), 14.
Germantown, Pa., 18, 23, 31, 147, 198, 199.
Germantown Telegraph, 32.
German Valley, N. J., 147.
Gerry, Mr., 83.
Gettysburg, battle of, 153, 155.
Gibbons, Louisa A., 67.
Gibbs, B., 196.
Gibraltar, 60.
Gibson.
  Chief Justice, 31.
  W. R., 191.
Gilbert, G., 185.
Gill, Mrs. Bennington, 115.
Gillespie, Capt., 126, 128, 129.
Glasgow, the Ship, 148.

INDEX.

Glencairn, family of, 109, 110.
Gnadenhutten, Pa., 50.
Goddard, Kingston, 24.
Golder, Howard, 19.
Gonanda, N. Y., 22.
Grampus, U. S. S., 13, 140.
Graves.
   Stephen, 39.
   Thankful, 39.
Gray.
   Edward, 222.
   Thomas, 222.
Greason, Robert, 72.
Green.
   Charles B., 199.
   John F., 199.
   Juliette H., 199.
   Mary G., 202.
Greene, General, 81.
Greenfield, Mass., 62.
Greenleaf, Mr., 87.
Green River, N. Y., 39, 44.
Grier, R. C., 30.
Griffin, Martin I. J., 11.
Ground Squirrel Bridge, battle of, 155.
Guaymas, Mexico, 119, 125.
Guernsey.
   Daniel G., 22.
   Henrietta M., 18, 22.
Gwynedd, 53.
Habersham, 84.
Haco, King of Norway, 105.
Haddonfield, N. J., 189.
Haen, Dr. de, 27, 28.
Halberstadt, 147.
Hale, Rev. Albert, 22.
Halidon Hill, battle of, 108.
Halifax, 57.
Hall.
   Grace, 66.
   Margaret, 67.
   Thomas, 36.
Halstead, 142,
Hamilton, U. S. S., 123.
Hammer, Henry M., 152.
Hampton Roads, Va., 19.
Hancock, John, 58.
Hanford.
   Lettice, 70.
   Mary, 140.
Harned.
   Delia, 120.

   Jonathan, 120.
   Nathaniel, 120.
Harper's Weekly, 20.
Harris.
   Florence, 68.
   Herbert Wood, 68.
   Reginald Foster, 68.
Harrisburg, Pa., 158.
Harrison.
   Alice K., 199.
   Caroline, 199.
   Charles, 198.
   Edward, 199.
   Francis, 199.
   Lillian M., 199.
   Mary R., 199.
   Robert, 199.
   Theo. H., 199.
   William E., 199.
Harrison, President, 23.
Hart.
   James H., 24.
   Sarah Byerly, 22, 24.
Harvey, Sarah R., 189, 195.
Haskin, Jane, 48.
Haskin-Foster Pedigree, 57, 61.
Hastings, battle of, 102, 103.
Havana, 124.
Haven.
   Catharine Dexter, 63.
   Elizabeth Craigie, 63, 87.
   Elizabeth F., 63.
   Lydia G., 87.
   Samuel, 59, 63, 87.
   Samuel Foster, 64, 65.
Havre, 124.
Hawes' Shop, battle of, 158.
Hayden.
   Anna G., 201.
   Charles E., 201.
   Eugene C., 201.
   Evelyn S., 201.
   Horatio H., 201.
   Martha M., 201.
   Mary G., 201.
   Sarah S., 201.
Hays, Matilda A., 201.
Hazard.
   Lorraine, 200.
   Samuel P., 11.
   Stanton L. H., 200.
   Virginia L. L., 200

INDEX.   293

William E., 200.
William P., 200.
Hedden, James, 153.
Hedge.
  Anna, 198.
  Henry, 198.
  Henry L., 198.
  Lyman, 198.
  Thomas, 198.
Heidelberg (Germ.), 42.
Hempstead.
  Charles W., 198.
  Lizzie, 198.
Hendrie.
  Anita, 191.
  Ann D., 182.
  Charles, 198.
  James D., 182.
  Joseph J., 182.
  Josephine, 182.
  Julia D., 182.
  William S., 177, 182.
Henri II., 109.
Henry I., 109.
Henry.
  Delia, 120.
  Harriet Eliza, 120.
  Mary, 118, 120.
  William, 120.
Hepburn.
  Adam, Sir, 109.
  Ann, 117.
  Elena Maria, 21.
  Elizabeth, 109.
  Hopewell, 18, 21, 31.
  James Francis, 21.
  Julia, 21.
  Laurence Cauffman, 21.
  Mary, 21.
  Samuel, 30.
  Sarah Cauffman, 21.
Hertell, M., 76.
Hickson, Sarah A., 49.
Hill, Elizabeth Blake, 119.
Hilliard.
  Catharine D., 63.
  Catharine Haven, 63.
  Catharine Lydia, 63.
  Edmund Bayfield, 64.
  Elizabeth Craigie, 63.
  Elizabeth Haven, 63.
  Foster Haven, 63.
  Frances, 63.
  Francis, 63.
  Francis William, 63.
  Frederick Burnham, 64.
  George Johnstone, 63.
  Haven, 63.
  Haven Johnstone, 64.
  Herbert Beeton, 64.
  Iredell, 63.
  Margaret Bergwin, 63.
  Maria Nash, 63.
  Samuel Haven, 64.
  Sarah McKean, 64.
  Timothy, 57.
Hinchenbrook, H. B. M. S., 33, 34.
Hingham, Mass., 62.
Historical Societies.
  Am. Antiquarian, 64.
  Am. Catholic, 11, 13, 14.
  Bangor (Me.), 67.
  California, 125.
  Massachusetts, 64.
  N. E. Hist-Genealog., 61, 63, 65, 67, 87.
  Pennsylvania, 271.
Hixson, Joseph R., 152.
Hoffman.
  Madame, 70.
  Mary M., 151.
Hoguet, Sarah L., 188.
Hokendauqua, Pa., 44.
Hollidaysburg, Pa., 43.
Holt.
  Betsey, 38.
  John, Sir, 38.
  William, 38.
Hopegood, 78.
Hopkins, Mary C., 202.
Hopkinson, F. 257.
Hoppin, 62.
Hornet, U. S. S., 124.
Horton, Sarah, 66.
Hours, Book of, 280.
Housel, George W., 149.
Howell, Susan, 56.
Huguenin, D. C., 134.
Hunnewell, Mo., 202.
Hunt.
  David, 188, 194.
  Helen D., 194.
  Isaac, 196, 244, 245, 249.
  James Henry Leigh, 196, 238, 244.

247, 248, 251, 254, 257.
John, 196.
Josephine A. D., 188.
Marie W., 194.
Mary, 214, 244, 249.
Vida Josephine, 194.
Huntington, Earl of, 105.
Huntley, Earl of, 110.
Huntsman, Edward, 199, 268.
Hurd.
  John, 57.
  Elizabeth, 57.
Ihrie, Chas. J., 158.
Indians, 71, 72, 245, 246.
Ingersoll, Lieut., 71.
Inman.
  Eliza Montgomery, 118.
  Mary Berrien, 118.
  William, 118.
  William Taylor, 118.
Insurance Companies.
  N. E. Mutual Life, 71.
Irvine (Scot.), 111, 113.
Irwin, W. H., 143.
Ivy Mills, Pa., 16, 17, 19.
Jackson, President, 69, 98, 116.
Jamaica Plain, Mass., 66, 68.
James I., 108.
  III., 110.
  IV., 110.
  V., 110.
  VI., 108, 111.
James.
  Charles E., 185.
  J. Walter, 150, 172.
  Ripley C., 185.
Jans, Anneke B., 146.
Jaques, P. L., 202.
Jarvis.
  Margaret, 66.
  William, 98.
Jefferson, Thos., 49.
Johnson, Eleazer, 59.
  Alexander R., 182.
  Alexander S., 191.
  Alexina, 191.
  Anne L., 191.
  Catharine E., 191.
  George E., 191.
  Georgia A., 191.
  Matilda W., 191.
  Rachel E., 191.

Richard A., 191.
Johnstone.
  Alice Ann, 64.
  Maria Nash, 63.
Johonnot, Zachary, 60.
Jones.
  Daniel, 152.
  William, 208.
Joy, Carrie H., 185.
Kauffman, Joseph, 13.
Kearsley, Dr. 204, 248.
Keim.
  Annetta F., 186.
  Augusta, 186.
  Daniel M., 181, 186,
  Esther de B., 186.
  Joseph de B., 186.
  Mary L., 18, 186.
  Mary S., 186.
  Thomas S., 136.
Kelly's Ford, battle of, 27.
Kennebec, Me., 72.
Kennedy.
  Catharine, 109.
  Lord, 109.
Kent, Duke of, 105.
Kimber, Mary, 175.
Kindred, To My, 9.
King.
  Emily R., 151.
  Joseph, 149, 150.
  Margaret R., 150.
  Rachel, 149, 150.
  Samuel, 151.
King Philip's War, 72.
Kinglake, 225.
Kingston (Can.), 222.
Kingston, Jamaica, 203.
Kingston, N, J., 117.
Kinnersley.
  Ebenezer, 197, 268,
  Esther, 196, 197.
Knox, Gen., 61.
Lafayette.
Lainshaw, estate of, 111, 112, 113.
  Castle of, 111.
Lamb, Charles, 247.
Lancaster, U. S. S., 119, 136.
La Paz, Cal., 119.
Largs, battle of, 106.
Lawrence, 62, 123.
  John, 116.

INDEX. 295

Lieutenant, 74, 79.
Nathaniel, 116.
Thomas, 116.
William, 116.
Lawrenceville, N. J., 43.
Lawson, Surg., 142.
Leaflets, Social and Scientific, 265.
Leghorm, 260.
Lehigh, Water Co., 156.
Leigh, Hon. W., 196.
Lennox.
    Earl of, 108.
    Margaret, 108.
Levant, H. B. M. S., 208.
Lewes, Del., 18.
Lewis, Dr., 68.
Leavenworth, Fort, 154.
Lewisburg, Pa., 41.
Lexington, battle of, 249.
Libby, Cora, 192.
Liberty, Sons of, 58.
Liberty Tree, 58.
Lincoln, Prest., 153.
Linington, Sarah B., 176, 180, 212.
Lisbon, 98.
Litle, Virginia, L., 198, 199.
Little Falls, N. Y., 39, 42, 43.
Little York (Toronto), 123.
Liverpool, 264.
Livingston, U. S. Minister, 124.
Lloyd.
    Archibald T., 195.
    Cornelia P. V., 195.
    Ernest M., 195.
    Henry A., 180, 195.
    Henry D., 195.
    James Hendrie, 11, 189, 190, 195.
    James P., 195.
    Julia D. H., 190.
    Julia M., 195.
    Marion, 195.
    Martin V., 195.
    Susan P. N., 195.
    Virginia G., 195.
London, Eng., 17, 25, 57, 60, 64, 94.
Longfellow, 7, 79.
Lorraine.
    Beauregard, 198.
    Celestine F., 198.
    Claude, 198.
    Claude L., 198.
    Elizabeth S., 198, 199.
    Eugene, 198.
    Frances, 198.
    Frank, 198.
    Grant, 198.
    John, 197, 198.
    John S., 198, 199, 200.
    Josephine, 198.
    Litle, 198.
    Lydia, 197, 198, 200.
    Madison J., 198.
    Martha, 198.
    Mary, 198, 200.
    Maude H., 198.
    Octavia, 198.
    Percy, 198.
    Stephen, 198.
Lost Names, 277.
Loudoun, Earl of, 114.
Louis XIV., 77, 78.
Louis XV., 217.
Louisville, Ky., 21.
Louisville Journal, 21.
Lowell, Mass., 63, 64.
Lowell, Miss, 85.
Lownes, William R., 182.
Loyall, Fort (Me.), 71, 72, 73, 74.
Lucan, Lord, 225.
Ludlow Castle, 104.
Lunger, Martha, 151.
Lyde, Nathaniel, 57.
Lyle.
    Arms of, 112, 122.
    Jean, 111, 112.
    John (Lord), 111.
    Lyman, George, 61.
McAllister.
    John A., 11.
    The family of, 62.
McClary, W., 153.
McCoskry, Bishop, 119.
McCullagh.
    Francis Hepburn, 23.
    Lawrence, 23.
    Mary, 23, 26.
    Mary Willcox, 23, 31.
    Robert Poalk, 18, 23, 31.
    Susan Rodney, 23.
    William, 23.
McDonough, Commodore, 118.
McElroy, M., 153.
McIlhenny, M., 176.
McKean, Emily Stewart, 40, 43.

McLane, Mr., 83.
McNeal, Mary, 41.
Macinac, Mich., 123.
Macpherson.
  John, 117.
  Margaret, 117.
Magnus, King of Norway, 105.
Maintenon, Madame de, 77, 78.
Manchester, Eng., 18.
Manassas, battle of, 155.
Manassas Gap, battle of, 155.
Mann, Susan A., 184.
Marblehead, Mass., 66.
Marshall.
  Emily, 61.
  Thomas, 58.
Marston.
  Anna Randall, 19, 20.
  Frank Dupont, 20.
  Henry Ward, 20.
  James Henry, 20.
  John, 19, 20, 58.
  Katie Lincoln, 20.
  Mary Van Weber, 20.
  Matthew Randall, 20.
Martinico, 208.
Mary, Queen of Scots, 110.
Masters.
  Sybilla, 175.
  Thomas, 175.
  William, 175.
Matamoras, Mex., 69.
Mattes.
  Mary G., 199, 202.
  Matt, 219.
Maxwell.
  Margaret, 108.
  Robert, 108.
Mayow, Col., 228, 233.
Mazatlan, Mex., 119, 125, 134.
Meadow Bridge, Va., 155.
Medal of Honor, U. S., 155.
Medford, Mass., 82.
Medical Student's Letters, A, 25.
Meiggs, George, 188.
Memory of the Just, The, 23, 31.
Memphis Eagle, 21.
Mendenhall, William White, 50.
Mercein, Mary A., 200.
Merino Sheep, 97.
Merrimac, C. S. S., 19, 20.
Mesmaker, Johannes de, 62.

Middleburg, battle of, 155.
Mifflin, Gov., 18, 208.
Military Serv. Inst., U. S., 155.
Miller.
  Emma, 183, 192.
  George, 70.
  Lydia Adelia Clark, 70.
  Mary D. Gibbons, 70.
Mills, family of, 63.
Milton, Pa., 30.
Misroon, Lieut., 130.
Mitchell, 63.
  Catharine, 202.
Monitor, U. S. S., 19, 20.
Mons Gomerici, 101.
Mons Gomeris, 101.
Monte Gomero, 101.
Montgomerie.
  Agnes, 108, 110.
  Alan, 106.
  Alexander, 107, 108, 109, 110, 115, 116.
  Anna, 115.
  Anne, 108.
  Burnet, 116.
  Catharine, 110, 114.
  Christian, 111.
  Elizabeth, 108, 110, 111, 114.
  Gabriel, 108, 109.
  George, 108, 114.
  Helene, 109, 111, 116.
  Henry, 1061.
  Hugh, 102, 104, 105, 106, 107, 108, 109, 110, 112, 113.
  Isabel, 108, 111, 115.
  James, 107, 112, 113, 115, 116, 123.
  Jane, 115.
  Jean, 112.
  Jeannette, 108, 110.
  John, 106, 107, 108, 109, 110, 111, 112, 113, 114, 115.
  Mabel, 104.
  Margaret, 108, 110, 114.
  Marjory, 107, 110.
  Mariot, 112.
  Maud, 104, 110.
  Murthaw, 106.
  Neil, 110, 111.
  Philip, 104, 105.
  Robert, 104, 105, 106, 108, 109, 110, 115, 117.
  Roger, 100, 101, 102, 103, 104, 112,

INDEX. 297

113.
Sybille, 104.
Thomas, 108, 1.
William, 102, 106, 110, 112, 113, 114, 115, 116, 123.
Montgomerie-Cuninghame feud, 110.
Montgomery.
  Alexander, 116.
  Alexander Maxwell, 118.
  David Edwards, 121.
  Delia Henry, 120.
  Helen Vredenbergh, 121.
  Henry, 155.
  Henry Edwards, 121.
  John Berrien, 118, 119, 120, 123, 125, 140, 157.
  John Elliott, 120, 121.
  Julia, 118.
  Julia Maria, 120.
  Letitia, 118.
  Lucy, 116.
  Margaret Eaton, 117.
  Maria S., 117.
  Martha, 116.
  Mary Henry, 121.
  Nathaniel Lawrence, 118.
  Richard (Gen.), 117.
  Robert, 116.
  Samuel Lawrence Ward, 121.
  Sarah, 116.
  Thomas Berrien, 118.
  Thomas Harrison, 11, 100.
  Thomas West, 116, 123.
  William Henry, 120, 121.
Montgommeri, 101.
Montreal, 72.
Moreau.
  Gen., 98.
  Monsieur, 98.
Morlaix, France, 62, 96, 98.
Morris, Robert, 18.
Morristown, N. J., 63, 181.
Mortain, Stephen, Count of, 105.
Morton, M. Louis, 182, 191.
Moulton, Marcia, 198.
Mount Holly, N. J., 180, 184, 185.
Muirheid, William, 149.
Mundegumbrie, 101.
Munjoy Hill, 73.
Mure.
  Archibald, 106.
  Margaret, 111.

Marion, 112.
William, Sir, 112.
Naaman's Creek, Pa., 50.
Napoleon and Benjamin West, 274.
Natchez, U. S. S., 170.
Naval Asylum, U. S. (Bhlrc.), 118.
Naylor, Sarah, 179.
Nazareth Hall, 40.
Neff, Mr., 164.
Nelson, Admiral, 32.
Neuwied, 147.
Newark, Canada, 132.
New Berne, N. C., 62, 66, 72.
New Bridge, battle of, 155.
New Britain, Pa., 175, 178, 179, 181.
New Briton, H. B. M. S., 33.
Newburyport, Mass., 81.
New Canaan, N. Y., 22.
Newell.
  Edward Harvey, 195.
  George Harvey, 195.
  Louis Henry Field, 195.
  Marie Louise, 195.
  Rebecca Woodside, 189.
  Sarah R. H., 195.
  Susan B. D., 189.
  Susan Dunlap, 189.
  Wm. C., 182, 189, 195.
Newell, Mrs. S. C., 115.
New Haven, Conn., 37, 40, 146.
New Hampshire, 72.
New Hampton, 149.
New Holland, 146.
New Orleans, 21, 116, 160, 161.
New Orleans Crescent, 21.
Newport News, 20.
Newton, L. I., 116.
Niagara, U. S. S., 103.
Niles' Register, 274.
Nolan, Captain, 225.
Nonesuch, U. S. S., 146.
Nonconformist's Memorial, 223.
Norfolk, Va., 116, 125, 136.
Norristown, Pa., 15, 157.
North Carolina, U. S. S., 141.
Notre Dame, U. S. S., 33, 34, 3
Nova Cæsaria, 147.
Oat, Sarah, 181, 188.
O'Brien,
  Lafracoth, 105.
  Murtagh, 105.
Odenheimer,

Bishop, 155.
Francis B., 117.
William H., 118.
Old Church, battle of, 155.
Old Ironsides, 145.
Oldman, S., 205.
Oldman & Shewell, firm of, 175, 203.
One of the Old Navy, 120, 140.
Ontario, U. S. S., 124.
Opequan, battle of, 154, 155.
Orne, Elizabeth, 17, 19.
O'Shanter, Tam, 112.
Otis.
   Har. G., 61.
   Elizabeth Gray, 61.
   George Harrison, 61.
   James William, 61.
   Mary Foster, 61.
   Sallie, 61.
   Sophia Harrison, 61.
Otterbourne, battle of, 107.
Pacific Mail S. S. Co., 22.
Padelford.
   Edward, 62.
   Marion, 62.
Paget, Lord, 220.
Paige's History of Cambridge, 57.
Paine, Thomas, 250.
Painswick, Eng., 174.
Painswick Hall, Pa., 18, 21, 175, 176, 177, 178, 179, 180, 182, 184, 185, 207, 208.
Painter.
   Ann.
   Armstrong, 49.
   Edward Lyon, 50.
   Evelyn, 50.
   Francis Bennett, 49.
   Lilian Churchman, 49.
   Margaret Churchman, 50.
   Milton, 50.
   Peasley Mary, 52.
   William, 49.
Palatinate, 147.
Paris, France, 65, 117.
Parker's Island, 78.
Parkin, Sarah, 183, 191.
Parnell.
   Charles Stewart, 69, 98.
   Elias, 67.
   Henry, 49, 98, 99.
   Isaac, 66, 67, 79.
   Jacob, 67.
   James, 67, 78, 79.
   John, 66, 67, 78 79.
   Margaret, 67.
   Mary, 65, 66, 67.
   Sarah, 67.
   Stephen, 67.
Partridge, Samuel, 58.
Paterson, Hannah K.
   Joseph S.
   Margaret A. B. C.
   Thomas Currie, 185.
Patterson, James, 188.
Paul, 16.
Paulding, Commodore, 19.
Paxinosa Improvement Co., 156.
Payton, Catharine, 52.
Penell, Mary, 49.
Penn.
   Seal of, 55.
   William, 10, 55, 147, 209, 216, 224.
Pennsylvania.
   Hospital, 30.
   The Indians in, 52.
Pennsylvania Loyalist and George III., 270.
Penobscot, 72.
Penobscot Bay, 72.
Pensacola, U. S. S. 124.
Perron.
   Marie Hortense, 61, 96.
Perseus, H. B. M. S., 33, 34.
Pequonnock, Conn., 140.
Peytona, Steamer, 143.
Philadelphia, Pa., 11, 13, 15, 16, 17, 18, 19, 20, 22, 23, 24, 25, 30, 31, 32, 33, 52, 53, 60, 93, 124, 158, 175, 176, 177, 183, 185, 198.
   High School, 41.
   Trust and Safe Deposit Co., 22.
Phillipsburg, N. J., 149, 156.
Phillips.
   Ida L., 184, 192.
   John, 79.
   Wm., 58.
Phips.
   Elizabeth, 86.
   Spencer, 86.
Phippsburgh, Md., 78, 87.
Phipps.
   Augustus, 276.
   George, 276.

Phyllis, 210.
Pigot and Booth, Messrs., 28.
Pinckney, 209.
Pierce.
  Anna, 48.
  Caleb, 48.
  Rebecca, 48.
Pinkie, battle of, 111.
Pitt, Mr., 263.
Pitts.
  John, 86.
  James, 59.
Pittsburg, 158.
Pittsfield, Mass., 97.
Plymouth, Mass., 66.
Plymouth, N. C., 63.
Plymouth Rock, 37.
Pollock, Sarah, 201.
Polly, U. S. S., 35, 36.
Poplar Grove, N. J., 16.
Port Neuf. Sieur, 72, 77, 78.
Portland, Me., 61, 71.
Portsmouth, O., 180, 185.
Portsmouth, Eng., 208.
Portsmouth, U. S. S., 119, 120, 125.
Potter, I., 143.
Potts, J. Elwood, 191.
Pratt.
  Catharine Chase, 64.
  Elizabeth, 64.
  Francis Hilliard, 64.
  Frederick Haven, 64.
  Frederick S., 64.
Prentice, Geo. D., 21.
Price, Ezekiel, 59.
Princeton, 117.
Prussia, King of, 29.
Pueblo, Mexico, 143.
Pullman Car Co., 155.
Putnam, General, 81.
Quaker, Missionary A, 47, 51.
Quay, Samuel, 116.
Quebec, Siege of, 72, 117.
Quinton.
  Margaret, 111.
  Mure, Laird of Sheldon, 111.
Quitman, J. A., 141, 143.
Rachel, Ship, 205.
Raglan, Lord, 225, 226.
Ralston, A. G. & Co., 22.
Ramsdell, Jos., 79.
Ramsey, Col., 162.

Rand, Olive G., 193.
Randolph, U. S. S., 15, 17.
  Loss of, 32.
Ransom, Charles, 198.
Read, Adjt.-Gen., 179.
Recollects, Order of the, 15.
Rector, Father, 17, 26.
Reed.
  A. W., 50.
  Martha, 50.
  Mary, 58.
Reeder, Gov., 153.
Reidesel, Baroness, 88.
Reigler, Elizabeth, 43.
Relic of Seventy-six, A, 93.
Remembrancer (London), 33.
Revere, Paul, 58.
Rinek, Mary Elizabeth, 149, 152.
Roanoke, U. S. S., 136.
Roberts, Martha R., 181, 186.
Robeson, Hannah, 199, 200.
Robinson, Gov., 178.
Rockland, Del., 181.
Rodenbach, 144.
Rodenbergh, 146.
Rodenberg, Pointe, 146.
Rodenbock, 144.
Rodenborch, 146.
  Lucas, 146.
Rodenbough & Bro., firm of, 156.
Rodenbough Bro. & Son, firm of, 156.
Rodenbough.
  Adam, 148.
  Ada Vickers, 152.
  Adelia, 157.
  Albert Churchman, 156.
  Ann, 149.
  Charles, 149, 150, 151, 158, 171, 172.
  Charles Russel, 156.
  Clara Ann, 152.
  Dorcas Adaline, 153.
  Elijah, 148, 149, 151.
  Elisha, 149.
  Elizabeth, 148, 149, 151, 152.
  Elizabeth Ann, 157.
  Emily, 172, 173.
  Emily Chidsey, 152.
  Euphemia Miller, 153.
  Frances Josephine, 157.
  George, 151.

INDEX.

George Smith, 152, 157.
Hannah Crawford, 157.
Hattie Grove, 154.
Heinrich, 148.
Henry, 148, 149.
Henry Shepps, 157.
Henry Smith, 153, 157.
Herbert, 148, 152.
James, 149.
James Foster, 155.
Joseph Kinnersley Swift, 149, 150, 156.
Josiah, 153.
John, 148.
John Calvin, 153.
John Hockenberry, 149, 152.
John Ner, 157.
John Peter, 148.
Lucy Fisher, 152.
Lydia Caroline, 153.
Margaret, 139.
Mary, 152.
Mary McCullagh, 155.
Morris, 149.
Nina, 155.
Peter, 148.
Rachel, 149, 150.
Rebecca, 152.
Samuel Leigh, 149, 150, 152.
Sarah, 147.
Sarah Ann, 153.
Stanley Leigh, 152.
Stewart, 151.
Susan Martha, 153.
Theodore Frelinghuysen, 157.
Theophilus Francis, 150, 153, 154.
William, 148, 151.
Willie Crawford, 157.
Rodenburg, 146.
Rodney, Wm., 181.
Roeloffse, Catrine, 146.
Royston, Eng., 222.
Rupp's "Names, etc.," 147.
Sallows.
    Richard, 175.
    Sarah, 175.
Sandyford, Pa., 201.
Sandy Hook, N. Y. S., 146.
Scarborough, Eng., 222
Scott.
    General, 141.
    Miss, 151.

Sir W., 276.
Schott, Emily A., 190, 202.
Second Dragoons, 155.
Seitz, Lillian H., 156.
Sellard, John, 152.
Shakamakson, 219.
Shakers, Community of, 166.
Shatwell, Clara Ann, 149, 152.
Shawell.
Shewell.
    Ann, 221, 222.
    Ann Louisa, 183, 191.
    Ann Thomas, 183.
    Augusta, 184.
    Benjamin, 197.
    Captain, 221, 244, 249.
    Charles, 178, 182.
    Charles Auguste Fiot, 187.
    Charles T., 192.
    Clara Parkin, 191.
    Cynthia, 178.
    Daniel Linington, 181, 220.
    De Benneville Brown, 187, 194.
    Edith, 188.
    Edward, 222, 224.
    Edward Davis, 184.
    Edward Granville, 181, 193.
    Edward Stone, 179, 184.
    Edward Warner, 224.
    Eliza, 183.
    Elizabeth, 175, 176, 179, 196, 197, 198, 259, 261, 264, 265, 266, 267, 268.
    Emily Cauffman, 183, 191.
    Emma de Benneville, 193.
    Esther Brown, 187.
    Esther de Benneville, 181, 187.
    Francis, 197.
    Frederick George, 221, 222, 225, 237.
    Frederick Seymour, 184, 192.
    George Edward, 183, 191.
    George Maunsell, 222.
    George Stuart, 179, 183, 184, 192.
    Hannah, 178, 196.
    Helen, 188.
    Helene, 192.
    Henri Linington, 193.
    Henry, 187.
    Horace Newton, 191.
    James Worth, 181.
    Jane, 178.

INDEX. 301

Joseph, 175, 178, 196, 197, 205, 220, 221.
Joseph Brown, 181, 188.
John, 224.
John Kimber, 175, 178, 183.
John, Sir, (Eng.), 121.
Julia, 176, 182.
Juliana, 175.
Julia Abbott, 194.
Julia Churchman, 187.
Kate, 188.
Katie M., 192.
Laughlin Currie, 183.
Laura Davis, 194.
Linington Daniel, 181,186, 187,221.
Linington Roberts, 184, 193.
Lowell Ackerman, 184.
Louise, 179, 183, 192.
Lydia, 197.
Margaret, 178.
Marie Isabel, 184, 192.
Martha Roberts, 187, 194.
Mary, 176, 178, 196, 197, 247.
Mary B., 192.
Mary Elizabeth, 183.
Mary Linington, 181, 185.
Mary P., 192.
Mary Roberts, 187.
Mary Shannon, 194.
Mary W., 182.
Nathaniel, 176, 177, 178, 211, 212.
Oliver Fuller, 187.
Rachel, 184.
Rebecca Wallace, 182.
Robert, 175, 176, 178, 195, 196, 203, 204, 209, 210, 211, 213, 257, 266, 268.
Robert A., 184.
Robert Edward, 192.
Robert Linington, 194.
Roberts.
Sallows, 175, 212.
Sarah, 170, 178, 197, 204, 209, 266.
Sarah Falconer, 176.
Sarah Linington, 181, 187, 193.
Stephen, 175, 196, 197, 205, 244, 245, 246, 247, 255, 262.
Susan Dunlap, 178.
Thomas, 175, 176, 178, 180, 181, 207, 213, 222, 223, 224, 256, 257.
Thomas Fassitt, 181, 187, 220, 258.
Thomas Roberts, 187, 194.

Thomas Thomas, 183.
Walter, 174, 175, 195, 209, 211.
Walter Dickinson, 179, 183, 191, 192.
William, 176, 196.
Shewell, family of England, 220, 237.
Sheetz, Mary Ann, 199, 201.
Shepps, Magaretta Smith, 157.
Sherer, Joseph, 151.
Sherman, Anna, 151.
Sheridan, Gen., 154.
Shields, General, 142.
Ship that sailed, The, 144.
Shippen, Dr., 204.
  Abigail, 206.
Shippenburg, Pa., 159.
Shoemaker, Samuel, 270.
Showers, Ida, 185.
Sill.
  Harold Montgomery, 190.
  John Todhunter, 190, 182.
  Joseph, 190.
  Sarah, C. D., 190.
Sims, Buckridge, 203, 204, 206.
Sims, Buckridge, Mrs., 175.
Skerrett, Rose, 193.
Slocum, Susan C., 184, 192.
Smith.
  George, 201.
  Joseph Beddome, 197.
  Margaret, 152.
  Sarah, 149, 152.
Snyder, Robert Curry, 153.
Society, Army of Potomac, 155.
Society, P. G. F. P., 220.
Soldiers Home, 155.
Spence, Edw., 206, 214.
Stagner, Anne, 184, 192.
Stamps, British, 203.
St. Louis, 140, 198.
St. Lucia, 204.
St. Martins-in-the-Field, 264
Stearns.
  George A., 202.
  Georgia Ann, 202.
  Willard Dickerson, 202.
Stewart, John, 150.
Stockdale, Julia, 199.
Stockton, Commodore.
Stone.
  James, 208.
  Sarah, 175.

Stoneman Raid, Va., 155.
Strader, Lydia P., 181.
Strephon, 264.
Strong, Caroline, 191.
Sweeney, T. W., 143.
Swift.
  Amelia Elizabeth, 200.
  Anna, 201.
  Arthur Woodruff, 202.
  Beates Robeson, 200.
  Catharine, 199.
  Caroline, 199.
  Charles, 199.
  Charles F., 201.
  Charles Dupont Breck, 200.
  Charles Kinnersley, 201.
  Clement Kinnersley, 201.
  Douglas Pollock, 201.
  Edward, 197, 198, 199, 200.
  Edward Clement, 202.
  Edward Robeson, 201.
  Edward Schott, 202.
  Elizabeth Shewell, 202, 265, 266, 267.
  Emila Eliza, 207.
  Eugene Lee, 202.
  Eugene Capella, 202.
  Francis Bacon, 201.
  Francis Joseph, 201.
  Frederick, 202.
  Frederick Ellis, 202.
  Gab. Dupont Breck, 200.
  George, 201.
  George Breck, 200.
  George Joseph, 201.
  Helen Mercein, 201.
  Henry, 109, 201.
  Henry Thomas, 201.
  James Mercein, 291.
  Jane, 201.
  Jane Galloway, 199.
  John, 198, 199, 200.
  John Henry, 202.
  Jos., 255, 266, 267.
  Joseph, 238, 198.
  Joseph Kinnersley, 199.
  Joseph Robeson, 200.
  Katherine Mattes, 202.
  Lawrence Dudley, 202.
  Louise, 199.
  Louise Mercein, 201.
  Marguerite, 199.
  Mary, 199, 202.
  Mary Anna, 202.
  Mary Frances, 201.
  Penelope, 202.
  Robeson Kinnersley, 201.
  Robert Bickley, 199.
  Roy Wright, 202.
  Samuel, 199.
  Sarah, 200.
  Stanbury Mercein, 200.
  William Breck, 200.
  William Frederick, 202.
  William Green, 202.
Sword, Capt., 238.
Talons.
  Mabel de, 102.
  William de, 102.
Talwin.
  Elizabeth.
  John, 222.
Talleyrand, 82.
Tamenend, 209, 210.
Tamenen, 209.
Tamenand, 209.
Tamany, St., 209.
Tamany, Society of, 210.
Tatamy, Moses, 209.
Teedyuscung, 53, 54.
The Mother of Leigh Hunt, 247.
Theresa, N. Y., 63.
Thom, George, 143.
Thomas.
  Ann, 179, 183.
  Gov., 147.
  Iron Co., 40
  R. N., 24.
Thompson.
  Anna, 38.
  Mary, 199.
Thorndyke, Israel, 61.
Thorntoun, (Scot), 105.
Tibbetts, Mercy, 86.
Todd, John Allen, 153.
Todd's Tavern, battle of, 154, 155.
Tracey, Nathaniel, 81, 87.
Trappe, Pa., 157.
Treadwell, Prof., 99.
Trenton, N. J., 158.
Trevillian Station, battle of, 153, 154, 155.
Trumbull, John, 88, 271.
Trump.

INDEX. 303

Chas., 199.
Frances Caroline, 199.
John, 199.
Tucker, Wm., 298.
Tudor.
   Delia, 98.
   Frederick, 98.
   Henry, 62, 98.
   Henry J., 98.
Tustin & Shewell, firm of, 188.
Twiggs, Major, 142.
Tyson, David, 180.
Uhler.
   Emily H. C., 24.
   Emily Hudson, 24.
   Florence, 24.
   George, 24.
   Jonathan Knight, 22, 24.
   Rebecca K., 24.
United States Naval School, 69.
Universalist Creed, 216.
Upper Freehold, N. J., 123.
Upperville, battle of, 155.
Ustick, Thomas, 178.
Vallego, General, 126.
Valparaiso, 118.
Vanderveer's Academy, 40.
Van Dyke.
   Harold Meredith, 189.
   John Parker, 189.
Van Rensselaer.
   Jeremiah, 62.
Vassall.
   Henry, 87.
   House, 80, 81.
   John, 80, 86, 87.
   Leonard, 86.
Vera Cruz, Mexico, 141, 143.
Vicksburgh, Miss., 20.
Victoria, Queen, 82.
Vienna, Austria, 17, 25, 26, 28, 29.
Vincent, Capt., 15, 34.
Virgil, 218.
Voltaire, 83, 84.
Voorhees.
   Cornelius Polhemus, 195.
Wace, Robert, 102.
Wade, Margaret, 17.
Wallace.
   Jane, 178, 182.
   Robert, 182.
Waller.

Elizabeth, 141.
Harriet, 141.
Mary G., 141.
W. E. H. W. G., 141.
Wallingford, Conn., 40.
Walters, Sarah, 39, 40.
War.
   For the Union, 151, 153, 154, 155, 190, 194.
Ward, 62.
Wardell, Johana, 116.
Ware, 68.
Washington, D. C., 155.
   Gen., 179.
   Berrien Card Table, 117, 121.
   Mrs., 80.
   Pa, 161.
Warren, Joseph, 58.
Waterford, N. Y., 22.
Waterloo Survivor, A., 224.
Watson, Lieut.-Col., 143.
Wells.
   John D., 117.
   Mary, 62.
   Sarah E., 68.
Wellesley, Dr., 276.
Wendell.
   Oliver, 58.
   Thomas, 58.
Wentworth, Elmer Ellsworth, 68.
West.
   Benjamin, 175, 180, 196, 247, 250, 255, 256, 257, 258, 259, 260, 261, 262, 263, 264, 265, 270, 275, 276.
   Benjamin, Napoleon and, 274.
   Elizabeth S., 180, 196.
   Emma, 116.
   Mrs., 214, 257, 265, 268, 270, 273.
   Raphael Lamar, 196, 276.
   Sarah, 48.
Weathersfield, Vt., 98.
White, William, 255, 257.
Whiting, de Garmo, 118.
White, Townsend, 210.
Who sent out his Argosies, 244.
Wiener, Pauline, 190.
Widdifield, Caspar, 182, 190.
Wilson.
   James Grant, 11.
   John, 60.
   Sir Robert, 276.
Willcox.

Caroline, 19.
Edward, 19.
Eliza.
Elizabeth, 17.
Elizabeth R., 19.
Ellen, 19.
Henry, 19.
James, 17, 19.
John, 17, 19.
Joseph, 19.
Joseph Cauffman, 17.
Mark, 14, 16, 17, 19.
Mary, 19.
Mary Elizabeth, 19.
Thomas B., 19.
William J., 19.
William, 188.
William and Mary, 71.
William the monk of Jumieges, 102, 103.
Williams.
  Catharine A., 39, 42.
  Jonathan, 58, 59.
  Nellie, 41.
William III., 38, 216.
William Rufus, 104.
Williamsport, battle of, 155.
Wildes, George & Co., 181.
Wilkes, Henrietta N., 193.
Wilkinson, Gen., 179.
Wilmarth, L. Clark, 21.
Winchester, battle of, 154, 155.
Winchester, Elhanan, 212, 217.
Winchester, General, 167, 170.
Winthrop, John, 58.
Winton.
  William, 144.
  Margaret, Countess of, 110.
Wolfenbüttel, 147.

Wolverton.
  Ann Elizabeth, 151.
  Benjamin, 151.
  Charles, 151.
  Chester, 151.
  Ebenezer, 149, 151.
  Edwin, R., 151.
  Eliza, 151.
  Elizabeth, 151.
  Henry, 151.
  Jonathan, 151.
  Thomas, C., 151.
Wood.
  David, 67.
  E. P., 120.
  James P., 186.
Woodbridge.
  Rev. Dr., 140.
  N. J., 120.
Woodlands Cemetery (Phila.), 51, 50.
Woodruff, C. H., 187.
Worden, Capt., 20.
Wright.
  Nathaniel, 153.
  Peter & Sons (Phila.), 23.
Yellow Tavern, battle of, 155.
Young.
  Alfred F., 187.
  Ann, 148.
  Cora de Benneville, 188.
  Esther de, B. S., 187.
  Fanny G., 188.
  Henry Dupont, 188.
  John E., 181, 188.
  Kate Roe, 188.
  Mary, 188.
  Sarah Linington, 188.
Zanesville, O., 162, 165.
Zephyr. II.B.M.S., 208.

www.ingramcontent.com/pod-product-compliance
Lightning Source LLC
Chambersburg PA
CBHW032353230426
43672CB00007B/682